IFIP Advances in Information and Communication Technology   **554**

Editor-in-Chief

Kai Rannenberg, Goethe University Frankfurt, Germany

Editorial Board Members

TC 1 – Foundations of Computer Science
  Luís Soares Barbosa⊕, *University of Minho, Braga, Portugal*

TC 2 – Software: Theory and Practice
  Michael Goedicke, University of Duisburg-Essen, Germany

TC 3 – Education
  Arthur Tatnall⊕, *Victoria University, Melbourne, Australia*

TC 5 – Information Technology Applications
  Erich J. Neuhold, University of Vienna, Austria

TC 6 – Communication Systems
  Burkhard Stiller, University of Zurich, Zürich, Switzerland

TC 7 – System Modeling and Optimization
  Fredi Tröltzsch, TU Berlin, Germany

TC 8 – Information Systems
  Jan Pries-Heje, Roskilde University, Denmark

TC 9 – ICT and Society
  David Kreps⊕, *University of Salford, Greater Manchester, UK*

TC 10 – Computer Systems Technology
  Ricardo Reis⊕, *Federal University of Rio Grande do Sul, Porto Alegre, Brazil*

TC 11 – Security and Privacy Protection in Information Processing Systems
  Steven Furnell⊕, *Plymouth University, UK*

TC 12 – Artificial Intelligence
  Eunika Mercier-Laurent⊕, *University of Reims Champagne-Ardenne, Reims, France*

TC 13 – Human-Computer Interaction
  Marco Winckler⊕, *University of Nice Sophia Antipolis, France*

TC 14 – Entertainment Computing
  Rainer Malaka, University of Bremen, Germany

IFIP – The International Federation for Information Processing

IFIP was founded in 1960 under the auspices of UNESCO, following the first World Computer Congress held in Paris the previous year. A federation for societies working in information processing, IFIP's aim is two-fold: to support information processing in the countries of its members and to encourage technology transfer to developing nations. As its mission statement clearly states:

> IFIP is the global non-profit federation of societies of ICT professionals that aims at achieving a worldwide professional and socially responsible development and application of information and communication technologies.

IFIP is a non-profit-making organization, run almost solely by 2500 volunteers. It operates through a number of technical committees and working groups, which organize events and publications. IFIP's events range from large international open conferences to working conferences and local seminars.

The flagship event is the IFIP World Computer Congress, at which both invited and contributed papers are presented. Contributed papers are rigorously refereed and the rejection rate is high.

As with the Congress, participation in the open conferences is open to all and papers may be invited or submitted. Again, submitted papers are stringently refereed.

The working conferences are structured differently. They are usually run by a working group and attendance is generally smaller and occasionally by invitation only. Their purpose is to create an atmosphere conducive to innovation and development. Refereeing is also rigorous and papers are subjected to extensive group discussion.

Publications arising from IFIP events vary. The papers presented at the IFIP World Computer Congress and at open conferences are published as conference proceedings, while the results of the working conferences are often published as collections of selected and edited papers.

IFIP distinguishes three types of institutional membership: Country Representative Members, Members at Large, and Associate Members. The type of organization that can apply for membership is a wide variety and includes national or international societies of individual computer scientists/ICT professionals, associations or federations of such societies, government institutions/government related organizations, national or international research institutes or consortia, universities, academies of sciences, companies, national or international associations or federations of companies.

More information about this series at http://www.springer.com/series/6102

Ioannis N. Athanasiadis · Steven P. Frysinger ·
Gerald Schimak · Willem Jan Knibbe (Eds.)

Environmental Software Systems

Data Science in Action

13th IFIP WG 5.11 International Symposium, ISESS 2020
Wageningen, The Netherlands, February 5–7, 2020
Proceedings

 Springer

Editors
Ioannis N. Athanasiadis (iD)
Wageningen University and Research
Wageningen, The Netherlands

Steven P. Frysinger
James Madison University
Harrisonburg, VA, USA

Gerald Schimak
Austrian Institute of Technology GmbH
Vienna, Austria

Willem Jan Knibbe
Wageningen University and Research
Wageningen, The Netherlands

ISSN 1868-4238   ISSN 1868-422X (electronic)
IFIP Advances in Information and Communication Technology
ISBN 978-3-030-39817-0   ISBN 978-3-030-39815-6 (eBook)
https://doi.org/10.1007/978-3-030-39815-6

This Springer imprint is published by the registered company Springer Nature Switzerland AG
The registered company address is: Gewerbestrasse 11, 6330 Cham, Switzerland

Preface

This book contains the papers presented at the 13th International Symposium on Environmental Software Systems (ISESS 2020), held during February 5–7, 2020, in Wageningen, the Netherlands. ISESS was initiated in 1995 as a forum to present and discuss research fundamentals and state-of-the-art applications in environmental informatics. Over the years, it has also evolved into a networking event for academics and industry experts focused on the intersection of software engineering, data science, and environmental sciences.

The ISESS conference series is organized by the Working Group 5.11 Computers and Environment of the International Federation for Information Processing (IFIP). The mission of **IFIP WG 5.11** is to foster environmental informatics and advance the state of the art of information science applications for environmental research, monitoring, assessment, management, and policy. To achieve this mission, IFIP WG 5.11 brings together researchers who deal with environmental challenges and try to provide solutions using forward-looking and leading-edge information technology. The conference connects acadamia and industry to overcome a manifold of technology changes and dynamics by using their best knowledge to improve our environment, and therefore the well-being of our society. Previous editions of the conference have been held in Zadar, Croatia (2017), Melbourne, Australia (2015), and Neusiedl am See, Austria (2013).

The theme of ISESS 2020 was **Data Science in Action**, and aimed to serve as a forum to present primary research in data science and its applications in the social, environmental, and green life sciences. The present volume includes 25 papers that have been reviewed by at least 2 members of the Program Committee. A wide range of topics is covered including data mining, artificial intelligence, high performance and cloud computing, visualization and smart sensing for environmental, earth, agricultural, and food applications.

The program also included an invited talk by Prof. Steven P. Frysinger on user engagement, discussing how environmental data science may end up helping real decision makers to make better environmental decisions and carry out more effective environmental management.

ISESS 2020 was organized by the Wageningen Data Competence Centre and was part of a broader event: the **Wageningen Data Science Week**. During this week a variety of activities were organized at the Wageningen University Campus, including crash courses, a data sprint hackathon, workshops, a movie, research project meetings, and an information market. This further fostered the discussion about the requirements and potential advances of data science applied in environmental sciences.

December 2019

Ioannis N. Athanasiadis
Steven P. Frysinger
Gerald Schimak
Willem Jan Knibbe

Organization

The 13th International Symposium on Environmental Software Systems (ISESS 2020) was organized by the Wageningen Data Competence Center on behalf of the IFIP Working Group 5.11 Computers and Environment. It was held during February 5–7, 2020, in Wageningen, The Netherlands.

Steering Committee

Ioannis N. Athanasiadis	Wageningen University & Research, The Netherlands
Ralf Denzer	Cismet GmbH, Germany
Steve Frysinger	James Madison University, USA
Sjoukje A. Osinga	Wageningen University & Research, The Netherlands
Gerald Schimak	Austrian Institute of Technology, Austria

General Chairs

Ioannis N. Athanasiadis	Wageningen University & Research, The Netherlands
Willem Jan Knibbe	Wageningen University & Research, The Netherlands

Local Organization

Chantal Hukkelhoven	Wageningen University & Research, The Netherlands
Renee Logtenberg	Wageningen University & Research, The Netherlands
Saskia van Marrewijk	Wageningen University & Research, The Netherlands
Mariet van Pluuren	Wageningen University & Research, The Netherlands
Hedy Wessels	Wageningen University & Research, The Netherlands

Program Committee

Ivan Andonovic	University of Strathclyde, UK
Robert Argent	Bureau of Meteorology, Australia
G. Blair	Lancaster University, UK
Christopher Brewster	TNO, The Netherlands
Arne Broering	Siemens AG, Germany
Vladimir Crnojević	BioSense Institute, Serbia
Susan Cuddy	CSIRO, Australia
Steve Davy	TSSG, Ireland
Marcello Donatelli	CREA, Italy
Omar El-Gayar	Dakota State University, USA
Marina Erechtchoukova	York University, Canada
Peter Fischer-Stabel	Trier University of Applied Sciences, Germany

Barak Fishbain	Technion - Israel Institute of Technology, Israel
Spyros Fountas	Agricultural University of Athens, Greece
Frank Fuchs-Kittowski	HTW Berlin, Germany
Karina Gibert	Universitat Politècnica de Catalunya, Spain
Jonathan Goodall	University of Virginia, USA
Daryl Hepting	University of Regina, Canada
Stefan Jensen	European Environment Agency, Denmark
Ari Jolma	Simosol Ltd., Finland
Claudia Kamphuis	Wageningen University & Research, The Netherlands
Argyris Kanellopoulos	Wageningen University & Research, The Netherlands
Pythagoras Karampiperis	SCiO P.C., Greece
Kostas Karatzas	Aristotle University of Thessaloniki, Greece
Derek Karssenberg	Utrecht University, The Netherlands
Albert Kettner	INSTAAR and University of Colorado, USA
Lammert Kooistra	Wageningen University & Research, The Netherlands
Dimitris Kremmydas	Joint Research Center - European Commission, Spain
Olivier Le Gall	Inra, France
Jose Lorenzo	Atos, Spain
Oskar Marko	BioSense Institute, Serbia
Jiri Nossent	Flanders Hydraulics Research, Belgium
Sjoukje A. Osinga	Wageningen University & Research, The Netherlands
Suzanne Pierce	The University of Texas at Austin, USA
Tomas Pitner	Masaryk University, Czech Republic
Gary Polhill	The James Hutton Institute, UK
Nigel W. T. Quinn	Berkeley National Laboratory, USA
Stefan Reis	Centre for Ecology & Hydrology, UK
Andrea-Emilio Rizzoli	Dalle Molle Institute for Artificial Intelligence (IDSIA), Switzerland
François Robida	BRGM, France
Gerald Schimak	Austrian Institute of Technology, Austria
Katharina Schleidt	Datacove, Germany
Miquel Sànchez-Marrè	Universitat Politècnica de Catalunya, Spain
Christos Tachtatzis	University of Strathclyde, UK
Bedir Tekinerdogan	Wageningen University & Research, The Netherlands
Jan Top	Wageningen University & Research, The Netherlands
Devis Tuia	Wageningen University & Research, The Netherlands
Simon Willcock	Bangor University, UK
Volker Wohlgemuth	HTW Berlin, Germany

Additional Reviewers

| Javier Cardona | University of Strathclyde, UK |
| Christopher Davison | University of Strathclyde, UK |

Engaging Users: How to Make Decision Support Systems Relevant to Real Environmental Decision Makers (Abstract of Invited Talk)

Steven P. Frysinger

James Madison University, Harrisonburg, VA 22807, USA
frysinsp@jmu.edu

Abstract. Those of us who have been involved with environmental informatics for a while know that only a fraction of the impressive technology we develop actually ends up helping real decision makers to make better environmental decisions and carry out more effective environmental management. This is because our community is largely composed of scientists and engineers specialized in computer science and environmental science, while the people who really need to use the fruits of our labors are usually not from these fields. Most of us aren't trained to connect our work to them. The true value of our effort isn't measured by papers written and talks presented, but by the degree to which our technology is used by environmental decision makers in the real world. This talk is a "call to arms" to break down that barrier: to engage the environmental end-users with our research and our designs, and to assess our effectiveness by measuring THEIR effectiveness when using our technology.

Keywords: EDSS · Environmental decisions · Human factors

Contents

Unsupervised Learning of Robust Representations for Change Detection on Sentinel-2 Earth Observation Images

Michelle Aubrun[1]([⊠]), Andres Troya-Galvis[1], Mohanad Albughdadi[2], Romain Hugues[1], and Marc Spigai[1]

[1] Thales Alenia Space, 26 avenue Jean François Champollion, 31100 Toulouse, France
{michelle.aubrun,andres.troya-galvis,romain.hugues, marc.spigai}@thalesaleniaspace.com
[2] TerraNIS, 12 avenue de l'Europe, 31520 Ramonville-Saint-Agne, France
mohanad.albughdadi@terranis.fr

Abstract. The recent popularity of artificial intelligence techniques and the wealth of free and open access Copernicus data have led to the development of new data analytics applications in the Earth Observation domain. Among them, is the detection of changes on image time series, and in particular, the estimation of levels and superficies of changes. In this paper, we propose an unsupervised framework to detect generic but relevant and reliable changes using pairs of Sentinel-2 images. To illustrate this method, we will present a scenario focusing on the detection of changes in vineyards due to natural hazards such as frost and hail.

Keywords: Change detection · Unsupervised method · Artificial intelligence · Sentinel-2 data · Vineyard use case

1 Introduction

With the advent of the Copernicus program and its wealth of free and open data, the Earth Observation (EO) domain is increasingly adopting automatic or semi-automatic data analytics applications, based on artificial intelligence techniques.

Using the spectral richness (13 bands), the fine temporal (few days) and spatial resolution (10 meters per pixel) of Sentinel-2, a lot of use cases can be carried out in diverse sectors, and in particular those related to vineyard health assessment. Wine-making is one of the largest industries that represents a turnover of several billions of euros in France. However, this industry faces severe meteorological challenges such as frost and hail, that can cause significant loss in wine production. After such meteo-rological events, winemaking farmers need to evaluate the level of damage that occurred in their vineyards in order to receive subsidies from the state and the European insurances. Additionally, insurance companies must also estimate the damage levels using field visits in order to check the information provided, which is non-trivial and requires a huge budget and workforce. Coupling these Copernicus data with an

I. N. Athanasiadis et al. (Eds.): ISESS 2020, IFIP AICT 554, pp. 1–6, 2020.
https://doi.org/10.1007/978-3-030-39815-6_1

appropriate change detection model will allow farmers and insurance companies to easily build a complete damage profile of the vineyards in case of any natural hazard.

In this context, a generic change detection application on Sentinel-2 time series was developed as part of CANDELA [1], an H2020 research and innovation project. Since the tool provides generic changes, many use cases can take full advantage of it in order to save time, effort and budget.

The rest of this article is structured as follows. Section 2 presents a brief review of existing change detection methods. Section 3 describes the methodology, and Sect. 4 is dedicated to the experiments and results obtained on the selected use case. Finally, Sect. 5 discusses our conclusions and future work perspectives.

2 Related Work

Change detection is a well-known problem in the remote sensing community, thus several approaches have been developed to tackle this problem. The most classical approaches rely on pixel difference, image regression, image rationing, radiometric index difference, and metrics based on mutual information or correlation indexes [2]. Other approaches compute a distance metric on manually engineered feature spaces such as the Laws filters presented in [3]. Although these methods are fast and easy to interpret, they are sensitive to noise and often detect subtle but irrelevant changes.

Other approaches rely on machine learning to classify the image pixels into relevant classes and then verify that the class of a given area has not changed between the two images [4, 5]. Such methods provide additional information about the nature of the changes, but they are very task-specific and require labeled data in order to learn the classifier in the first place.

More recently, some approaches start making use of deep learning techniques such as Generative Adversarial Networks [6] or U-Net [7] to infer the change map directly from the two images.

Since labeled data is scarce and expensive to produce, we propose an unsupervised framework to detect generic but relevant changes between pairs of Sentinel-2 images.

3 Methodology

3.1 Change Detection Service

The proposed Change detection service has been implemented on Candela platform. As seen in Fig. 1, the pipeline is composed of several modules. The first one, named Jpeg2Tiff, consists in extracting the bands of interest, resampling them to get the same spatial resolution for all bands and concatenating them to obtain a single geoTiff image for each Sentinel-2 product. The second module, named Preprocess, verifies that all images provided represent exactly the same area and sorts them in the chronological order. And the last module, named ChangeDetect, computes the change detection maps for each pair of consecutive images of the time-series.

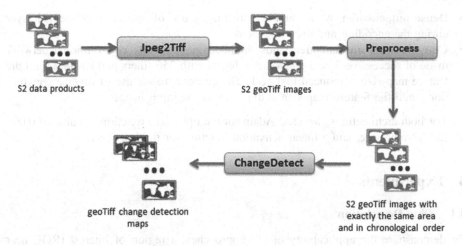

Fig. 1. Change detection pipeline

3.2   Framework

The proposed framework to generate the change detection map consists in projecting the image pixel space into a more robust feature space which is learnt by a neural network E. Then, computing a distance metric M between two encoded images in order to determine a change score. This whole framework can be described as follows:

$$C(X_1, X_2) = M(E(X_1), E(X_2)) \qquad (1)$$

where X_1 and X_2 are the two images to be compared, which are split into individual $n \times n$ patches on which the encoding and the subsequent distance are computed.

3.3   Approach and Implementation

In order to generate models of robust representations, an unsupervised approach based on stacked autoencoders [8–10] was explored. Stacked autoencoders consist in two sub-networks, the first one is used to compress the input data into a fixed-length representation, while the second one tries to decompress this representation in order to obtain the initial data back. The networks are trained from only one image by minimizing the following loss:

$$L(x, e, d) = MSE(x, d(e(x))) \qquad (2)$$

where x is an input image, e is the encoder network, d is the decoder network, and MSE is the mean squared error. In conclusion, the decoder network learns to reconstruct the input image from a compressed representation, forcing the encoder network to capture the main features of the image and discarding the noise.

Two different architectures of stacked autoencoders have been implemented:

- **Dense autoencoder** whose architecture makes use of one fully connected layer during the encoding and decoding steps.
- **Convolutional autoencoder** whose architecture is a fully convolutional network made of successive 3×3 convolution layers with 256 filters and stride 2 until the feature map size is reduced to 1×1. The decoder makes use of inverse convolutions until the feature map size is the same as the input image.

For both architectures, we used Adam for the optimizer function, a value of 0.001 for the learning rate, and a linear activation function for the last layer.

4 Experiments

4.1 Data Description

To demonstrate the applicability of our approaches, a region of interest (ROI) near Bordeaux in France, well-known for its wine and affected by frost on 27th April 2017, was selected (−0.3868367W, 44.5202483N: 0.1090724E, 44.7963392N). Two optical Sentinel-2 Level-2A (atmospherically corrected) data products of the T30TYQ tile with low cloud cover on the ROI were used for the analysis. One acquired during 19th April 2017 (before the frost) and the other during 29th April 2017 (after the frost). These products contain 13 spectral bands in the visible, near infrared and shortwave infrared part of the spectrum with different spatial resolutions.

To quantify the level of change (low, middle or high) at vineyard parcel level, a vector dataset containing 11355 parcels from the French Parcel Registration System [11] was also used.

4.2 Settings

The training data come from a Sentinel-2 Level-2A image from Toulouse with low cloud cover. This image have been tiled into normalized patches of $5 \times 5 \times N$ pixels with N the number of bands. For our vineyard use case, we have decided to consider all the bands at 10 and 20 meters of resolution, what represents 10 bands, and resample them according to the blue band. Thus, our models were trained on 65536 patches of $5 \times 5 \times 10$ pixels selected randomly by the algorithm for 10 epochs. The models are based on the architectures presented in Sect. 3.3 and provide a 25-dimensional vector that corresponds to an encoded representation of the patch in another feature space. Thus, the shapes of the different layers for the dense encoder are $5 \times 5 \times 10 \rightarrow 1 \times 250 \rightarrow 1 \times 25$, and for the convolutional encoder are $5 \times 5 \times 10 \rightarrow 3 \times 3 \times 256 \rightarrow 2 \times 2 \times 256 \rightarrow 1 \times 1 \times 256 \rightarrow 1 \times 1 \times 25$. Both models are available on Candela platform.

The testing data correspond to the two images of our vineyard use case. The same pre-processing procedure as the training image was applied to encode all possible patches. Finally, the L2 distance between each pair of encoded feature vectors have been chosen to measure the amount of change.

4.3   Results

To evaluate the performance of our method, we have asked an expert, who has a dual competence in remote sensing and agronomy and whose job is to extract accurate and relevant information from images, to create a ground truth of change levels from the Sentinel-2 Level-2A images. As the analysis takes a lot of time, the ground truth has been done on an area that contains 253 parcels. Figure 2 shows the ground truth, the results generated by our framework with using both models described in Sect. 4.2 and the result generated by our framework without applying any model. We can see that the results generated by our approach seem more similar to the ground truth than the approach where data are not projected into a learnt feature space. To quantify these similarities, we have extracted the median values of the different change detection maps at parcel level and considered the correlation coefficients as the evaluation metric. The correlation coefficient values were 0.79, 0.80 and 0.56 for respectively the frameworks with the dense encoder, the convolutional encoder and without encoder. These scores prove the efficiency of our approaches compared with classic approaches.

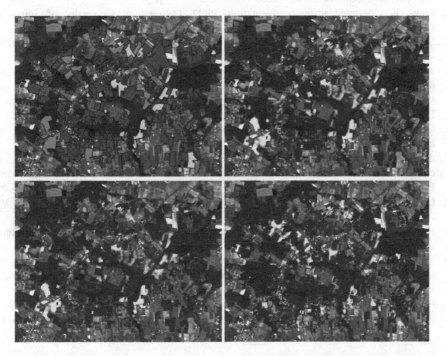

Fig. 2. Comparison of change detection results get by a Remote Sensing Expert (up-left), dense encoder (up-right), convolutional encoder (down-left) and without encoder (down-right). Change levels; violet: low, orange: middle, yellow: high (Color figure online)

5 Conclusion

In this study, we have demonstrated on a real use case the effectiveness of our unsupervised approaches to provide trustworthy change detection maps. These approaches lead to generic change level maps, but coupling with vector datasets, the type of changes can be specified and the percentage of changes estimated. Thus, these results may facilitate the work of many operators in different sectors.

Acknowledgements. The work presented in this paper was supported by the H2020 CANDELA project under grant agreement No. 776193.

References

1. CANDELA project. http://www.candelah2020.eu/
2. Singh, A.: Review article digital change detection techniques using remotely-sensed data. Int. J. Remote Sens. **10**(6), 989–1003 (1989)
3. Laws, K.: Textured image segmentation. Ph.D. Dissertation, University of Southern California (1980)
4. Serra, P., Pons, X., Saurí, D.: Post-classification change detection with data from different sensors: Some accuracy considerations. Int. J. Remote Sens. **24**(16), 3311–3340 (2003)
5. Alboody, A., Sedes, F., Inglada, J.: Post-classification and spatial reasoning: new approach to change detection for updating GIS database. In: 3rd International Conference on Information and Communication Technologies, pp. 1–7. From Theory to Applications, Damascus (2008)
6. Gong, M., Niu, X., Zhang, P., Li, Z.: Generative adversarial networks for change detection in multispectral imagery. IEEE Geosci. Remote Sens. Lett. **14**(12), 2310–2314 (2017)
7. de Jong, K.L., Bosman, A.S.: Unsupervised change detection in satellite images using convolutional neural networks. In: International Joint Conference on Neural Networks, Budapest (2019)
8. LeCun, Y.: Modèles connexionistes de l'apprentissage. Ph.D. thesis, Université de Paris VI (1987)
9. Planinsic, P., Gleich, D.: Temporal change detection in sar images using log cumulants and stacked autoencoder. IEEE Geosci. Remote Sens. Lett. **15**(2), 1–5 (2018)
10. Mou, L., Ghamisi, P., Zhu, X.X.: Unsupervised spectral-spatial feature learning via deep residual Conv-Deconv network for hyperspectral image classification. IEEE Trans. Geosci. Remote Sens. **56**(1), 391–406 (2018)
11. French Parcel Registration System. https://www.data.gouv.fr/en/datasets/registre-parcellaire-graphique-rpg-contours-des-parcelles-et-ilots-culturaux-et-leur-groupe-de-cultures-majoritaire/

Dietary Intake Assessment: From Traditional Paper-Pencil Questionnaires to Technology-Based Tools

Elske M. Brouwer-Brolsma[✉] [ID], Desiree Lucassen,
Marielle G. de Rijk, Anne Slotegraaf, Corine Perenboom,
Karin Borgonjen[ID], Els Siebelink, Edith J. M. Feskens[ID],
and Jeanne H. M. de Vries[ID]

Division of Human Nutrition and Health, Wageningen University,
Wageningen, The Netherlands
elske.brouwer-brolsma@wur.nl

Abstract. Self-reported methods of recall and real-time recording are the most commonly used approaches to assess dietary intake, both in research as well as the health-care setting. The traditional versions of these methods are limited by various methodological factors and burdensome for interviewees and researchers. Technology-based dietary assessment tools have the potential to improve the accuracy of the data and reduce interviewee and researcher burden. Consequently, various research groups around the globe started to explore the use of technology-based tools. This paper provides an overview of the: (1) most-commonly used and generally accepted methods to assess dietary intake; (2) errors encountered using these methods; and (3) web-based and app-based tools (i.e., Compl-eat™, Traqq, Dutch FFQ-TOOL™, and "Eetscore") that have been developed by researchers of the Division of Human Nutrition and Health of Wageningen University during the past years.

Keywords: Technology-based dietary intake assessment · App · Sensors · Biomarkers · FFQ · Recall · Food record · Dietary history

1 Assessing Dietary Intake: Why?

Scurvy was a major cause of disability and mortality among long-distance sailors for decades [1]. In 1497, the Portuguese explorer Vasco da Gama lead an expedition to India and reported that crew members with scurvy recovered days after eating fresh oranges. Yet, another 150 years passed before scurvy was finally acknowledged as being caused by malnutrition [1].

Fortunately, our understanding of how diet influences the human body evolved more rapidly during the past decades, and nutrient-related diseases considerably decreased. Accurate dietary assessment played an important role in these developments by generating quantitative information on the intake of foods, energy, and/or nutrients. The demand for quantitative information on dietary intake is still high, now more and more focusing on the exploration of diet-related determinants of today's challenges

I. N. Athanasiadis et al. (Eds.): ISESS 2020, IFIP AICT 554, pp. 7–23, 2020.
https://doi.org/10.1007/978-3-030-39815-6_2

such as obesity and (age-related) non-communicable diseases (NCD) [2, 3]. More specifically, around 39%, 40%, 39% and 9% of the population is faced with one or more cardiometabolic risk factors, e.g., overweight [4], hypertension [5], hypercholesterolemia [6], and/or hyperglycaemia, respectively [7].

Consequently, many studies nowadays focus on the identification of modifiable dietary factors affecting the development of obesity and NCD risk. Nutritional epidemiologists for instance focus on potential associations between dairy consumption and body weight development or diabetes risk using data of large observational cohort studies [8, 9]. Dietary intake is estimated and included in the model as the exposure factor and various health parameters (e.g., body weight, waist circumference, fasting blood glucose and insulin and/or self-reported disease prevalence) are assessed and included in de model as the outcome. In addition, potentially relevant information is obtained on a large range of characteristics related to demographics, lifestyle, medical (family) history, etc. Subsequently, statistical modelling results in e.g., βs showing whether or not an increase in dairy intake is associated with an increase or decrease in body weight, or risk estimate indicating whether or not diabetes risk is associated with a certain dairy intake level (e.g., 2 glasses of milk per day) relative to a reference level (e.g., no milk consumption). Dietary intake assessment is also an important component of dietary intervention studies. By modifying the consumption of a nutrient, food or diet in a controlled way and monitoring the potential impact on a selected health parameter, intervention studies are key to provide more certainty on whether or not there is actual causality between a nutrient, product or dietary pattern and a certain health outcome [10]. Dietary assessment is also performed by various national organisations in order to monitor the intake of foods and nutrients of the general population, which serves the formulation and evaluation of food policy [11]. Finally, a very important non-research related application of dietary assessment is the health-care setting where it is used to prevent or treat diseases caused by malnutrition or disease-related malnutrition. Dietary assessment allows the health-care professional to diagnose and provide feedback on the nutritional status of the patient and to educate the patient to improve dietary habits.

2 Assessing Dietary Intake: How?

Currently, self-report methods are the most commonly used dietary assessment methods, which can be roughly divided in methods of recall and methods of real-time recording.

2.1 Methods of Recall

In research, 24-hour recalls and food frequency questionnaires (FFQ) are the most commonly used methods of recall. In the health-care setting, the dietary history method is the most commonly-used approach.

24-hour Recall

The 24-hour recall is an open-ended method to generate detailed information on all foods and drinks consumed during the previous 24 h (i.e., actual intake), usually starting with breakfast on the previous day. On the individual level, data of 2–3 24-hour recalls can be used to gain insight in the habitual intake of commonly consumed foods; ≥ 3 days are needed to capture the day-to-day variation of a variety of nutrients and foods that are episodically consumed such as vitamin A, vitamin C, cholesterol, and fish [12]. The required observation period for interviewees with a stable food pattern is usually shorter than the required observation period for interviewees with a varied food pattern due to less day-to-day variation. At our department, 24 h-recalls are often carried-out by trained dietitians, either face-to-face or by telephone. In general, the interview can be completed in approximately 30 min, whereas food coding by the dietitian requires another 30–60 min. Our dietitians perform the 24-hour recall according the multiple-pass method [13, 14]. Due to the workload related to this method it is expensive to use face-to-face or phone-based 24-hour recalls in research, which limits its use to small-scale studies. Fortunately, recent technological innovations lead to the development of various self-administered web-based 24-hour recalls all over de world. Obviously, it is of key importance that these new tools are just as accurate as the dietitian-guided recalls. So far, validation studies of web-based recalls show promising results, but also clues for further improvements [15–22].

Dietary History Method

The dietary history method is the most commonly used method in the clinic, but less often used in the research setting. Similar to the 24-hour recall, the dietary history is an open-ended method to generate detailed information (i.e., type and amount) of all foods and drinks consumed, and is usually performed by a dietitian. The difference between the two methods is the addressed time-window. Where the 24-hour recall focusses on the previous day, the dietary history aims to assess a typical weekly or monthly pattern. Therefore, a 24-hour recall or food record can be a first step of a dietary history, but additional information on foods, drinks, and meals consumed on other days is warranted to obtain insight in the habitual intake. Information on habitual intake can be obtained by requesting for alternatives for the foods reported during the 24-hour recall; this process may be supported by addressing time and location of food consumption, differences between week days and weekends, cooking methods, etc. Clearly, the dietary history is a comprehensive and time-consuming method and may require up to 30–90 min to complete depending on the aim of the interview [23]; the use of photographs, food models or food packages may aid the procedure. Perceptibly, interviewees with irregular eating patterns are a challenge [24].

Food Frequency Questionnaire

A Food Frequency Questionnaire (FFQ) is a fixed-food list - with or without portion size descriptions - inquiring for the consumption frequency of foods and beverages over the past month, past three months, or year (i.e., habitual intake). FFQs can be interviewer-based and self-administered. In general, an extensive FFQ that addresses macronutrients and the majority of the micronutrients can be completed in approximately 45 min. FFQs are primarily designed to rank interviewees according to their intakes and not to estimate absolute intakes. Nevertheless, in case of nutrients or foods with a large day-to-day variability (e.g., fish and alcohol), an FFQ may be more accurate than other methods also in terms of absolute intakes. Important benefits of an FFQ are that the administration and processing is very efficient. We can easily process several thousand FFQs at once and the output is relatively easy to convert to computer ready-data, making the FFQ a very practical method for use in large-scale studies. However, in contrast to a recall, dietary history or food record, the use of validated FFQs requires intensive preparation before it can be send to the interviewees. The first step involves the identification of food items that are contributing most to the relevant energy and nutrient intakes in the target population, which obviously depends on the research questions to be addressed. To identify these food items, researchers in the Netherlands currently use the results of the Dutch National Food Consumption Survey (DNFCS) [25] - collected through two 24-h recalls - and generally aim to cover at least 80% of the absolute intake level and between-person variability of each nutrient under study [26]. Thus, each FFQ is tailored depending on the research question(s) and the population of interest. It should be emphasized that this process requires the availability of detailed food consumption data for the population under study, which are not (yet) available for many low-and middle income countries [11]. The second step involves the validation of the FFQ, which is ideally performed using validated recovery markers/techniques such as urinary nitrogen (for protein), potassium, sodium, and doubly labelled water, which are able to estimate absolute nutrient intakes [27]. Blood carotenoids and n-3 fatty acids can be used to assess the relative validity (i.e. ranking) for the intake of fruit/vegetables and fish intake (concentration markers), respectively [28–30]. However, no other markers are available yet [31]. Although the duplicate portion technique could serve as an alternative method for the use of validated biomarkers [32], validation studies are often conducted using other self-reported dietary assessment methods (sharing correlated errors) as the reference method (e.g. 24 h-recalls, food records) [33]. Besides this validation step, FFQs also require continuous updating due to new research questions and continuously changing availability of products. Thus, all in all, the development and maintenance of FFQs is a skilled task, time-consuming, and expensive. Fortunately, also this research area substantially developed in terms of automatization during the past years [34–38].

2.2 Methods of Real-Time Monitoring

Food Record

Food records are open-ended and generate detailed information (i.e., amount and type) on all foods and drinks consumed during the recording period. Similar to the 24-hour recall, a one day food record provides information on actual food and nutrient intake; 2–3 day food records provide information on the habitual intake of commonly consumed foods on the individual level. More days are needed to cover the nutrients and foods that are less commonly consumed [12]. The completion time of a one-day food record is approximately 30 min distributed over the day. In theory, multiple (i.e., 7 day) *weighed* food records are the most accurate self-reported dietary assessment method;

the so-called "gold standard" [39]. In case of weighed food records, the interviewee is instructed to weigh all foods and drinks consumed, ideally using scales with an accuracy up to 1 g. Following a demonstration on the weighing and reporting of consumed foods (i.e., food type such as white bread vs. whole-wheat bread, food brands, recipe details) the interviewee receives a simple notebook. A disadvantage of dietary records is that they are prone to reactivity bias, very intrusive for interviewees and also time-consuming and labour-intensive for dietitians due to the food coding. Weighed food records can be very useful in dietary studies, but weighed food records are not feasible for use in large-scale studies. The *non-weighed* food record largely follows the same procedure, but is less intrusive as food quantity is estimated, using e.g., standard portion-sizes and household measures. Obviously, this procedure requires more from the dietitian in terms of the interpretation of the portion size estimates and is thus less precise compared to the weighed food record. Fortunately, also for the food record, technological inventions have led to promising innovations, including the use of mobile devices. Whereas the more basic apps still collect dietary intake data through descriptive text [40], other apps are also exploring the potential of before and after photography, which provides additional information on consumed portion sizes and potentially undocumented foods [41].

Duplicate Portions
Similar to the 24-hour recall and food record, the duplicate portion method is open-ended and provides information on actual intake in case of a 24-hour collection period; ≥ 3 days may provide information on the habitual intake of commonly consumed foods and nutrients on the individual level. Distinct from the other methods, the duplicate portion method involves the collection of a second identical portion of all foods and drinks consumed - whether in combination with a weighed food record or not - in a cool box. Cool boxes are collected the following day; foods are weighed, homogenised in a blender, freeze dried and chemically analysed for nutrient composition [32, 42]. Clearly this method is very intrusive, labour-intensive and expensive, and therefore it is not often used. However, the duplicate portion method may be valuable when local food composition data are lacking, food composition tables do not contain information on specific compounds, validating other self-report dietary assessment methods or biomarkers, or exploring determinants associated with misreporting of dietary intake.

2.3 Nutrient and Food Calculations

Except for the duplicate portion method, average daily nutrient intakes for the 24-hour recall, dietary history, FFQ and food record are usually calculated by multiplying the consumption frequency with portion sizes (in grams) and nutrient content as indicated in the Dutch food composition table [43]. Note that, depending on the design of the FFQ, a weighed estimate of multiple food codes may be assigned to an item due to the fixed nature of the questionnaire.

3 True vs. Measured Diet: Sources of Measurement Error

Studies exploring diet–disease associations often show mixed findings [44, 45]; varying from null associations, beneficial associations to adverse associations. Inconsistencies may relate to various factors, including study population (e.g., healthy vs. health-compromised population), variation in the exposure (e.g., population with high intakes of a certain food or nutrient vs. population with a low intake) or outcome (e.g., low vs. high prevalence of a certain disease) under study, the covariates considered (e.g. inadequate vs. satisfactory correction for covariates) or the applied statistical approach (e.g., may affect statistical power to detect potential associations). Methodological issues related to the assessment of the exposure (i.e., dietary factor) are also commonly discussed. Indeed, it is indisputable that above described methods have their limitations that introduce measurement error, which can be "intake-related" (reflecting the correlation between the error and true intake) or "person-specific" (errors related to the interviewee's personal characteristics) [46]. Besides, errors can be systematic/ differential or random/non-differential [46]. To be more specific, a shared factor for all methods of recall (i.e., recall, dietary history and FFQ) is its sensitivity to memory-related bias. To illustrate, dietary estimates obtained by dietary history have been shown to overestimate the consumption of healthy foods and underestimate the consumption of snacks, drinks and alcoholic beverages (e.g., socially desirable responses). Moreover, although the dietary history aims to obtain information on the habitual diet, the estimated diet may be more likely to reflect the past 7 days rather than the diet over a longer period. Other shared sources of errors for these three methods as well as the *non-weighed* food record include the inaccurate estimation of portion sizes and errors in food composition tables. An additional source of measurement error for the FFQ is the large supply of available foods, which cannot be fully reflected in a fixed-food list. Additionally, reporting's obtained through food record as well as duplicate portion method may be influenced by the fact that interviewees are made aware of their habits while recording/collecting. To limit this source of error it is therefore important to emphasize that interviewees should not change their usual intake at the time of recording/collecting (reactivity bias). The duplicate portion method is least influenced by abovementioned sources of error: there is no memory-related bias, no bias due to errors in food consumption tables, and errors in portion sizes are also unlikely. Still, interviewees may forget to collect foods resulting in underestimated food intakes [32]. So in the end, dietary assessment will give you more or less an indication of what people eat, but it is very difficult to get a very precise estimate.

4 Assessing Dietary Intake: Which Method to Use?

The dietary assessment method to choose eventually depends on your research question and target population [47]. To select the most appropriate and cost effective method for a specific research question it is important to weigh the benefits and the weaknesses, e.g., available tools, resources and expertise, interviewee burden, researcher burden, costs, and validity and reproducibility. Considerations may relate to the range of foods or nutrients of interest, how the data will be analysed and presented (i.e., group vs. individual level and absolute intakes vs. relative intakes), and to the targeted time-frame (i.e., actual vs. habitual intake and recall vs. real-time recording). In terms of the target population important considerations may relate to the sample size, age of the interviewees (e.g., young children and older adults may experience difficulties when working with some of the tools), educational level/literacy, motivation, ethnicity, disabilities (e.g., vision or hearing problems), country, and available resources and expertise (e.g., internet access or not, availability of dietitians).

5 Innovations

It may be clear that each tool has it strengths and it weaknesses. Up to 15–20 years ago, above presented methods were completely paper-pencil based, which shifted more and more towards web-based and smartphone-based tools throughout the past decade. The current pace of technological development is very valuable to improve our methods, i.e., reduce sources of error, increase user-friendliness, and decrease workload of dietitians and/or researchers. Due to the absence of a dietitian/researcher, data obtained through web-based/smartphone-based tools are for instance expected to be less biased by social desirable answers. Web-based and smartphone-based tools are also assumed to be less burdensome for the interviewees as they can complete the dietary assessment at a time and location that is convenient for them.

5.1 Compl-eat™

New technological opportunities allowed us to develop a self-administered Dutch web-based dietary 24-hour recall tool, entitled Compl-eat™ [22]. Contrary to the traditional method, the web-based tool is not guided by a research dietitian. At 6.00 AM, the interviewee receives an invite to complete the recall through e-mail; the invite remains effective until midnight that same day. The tool is introduced by two short instruction videos explaining how to: (1) select food items from the food list (2 min 16 s) and (2) report details (type and amount) of the consumed foods (2 min 26 s). Portion sizes can be reported in commonly-used household measures, standard portion sizes or in grams/litres. Compl-eat™ does not contain images. Identical to the traditional 24 h-recall, interviewees are requested to report their dietary intake of the previous day, starting in the morning after waking up till the next morning. Moreover, comparable to the traditional 24 h-recall, the web-based tool is based on the multiple-pass method, ensuring proper guidance while reporting the consumed foods [13, 14]. Compl-eat™ contains an extensive food list based on the Dutch food composition table (NEVO) [43], including most commonly-used synonyms as well as previously entered foods and recipes. This food list is flexible and can be easily modified in order to be tailored to specific research questions or updated to include new food items. In theory, this food list can be replaced with non-Dutch food lists. Compl-eat™ also comprises a recipe module, which facilitates the reporting of a complete dish by selecting or modifying a standard recipe. Besides, the interviewee has the option to enter all ingredients of an original recipe in combination with the consumption amount of the meal. Yield and retention factors (i.e., retained weight and nutrients after cooking) are automatically taken into account. Interviewees also have the possibility to include notes to clarify their input. After each eating occasion, interviewees receive prompts to report on commonly omitted foods (i.e., sugar and/or milk in coffee/tea, oils and fats used in the preparation of dishes, snacks/candies and fruits). Generally, all web-based 24-hour recalls are checked by research dietitians for completeness, unusual portion sizes and notes entered by the interviewee. Identified errors and notes are processed according to a standardised protocol, using standard portion sizes and recipes. Interviewees are not contacted for clarifications. Examples of errors include the report of 125 cups of coffee instead of one cup of 125 g. Notes may relate to a food consumed, but could not be identified in the food list. The computation module of Compl-eat™ subsequently calculates food, food groups, and energy and nutrient intakes where different output formats can be selected. Interviewees require on average 40–45 min to complete the web-based recall (including login time, watching the instruction videos and entering the food items), which is 10–15 min more compared to the traditional recall method. However, the dietitians can process the recalls in 5-10 min, whereas approximately 90 min are needed to complete the interview and coding according to traditional method.

5.2   Traqq

Recently, the development of the app called "Traqq" was initiated. Traqq can serve as a recall and food record, and can be used to collect data on one or more pre-specified full days. Besides, Traqq can be programmed to send random notifications over a longer period of time. In case of the food record module, interviewees are able to enter consumed foods throughout the day. In case of the recall module, the interviewee receives a notification on the smartphone prompting to complete the recall. By ticking the notification/opening the app, the interviewee obtains access to an extensive food list based on the Dutch food composition Table (1463 items) with additional synonyms (1019 items) [43]. If desired, this food list can be adjusted to fit different research purposes. Following the selection of a food item, the interviewee is prompted to select a portion size. Portion sizes can be reported in household measures (e.g., cups, spoons, glasses), standard portion sizes (e.g., small, medium, large), and weight in grams. Traqq also contains a "My Dishes" option where the interviewee can select all ingredients of an original recipe in combination with the quantity of the meal consumed. Yield and retention factors (i.e., retained weight and nutrients after cooking) are automatically taken into account. The recall closes after submission of the entered foods; data are stored on a secured server. The validation study of Traqq is currently ongoing with the first results expected early 2020. Screenshots of Traqq are displayed in Fig. 1.

Fig. 1. Screenshots of Traqq.

5.3   The Dutch FFQ-TOOL™

The Dutch FFQ-TOOL™ is a data-driven web-based computer system developed to generate (Fig. 2) and process tailored FFQs (Fig. 3) - i.e., for nutrients of interest and population under study - by standardized, reproducible, relatively fast and flexible procedures [38]. The FFQ-tool has three main functionalities, i.e., 'selection of food items', 'question generation', and 'nutrient and food calculations'. The selection of food items is a semi-automated process. The FFQ-tool uses data from the DNFCS [25] to tailor the FFQ to the nutrients and population of interest, which is comparable to the procedure used to develop paper-based FFQs. Generally, researchers aim to cover about 80% of the absolute intake level and 80% of the between-person variability of each nutrient under study [48, 49]. The FFQ-tool indicates to which extent an item contributes to the total intake or the variation in intake for the nutrient(s) of interest for each aggregation level. Depending on the research question, the researcher subsequently selects the most suitable aggregation level and related food items. Thereafter, the selected food items are automatically translated to standard questions. Once the FFQ is completed, food, and energy and nutrient intake is computed through the computation module of the FFQ-TOOL™, which is facilitated by attached (Dutch) food composition tables.

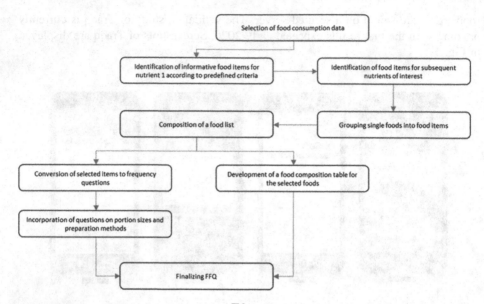

Fig. 2. Overview of the Dutch FFQ-TOOL^{TM} to develop and process FFQs. Figure adapted from PhD-thesis Marja Molag entitled "Towards Transparent Development of Food Frequency Questionnaires. Scientific basis of the Dutch FFQ-TOOL^{TM}: a computer system to generate, apply and process FFQs" [38].

5.4 Eetscore

The "Eetscore" is a self-administered web-based screener to assess habitual diet quality during the previous month. In contrast to above described methods and associated tools, the "Eetscore" is a relatively short FFQ specifically developed to fulfil the demand for a shorter and less burdensome questionnaire. It is not the primary aim to obtain quantitative food or nutrient intakes when administrating the "Eetscore". The "Eetscore" can be completed in approximately 10–15 min and therefore interviewee and researcher burden as well as the associated costs are relatively low. The "Eetscore" is also the only tool providing immediate personal dietary advice after submission of the questionnaire. However, if desired, the "Eetscore" can also be administered without the advice module. The "Eetscore" is based on the Dutch Health Diet-index (DHD-index). The DHD-index was developed in 2012 [50] by the Division of Human Nutrition and Health of the Wageningen University and based on the Dutch dietary guidelines of 2006 [51]. The first version of the Eetscore FFQ was developed in 2015 and called the Dutch Healthy Diet-FFQ (DHD-FFQ), reflecting the nine (nutrient-based) dietary components of the DHD-index [50]. In 2017, the DHD-index was adapted to the Dutch dietary guidelines 2015 [52] – which are food-based instead of nutrient-based - and called the Dutch Healthy Diet 2015-index (DHD15-index) [53]. The DHD15-index includes fifteen components, including vegetables, fruit, whole-grain products, legumes, nuts, dairy, fish, tea, fats and oils, coffee, red meat, processed meat, sweetened beverages and fruit juices, alcohol, and salt. For each component an

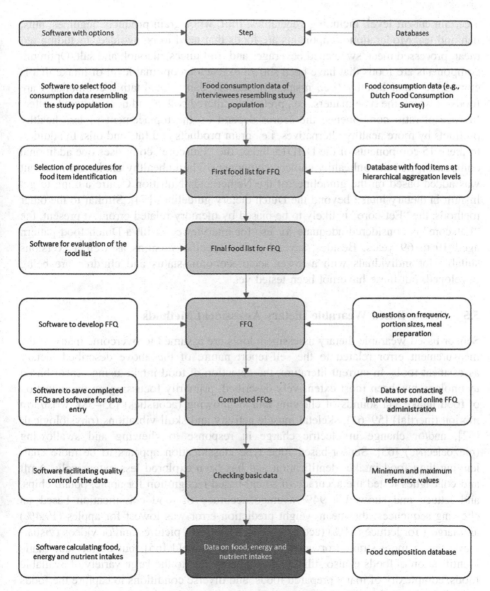

Software with options	Step	Databases
Software to select food consumption data resembling the study population	Food consumption data of interviewees resembling study population	Food consumption data (e.g., Dutch Food Consumption Survey)
Selection of procedures for food item identification	First food list for FFQ	Database with food items at hierarchical aggregation levels
Software for evaluation of the food list	Final food list for FFQ	
Software to develop FFQ	FFQ	Questions on frequency, portion sizes, meal preparation
Software to save completed FFQs and software for data entry	Completed FFQs	Data for contacting interviewees and online FFQ administration
Software facilitating quality control of the data	Checking basic data	Minimum and maximum reference values
Software calculating food, energy and nutrient intakes	Data on food, energy and nutrient intakes	Food composition database

Fig. 3. Software and databases in the Dutch FFQ-TOOL^{TM} to generate and process FFQs. Figure adapted from PhD-thesis Marja Molag entitled "Towards Transparent Development of Food Frequency Questionnaires. Scientific basis of the Dutch FFQ-TOOL^{TM}: a computer system to generate, apply and process FFQs" [38].

interviewee can score from 0 to 10; the total score of the DHD15-index ranges from 0 to 150. The scoring depends on the component type, which can be an adequacy component, moderation component, optimum component, qualitative component and ratio component. Adequacy components are foods which require an intake level above a certain cut-off level, including vegetables, fruit, wholegrain products, legumes, nuts, fish and tea. Moderation components are foods that need to be avoided, including red meat, processed meat, sweetened beverages and fruit juices, alcohol, and salt. Optimum components are foods that have been shown to reach an optimal level of intake that is considered most healthy (i.e., n-shaped), namely dairy. Qualitative components are foods of which the type matters, i.e., preferably filtered coffee and not unfiltered coffee. In case of ratio components, the scores depend on the replacement of less healthy products by more healthy alternatives, i.e., grain products and fats and oils. In addition to these 15 components of the DHD15-Index, the "Eetscore" comprises one additional component, i.e., the unhealthy choices component. The unhealthy choices component was added based on the guidelines of the Netherlands Nutrition Centre aiming to get insight in dietary intake beyond the Dutch dietary guidelines [54]. Similar to the other methods, the "Eetscore" is likely to be biased by memory-related error. At present, the "Eetscore" is considered adequate for use for interviewees with a Dutch food pattern aged 19 to 69 years. Besides, several patient-specific versions as well as versions suitable for individuals with a lower socio-economic-status and children are being developed, but these have not been tested yet.

5.5   Sensor-Based Wearable Dietary Assessment Methods

Sensor-based wearable dietary assessment tools are assumed to overcome many of the measurement error related to the self-report nature of the above described dietary assessment tools. In current literature, the detection of food intake using sensor-based technology has been most extensively described, primarily focussing on the detection of food intake via sounds of chewing and swallowing (acoustics) [55–58], wrist/arm motion (inertial) [59–61], skeletal muscle activity and skull vibrations (physiological) [62], and/or change in electric charge in response to chewing and swallowing (piezoelectric) [63]. Sensor-based food type classification appears to be more challenging than food intake identification and has been explored less extensively. Amft and colleagues tested the accuracy of sound-based recognition for apple, potato chips, and lettuce and showed a 94% average accuracy of food classification based on chewing sequences; the mean weight prediction error was lowest for apples (19.4%) and largest for lettuce (31%) (acoustic) [64]. The use of pictures and/or videos (visual) may seem a more straightforward approach in this field [65], but correct automatic identification of foods is also still a huge challenge due to the large variety of available foods, complexity of many prepared foods, and diverse conditions to capture the foods (e.g., lighting, position) [66]. In terms of portion size estimation, the use of camera's is developed somewhat more [66–68]. Still, current methods do not allow the use of sensors for detailed quantification of food, energy and nutrient intake for use in nutrition and health research yet. Therefore, in future studies we aim to contribute to this work by piloting various independent sensors to examine whether the combination of two or more sensors can provide a valuable addition to the currently used dietary assessment methods.

5.6   Biomarkers

Finally, even though not directly related to the technology-based work described above, work within the division of human nutrition and health also focusses on the identification of nutritional biomarkers as a complementary or alternative measure of dietary intake. Biological markers for dietary intake are considered more objective than the self-reported dietary intake methods, e.g., not affected by memory, social desirability and/or errors in food composition tables. As mentioned earlier, there are few well-validated nutritional biomarkers, but metabolomic techniques now provide a unique opportunity to measure up to thousands of metabolites at once providing valuable information on the food metabolome using a variety of body tissues [31, 69, 70].

6   Conclusion

The methods to assess diet substantially enhanced during the past decades, predominantly in terms of cost- and time-effectiveness, labour-intensiveness and interviewee and researcher burden. However, novel tools still share various methodological issues with the traditional self-report methods. New technology-based opportunities will help to further improve current tools (e.g., by updating app-based recalls such as Traqq with photo, video and/or chat functionalities to facilitate better food identification and portion size estimations), develop new wearable sensor-based tools to quantify food, energy, and nutrition intake, identify novel biomarkers, and potentially even integration of the various approaches.

References

1. Carpenter, K.J.: The discovery of vitamin C. Ann. Nutr. Metab. **61**, 259–264 (2012)
2. Worldwide trends in body-mass index, underweight, overweight, and obesity from 1975 to 2016: a pooled analysis of 2416 population-based measurement studies in 128.9 million children, adolescents, and adults. Lancet (London, England), vol. 390, pp. 2627–2642 (2017)
3. Global, regional, and national incidence, prevalence, and years lived with disability for 310 diseases and injuries, 1990–2015: a systematic analysis for the Global Burden of Disease Study 2015. Lancet (London, England), vol. 388, pp. 1545–1602 (2016)
4. https://www.who.int/gho/ncd/risk_factors/overweight_obesity/obesity_adults/en/
5. http://www.who.int/gho/ncd/risk_factors/blood_pressure_prevalence_text/en/
6. http://www.who.int/gho/ncd/risk_factors/cholesterol_text/en/
7. http://www.who.int/gho/ncd/risk_factors/blood_glucose_text/en/
8. Brouwer-Brolsma, E.M., Sluik, D., Singh-Povel, C.M., Feskens, E.J.M.: Dairy shows different associations with abdominal and BMI-defined overweight: cross-sectional analyses exploring a variety of dairy products. Nutr. Metab. Cardiovasc. Dis. **28**, 451–460 (2018)
9. Brouwer-Brolsma, E.M., Sluik, D., Singh-Povel, C.M., Feskens, E.J.M.: Dairy product consumption is associated with pre-diabetes and newly diagnosed type 2 diabetes in the lifelines cohort study. Br. J. Nutr. **119**, 442–455 (2018)

10. Staudacher, H.M., Irving, P.M., Lomer, M.C.E., Whelan, K.: The challenges of control groups, placebos and blinding in clinical trials of dietary interventions. Proc. Nutr. Soc. 76, 203–212 (2017)
11. Huybrechts, I., et al.: Global comparison of national individual food consumption surveys as a basis for health research and integration in national health surveillance programmes. Proc. Nutr. Soc. 76, 549–567 (2017)
12. Willett, W.C.: Nutritional Epidemiology. Oxford University Press, Inc., New York (2013)
13. Moshfegh, A.J., et al.: The US department of agriculture automated multiple-pass method reduces bias in the collection of energy intakes. Am. J. Clin. Nutr. 88, 324–332 (2008)
14. Blanton, C.A., Moshfegh, A.J., Baer, D.J., Kretsch, M.J.: The USDA automated multiple-pass method accurately estimates group total energy and nutrient intake. J. Nutr. 136, 2594–2599 (2006)
15. Touvier, M., et al.: Comparison between an interactive web-based self-administered 24 h dietary record and an interview by a dietitian for large-scale epidemiological studies. Br. J. Nutr. 105, 1055–1064 (2011)
16. Subar, A.F., et al.: The automated self-administered 24-hour dietary recall (ASA24): a resource for researchers, clinicians, and educators from the national cancer institute. J. Acad. Nutr. Diet. 112, 1134–1137 (2012)
17. Foster, E., et al.: Validity and reliability of an online self-report 24-h dietary recall method (Intake24): a doubly labelled water study and repeated-measures analysis. J. Nutr. Sci. 8, e29 (2019)
18. Arab, L., Wesseling-Perry, K., Jardack, P., Henry, J., Winter, A.: Eight self-administered 24-hour dietary recalls using the internet are feasible in African Americans and Whites: the energetics study. J. Am. Diet. Assoc. 110, 857–864 (2010)
19. Greenwood, D.C., et al.: Validation of the Oxford WebQ online 24-hour dietary questionnaire using biomarkers. Am. J. Epidemiol. 188, 1858–1867 (2019)
20. Wark, P.A., et al.: Validity of an online 24-h recall tool (myfood24) for dietary assessment in population studies: comparison with biomarkers and standard interviews. BMC Med. 16, 136 (2018)
21. Timon, C.M., et al.: Comparison of a web-based 24-h dietary recall tool (Foodbook24) to an interviewer-led 24-h dietary recall. Nutrients 9, 425 (2017)
22. Meijboom, S., et al.: Evaluation of dietary intake assessed by the Dutch self-administered web-based dietary 24-h recall tool (Compl-eat™) against interviewer-administered telephone-based 24-h recalls. J. Nutr. Sci. 6, e49 (2017)
23. Moran Fagundez, L.J., Rivera Torres, A., Gonzalez Sanchez, M.E., de Torres Aured, M.L., Perez Rodrigo, C., Irles Rocamora, J.A.: Diet history: method and applications. Nutr. Hosp. 31(Suppl 3), 57–61 (2015)
24. Bloemberg, B.P., Kromhout, D., Obermann-De Boer, G.L., Van Kampen-Donker, M.: The reproducibility of dietary intake data assessed with the cross-check dietary history method. Am. J. Epidemiol. 130, 1047–1056 (1989)
25. van Rossum, C.T.M., et al.: The diet of the Dutch: Results of the first two years of the Dutch National Food Consumption Survey 2012–2016. Dutch Institute for Public Health and the Environment (2016)
26. Brouwer-Brolsma, E.M., et al.: A national dietary assessment reference database (NDARD) for the dutch population: rationale behind the design. Nutrients 9, 1136 (2017)
27. Jenab, M., Slimani, N., Bictash, M., Ferrari, P., Bingham, S.A.: Biomarkers in nutritional epidemiology: applications, needs and new horizons. Hum. Genet. 125, 507–525 (2009)
28. Brevik, A., Andersen, L.F., Karlsen, A., Trygg, K.U., Blomhoff, R., Drevon, C.A.: Six carotenoids in plasma used to assess recommended intake of fruits and vegetables in a controlled feeding study. Eur. J. Clin. Nutr. 58, 1166–1173 (2004)

29. Al-Delaimy, W.K., et al.: Plasma carotenoids as biomarkers of intake of fruits and vegetables: individual-level correlations in the European Prospective Investigation into Cancer and Nutrition (EPIC). Eur. J. Clin. Nutr. **59**, 1387–1396 (2005)
30. Saadatian-Elahi, M., et al.: Plasma phospholipid fatty acid profiles and their association with food intakes: results from a cross-sectional study within the European prospective investigation into cancer and nutrition. Am. J. Clin. Nutr. **89**, 331–346 (2009)
31. Brouwer-Brolsma, E.M., et al.: Combining traditional dietary assessment methods with novel metabolomics techniques: present efforts by the food biomarker alliance. Proc. Nutr. Soc. **76**, 619–627 (2017)
32. Trijsburg, L., et al.: Comparison of duplicate portion and 24 h recall as reference methods for validating a FFQ using urinary markers as the estimate of true intake. Br. J. Nutr. **114**, 1304–1312 (2015)
33. Cade, J., Thompson, R., Burley, V., Warm, D.: Development, validation and utilisation of food-frequency questionnaires - a review. Public Health Nutr. **5**, 567–587 (2002)
34. Kristal, A.R., et al.: Evaluation of web-based, self-administered, graphical food frequency questionnaire. J. Acad. Nutr. Diet. **114**, 613–621 (2014)
35. Fallaize, R., et al.: Online dietary intake estimation: reproducibility and validity of the Food4Me food frequency questionnaire against a 4-day weighed food record. J. Med. Internet Res. **16**, e190 (2014)
36. Labonte, M.E., Cyr, A., Baril-Gravel, L., Royer, M.M., Lamarche, B.: Validity and reproducibility of a web-based, self-administered food frequency questionnaire. Eur. J. Clin. Nutr. **66**, 166–173 (2012)
37. Wise, A., Birrell, N.M.: Design and analysis of food frequency questionnaires–review and novel method. Int. J. Food Sci. Nutr. **53**, 273–279 (2002)
38. Molag, M.: Towards transparent development of food frequency questionnaires. Scientific basis of the Dutch FFQ-TOOLTM: a computer system to generate, apply and process FFQs. Division of Human Nutrition and Health. Ph.D. Wageningen University, Wageningen (2010)
39. Cameron, M.E., van Staveren, W.A.: Manual on Methodology for Food Consumption Studies. Methods for Data Collection at an Individual Level. Oxford University Press, Oxford (1988)
40. Eldridge, A.L., et al.: Evaluation of new technology-based tools for dietary intake assessment-an ILSI Europe dietary intake and exposure task force evaluation. Nutrients **11**, 55 (2018)
41. Boushey, C.J., Spoden, M., Zhu, F.M., Delp, E.J., Kerr, D.A.: New mobile methods for dietary assessment: review of image-assisted and image-based dietary assessment methods. Proc. Nutr. Soc. **76**, 283–294 (2017)
42. Trijsburg, L., et al.: BMI was found to be a consistent determinant related to misreporting of energy, protein and potassium intake using self-report and duplicate portion methods. Public Health Nutr. **20**, 598–607 (2017)
43. Dutch Institute for Public Health and the Environment, R.: NEVO-tabel. Nederlands Voedingsstoffenbestand 2011. Voedingscentrum (2011)
44. Gijsbers, L., Ding, E.L., Malik, V.S., de Goede, J., Geleijnse, J.M., Soedamah-Muthu, S.S.: Consumption of dairy foods and diabetes incidence: a dose-response meta-analysis of observational studies. Am. J. Clin. Nutr. **103**, 1111–1124 (2016)
45. Schwingshackl, L., et al.: Food groups and risk of hypertension: a systematic review and dose-response meta-analysis of prospective studies. Adv. Nutr. **8**, 793–803 (2017). (Bethesda, Md.)
46. Kipnis, V., et al.: Structure of dietary measurement error: results of the OPEN biomarker study. Am. J. Epidemiol. **158**, 14–21 (2003). Discussion 22-16

47. Cade, J.E., et al.: DIET@NET: best practice guidelines for dietary assessment in health research. BMC Med. **15**, 202 (2017)
48. Eussen, S.J., et al.: A national FFQ for the Netherlands (the FFQ-NL1.0): development and compatibility with existing Dutch FFQs. Public Health Nutr. **21**, 2221–2229 (2018)
49. Sluik, D., et al.: A national FFQ for the Netherlands (the FFQ-NL 1.0): validation of a comprehensive FFQ for adults. Br. J. Nutr. **116**, 913–923 (2016)
50. van Lee, L., et al.: Evaluation of a screener to assess diet quality in the Netherlands. Br. J. Nutr. **115**, 517–526 (2016)
51. Health Council of the Netherlands: Guidelines for a healthy diet 2006. Health Council of the Netherlands (2006)
52. Health Council of the Netherlands: Guidelines for a healthy diet 2015. Health Council of the Netherlands (2015)
53. Looman, M., et al.: Development and evaluation of the Dutch Healthy Diet index 2015. Public Health Nutr. **20**, 2289–2299 (2017)
54. https://www.voedingscentrum.nl/nl/gezond-eten-met-de-schijf-van-vijf/omgaan-met-product en-buiten-de-schijf-van-vijf.aspx
55. Bi, Y., Lv, M., Song, C., Xu, W., Guan, N., Yi, W.: AutoDietary: a wearable acoustic sensor system for food intake recognition in daily life. IEEE Sens. J. **16**, 806–816 (2016)
56. Lopez-Meyer, P., Schuckers, S., Makeyev, O., Sazonov, E.: Detection of periods of food intake using support vector machines. In: Proceedings of Annual International Conference of the IEEE Engineering in Medicine and Biology Society, Annual Conference 2010. IEEE Engineering in Medicine and Biology Society, pp. 1004–1007 (2010)
57. Olubanjo, T., Moore, E., Ghovanloo, M.: Detecting food intake acoustic events in noisy recordings using template matching. In: 2016 IEEE-EMBS International Conference on Biomedical and Health Informatics (BHI), pp. 388–391 (2016)
58. Päßler, S., Fischer, W.: Acoustical method for objective food intake monitoring using a wearable sensor system. In: 2011 5th International Conference on Pervasive Computing Technologies for Healthcare (PervasiveHealth) and Workshops, pp. 266–269 (2011)
59. Ye, X., Chen, G., Gao, Y., Wang, H., Cao, Y.: Assisting food journaling with automatic eating detection. In: Proceedings of the 2016 CHI Conference Extended Abstracts on Human Factors in Computing Systems. ACM, San Jose (2016)
60. Ye, X., Chen, G., Cao, Y.: Automatic Eating Detection using head-mount and wrist-worn accelerometers. In: 2015 17th International Conference on E-health Networking, Application and Services (HealthCom), pp. 578–581 (2015)
61. Amft, O., Junker, H., Troster, G.: Detection of eating and drinking arm gestures using inertial body-worn sensors. In: Ninth IEEE International Symposium on Wearable Computers (ISWC 2005), pp. 160–163 (2005)
62. Farooq, M., Fontana, J.M., Sazonov, E.: A novel approach for food intake detection using electroglottography. Physiol. Meas. **35**, 739–751 (2014)
63. Kalantarian, H., Alshurafa, N., Sarrafzadeh, M.: A wearable nutrition monitoring system. In: 2014 11th International Conference on Wearable and Implantable Body Sensor Networks, pp. 75–80 (2014)
64. Amft, O., Kusserow, M., Troster, G.: Bite weight prediction from acoustic recognition of chewing. IEEE Trans. Bio-med. Eng. **56**, 1663–1672 (2009)
65. Sun, M., et al.: eButton: a wearable computer for health monitoring and personal assistance. In: Proceedings of the Design Automation Conference, pp. 1–6 (2014)
66. Puri, M., Zhiwei, Z., Yu, Q., Divakaran, A., Sawhney, H.: Recognition and volume estimation of food intake using a mobile device. In: 2009 Workshop on Applications of Computer Vision (WACV), pp. 1–8 (2009)

67. Jia, W., et al.: Accuracy of food portion size estimation from digital pictures acquired by a chest-worn camera. Public Health Nutr. **17**, 1671–1681 (2014)
68. Shang, J., et al.: A pervasive dietary data recording system. In: 2011 IEEE International Conference on Pervasive Computing and Communications Workshops (PERCOM Workshops), pp. 307–309 (2001)
69. Michielsen, C., Almanza-Aguilera, E., Brouwer-Brolsma, E.M., Urpi-Sarda, M., Afman, L. A.: Biomarkers of food intake for cocoa and liquorice (products): a systematic review. Genes Nutr. **13**, 22 (2018)
70. Michielsen, C., Hangelbroek, R.W.J., Feskens, E.J.M., Afman, L.A.: Disentangling the effects of monounsaturated fatty acids from other components of a mediterranean diet on serum metabolite profiles: a randomized fully controlled dietary intervention in healthy subjects at risk of the metabolic syndrome. Mol. Nutr. Food Res. **63**, e1801095 (2019)

Computational Infrastructure
of SoilGrids 2.0

Luís M. de Sousa[1]([✉]) [iD], Laura Poggio[1] [iD], Gwen Dawes[2] [iD], Bas Kempen[1] [iD],
and Rik van den Bosch[1]

[1] ISRIC - World Soil Information,
Wageningen, The Netherlands
luis.desousa@isric.org
[2] FB-IT, Wageningen University and Research,
Wageningen, The Netherlands

Abstract. SoilGrids maps soil properties for the entire globe at medium spatial resolution (250 m cell side) using state-of-the-art machine learning methods. The expanding pool of input data and the increasing computational demands of predictive models required a prediction framework that could deal with large data. This article describes the mechanisms set in place for a geo-spatially parallelised prediction system for soil properties. The features provided by GRASS GIS – *mapset* and *region* – are used to limit predictions to a specific geographic area, enabling parallelisation. The Slurm job scheduler is used to deploy predictions in a high-performance computing cluster. The framework presented can be seamlessly applied to most other geo-spatial process requiring parallelisation. This framework can also be employed with a different job scheduler, GRASS GIS being the main requirement and engine.

Keywords: Digital Soil Mapping · High-performance computing · GRASS GIS

1 Introduction

Soil is key in the realisation of a number of UN Sustainable Development Goals by providing a variety of goods and services. Soil information is fundamental for a large range of global applications, including assessments of soil and land degradation, sustainable land management and environmental conservation. It is important to provide free, consistent, easily accessible, quality-controlled and standardised soil information. Spatial soil information is often available as maps of soil properties, e.g. pH, carbon content, texture information. Soil is a 3D body and the maps should describe the landscape (i.e. horizontal) variability as well as the vertical (i.e. along the soil depth) variability. Often, such maps are produced using a Digital Soil Mapping (DSM) approach [7], creating a statistical model between the properties measured at known locations and environmental covariates describing the soil forming factors [9]. In recent years machine learning

© IFIP International Federation for Information Processing 2020
Published by Springer Nature Switzerland AG 2020
I. N. Athanasiadis et al. (Eds.): ISESS 2020, IFIP AICT 554, pp. 24–31, 2020.
https://doi.org/10.1007/978-3-030-39815-6_3

methods [4] were used to develop such models. Once the model is calibrated and evaluated, it is used to predict soil properties at non visited locations.

SoilGrids is based on a DSM system that produces geo-spatial soil information fulfilling two main goals: (1) be a source of consistent soil information to support global modelling, and (2) provide complementary information to support regional and national soil information products in data deprived areas. The main target user groups are policy makers and land management services in countries that lack the means to produce such information, as well as scientists developing other models and tools requiring soil data as input.

SoilGrids is of a series of maps for different soil properties following the specifications of the GlobalSoilMap project [1]. The production of a soil property map consists of different steps: the fitting of a model, the evaluation of that model and finally the prediction for each raster cell at the global scale with a spatial resolution of 250 m. Six depth intervals are currently considered and prediction uncertainty is quantified. The total computation time required for a single soil property exceeds 1 500 CPU-hours. Parallelisation is therefore fundamental, requiring up to hundreds of CPUs.

This article outlines the computational infrastructure (hardware and software) employed to compute the latest SoilGrids products in a high-performance computing (HPC) cluster, focusing in particular on the parallelisation and the resource management for global DSM modelling.

2   General Framework

SoilGrids requires an intensive computational workflow, including different steps and integrating different software. SoilGrids is entirely based on open source software. The inputs to SoilGrids currently comprise observations from 250 000 soil profiles and a selection from over 400 global raster characterising soil forming factors: morphology (e.g. elevation, landform), vegetation information (e.g. NDVI and other indices), climate (e.g. precipitation, land surface temperature) and human factors (e.g. land use/cover).

Gathering and harmonising soil profile observations is one of the core work-streams performed by ISRIC, with the World Soil Information System (WoSIS) [2] being its most visible product. These observations are maintained in a relational database hosted by PostgreSQL [10], from which they are directly sourced for modelling. Environmental covariates are ingested into GRASS GIS [6,11], thus being automatically normalised to a unique raster cell matrix (of 250 m cells). Previous SoilGrids releases were computed on the millenary Marinus of Tyre map projection [16], a popular projection in environmental modelling. However, this projection expands the surface area of the globe by about 60%. With the increasing size of inputs and outputs in SoilGrids, this overhead urged the switch to an equal-area map projection. The Homolosine projection [5] was selected, since among those projections supported by open source software, is the one that best preserves the shapes of lands masses [17]. The size of each output raster was thus reduced in over 10^{12} cells.

The general framework of SoilGrids is described in Fig. 1. The main steps are:

1. creation of a regression matrix that overlays soil profile data with environmental covariates.
2. fitting of the regression model. Currently this step is based on state-of-the-art machine learning methods, able to produce a measure of the uncertainty of the predictions, namely Quantile Regression Forests (QRF) [8].
3. prediction with the model at global scale.

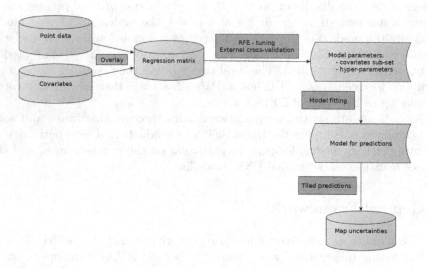

Fig. 1. General framework of SoilGrids.

3 HPC Infrastructure

SoilGrids is currently computed on Anunna, an HPC cluster managed by Wageningen University and Research (WUR). Anunna provides more than 2 000 CPUs in an heterogeneous set of compute nodes. The majority of compute nodes provide 12 GB of RAM per CPU. Storage is managed by the Lustre distributed file system [15].

The Slurm Workload Manager [20] is used to manage the cluster workload. Slurm offers a large range of flexibility. The user may restrict computation to a specific type of node, require an exact number of CPUs to use in parallel, set the number of CPUs required by each process, set a computation time limit, request a specific amount of memory and declare the exact software packages to load at computation time. These settings are defined in a configuration file (the Slurm file), where the user sets the programmes to run and their parameters.

4   Parallelisation of Global Scale Geo-Spatial Computations

SoilGrids requires the integration of a number of software. The two key components are GRASS GIS [6,11] and R [13]. GRASS GIS is used to store the input data and as the engine to control the parallelisation of the predictions. R is used for the statistical modelling, i.e. to calibrate, fit and compute the predictions using the QRF model.

The GRASS GIS *mapset* and *region* features are used to set up parallelisation. *Location* is a directory which contains GRASS GIS *mapsets*, which are its sub-directories. All data in one *location* must refer to the same spatial reference system (SRS). *Mapsets* contain the actual data, they are a tool for organising maps in a transparent way and provide isolation between different tasks to prevent data loss. GRASS GIS is always connected to one particular *mapset*. *Mapsets* are used to store maps related to a project, a specific task, issue or sub-region. Besides the geo-spatial data, a *mapset* holds the resolution and extent of the current computational region. In this version of SoilGrids, the SRS used for the GRASS *location* is the Homolosine projection applied to the WGS84 datum.

Prior to prediction, a global tessellation is created dynamically using the GRASS module r.tile, dividing land masses into square tiles of a given side (Fig. 2). Predictions are then executed independently, and in parallel, within each of these tiles.

Fig. 2. Land masses tessellated with tiles of 450 km in side.

A Slurm file is used to start up each individual prediction process. The prediction process receives as argument the identifier of one of the tiles in the tessellation. The process then creates a temporary *mapset*, setting its *region* to the extent of the tile it is tasked to process. The temporary *mapset* works as a geo-spatial sand box for the prediction process. The prediction process loads data from GRASS within the extent of the tile, as set by the GRASS *region*. The prediction process is controlled by R software linked to GRASS with the rgrass7 package [3]. The result is saved to disk as a GeoTIFF file and the temporary *mapset* deleted (Fig. 3).

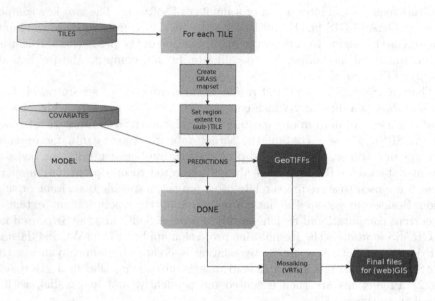

Fig. 3. Predictions occur in parallel in each of these tiles.

5   Resources Management with (sub-)tiling

Prediction models developed with the R language may require a large amount of RAM, i.e. tens of GBs of RAM to execute predictions for a single tile under 1 MB in size. The obvious strategy to tackle memory constraints would be to reduce the size of the tiles used to set up the temporary GRASS *mapsets*. However, this can soon result in tens of thousands of GeoTIFF files. Such large numbers can be excessive for some file systems, and complicate the functioning of command line tools [19].

In the case of SoilGrids, a different strategy was applied to address resource constraints, i.e. sub-tiling. The prediction process sub-divides the tile in equal-size sub-tiles. Within the temporary GRASS *mapset*, the prediction process successively sets the *region* to each of these sub-tiles and invokes the general prediction model. The output computed within each sub-tile is finally saved into a folder named after the prediction tile. The end result is a collection of folders, one per tile, each containing as many GeoTIFF files as the number of sub-tiles contained in the tile.

6   Assemblage of Prediction Files

The sub-tilling strategy can result in a very large number of GeoTIFF files. For example, a three-by-three sub-tiling matrix applied to tiles of 200×200 km results in over 50 000 GeoTIFF files covering the globe's land masses. All these files must then be aggregated to produce a single asset, easily manageable by end users. The Virtual Raster Tiles (VRT) format [12] introduced by the Geospatial Data Abstraction Library (GDAL) is a suitable solution, as it provides a simple and lightweight way to mosaic geo-spatial data. A VRT is in essence a XML file that patches together various contiguous rasters in the same SRS into a mosaic. As the GDAL library is used as I/O driver by most GIS programmes this format is widely supported.

GDAL provides a specific tool for the creation of VRT mosaics: gdalbuildvrt. It can take as input a file with the list of rasters to include in the output VRT. Another GDAL tool, gdaladdo, can afterwards be employed to create overviews for the VRT. These overviews are stored in a companion file to the original VRT. The end user needs only to point a GIS programme to the VRT file to load the full raster mosaic. With the overviews created, access is fast and fluid at different map scales.

The VRT format is also useful to simplify the re-projection of large rasters. Another GDAL tool – gdalwarp – can be applied directly to a VRT file, creating a second VRT file encoding the parameters of the specified output SRS. No transformations are conducted on the rasters themselves, thus a swift operation.

7   Reproducibility and Portability

The parallelisation scheme described in this article is directly portable to any system using Slurm where GRASS GIS and R can be installed. It is also applicable to any other system relying on a similar scheduling mechanism, such as Son of Grid Engine or Mesos [14]. In essence, any system able to spawn processes passing a tile identifier as parameter can be used to reproduce this set up. This solution can also be easily adapted to run on single machines with a large number of CPUs and managed by the GNU parallel tool [18].

While GRASS GIS is a key component in the approach described wherewith, alternative software can be used to similar ends. Certain raster formats, like GeoTIFF, store rasters in blocks of constant size. It is therefore possible to parallelise spatial computation on the basis of such blocks. GDAL in particular provides an API that facilitates the retrieval of these blocks. However, some pre processing might be necessary to guarantee that all rasters stack up, using blocks of equal size and spatial extent. The *mapset* and *region* features in GRASS are unique among open source software and perform this stacking of input rasters in a seamless way.

The parallelisation approach reported in this article can be applied to other types of modelling where results can be easily parallelised in space. The tiling mechanism is fully dynamic and independent of the underlying SRS. The size of both the main map tiles and its sub-tiles are parameters to the tiling routine, and expressed in number of raster cells, not map units. It is therefore straightforward to apply with different SRSs and computation extents. The main limitation of this approach is with problems that can not be easily parallelised in space, such as hydrological processes requiring continuity or interactions between catchments.

References

1. Arrouays, D., et al.: GlobalSoilMap: toward a fine-resolution global grid of soil properties. In: Advances in Agronomy, vol. 125, pp. 93–134. Academic Press (2014). https://doi.org/10.1016/B978-0-12-800137-0.00003-0
2. Batjes, N.H., Ribeiro, E., van Oostrum, A.: Standardised soil profile data to support global mapping and modelling (wosis snapshot 2019). Earth Syst. Sci. Data Discussions **2019**, 1–46 (2019). https://doi.org/10.5194/essd-2019-164. https://www.earth-syst-sci-data-discuss.net/essd-2019-164/
3. Bivand, R.: rgrass7: Interface between GRASS 7 geographical information system and R (2018). https://CRAN.R-project.org/package=rgrass7. r package version 0.1-12
4. Breiman, L.: Random forests. Mach. Learn. **45**(1), 5–32 (2001)
5. Goode, J.P.: The homolosine projection: a new device for portraying the earth's surface entire. Ann. Assoc. Am. Geogr. **15**(3), 119–125 (1925)
6. GRASS Development Team: Geographic Resources Analysis Support System (GRASS GIS) software, version 7.6.0 (2019). http://www.grass.osgeo.org
7. McBratney, A., Santos, M., Minasny, B.: On digital soil mapping. Geoderma **117**, 3–52 (2003). https://doi.org/10.1016/S0016-7061(03)00223-4
8. Meinshausen, N.: Quantile regression forests. J. Mach. Learn. Res. **7**(Jun), 983–999 (2006)
9. Minasny, B., McBratney, A.: Digital soil mapping: a brief history and some lessons. Geoderma **264**(Part B), 301–311 (2016). Soil mapping, classification, and modelling: history and future directions
10. Momjian, B.: PostgreSQL: Introduction and Concepts. Addison-Wesley, New York (2001)
11. Neteler, M., Mitasova, H.: Open Source GIS: A GRASS GIS Approach, vol. 689. Springer, Berlin (2013)
12. OSGeo Foundation: VRT - GDAL virtual format. https://gdal.org/drivers/raster/vrt.html (2019). Accessed 2019 Oct 09
13. R Core Team: R: A language and environment for statistical computing. R Foundation for Statistical Computing, Vienna, Austria (2019). http://www.R-project.org/. ISBN 3-900051-07-0
14. Reuther, A., et al.: Scheduler technologies in support of high performance data analysis. In: 2016 IEEE High Performance Extreme Computing Conference (HPEC), pp. 1–6. IEEE (2016)
15. Schwan, P., et al.: Lustre: building a file system for 1000-node clusters. In: Proceedings of the 2003 Linux Symposium, vol. 2003, pp. 380–386 (2003)
16. Snyder, J.P.: Flattening the Earth: Two Thousand Years of Map Projections. University of Chicago Press, Chicago (1997)
17. de Sousa, L.M., Poggio, L., Kempen, B.: Comparison of FOSS4G supported equal-area projections using discrete distortion indicatrices. ISPRS Int. J. Geo-Inf. **8**(8), 351 (2019)
18. Tange, O.: GNU Parallel 2018. https://doi.org/10.5281/zenodo.1146014

19. Thomas Koenig: sysconf manual page, in Linux Programmer's manual (2019). http://man7.org/linux/man-pages/man3/sysconf.3.html. Accessed 2019 Oct 15
20. Yoo, A.B., Jette, M.A., Grondona, M.: SLURM: simple linux utility for resource management. In: Feitelson, D., Rudolph, L., Schwiegelshohn, U. (eds.) JSSPP 2003. LNCS, vol. 2862, pp. 44–60. Springer, Heidelberg (2003). https://doi.org/10.1007/10968987_3

Defining and Classifying Infrastructural Contestation: Towards a Synergy Between Anthropology and Data Science

Christos Giovanopoulos[1]([⊠]) [iD], Yannis Kallianos[1] [iD],
Ioannis N. Athanasiadis[2] [iD], and Dimitris Dalakoglou[1]([⊠]) [iD]

[1] Vrije Universiteit Amsterdam, Amsterdam, The Netherlands
{c.giovamopoulos,d.dalakoglou}@vu.nl
[2] Wageningen University and Research, Wageningen, The Netherlands

Abstract. The last decade infrastructure systems have been under strain around the globe. The 2008 financial crisis, the so-called fourth industrial revolution, ongoing urbanisation and climate change have contributed to the emergence of an infrastructural crisis that has been labelled as infrastructural gap. During this period, infrastructure systems have increasingly become sites of public contestation with significant effects on their operation and governance. At stake has been the issues of access to infrastructure, their social and environmental consequences and the 'modern ideal' embodied in the design of those socio-technical systems. With this paper we apply a cross-disciplinary methodology in order to document and define the practices of this new wave of infrastructural contestation, taking Greece in the 2008–2017 period as the case study. The synthesis of quantitative and qualitative datasets with ethnographic knowledge help us, furthermore, to record tendencies and patterns in the ongoing phenomenon of infrastructural contestation (This study is part of infra-demos project (www.infrademos.net), which is funded by a VIDI grant awarded by the Dutch Organisation of Science, PI: Prof. Dimitris Dalakoglou, Dept. of Social and Cultural Anthropology, Vrije Universiteit Amsterdam).

Keywords: Infrastructural contestation · Infrastructural gap · Anthropology · Data sciences

1 Introduction

The last decade infrastructures have been increasingly noticeable as the terrain of socio-political contestation. Economic crisis, disruptive technologies and ongoing urban expansion - among other reasons - challenge the capacities of even the 'developed economies', to sustain their pre-crisis level of infrastructural provisions. This phenomenon, which has been labelled infrastructural gap (Authers 2015; Dalakoglou 2016; ODI 2016), challenges the modernist ideal of infrastructure development and questions its concomitant model of infrastructural governance. The role of infrastructure systems as safeguards of unhindered economic growth and social cohesion is at stake and has been contested by various movements in diverse forms. A recent example of such contestation has been the Yellow Vest protests in France that were concerned

I. N. Athanasiadis et al. (Eds.): ISESS 2020, IFIP AICT 554, pp. 32–47, 2020.
https://doi.org/10.1007/978-3-030-39815-6_4

initially with access to automobility, heating, and hydrocarbon-based energy. That movement, besides contesting the infrastructural and environmental policies of the French government, signified the break-up of the social contract between polity and citizenry that is facilitated by these infrastructural provisions.

This paper aims (A) to define infrastructural contestation, to create a typology of the phenomenon and to document its diversity and its scale and (B) to show trends and patterns within infrastructural contestation, with Greece as the case study. In order to achieve this, we have compiled datasets of events of grassroots contestation and socio-political struggles related to infrastructures during the 2008–2017 period. In the context of the infra-demos project, which seeks to critically understand the relationship between infrastructures, democracy and civil participation, we analyse these struggles both qualitatively and quantitatively using ethnographically embedded knowledge and digital tools. The latter enriches the affordances and capacities of the ethnographically acquired knowledge by making explicit quantitative correlations. The analysis and visualisation of large data-sets related to infrastructural contestation allow us to conceptualise the various representations of contestation. Moreover, this ongoing synergy between data science and anthropology, although a work in progress, enables us to detect processes towards a more active citizen engagement with infrastructure.

2 The Case Study and Beyond

The global financial crisis had sweeping consequences for infrastructural sustainability and provision within Europe. Increased austerity in public spending as well as privatisation of public assets affected the governance, maintenance and materialities of hard infrastructures[1]. The consequences for soft infrastructures (Filion and Keil, 2016) are even more evident, with reductions in funding for social provision and welfare services (Dalakoglou 2016). As such, the crisis – paired with neoliberal policies – has challenged the role of infrastructures in 'forming the base on which to operate modern economic and social systems' (Larkin 2013: 330).

Within that context while Greece may have been the most extreme case of crisis-stricken country in the EU, it is far from being unique (Dalakoglou and Agelopoulos 2018). The volatile financial recovery and the ongoing political uncertainty across the EU combined with the permeation and effects of disruptive technologies around the globe, have upset the foundations and legitimacy of the dominant infrastructural model. At the same time, infrastructural contestation has emerged as one of the main socio-political phenomena through which austerity, neoliberal policies, environmental risks and state legitimisation have been challenged.

Roads and other transport networks, water and sewage systems, communication and electricity networks, as much as welfare and state governance infrastructures have been subject to social dispute and conflicts. In addition to the aforementioned Yellow Vest protest against the allegedly pro-environment fuel tax and access to auto-mobility,

---

[1] Between 2006 and 2013 the total drop in the value of infrastructure deals was 80% (Linklaters 2014: 8).

heating etc. in France (2018–19), one can also mention the dynamic protests against the increase in public transport fares in Chile (2019), the water charges battle in Ireland (2015–16), the re-municipalisation of water systems (e.g. Paris 2010, Berlin 2013, Budapest 2012 and many more EU cities), the ongoing No-TAV movement in north Italy, struggles against the construction or expansion of airports (ZAD, France; Gatwick, UK) or for the utilization of former airports (Tempelhof, Berlin).

Making explicit the multifarious ways in which similar socio-political mobilisations contested infrastructure systems and flows in Greece during the same period provides insights and a method that can inform research in different frameworks. Those movements have rendered the infrastructural domain as one of the most important public sites of civil participation. On the one hand, they made visible power relations embedded in the technologies, governance and distribution of infrastructure systems, allowing their re-conceptualisation. On the other hand, the diverse (traditional and novel) modes of engagement with infrastructural systems arguably underline the potential for emerging, innovative and democratic forms of infrastructure participation.

3   Mapping Infrastructural Contestation

Our engagement with previous studies on the infrastructural gap and political mobil-isations (Crisis-scape.net 2014; Dalakoglou and Kallianos 2014, 2018; Giovanopoulos and Dalakoglou 2011) and pilot ethnographic fieldwork on sites where infrastructures were contested (solidarity schools and clinics, waste management, energy communi-ties) provided us with an empirical understanding of the significance and wider dynamic of infrastructural contestation. Thus, before proceeding to more precise and longer-term ethnographic fieldwork the need for systematic documentation of the phenomenon, its taxonomies and scales and by extension for a more precise definition of its content in practice became explicit to us.

Our mapping focuses on the grassroots aspect of infrastructure contestation and is composed by four dimensions: (1) a description of instances of socio-political antag-onism in regard to infrastructure; (2) the different types of those events according to their means of struggle/form of action; (3) the infrastructural fields those conflicts regard; and (4) the mode of infrastructure contestation each of the events relates to. Our aim has been to depict the realm of socio-technological interventions from below and highlight comparisons between them in order to visually explore patterns and draw some preliminary conclusions.

3.1   Method

In order to collect and digitise our dataset, we followed seven stages.

1. By building on thick and deep datasets acquired from our previous and pilot studies we created a broad but systematic timeline of socio-political conflicts that took place between 2008 and 2017. We did so according to their documentation in communication hubs (online media) of social movements. This initial timeline operated as guideline in outlining the two next steps.

2. While we confirmed the high degree of conflicts related to infrastructure at this point our research lacked a definition of the infrastructural fields at play. Thus we proceeded in their classification to specific categories (Table 1). In order to do so we drew from the report *Infrastructure for the 21st Century: Framework for a Research Agenda* by the National Research Council (1987) for the US Committee on Infrastructure Innovation, and from the definition provided by the Greek Centre for the Security Studies (Ministry of Public Order and Citizen Protection) according to the EU directive 2008/114/EC about 'European critical infrastructure' (Official Government Gazette 2011).

3. Next, we separated from the broader timeline of socio-political contestation those events that occurred around and were related to, to a greater or lesser degree, the infrastructural fields that we defined. Thus we formed the initial chronological line-up of instances of infrastructural contestation which constitutes the first dimension of our mapping.

4. We proceeded then in defining the second dimension of our mapping. This regarded the variation of the struggles and mobilisations related to infrastructures according to the means and kind of practices they employed. We classified the events in six categories: i. strikes & protests, ii. civil disobedience campaigns, iii. community struggles, iv. (infrastructure) self-management or recuperation, v. institutional and legal interventions and vi. generative endeavours linked to infrastructuring attempts. Such categories are not mutually exclusive. An event may involve more than one type of action. Analytically they are important because they indicate the connection between types of socio-political and infrastructural contestation. Most significantly they point out to the subjects and processes that are more prone to contest critically infrastructure systems. In addition, we drew a last category to include 'general events', mainly general strikes, that interacted with more specific and targeted movements around infrastructure.

5. The following step was to classify the recorded events according to the different ways in which they engage with and contest infrastructure. Thus, we defined a typology of infrastructure contestation (see Sect. 4 below), which forms the third dimension of our datasets. Central to the definition process has been the degree with which movements, forms of struggle and demands problematise, or not, the existing infrastructure paradigm.

6. Building on these initial findings and definitions we continued with a more thorough, focused and detailed search of events of infrastructural contestation. Our aim was to cover and map to the largest possible degree movements, campaigns and citizen initiatives which engaged with infrastructural contestation. This effort resulted in a list of 880 events.

7. The last part included the revisiting of our taxonomy of infrastructural contestation. Considering issues that were raised by the larger volume and variety of events and types of action that challenged the established infrastructure arrangements, we refined our definitions and typology of infrastructural contestation (see Sect. 4).

Table 1. Infrastructure type categorisation.

Infrastructure type	Subcategories
Transport & mobility	Airways/airports Bridges & canals Public transport (metro, bus, trains, etc.) Railways Roads Ports/sea transport
Energy	Gas pipelines, storage, distribution Oil production, storage, distribution Power-plants (oil, coalmines etc.) Power-grid Renewable energy power-plants (air, solar, water)
Water	Sewage network Water supply network Irrigation network Dams
Waste	Solid waste Hazardous waste Landfill sites Recycling plants
Communication & information systems	Public broadcasting services Telecommunication networks (analogue and digital) Media (press, radio, TV, digital)
Welfare infrastructures	Health care (hospitals, etc.) Social security (insurance – pension system) Education (schools, universities, etc.) Housing (temporary shelter) Recreation (parks, coastlines, public spaces, etc.)

3.2   Sources

The collection and composition of the datasets was one of the most challenging parts of the process. This was due to the magnitude of mobilisations that occurred in this period, due to the lack of any consistent recording of socio-political struggles[2] in Greece and due to the informal status of many of these grassroots movements unlike elsewhere in Europe (Institute of Citizen Studies 2016). While our mapping of events of infrastructural contestation is by no means exhaustive, we attempted a double task. First, to certify the validity of information regarding the events we documented. Second, to achieve a degree of representativeness in relation to the array of movements that

---

[2] Even the most organised and institutionalised social movements, such as the General Confederation of Trade-Unions of Greece (GSEE), kept records of the labour movement activities only between 2011–2017.

emerged around infrastructure during this period. In order to achieve this, we proceeded as follows:

1. By combining our initial mapping of socio-political antagonism and our ethnographically acquired knowledge we made a list of the movements and campaigns related to infrastructural contestation. This assisted a more focused research for, and use of, sources.

2. We looked for existing datasets that cover large parts of grassroots encounters with infrastructure. Those datasets include: the annual report on strikes and labour mobilisations of the Research Institute of the General Confederation of Greek Workers (INE-GSEE) published between 2011–2017 and unprocessed archival material for the 2008–2009 period which were made available to us; raw data of Prof. Serntedakis and Koufidi's research on "Conflictual and electoral cycle in crisis-ridden Greece" (2018) which cover the years 2009–2013 were kindly shared with us by the authors. From those datasets we retrieved the vast majority of infrastructural events related to labour strikes and protests.

3. In order to pin down the diffused activity of informal movements on infrastructural fields we scanned online hubs of social movements (athens.indymedia.org and kinimatorama.net) and hubs of the alternative and social solidarity economy (enallaktikos.gr and solidarity4all.gr). Through these sources we documented specific actions of grassroots infrastructural contestation and we identified struggles and initiatives which we then confirmed and explored more via other avenues.

4. The online media hubs (webpages and blogs) of movements and campaigns, 12 in total, and the online outlets and social media of citizens' initiatives which engaged in infrastructural contestation, 73 in total, have also been a significant source. These sources covered a big portion of campaigns (e.g. against mobile phone towers, road tolls and public transport price-hikes), of specific struggles related to infrastructure (e.g. against landfill construction in the town of Keratea, anti-privatisation struggles, or against mergers of public hospitals and schools), as well as of initiatives that created their own alternative infrastructures (e.g. solidarity clinics and schools).

5. Lastly, we resorted to an open internet search in order to retrieve information for specific events of infrastructural contestation that we had already identified. These sources included articles from the online editions of 11 newspapers with nationwide distribution, 32 regional and local media outlets, 9 online media sources, 3 special interest media, and 8 alternative media sources. In total 63 different sources.

While we acknowledge that our mapping is not exhaustive, by collecting and cross-checking between these sources we believe that our dataset offers a representative sample of the events and features of infrastructural contestation. However, we should also be attentive to unbalances between forms of infrastructural contestation that may be linked to the choice, or lack, of sources. The systematic recording of labour struggles by the trade unions' institute INE-GSEE for example may have contributed to an over-representation of infrastructural contestation related to labour issues and working conditions. We tried to counter such unevenness by performing a meticulous documentation of the informal and decentralised movements. We did this by using alternative media, and mainly their own sources, to record infrastructure related actions. In any case, judging by our findings, any such unbalance does not contradict our initial hypotheses for the increasing importance of infrastructural contestation, and for the growing tendency towards participation and reconfiguration of the existing infrastructural arrangements.

4 Modes of Infrastructural Contestation

Suggesting a typology of the modes of infrastructural contestation has not only been the most demanding task but also critical for the conceptualisation of infrastructural contestation. In order to explore the diverse characteristics that defined infrastructural contestation during the examined period we organised a typology based on the following criteria:

a. the ability to render infrastructure space as a site of socio-political antagonism,
b. the relationship between the expressed demands or actions of a movement, community or public and the infrastructure's function or transformation,
c. the form that this contestation has taken in relation to the operation of infrastructure (disruption, remodification, alternative use, innovation, etc.).

Based on the facts gathered so far, and on ethnographic affinity and knowledge we argue that we encountered at least six modes of infrastructural contestation.

4.1 Contestation of Labour and Working Conditions

Industrial actions in defense of labour rights and income (social security, pensions etc.) and resisting the deregulation of the labour market - which often involves technological changes - compose this type of contestation. Although most times this type does not explicitly refer to infrastructure per se, nevertheless it is central to the disruption (and efficacy) of infrastructural function and provision. According to Pasternak and Dafnos (2018: 740) '[T]he timely circulation of goods, services, information, resources, and energy through territory is critical to capitalism today, rendering acute the problem of blockades and resource extraction stoppages for the state'. Moreover, the attempts to restrict this disruptive power held by infrastructure employees (even by manual non-specialised workers) has often led to infrastructural 'innovation' (automation, robotics etc.).

4.2 Contestation for the Right to Access

This type concerns struggles for a fairer distribution of, and access to, infrastructure networks that are fundamental in sustaining everyday life (water, energy, transport etc.). This mode may interweave with demands for public investment on infrastructure development. It also relates to acts of civil disobedience for access to infrastructure (e.g. clandestine power connections) or with resisting unfair payments for infrastructural services (e.g. refusal to pay transport fares or road-tolls). Such actions have a very direct result in asserting the right to infrastructural use. However, while contestation over access accentuates the injustices in the distribution of infrastructure networks it does not always prompt a questioning of the infrastructural model. Yet, in specific contexts, such contestation type may cause growing financial leakages in infrastructural systems (power-grid, water supply, road system etc.) and thus enforce changes in the governance and operational mode of the infrastructure at stake.

4.3 Ownership and Governance Contestation

Modes of ownership and governance are among the most contested issues when it comes to infrastructure. The primarily state-funded and run infrastructural model of modernity has been under attack from neoliberal policies and governance the last 50 years (Graham and Marvin 2001), yet, the defense of infrastructures as public assets constitutes one of the most prominent types of infrastructural contestation still. Anti-privatisation struggles compose the majority of such kind of contestation and occurred in most of the large infrastructural systems in Greece (telecommunications, ports, energy etc.). Most of the times they blend with other modes of infrastructural contestation, usually labour strikes or struggles for the re-municipalisation of infrastructural provisions (e.g. water).

4.4 Contesting Infrastructural Effects

Here contestation usually concerns acts by local communities and movements against the social, environmental and financial effects of infrastructural development in a vicinity. Mobilisations against waste landfills, river dams, mobile phone towers, and industrial scale air-turbines are some examples of this kind of contestation. While such movements develop, largely, a critique of the top down developmental model in situ (within a local context), it is less often the case to see them moving on a wider critique of the infrastructure model itself. In addition, there are cases that refusal to infrastructural development has been associated with maintaining the local, traditional infrastructure and use (or disuse) of natural resources. However, those rebuffs should not be easily classified as a Not In My Back Yard approach, since they inform a critique of a wider economic and political framework of governance. There are examples (e.g. waste management) where movements and communities proceeded from denial to form their own proposals for alternative waste infrastructure system.

4.5 Contestation as Remodification of Infrastructure

Such form of contestation regards numerous collective and individual, but widespread, everyday uses of infrastructural systems that prompt their remodification. It involves cases in which a specific infrastructure is used by the public for purposes other than the ones which it was initially designed for (Filion and Keil 2016). In this way a certain level of re-purposing of the specific infrastructure takes place. Most of these cases unfold at the everyday molecular level. However, this type of contestation may also include collective attempts to transform the function and use of an infrastructure. Cases where public 'brown fields' were converted into parks, self-managed recreational spaces or urban-farms are some examples of contestation as remodification in Greece.

4.6 Transfigurative Contestation

This last type includes movements and attempts which experiment, design or develop alternatives to the dominant paradigm infrastructure with regard to engagement in acts of infrastructuring. Transfigurative contestation does not concern only attempts for more inclusive and equal redistribution of infrastructural provisions. It regards experimentation with infrastructure prototypes which aim to organise and facilitate processes of social transformation. In that sense it refers 'to infrastructure' as verb and not as a noun. It expands 'the right to infrastructure' from merely a meaning of 'access to' to a concept that claims the right to create infrastructure (Jiménez 2014). Thus, it opens up the notion of infrastructural contestation to participatory experiments of design in a process of democratisation (and commoning) of infrastructural systems. Examples of transfigurative contestation in Greece include self-organised solidarity clinics, solidarity schools, cooperative hydroelectric power-plants and/or renewable energy communities.

Having defined these six types of infrastructural contestation, according to our data and findings, we need to clarify a few points. First they are not mutually exclusive. This typology is proposed for analytical reasons and it aims to unveil how different agencies, interests and publics affect the technologies and operation of infrastructural systems. Thus many acts of socio-political contestation entailed more than one type of infrastructural contestation. More importantly, a particular struggle could evolve and include many different forms or instances of infrastructural contestation.

5 Open Data and Digital Visualisation

We have compiled a dataset that includes about 880 grassroots socio-political encounters with infrastructure, that span from 2008 to 2017. Some events existed in an instant in time (as in the case of one day strikes or one off protests), while others have been assigned a duration that spans across several days (as in the case of the operation of social pharmacies). Thus, events are associated with two dates: a compulsory start date, and an optional end date. However, some repetitive events correspond to long term campaigns (e.g. against the road tolls, or anti-privatisation struggles) but appear as instant events date-wise.

Each event is classified in three dimensions: according to the type of struggles and actions it employed, according to the infrastructural field in which it unfolded and according to the mode of infrastructural contestation it indicates. Each event can be associated with more than one types, fields and modes. Data have been organized in a spreadsheet, and will be published using an open license, on Zenodo.

To visualise the dataset, we have employed the Timeline Storyteller (Brehmer et al. 2017), an open-source expressive visual storytelling environment for presenting timelines in the browser or in Microsoft Power BI. Timeline Storyteller allows us to visualise different aspects of timeline data using a palette of timeline representations, scales and layouts, as well as controls for filtering, highlighting and annotation. The data storytelling approach intends to use quantitative date to convey multiple narrative points, and to explore the process of transforming data into visually shared stories (Lee et al. 2015). An example timeline is shown in Fig. 1, where the pattern identified shows that in the beginning of the crisis, during the period between 2008–2009, mobilisations mostly concerned 'against infrastructure effects' events, while from 2010 onwards, there was a rise of 'right to access' contestation events.

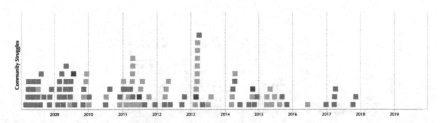

Fig. 1. Timeline of 'community struggle' type of events. (Legend below in Fig. 3)

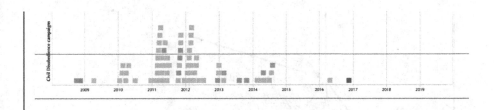

Fig. 2. Timeline of 'civil disobedience' type of events.

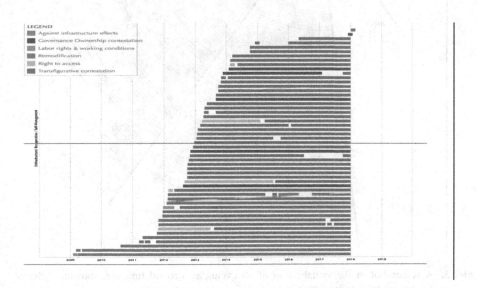

Fig. 3. Timeline of 'self-management/recuperation of infrastructures' type of events.

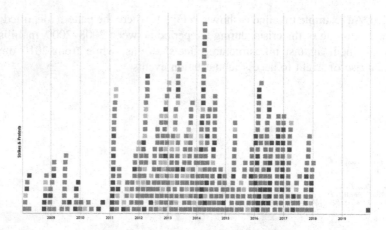

Fig. 4. Timeline of 'strike and protests' type of events

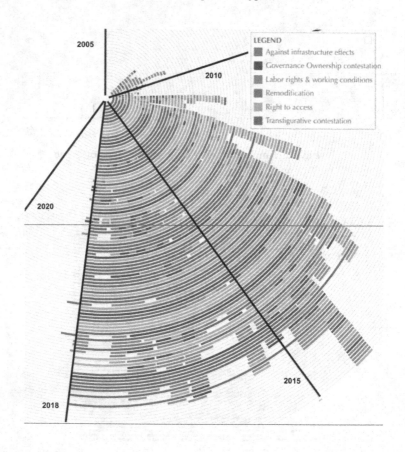

Fig. 5. A screenshot of the visualisation of all events as a round timeline, showing different modes of infrastructural contestation in colour (Color figure online)

6 Preliminary Findings from the Data Visualization

By applying this multi-layered visualisation which spans uninterrupted along a ten-year period (Jan. 2008–Dec. 2017), we were able to compare forms of socio-political interventions around various infrastructure systems with modes of infrastructural contestation. It also made possible the tracing of relations between modes of infrastructural contestation and of emerging trends and patterns. Within this context we can draw five preliminary observations:

1. Looking at the more general trend and mutations of types of contestation we see an explicit tendency from community struggles against infrastructural effects in 2008 and 2009 (Fig. 1), towards civil disobedience in 2011–2012 (Fig. 2) and from there to self-management/recuperation of infrastructures (Fig. 3). While this tendency does not relate to the evolution of a specific event or campaign, it maps a more general trend among various forms of infrastructural contestation. Thus it is revealing of the transformative processes that unfold and of the emerging tendencies for participatory infrastructuring.
2. The majority of the "strikes and protests" type relates predominantly with "labour rights" industrial disputes and to a smaller degree with anti-privatisation struggles (governance & ownership form of infrastructural contestation) and for "right to access" (Fig. 4). This information confirms the weak (and indirect) links of traditional forms of industrial action and the labour movement with transformative infrastructural processes.
3. By taking into account the number of incidents, regularity of appearance and duration of events most present incidents concern labour rights and working conditions, right to access and transfigurative contestation (Fig. 5 and points a. and d. below).
4. The vast majority of cases of transfigurative infrastructural contestation (64 out of 80 events in total, or, 80%) appear on the field of welfare infrastructure. This indicates that it is more likely participatory forms of infrastructuring to occur on the sphere of 'soft infrastructures', which relate to social reproduction and welfare.
5. Almost a tenth of the events documented (84 out of 880) concern "against infrastructural effects" type of contestation. The vast majority of them (75, or, 89%) concern 'community struggles' and largely opposition to the environmental effects of infrastructural development on the fields of waste management, telecommunication (radiation from mobile phone towers) and renewable energy power plants.

7 Remarks and Observations

These initial quantitative observations indicate the favourable areas for more thick description through qualitative enquiry. They also point toward certain directions in order to ethnographically understand better the phenomenon of infrastructural contestation. However, some preliminary points that can be made at this stage by synthesising our mapping and our qualitative thick datasets are:

a. While the majority of contestation involving infrastructural fields concerned labour issues (59%) and took the form of industrial actions and strikes, the most lasting infrastructural effect was exercised by other forms of socio-political contestation. Community struggles and mainly the generation of new infrastructures by the solidarity movement were more closely connected to forms of transfigurative contestation (Fig. 1 and point d. below).

b. Moreover, in regard to infrastructural contestation around labour and working conditions, one should note the non-direct effect of these struggles on infrastructure systems. The discourse of the social agents involved in these incidents lacked a wider critique of the interrelationship between power structures and the operation of the infrastructure within which they acted. The demands of these struggles predominantly concerned opposition to cuts and privatisation of (public) infrastructure. There have, however, been a few interesting exceptions of the labour issue developing into a critique of infrastructure operation, such as the attempt at self-management of the public hospital of Kilkis.

c. By the same token, only some of the cases of infrastructure contestation associated with the right to access or against the effects of infrastructure development seem to develop a critique of the dominant infrastructural model per se. For example, only recently some of the participants in the decade long struggle against solid waste management in Attica, (Fyli, Keratea and Grammatiko) seem to formulate alternative proposals about the infrastructure systems in question. However, such struggles represent processes of active participation in infrastructure planning, even if they just disclaim any infrastructure development.

d. While the number of generative forms of social contestation and of transfigurative paradigms represent a small proportion of instances of infrastructural contestation, they have a much larger time-span and thus transformative capacity. Moreover, qualitative evidence suggests that they include a wider number and variety of actors, users and infrastructural publics (Collier et al. 2016). In this way they often develop significant (and long lasting) participatory infrastructural potential, as is the case with solidarity schools, solidarity clinics and the few self-managed renewable energy power plants.

e. Another significant feature of our method regards the mapping of fluctuations (and interactions) of socio-political mobilisation and incidents of infrastructural contestation. Comparing the two dimensions one notices that they follow a common pattern. Most precisely that in this ten-year crisis period they peak around 2013–2014 and they retreat post-2015. However, a closer look at some parameters, such as time span of an event, provides some interesting qualitative differences regarding the degree that certain forms of mobilisation contest infrastructures and establish accumulatively long-term cases of infrastructural participation. Hence, they constitute examples where novel forms of socio-technical relations and infrastructural citizenship may be incubated.

8 Conclusions

Today infrastructures are increasingly approached as socio-technical systems that shape and are shaped by relationships of power. The post-2008 crisis besides its material consequences, including a serious gap in infrastructure development in Western Europe, has brought to the fore the socio-political role inherent to infrastructure and, thus, contested nature. A feature augmented by technological developments and environmental concerns. As Hill (2017) mentions the design of life-ecosystems in 21st century moves towards something "socially powerful: to shared systems, civic systems." In that context, the emerging digital, interactive and open source infrastructures, have to address an array of concerns around which infrastructural publics and users move and mobilise in both urban and rural environments.

By composing our datasets on infrastructural contestation we were able to visualise, to grasp, and outline the scale of the phenomenon. It enabled us also to determine and classify more precisely the forms that it takes and to make visible a number of quantitative dimensions with significant qualitative impact on the unfolding process. Such visualisation has also pointed out the social and political significance of certain infrastructure fields, trends and patterns, which can direct the ethnography towards specific sites of deeper research and thicker description regarding the qualities of the phenomenon. Moreover, the results can inform decisions regarding the design of new socio-technical systems and solutions able to register concerns (and also utilize knowledge capacities) of 'non-expert' but equally (in-situ) specialised users and communities (Collier et al. 2016). In doing so, 21st century infrastructure systems can not only install (productivity) optimisation sensors but become sentient platforms of the totality of the social and natural life.

The mapping of infrastructural contestation in Greece, despite its focus on grass-roots forms of infrastructural contestation – or rather because of it - documented the extended presence of the infrastructural gap that left almost no infrastructural field unaffected. Socio-political tensions have revealed, on the one hand, the infrastructural realm as a contested terrain between a variety of actors and publics; on the other hand, it revealed an increasing number of citizen-led movements that not only fight about or for infrastructure but also over it, namely demand a role to its function and structure. These movements did not refrain from building their own infrastructures where the existing ones failed and thus they should be approached as socio-technical transfiguration attempts.

Within the context of our study infrastructure systems are not only negotiated but emerge as a contested public sphere between differential positions and agencies. At the same time, they also emerge as a plateau of social innovation and participation, as many of our recorded examples demonstrate. Moreover, despite the fluctuations of such transformative endeavors, what it seems established is a permanent process and a variety of practices of infrastructuring, which maintain the potential for a more participatory, democratic and equally distributed infrastructural realm.

A focus on infrastructural contestation thus brings to the fore the variety of societal agents who emerge as constitutive actors in reshaping and recodifying infrastructure, something that challenges the idea that such socio-technical arrangements only become 'visible upon breakdown' (Star and Ruhleder 1996: 113). Events of disruption and blockade of infrastructural flows or acts of contestation that aim towards infrastructural change also manifest, if anything, awareness of both the fragile nature of infrastructure and its critical role in maintaining certain forms of power relations. Hence, when various publics around infrastructures emerge as mobilised subjects they unveil unjust power relations embedded in those socio-technical systems. More significantly, and ever more often, they claim an increasingly active role in their "right to infrastructure" (Jiménez 2014) the ecosystems in which they produce and re-produce and the future(s) they dream of.

References

Authers, J.: Infrastructures: Bridging the gap. Financial Times, 09 November 2015 (2015). http://www.ft.com/cms/s/0/0ac1a45e-86c8-11e5-90de-f44762bf9896.html#axzz4BAfbJc9q. Accessed 14 Oct 2019

Brehmer, M., Lee, B., Bach, B., Riche, N.H., Munzner, T.: Timelines revisited: a design space and considerations for expressive storytelling. IEEE Trans. Vis. Comput. Graph. 23, 2151–2164 (2017)

Collier, S., Mizes, C., von Schnitzler, A.: Preface: public infrastructures/infrastructural publics. Limn 7, 2–7 (2016). https://limn.it/articles/preface-public-infrastructures-infrastructural-publics/. Accessed 2 Sept 2017

Jiménez, A.C.: The right to infrastructure: a prototype for open source urbanism. Environ. Planning D: Soc. Space 32(2), 342–362 (2014)

Crisis-scape.net: Crisis-Scapes: Athens and beyond. Athens: Crisis-scape.net (2014)

Dimitris, D.: Infrastructural gap: Commons, state and anthropology. City 20(6), 822–831 (2016)

Dalakoglou, D., Agelopoulos, G.: Critical Times in Greece: Anthropological Engagements with the Crisis. Routledge, London (2018)

Dalakoglou, D., Kallianos, Y.: Infrastructural flows, interruptions and stasis in Athens of the crisis. City: Anal. Urban Trends Culture Theory Policy Action 18(4/5), 526–532 (2014)

Dalakoglou, D., Kallianos, Y.: 'Eating mountains' and 'eating each other': Disjunctive modernization, infrastructural imaginaries and crisis in Greece. Polit. Geogr. 67, 76–87 (2018)

Filion, P., Keil, R.: Contested infrastructures: tension, inequity and innovation in the global suburb. Urban Policy Res. 35(1), 7–19 (2016)

Giovanopoulos, C., Dalakoglou, D.: From ruptures to eruption: a genealogy of post-dictatorial revolts in Greece. In: Vradis, A., Dalakoglou, D. (eds.) Revolt and Crisis in Greece: Between a Present yet to Pass and a Future Still to Come. AK Press & Occupied London, London & Athens (2011)

Graham, S., Marvin, S.: Splintering Urbanism: Networked Infrastructures, Technological Mobilities and the Urban Condition. Routledge, London (2001)

Hill, D.: The Battle for the Infrastructure of Everyday Life (2017). https://medium.com/butwhatwasthequestion/the-battle-for-the-infrastructure-of-everyday-life-6c9b0572e57f

Institute of Citizen Studies, University of Geneva: Livewhat - Living with hard times: How citizens react to economic crises and their social and political consequences. Livewhat project, Geneva (2016). http://www.livewhat.unige.ch

Larkin, B.: The politics and poetics of infrastructure. Ann. Rev. Anthropol. 42, 327–343 (2013)

Lee, B., Riche, N.H., Isenberg, P., Carpendale, S.: More than telling a story: a closer look at the process of transforming data into visually shared stories. IEEE Comput. Graph. Appl. **35**(5), 84–90 (2015)

Linklaters. Set to Revive: Investing in Europe's Infrastructure (2014). https://www.linklaters.com/en/insights/thought-leadership/investing-europe-infrastruture/set-to-revive-investing-in-europes-infrastructure

National Research Council. Infrastructure for the 21st Century: Framework for a Research Agenda. The National Academies Press, Washington, DC (1987). https://doi.org/10.17226/798

ODI (Overseas Development Institute): Infrastructure development: ambition versus reality (2016). https://www.odi.org/opinion/10050-in-fographics-infrastructure-development-ambition-reality

Official Government Gazette: Presidential Decree 39/2011 of the Hellenic Republic concerning the Greek legislation adjustment to the relevant EU Directive EC 2008/114 of the European Council [In Greek] (2011). http://www.kemea.gr/images/documents/pd39-2011.pdf. Accessed 20 Oct 2019

Pasternak, S., Dafnos, T.: How does a settler state secure the circuitry of capital? Environ. Plann. D: Soc. Space **36**(4), 739–757 (2018)

Serntedakis, N., Koufidi, M.: Sygrousiakos kai eklogikos kyklos stin Ellada tis krisis (Conflictual and electoral cycle in crisis ridden Greece). elliniki Epitheorisi Politikis Epistimis **44**(1), 7–30 (2018). http://dx.doi.org/10.12681/hpsa.15919

Star, S.L., Ruhleder, K.: Steps toward an ecology of infrastructure: Design and access for large information spaces. Inf. Syst. Res. **7**(1), 111–134 (1996)

Automated Processing of Sentinel-2 Products for Time-Series Analysis in Grassland Monitoring

Tom Hardy[1]([✉]), Marston Domingues Franceschini[1],
Lammert Kooistra[1], Marcello Novani[1], and Sebastiaan Richter[2]

[1] Laboratory of Geo-Information Science and Remote Sensing,
Wageningen University, P.O. Box 47, 6700 Wageningen, The Netherlands
{tom.hardy,marston.franceschini,lammert.kooistra,
marcello.novani}@wur.nl
[2] Versuchs- und Bildungszentrum Landwirtschaft, Haus Riswick, Elsenpass 5,
47533 Kleve, Germany
sebastiaan.richter@lwk.nrw.de

Abstract. Effective grassland management practices require a good understanding of soil and vegetation properties, that can be quantified by farmers' knowledge and remote sensing techniques. Many systems have been proposed in the past for grassland monitoring, but open-source alternatives are increasingly being preferred. In this paper, a system is proposed to process data in an open-source and automated way. This system made use of Sentinel-2 data to support grassland management at Haus Riswick in the region around Kleve, Germany, retrieved with help of a platform called Sentinelsat that was developed by ESA. Consecutive processing steps consisted of atmospheric correction, cloud masking, clipping the raster data, and calculation of vegetation indices. First results from 2018 resembled the mowing regime of the area with four growing cycles, although outliers were detected due to a lack of data caused by cloud cover. Moreover, that year's extremely dry summer was visible in the time-series pattern as well. The proposed script is a primary version of a processing chain, which is suitable to be further expanded for more advanced data pre-processing and data analysis in the future.

Keywords: Grassland monitoring · Open-source system · Sentinel-2 · Cloud cover · Time-series analysis

1 Introduction

Efficient grassland management is beneficial to the cultivation of crops in a sustainable and cost-effective way. It is therefore important to quantify the spatial and temporal variation of such lands, in order to get a better understanding of soil and vegetation properties such as nitrogen (N) uptake and the health status of grasslands [1]. One way to quantify such features is based on farmers' experience, but this is increasingly being complemented by technologies such as remote sensing, which makes use of data derived from satellite and airborne based platforms [2].

© IFIP International Federation for Information Processing 2020
Published by Springer Nature Switzerland AG 2020
I. N. Athanasiadis et al. (Eds.): ISESS 2020, IFIP AICT 554, pp. 48–56, 2020.
https://doi.org/10.1007/978-3-030-39815-6_5

In recent years, many systems have been proposed and developed for the purpose of (grass)land monitoring, such as the *groenmonitor* (green monitor) initiated by Wageningen Environmental Research, aimed at providing the most recent vegetation information that was extracted from satellite imagery [3]. Another platform is Descartes Labs, which collects and processes open satellite data on a daily basis to prepare it for further analysis such as time-series to determine land cover change over time [4]. However, these initiatives are on a commercial basis for which it is hard to gain insight in the underlying processing chains, making open-source based platforms more and more attractive. One such platform is Google Earth engine aimed at environmental data-analysis on a planetary scale, making use of open-source data from satellite platforms such as Landsat and Sentinel [5]. Although it is a very promising platform to perform big data analysis in remote sensing, it is required to have programming skills to some extent, for instance in JavaScript, in order to perform such analyses.

This paper describes an alternative for developing a grassland monitoring system in an automated way, aimed at providing stakeholders with up-to-date information about the condition and cultivation status of grasslands throughout a growing season in an open-source platform. Stakeholders include for instance farmers, plant breeders, or companies providing agricultural services to those farmers and breeders. Moreover, this application could also be relevant for researchers at universities or research companies, to be able to use the obtained data and information for further research in relation to crop monitoring or environmental protection. The proposed information consists of time-series graphs and output maps of vegetation indices throughout a growing season for any chosen grassland (or land with other agricultural purposes) worldwide. For this paper, this information is derived from images obtained by Sentinel-2 satellites, which are part of an online and open source platform provided by the European Space Agency (ESA).

2 Methodology

For the study area described in Sect. 2.1, the proposed processing chain started with querying and harvesting Sentinel-2 satellite data (explained in Sects. 2.2 and 2.3). Next processing steps consisted of an atmospheric correction and extraction of these data for each individual parcel, which is further explained in Sects. 2.4 and 2.5. The final part of the workflow involved calculation and visualization of vegetation indices and cloud cover percentages for each given date (described in Sect. 2.6).

2.1 Study Area

The study area for this case study was Haus Riswick, located just east of the city of Kleve, Germany (Fig. 1). Haus Riswick is a teaching and research institution facilitated by the *Landwirtschaftskammer* (chamber of agriculture) from Nordrhein-Westfalen. The soil in that area consists of sandy, clay loam [6]. Data provided by Haus Riswick were geoJSON files representing the field boundaries from (experimental) grassland parcels located at Haus Riswick, as well as harvest data obtained during the days of mowing including its grassland yield expressed in dry matter content per hectare.

A geoJSON is a data exchange format based on JavaScript Object Notation (JSON), which is able to contain a variety of geospatial attributes [7]. For this case study, the data from the field *Lenzen Große Weide* (the blue polygon in Fig. 1) were used.

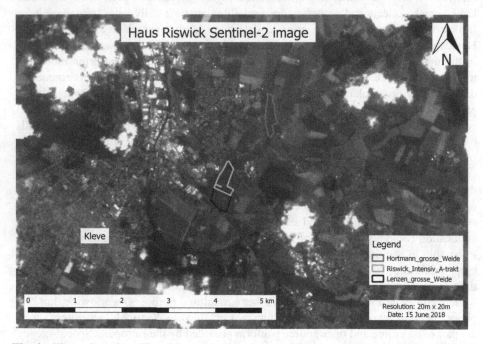

Fig. 1. The region where Haus Riswick is located (east of the city of Kleve), including three of its grassland parcels. Only data from the field *Lenzen Große Weide* were used in this paper (Color figure online).

2.2 Sentinel-2 Satellite Data

Besides the field data from Haus Riswick, earth observation data recorded with Sentinel satellites were addressed for this application. Sentinel satellites are being developed especially for the Copernicus program, one of ESA's earth observation programs aimed at improving environmental management and monitoring the impact of climate change worldwide [8]. For this program, a number of satellites are launched, such as weather satellites and satellites for land- and ocean monitoring. This project made use of data obtained from the two Sentinel-2 satellites (2A and 2B, which both sense the earth in parallel), designed to obtain high resolution (currently 60 m, 20 m and 10 m) optical images for land monitoring worldwide [9].

One way to obtain Sentinel-2 imagery would be by means of the Open Access Hub, which is part of the ESA Copernicus program. This platform has been developed with the aim to offer free and open access to data recorded by the different Sentinel satellites. Those data can be viewed and retrieved one by one via an interactive web viewer [10], based on a number of search criteria such as sensing period, sensing mode, satellite platform, and product type. This may be useful for anyone who is occasionally interested in only one or two images for a specific location. However, when a larger number of images is needed, this process becomes laborious and time-consuming. In that case, a platform such as the Sentinelsat Application Programming Interface (API) [11], which is aimed at being used in a scripting interface to query and harvest Sentinel data, could be a more effective approach.

2.3   Harvesting Sentinel-2 Data with Sentinelsat API

For the application in this case study, the data were accessed with help of the Sentinelsat API used in Jupyter notebooks, which is an open-source platform for interactive computing, coding and data analysis in programming languages such as R and Python [12]. The API was used to harvest, (pre-)process and analyze all input data in an automated way. Based on parameters and input data such as a given range of dates, the field's geoJSON file providing the geographical extents, cloud cover percentage, and other (meta)data, large batches of Sentinel-2 products could be downloaded at a time. Those products consisted of images with a size of 100×100 km^2 for a region in the world matching the location of the input geoJSON file. For most areas in the world, two or three images each week are recorded by either of the two Sentinel-2 satellites. For each of those days, a check was made to see whether a level-2A or a level-1C product was available for the location. A level-1C product contains top-of-atmosphere (TOA) reflectance, while level-2A products contain bottom-of-atmosphere (BOA) reflectance. It was preferred to make use of level-2A imagery, since level-1C products gave inconsistent analysis results because of distortions in atmospheric reflectance. However, if a level-2A image was not available for a given date, a level-1C product was downloaded nonetheless. Consequently, such product was processed to level-2A with help of the Sen2cor tool.

2.4   Atmospheric Correction with Sen2cor Processing Tool

The sen2cor tool has been developed as part of the ESA STEP science toolbox and has the purpose to perform pre-processing on level-1C (TOA) images based on a scene classification, and atmospheric, terrain and cirrus correction, leading to Level-2A (BOA) products [13]. The sen2cor tool is a standalone package and can be freely obtained from the ESA STEP website [14]. The package contains a batch file that was accessed through a python script to automatically process level-1C products to level-2A images.

2.5   Extracting Data Based on Field Boundaries

After downloading and levelling up of Sentinel-2 products, all raster bands for each date with a resolution of 20 m were clipped according to the *Lenzen Große Weide* field's geoJSON file for from Haus Riswick. For a resolution of 20 m, the RGB bands, three Red-edge bands, one NIR band, two SWIR bands and a cloud mask were available. The function GDALWarp, part of the GDAL library for fast processing of raster and vector data [15] was used to clip all raster bands according to the input field boundary. Besides raster bands and the geoJSON representing this boundary, other input parameters for GDALWarp were for instance input and output coordinate reference system, output format (such as a GeoTIFF file), output resolution and resampling method of the pixels.

2.6 Calculation and Visualization of Vegetation Indices

From the different Sentinel-2 bands, vegetation indices were calculated. For the initial version of the processing chain, three indices were included: NDVI, WDVI, and a Red Edge index that made use of the sharp increase in reflectance between Red and NIR, useful to quantify leaf chlorophyll content in crops [16]. Its equation is as follows, where RE_{band7} and RE_{band5} represent Sentinel-2 bands with wavelengths in respectively the higher and lower regions of the Red Edge slope:

$$CI_{red\,edge} = \frac{RE_{band7}}{RE_{band5}} - 1 \qquad (1)$$

For each Sentinel-2 product, an extra masking band was available. This band was a classification raster with classes representing cloud probability, cloud shadow, vegetation, unvegetated pixels, water, cirrus, and snow. The vegetation index raster was masked according to this masking band [17]. This information was visualized by raster maps for each date in range of dates on which either of the two Sentinel-2 satellites recorded data (given that the maximum cloud cover was not exceeded). For presentation purposes, these maps were compiled in GIF animations showing the crop growth over time in a more dynamic way.

For each date in the input date range, the vegetation index mean and standard deviation were calculated based on the Sentinel-2 pixels located within the field boundary. The cloud cover percentage was calculated by dividing the number of cloud-masked pixels by the total number of pixels within the field boundary. Raster datasets containing more cloud-masked pixels than the selected cloud cover threshold were discarded. For the selected range of dates, vegetation index means and standard deviations, as well as cloud cover were visualized by means of time-series charts.

3 Results

The aim of the proposed application is to generate relevant information from open-source data, based on a limited number of input parameters. Ideally, those parameters should include start- and end date, which vegetation index to calculate as described in Sect. 2.4, and maximum cloud cover percentage for visualization of results. However, in order to guarantee a smoother data processing workflow, additional parameters such as main working directory, folder paths to input and output locations, and the location of the field boundary shape- or geoJSON file should be provided in the Python script as well.

Based on these input parameters and the workflow in the script, information as depicted in Figs. 2 and 3 was created. Figure 2 shows the Red Edge index calculated according to eq. 1, for nine selected days during the growing season of 2018. For this

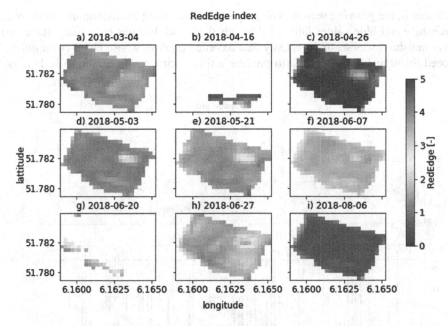

Fig. 2. Red Edge on March 4 (a), April 16 (b), April 26 (c), May 3 (d), May 21 (e), June 7 (f), June 20 (g), June 27 (h), August 6 (i), 2018 (Color figure online)

specific case study, that index ranged roughly between values of 0 and 5, where red colors represent values closer to zero and green colors imply values closer to 5. For most maps depicted in Fig. 2, 100% (so zero percent cloud cover) of pixels were available, but Figs. 2b and g were greatly hindered by cloud cover. In addition, almost in the north-east of this field a divergent patch of pixels is visible in some of the maps, which is a location with experimental plots having a different mowing regime than the rest of the field. The mowing dates for the field *Lenzen Große Weide* in 2018 were April 26, May 26, July 12, and October 9, indicating a season with four growing cycles. On the one hand, the data for the map in for instance Fig. 2c was recorded just before harvesting of the field, clearly depicted by high values in Red Edge index. On the other hand, the data for Fig. 2d was taken not long after mowing, which is represented by lower Red Edge values. Similar patterns were also observed for the dates close to the other three moments of harvesting. Lastly, the map in Fig. 2i shows very low values in Red Edge, which was caused by the extremely dry summer of 2018.

Figure 3a shows time-series containing the mean and standard deviation of the selected vegetation index, and Fig. 3b depicts the cloud cover percentage for the given range of dates. The mowing dates described earlier are also resembled in Fig. 3a, since large drops in Red Edge are visible for those moments in the growing season. However, also large decreases in Red Edge are visible on for instance April 16, as well as a pattern containing very low values for the months July and August. One explanation for the first issue is the large influence of cloud cover, while the second issue was caused by the very dry summer of 2018. Figure 3b shows the cloud cover range for each date in the growing season, with grey values exceeding the maximum cloud cover percentage and blue values falling below this threshold. For this case study, the cloud cover threshold was set to 90%. Only data recorded on days whose cloud cover did not exceed this threshold were used to produce a time-series output as shown in Fig. 3a.

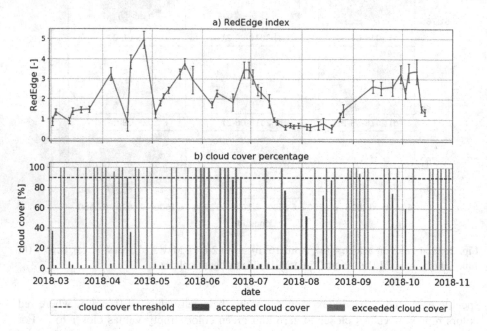

Fig. 3. Red Edge index (a) and cloud cover percentage (b) from March 1 till October 31, 2018 (Color figure online)

4   Discussion

In this paper, an alternative was proposed with a first version of a processing chain for extracting, processing and analyzing satellite-based data for grassland monitoring in an automated and open-source way, aimed at stakeholders resembling agribusiness companies and researchers to support their services and research practices. The development and primary testing of this processing chain was mainly conducted on a university's notebook. However, a notebook's or PC's processing memory and storage capacity are limited, which is one reason to upscale the processing workflow to a cloud computing environment for more efficient data processing and analysis in the future. Moreover, this system could still be enhanced to perform more advanced data (pre) processing and analysis, for instance by creating a more elaborated atmospheric correction algorithm and the inclusion of additional vegetation indices. For instance, atmospheric correction was merely performed with help of the sen2cor tool developed by ESA. A great variability in radiometry was observed comparing Sentinel images of multiple days. Therefore, many processing parameters could have been changed in configuration files (xml files as part of a Sentinel product's metadata) to be used in the sen2cor tool for each day separately. These options were considered, but were not included in the pre-processing chain, since this was tough to implement in an automated way. An alternative to the sen2cor tool could have been MACCS/MAJA, which has a more elaborated workflow in comparison to the sen2cor tool, since it includes more advanced weather analysis, cloud detection and atmospheric correction in its algorithm [18]. In addition, ESA has been started to process all Sentinel L1C data to L2A in retrospect, so the sen2cor tool might become obsolete in the future.

The next step was to discard vegetation images with a cloud cover more than a given threshold (90% was used for this case study, see Fig. 3b). One way to deal with this issue would be to lower the cloud cover threshold, which would lead to more accurate vegetation index output for the remaining data, but also to a loss of data not meeting the cloud cover threshold requirement. For instance, the maps in Figs. 2b and d were greatly influenced by cloud cover, which is resembled by the outliers in Fig. 3a for the dates on April 16 and June 20. In conclusion, the cloud cover percentage threshold is a trade-off that the end-user of this monitoring system should decide upon. Another way to improve this process would be to take a sequence of images in time as input, and systematically replace disturbed pixels from one image by clean pixels from a subsequent or previous image. Clean pixels are pixels that do not containing cloud cover or NA values. This replacing process could for example be performed by the sen2three tool, which was developed as part of the ESA STEP program as well [19]. However, this tool takes a sequence of Sentinel L2A images and merges them into one clean composite image. Since data was limited already, this could have had a disadvantageous effect on time series output such as in Fig. 3a.

5 Conclusions

The main goal of this paper was to develop and provide insight in the processing workflow of a grassland monitoring system in an open-source and automated way. In such workflow, processing steps are required to get from input data to output representing useful information for grassland management practices, and to compare that output to information derived from airborne or ground based data.

The higher the cloud cover threshold, the more data is available to create a time-series, but also the lower the accuracy becomes. Lowering this threshold leads to a loss of data but also to an increase in accuracy. This is a trade-off that should be decided upon by the end-user of the monitoring system.

Despite the outliers caused by a lack of pixels due to cloud cover, first results gave insights about the mowing regime over time, which could support optimizing and managing a grassland system in a more effective way. These results and data could be useful as well to elaborate on in further research.

The proposed script was a preliminary version of a processing change, which is ready to be further enhanced and expanded with coding for more advanced data pre-processing and data analysis in the future.

6 Further Research

- Further develop processing chain for more elaborate pre-processing and analysis steps such as atmospheric correction and the inclusion of extra vegetation indices.
- Further develop processing chain to make it suitable to include airborne based data.
- Translate time-series information into crop biomass information for the different cycles in a growing season.
- Upscale the processing chain to a cloud computing environment for more efficient data processing and analysis.

Acknowledgements. This work was supported by the SPECTORS project (143081), which is funded by the European cooperation program INTERREG Deutschland-Nederland.

References

1. Capolupo, A., Kooistra, L., Berendonk, C., et al.: Estimating plant traits of grasslands from UAV-acquired hyperspectral images: a comparison of statistical approaches. ISPRS Int. J. Geo-Inf. **4**(4), 2792–2820 (2015). https://doi.org/10.3390/ijgi4042792
2. Mulla, D.J.: Twenty five years of remote sensing in precision agriculture: key advances and remaining knowledge gaps. Biosyst. Eng. **114**, 358–371 (2012). https://doi.org/10.1016/j.biosystemseng.2012.08.009
3. Wageningen Environmental Research Groenmonitor. http://www.groenmonitor.nl/
4. DescartesLabs. https://www.descarteslabs.com/
5. Gorelick, N., Hancher, M., Dixon, M., et al.: Google Earth Engine: Planetary-scale geospatial analysis for everyone. Remote Sens. Environ. **202**, 18–27 (2017). https://doi.org/10.1016/j.rse.2017.06.031
6. Haus Riswick. http://www.riswick.de
7. Butler, H., Daly, M., Doyle, A., et al.: The GeoJSON Format. RFC Editor (2016)
8. ESA Copernicus. https://m.esa.int/Our_Activities/Observing_the_Earth/Copernicus/Overview3
9. ESA Copernicus data products. https://www.esa.int/Our_Activities/Observing_the_Earth/Copernicus/Sentinel-2/Data_product
10. ESA Copernicus Scihub. https://scihub.copernicus.eu/dhus/#/home
11. ESA Copernicus Scihub API Hub. https://scihub.copernicus.eu/twiki/do/view/SciHubWeb Portal/APIHubDescription
12. Wille, M., Clauss, K.: Sentinelsat. https://sentinelsat.readthedocs.io/en/stable/#
13. ESA S2A processing user guide. https://earth.esa.int/web/sentinel/user-guides/sentinel-2-msi/processing-levels/level-2
14. ESA STEP. http://step.esa.int/main/third-party-plugins-2/sen2cor/
15. Warmerdam, F., Rouault, E.: GDALWarp. https://gdal.org/programs/gdalwarp.html
16. Gitelson, A.A., Viña, A., Ciganda, V.S., et al.: Remote estimation of canopy chlorophyll content in crops (2005)
17. ESA S2A processing algorithm. https://earth.esa.int/web/sentinel/technical-guides/sentinel-2-msi/level-2a/algorithm
18. CESBIO multitemp MACCS/MAJA tool. https://labo.obs-mip.fr/multitemp/maccs-how-it-works/
19. ESA Sen2Three tool. http://step.esa.int/thirdparties/sen2three/1.1.0/sen2three-1.1.0.htmldoc/index.html

CLARITY Screening Service for Climate Hazards, Impacts and Effects of the Adaptation Options

Denis Havlik[1(✉)], Gerald Schimak[1], Patrick Kaleta[1], Pascal Dihé[2],
and Mattia Federico Leone[3]

[1] AIT Austrian Institute of Technology GmbH,
Giefinggasse 4, 1210 Vienna, Austria
denis.havlik@ait.ac.at
[2] cismet GmbH, Saarbrücken, Germany
[3] University of Naples "Federico II", Naples, Italy

Abstract. The CLARITY project (www.clarity-h2020.eu) aims to implement a new generation of climate services that allow the service users to perform an initial assessment of the expected climate change effects in the project area, as well as an initial assessment of the need for and of the usability of the adaptation options in the early project planning phase. The target users of this service are the consultants and urban planning experts that aren't climate change experts but need to produce standardized reports indicating the climate hazard, exposure and impact data, as well as the expected impact of the adaptation options in the project area, as a part of the project planning. The initial implementation of this service uses the available open data to calculate the local heat hazard, population exposure and related impact indicators at the project location on the fly. In the initial implementation, the heat related can be automatically calculated for more than 400 European cities, with a spatial resolution of 500×500 m^2. Extension to the flooding hazards and related impacts is in implementation. This article will describe in more detail the workflow and the technical implementation of the CLARITY screening service and discuss the value, potential and the limitations of the current service implementation.

1 Introduction/Methodology

1.1 Introduction

In recent years, the representation of climate information in a way to support decision making has been gaining momentum. Worldwide, these climate services are emerging as an essential tool to connect the advances in climate science with the domains of climate change adaptation.

The EU promotes climate resilience in different ways, e.g. by encouraging its member states to develop their own comprehensive climate adaptation plans [1], but also by providing support to individual projects by helping infrastructure developers in the identification of steps they can take to make investment projects climate resilient [2].

© IFIP International Federation for Information Processing 2020
Published by Springer Nature Switzerland AG 2020
I. N. Athanasiadis et al. (Eds.): ISESS 2020, IFIP AICT 554, pp. 57–71, 2020.
https://doi.org/10.1007/978-3-030-39815-6_6

To provide customized support for urban and infrastructure planners, the CLARITY (Integrated Climate Adaptation Service Tools for Improving Resilience Measure Efficiency) project, funded through the European Union (EU) funding framework Horizon-2020, aims at providing an integrated Climate Services Information System (CSIS) to ease climate-proof urban infrastructure planning. CSIS guides users through several steps to obtain a project and location-specific assessment of climate change risks, as well as an evaluation of possible adaptation options.

In this paper, we shall explain the underlying CLARITY CSIS methodology, present the currently implemented CSIS application workflow and user interfaces and discuss the advantages, shortcomings and further development of the service.

1.2   CLARITY and the EU-GL Methodology

The CLARITY CSIS methodology is based on the "Non-paper Guidelines for Project Managers: Making vulnerable investments climate resilient" [3] and has been updated to comply with the IPCC-AR5 approach [4] by the CLARITY consortium [5]. The following Table 1 gives a summary of the changes, as compared to the workflow proposed in the original EU-GL document:

Table 1. Comparison of the 7 modules from the Climate Resilience Toolkit as presented in the EU-GL non-paper guidelines for project managers [3] and the 7 modules adapted for the CLARITY project.

EU-GL	CLARITY
1. Identify Climate Sensitivity	1. Characterize Hazard (HC)
2. Evaluate Exposure	2. Evaluate Exposure (EE)
3. Assess Vulnerability	3. Vulnerability analysis (VA)
4. Assess Risks	4. Assess Risks and Impact (RA & IA)
5. Identify adaptation options	5. Identify adaptation options (IAO)
6. Appraise options	6. Appraise adaptation options (AAO)
7. Implement	7. Implement/Integrate Adaptation Action Plans (IAAP)

In line with the updated approach as outlined in the IPCC-AR5, the Hazard and exposure are independent variables of time and space, vulnerability is largely independent of time and space and the risk and impact evaluation are derived by the general relation:

$$R\,(or\,I) = H\,x\,E\,x\,V.$$

Main difference between the risk and impact calculation is in the meaning of the "hazard" variable (H). In simple terms, the impact is a real or estimated damage resulting from a specific hazard event, whereas the risk is a probabilistic quantity that sums up all the possible damage for all the possible events in a certain period, weighted by the relative probability of the event.

For a concrete example of heat mortality (Fig. 1), this formula translates to "heat mortality (impact) is a function of the heat hazard intensity (e.g. duration of the heat episode) and the number of people in the area, as well as on their vulnerability to the heat hazard".

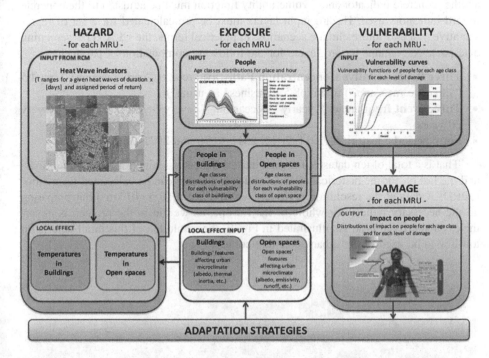

Fig. 1. Impact (damage) calculation example: impact of heat wave on human health.

Depending on the study scope, the elements at risk (population in Fig. 1) can be disaggregated in various vulnerability classes, e.g. by age (old people are more vulnerable than young ones) or by the socioeconomic status (poor people are more vulnerable than rich ones). Moreover, the vulnerability is almost location-independent. That is, the heat vulnerability of the population can be considered virtually the same in all of the southern Europe, but a different vulnerability curve must be used in the colder regions.

1.3 Screening Methodology: Simplifications and the Data Preparation

CLARITY methodology is applicable to studies with different complexity levels. In "expert" studies, the methodology is followed by the experts and merely the results of the work are presented using the CLARITY CSIS tool, whereas the "screening" calculations are performed automatically and nearly in the real-time. To achieve this, several simplifications need to be implemented.

For the start, the screening requires a pre-computed "screening data package" that contains a accurate but spatially relatively coarse hazard indicators, exposure and vulnerability data, as well as the high-resolution land cover data. Within the data package, the abstract notion of a "hazard" must be replaced by a concrete hazard indicator, e.g. a "heat hazard" by a "number of consecutive tropical nights" or a by another concrete indicator and a vulnerability function must be adjusted to the concrete hazard indicators used. Hazard input layers must be pre-calculated for a set of representative past and future climate scenarios. In practical terms, the CLARITY screening data package contains hazard layers for the following combination of parameters:

- **Three Representative Concentration Pathways:** rcp2.6 ("early response"), rcp4.5 ("effective measures") and rcp8.5 ("business as usual")
- **Three event frequencies:** "yearly", "occasional" (every 5 years) and "rare" (every 20 years)
- **Four periods:** historical, 2011–2040, 2041–2070 and 2071–2011

That is a total of ten datasets for each hazard indicator – nine for the future climate and the last on for the historical climate[1]. Such indicators can be calculated from euro-CORDEX data at the resolution regional level (typically 10×10 km^2) but preparing all the necessary indices for whole of the Europe, as we did in the project, is nevertheless a nontrivial task. As illustrated in Fig. 2, the resolution of this input data is far too low to be used in the urban screening context.

Fig. 2. Number of "hot days" in the wider Vienna region, resolution 10×10 km^2, historical data.

To account for the "urban heat islands" and similar urban microclimate effects, all the indicators must be available at a 500×500 m^2 grid resolution or higher (e.g. 250 m or 100 m resolution would be even better). This type of downscaling can be

---

[1] Actually 20, since a standard deviation layer is provided for each data layer, representing the variation between predictions by different climate models.

performed as a part of an "expert study" for a smaller region, but a calculation for the whole Europe is not practical. Moreover, the expert studies tend to be rather expensive and preparing them can take weeks or even months.

To overcome this issue, CLARTIY consortium has developed a simplified down-scaling models for each of the indicators that calculates the "local effects" (urban-scale variations) by superposing the high-resolution land cover data on e.g. terrain, building fabric, paving materials, green fraction, albedo, emissivity, shading conditions, and run-off coefficient on the lower resolution input data. The necessary high-resolution data has been extracted from (mainly) Copernicus datasets, as illustrated in the Fig. 3.

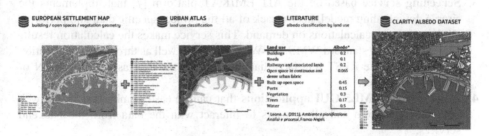

Fig. 3. Example of information extraction from Copernicus datasets to derive the "albedo" dataset used in the CLARITY Urban Microclimate simplified model

The resulting urban-scale data is not as accurate as the results of a fully-fledged and validated expert study. However, the advantage is that the results can be calculated very quickly and cost efficiently. In our service prototype, the calculation typically takes 15–20 min on a simple server (no supercomputing facility necessary), even for relatively large areas[2].

A second advantage of this approach is that the effect of (some) adaptation options can be calculated by changing the characteristics of the land cover and re-calculating the local effects. E.g., the "cool paving" adaptation option changes the albedo and emissivity of the roads and build up open spaces, whereas the "green roofs" change the albedo, emissivity and the runoff coefficient, and introduce additional cooling through evapotranspiration.

Within the project, the simple downscaling models were developed: one for the heat hazard and one for the flooding hazard. At a time of writing this article, only the heat hazard model has been fully implemented in the CLARITY CSIS and the validation is under way. Full report on these models, and on the validation results, will be provided in a separate publication.

---

[2] In our service prototype, an "urban heat" screening calculation for an area of up to 500 km^2 is finished in 15–20 min.

2   CSIS Screening Workflow Implementation

2.1   CSIS Overview

The CLARITY CSIS is composed of four main components:

1. The **web integration platform** providing such functions as the user management, workflow management and data package management. This web platform is based on the Drupal 8 web application framework [6].
2. WMS/WFS **servers hosting the static (input) geospatial data** that is necessary for the functioning of the service.
3. **Screening service** based on the AIT EMIKAT platform [7] that implements the simple downscaling model, keeps track of all the project specific data and performs all the necessary calculations on demand. This service makes the calculation results available through standard WMS and WFS service as well as through an application specific read/write REST interface that can provide the data as e.g. GeoJSON or simple CSV tables.
4. A set of the **HTML5 GUI applications** that can be easily embedded in the web integration platform and allow users to interact with the data from the backend services.

From the end-user, point of view, the GUI is the application. Therefore, this paper mainly concentrates on the implementation of the screening study workflow. More information on the technical details of the implementation is available in [8].

2.2   Prior to a Study: System Configuration and Data Management

Hidden from the end-users, the CSIS web integration platform allows the users with higher privilege level to define different types of the studies and the data packages that can be used with these study types. CLARITY data package is modelled similarly to a frictionless data package [9], and consists of:

- Metadata that describes the structure and contents of the package ("descriptor")
- A set of "resources" such as data files that form the contents of the package

Moreover, each "resource" is a self-describing rich data set containing not only the links to the local data file(s) and/or service(s) providing the resource data on demand, but also the information about the data provenance, authors, licenses, and on the type of the data provided by this resource.

In contrast to the generic frictionless data package, the CLARITY data package specification imposes some constraints on the data and extends the descriptor with additional properties which ensure that data contained in a CLARITY data package is valid and suitable for being ingested and processed by CLARITY Services. On a technical level, a CLARITY data package is implemented as a set of related Drupal 8 "node" and "taxonomy" data types.

Data packages can be either imported in the CSIS from a JSON representation thereof or edited online using a relatively comfortable GUI interface. Once it is incorporated into the system, this data can be used both within the CSIS web integration platform and accessed by external services, either through a default JSON: API [10] or through a custom REST GET interface that outputs the complete data package at once and in a form that is (mostly) compatible with the frictionless data package JSON schema. Full CLARITY data package specification can be found at [11].

Second important configurable element of the CSIS integration platform is the "study template". Study template consists of a set of the study-step templates corresponding to the steps in the CLARITY CSIS methodology. The integration platform provides an easy to use GUI for study template configuration that allows the system administrator to determine which of the methodology steps shall be covered by the specific study type and how each of the study step will look like.

As already mentioned, the way how the data is presented in a study is largely determined by the HTML5/JavaScript embedded applications and not by the integration platform itself. These applications are almost completely independent from the underlying integration platform and merely inherit some input parameters from it. Study templates provide placeholders where either such HTML5 applications or the Drupal views can be easily embedded. Finally, the study template also determines if some external data models need to be triggered by the study or not and how to do so. At a time of writing this article, only the "Urban infrastructure" screening model has been implemented, but we are also working on a "transport infrastructure screening".

2.3 Starting a New Study

CLARITY CSIS studies are implemented as Drupal 8 groups, with the group itself containing the study context data and the actual study data modelled as group nodes. From the user perspective, starting a new screening study is as simple as clicking on the "Create a new study" button and filling in the initial context data (Fig. 4).

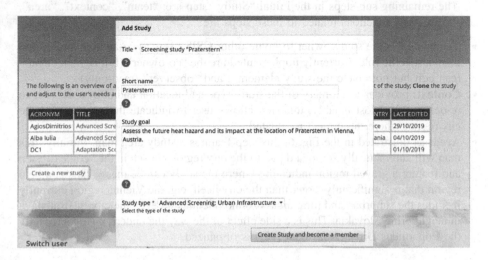

Fig. 4. Adding a new study

Once this is done, the user is redirected to a study workspace, and provided with an introduction to CSIS methodology. The study workspace is illustrated in Fig. 5.

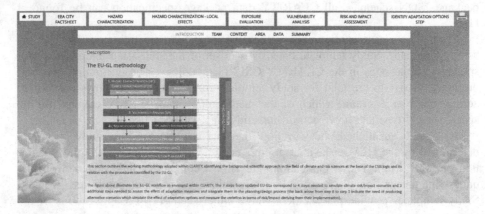

Fig. 5. Study workplace

2.4   Study Workspace

Study workspace is a separate area on the CSIS that is dedicated to a specific study. It is implemented as a Drupal group and structured in the study steps (first row in in Fig. 5), with each step featuring several sub-steps (second row in in Fig. 5). Both the steps and the sub-steps are configurable through study-type templates, but each study step starts with the introduction and ends with a summary. While the introduction merely provides the contextual help, the summary sub-step provides a preview of the study report section corresponding to the current study step. Complete report can be accessed and printed or saved as PDF by clicking on the printer icon (right-top corner in Fig. 5).

The remaining sub-steps in the initial "Study" step are: "team", "context", "area", and "data". The functions related to these steps are:

- **Team:** allows the study owner to invite other CSIS users as co-authors and assign them a specific role. Currently implemented are the "co-owner" (full rights), "team" (can edit but not delete the study elements) and "observer" (read-only)
- **Context:** provides a summary of the study type and location and allows the user to re-define this. Most notably, this step allows user to indicate the country and the city/region where the project is situated.
- **Area:** as illustrated in the Fig. 6, this step features a study area map. Initially, this map will automatically zoom and pan to the city/region chosen in the "context" step and feature a greyed region indicating where the study can be made. This can be a region that is significantly larger than the city itself, e.g. the Vienna region currently includes the suburban and rural areas around Vienna and even the city of Bratislava in neighboring Slovakia. This is a side effect of the way the underlying data (mainly the Copernicus Urban Atlas data [12]) is organized.

By clicking on the "toggle edit" button, the user can define a study area within this region. For illustration, a rather large area in the Neusiedl lake region has been selected in the Fig. 6.

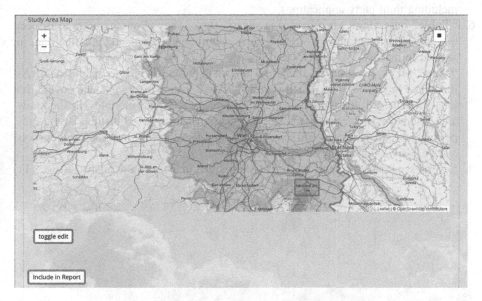

Fig. 6. Choosing the study area

The "include in report" button at the left-bottom corner of the Fig. 6 allows the user to take a map screenshot, add a comment to it and include the result in the future project report. This generic feature that appears again and again in the study workflow and allows the users to configure any interactive application that is embedded in the screening workflow, include the result in the report and comment the findings.

- **Data:** here is where the user can choose a data package to be used in this study. Choice of the data package has a profound consequence on the data that will be available in the study. E.g., two data packages could provide data with different resolution/quality or even different type of data (different hazards, elements at risk, vulnerabilities, adaptation options).

Once the data package has been chosen, a "N out of 20 processes have finished. In general calculations take about 10–15 min depending on the size of the Study area." will be shown to the user indicating that the calculation has been started in the background.

2.5 Data Visualization

What user needs to do to produce a study report now is to click through each of the steps and through all of the sub-steps shown on the screen, read the instructions provided in the contextual help, interact with the embedded applications and decide which data they wish to have included in the report. Currently, the screening workflow includes the following interactive applications (Fig. 7):

5. First workflow step includes the **EEA city factsheet**, as a proof of concept for including third party applications.
6. **"Table" data views** are provided at several steps. They allow the users to inspect the data values and allow sorting by any column and downloading of the data in several formats (CSV, JSON, GeoJSON).
7. **"Map" views** are used in almost all steps, to visualize the geospatial data. As illustrated in Figs. 8, 9 and 10, it is already possible to compare the land cover with local heat hazard distribution, population density and heat mortality in the study area. Moreover, this comparison can be made for various combinations of the time period, emission scenario end event frequency and the resulting map screenshots can be easily included in the study report
8. Several **scenario comparison views** are provided in the scenario analysis (Fig. 11).

Fig. 7. Prater area: land cover (green is the prater Park area) (Color figure online)

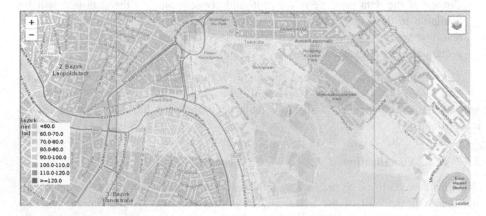

Fig. 8. Prater area: mean radiant temperate (event frequency: yearly, rcp4.5, period: 2040–2071); temperature not calibrated but in a plausible range.

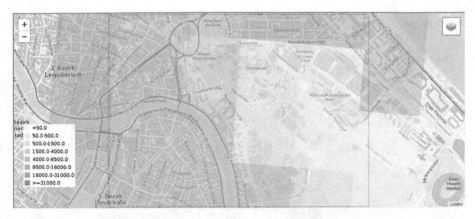

Fig. 9. Prater area: population exposure; scale: number of people living in the 500 × 500 m^2 area

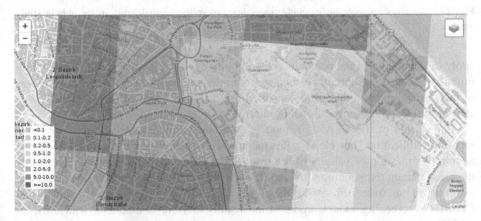

Fig. 10. Prater area: mortality (event frequency: yearly, rcp4.5, period: 2040–2071); units are "people per 500 × 500 m^2 area".

2.6 Screening Model Calibration and Validation

CLARITY urban heat impact screening includes the calculation of the Ambient temperature T_A, Mean Radiant temperature T_{MRT}, and the simplified Universal Thermal Climate Index (T_{UTCI}) [13], as well as the downscaling of the population density and the calculation of a severe heat impact on population ("mortality") index – all at a 500 × 500 m^2 spatial scale.

T_{MRT} is calculated by applying a PLINIUS (CLARITY) simplified model, which is based on the SOLWAY model that was developed by Lindberg et al. [14], whereas the simplified T_{UTCI} calculation was performed for a reference environment with a wind speed (v_a) of 0.5 m s-1 at 10 m height (approximately 0.3 m s-1 at 1.1 m), as defined by the International Society of Biometeorology Commission. Similar simplifications

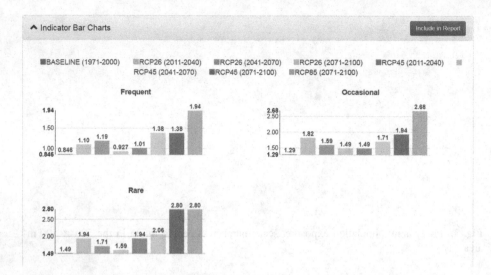

Fig. 11. Scenario comparison example: mortality pro million inhabitants in the whole study area.

apply to calculation of the population distribution (exposure), whereas the vulnerability function, is based on mortality estimates from previous heat waves and the experiences of the medical experts that were consulted by PLINIUS. Similar simple models have also been developed for the flooding hazards.

Full details of the CLARITY models and their validation will be disclosed in a separate publication, but clearly, the models we use are extremely simplified, thus raising the question of validity of the results. Our initial tests have indeed shown that the mean radiant temperature provided by our screening model is higher than expected, resulting in an overestimate for the T_{UTCI} as well. A closer analysis shows that CLARITY screening model produces the results that are comparable with those of SOLWAY but higher than those provided by e.g. Grasshopper and higher than suggested by available measurements.

On the other hand, the Figs. 8, 9, 10 and 11 clearly show that the models used provide plausible variations at a local scale. E.g., the temperatures are lower in the park area than in the city center; mortality scales with population density and heat index values; and mortality is higher in the "hotter" scenarios (rcp8.5, end of the century, rare events) than in the "colder" ones (historical and near-future data, lower RCP scenarios, yearly and occasional events).

Our working assumption is that the T_{MRT}, which is calculated for the noon at the warmest day in the year is not representative for the T_{UCTI} and mortality and needs to be scaled down to obtain more representative results. The calibration is currently performed against the Naples data and will be followed by validation in the Linz, Austria and Stockholm, Sweden, where the CLARITY expert studies are available. The details on the modeling used as well as the results of the calibration and validation will be published separately.

Table 2. Examples of adaptation options and their effects on the input parameters for the simplified downscaling models

Adaptation option	Effects	Applicable to
Cool roofs - Dark (Waterproof aluminium coated membrane)	Albedo = 0.45; Emissivity = 0.60	Buildings
Cool roofs - Light (Mineral membrane coated white reflex ultra)	Albedo = 0.86; Emissivity = 0.90	Buildings
Green roofs - Extensive	Albedo = 0.26; Emissivity = 0.96; Runoff = 0.35	Buildings
Green roofs - Intensive	Albedo = 0.2; Emissivity = 0.97; Runoff = 0.2	Buildings
Reflective surfaces - Dark (Cool flooring, Cool coated)	Albedo = 0.3; Emissivity = 0.90	Built open spaces, roads
Reflective surfaces - Light (Cool flooring, Cool coated)	Albedo = 0.6; Emissivity = 0.80	Built open spaces, roads

2.7 Adaptation Options

As indicated in the Sect. 1.3, the "local effect" models can be used both to calculate the variation of the hazard due to urban fabric and to calculate the effects of the adaptation options at the same scale. At a time of writing this article, we have defined several adaptation options that can be used in the screening study (Table 2) and implemented a simple mechanism for the administrators to indicate which adaptation options should be offered in a data package and for the end-users to indicate which adaptation options they wish to test in the screening study.

The initial values for the "effects" are a result of an offline study in the Naples area and haven't been validated at other locations yet. That is, they may change in the future.

Fortunately, the adaptation options, including their effects and the data layers they are applicable to, are defined in the CSIS web integration platform and not hardcoded in the backend server. As a result, they can be easily reconfigured by the CSIS user with sufficient privileges, using the web interface and without any changes to the backend server.

2.8 The Future

CLARITY CSIS service is implemented as a "proof of concept" and its development will continue for another six months within the scope of the CLARITY project. Main planned developments include:

- Adding support for the "flooding hazard screening" including the simple downscaling models, buildings exposure, flood vulnerability and damage indicators to the screening study.

- Implementing the application workflow for assessing the effects of the adaptation options.
- Implementing the "traffic infrastructure screening" study type, in addition to the "urban infrastructure" one.
- Validating all the models used in the screening against sensor measurements and against the results of the (more accurate) model results from the CLARITY expert studies.
- Improving and extending of the data visualisation methods. For example, the data views used by the table applications need to be redesigned and labels and units need to be added to the map legend(s). Furthermore, we plan to implement an application that will visualise the relevant indicator for the four time periods and the three RCP scenarios in one compact x-t graph.
- Improving the application usability. For example, the application currently allows the user to define one combination of the time period, rcp scenario and the event frequency as a named "application present". This preset is used in some parts of the workflow to decide what data needs to be visualised. In the future, this will be extended to allow the users to define several presets and supported by all the embedded applications.

3 Conclusion

At a time of writing this article (November 2019), the CSIS application is implemented at a "proof of concept", the results appear plausible and the work on validation of the heat related indices is under way.

Once the features listed in Sect. 2.8 have been implemented, the CSIS service will turn into a very feature rich demonstrator that will allow the users to easily perform a two types of screening studies (urban and traffic infrastructure) for two key hazards (heat and flood), at least two elements at risk types (population and buildings in the urban infrastructure study type) and a limited number of adaptation option types in most of the Europe.

Apart from the uncertainties concerning the validation of the simple downscaling and impact models, the remaining implementation work is straightforward and the probability of not reaching these goals therefore considered very low.

Depending on the results of the model validation, two things can happen: either the simple models are found to be good enough for use with the EU-wide data package (as is or with additional tuning), or we will find out that they need to be configured and fine-tuned for use in a specific region. In both cases, the CSIS service could be relatively easily turned into a sustainable service offer that can provide the users with initial estimates of the future hazards and their impacts, as well as of the usability of the selected adaptation options.

Currently, we are looking for the partners interested in industrialization and exploitation of the project results. Early testers interested in the application are kindly asked to open a user account at the https://myclimateservices.eu/en platform and request a guided tour through the CSIS application or join one of the CSIS webinars.

Acknowledgement. This project has received funding from the European Union's Horizon 2020 research and innovation programme under grant agreement n° 730335. The information and views set out in this publication are those of the author(s) and do not necessarily reflect the official opinion of the European Union.

References

1. Delbeke, J., Vis, P.: EU Climate Policy Explained, European Union, Brussels (2016)
2. European Commission: An EU Strategy on adaptation to climate change, European Commission, Brussels (2013)
3. European Comission, Directorate-general Climate Action: Non-paper Guidelines for Project Managers: Making vulnerable investments climate resilient, European Comission, Brussels
4. Stocker, T.F., et al. (eds.): IPCC, Climate Change 2013: The Physical Science Basis. Contribution of Working Group I to the Fifth Assessment Report of the Intergovernmental, p. 1535. Cambridge University Press, Cambridge (2013)
5. Zuvela-Aloise, M. (ed.) CLARITY consortium: D3.1 Science support plan and concept. CLARITY, Vienna (2018)
6. Tomlinson, T.: Engineering drupal. In: Enterprise Drupal 8 Development For Advanced Projects and Large Development Teams, pp. 29–44. Apress, Berkeley (2017)
7. AIT Austrian Institute of Technology GmbH. EMIKAT – Emissionskataster (2019). http://www.emikat.at. Accessed 15 Nov 2019
8. Esbri, M.A., Havlik, D. (eds.): CLARITY consortium: D1.3 CLARITY CSIS V1. CLARITY, Vienna, Austria (2019)
9. Walsh, P., Pollock, R.: Data package. https://frictionlessdata.io/specs/data-package/. Accessed 15 Nov 2019
10. Sullice, G., Bosch, M.A., Leers, W., Tolboom, C.: JSON:API (2019) https://www.drupal.org/docs/8/modules/jsonapi. Accessed 15 Nov 2019
11. Esbri, M.A.: CLARITY Data Package Specification, Documentation and Examples (2019). https://github.com/clarity-h2020/data-package. Accessed 15 Nov 2019
12. COPERNICUS: Urban Atlas (2012). https://land.copernicus.eu/local/urban-atlas/urban-atlas-2012. Accessed 15 Nov 2019
13. Błażejczyk, K.: Mapping of UTCI in local scale (the case of Warsaw). Prace i Studia Geograficzne, WGSR UW, Nr. **47**, 275–283 (2011)
14. Lindberg, F., Holmer, B., Thorsson, S.: SOLWEIG 1.0–Modelling spatial variations of 3D radiant fluxes and mean radiant temperature in complex urban settings. Int. J. Biometeorol. **7**, 697–713 (2008)

Diet Modelling: Combining Mathematical Programming Models with Data-Driven Methods

Ante Ivancic[✉], Argyris Kanellopoulos, and Johanna M. Geleijnse

Wageningen University and Research, Wageningen, The Netherlands
{ante.ivancic,argyris.kanellopoulos,marianne.geleijnse}@wur.nl

Abstract. Mathematical programming has been the principal work-horse behind most diet models since the 1940s. As a predominantly hypothesis-driven modelling paradigm, its structure is mostly defined by a priori information, i.e. expert knowledge. In this paper we consider two machine learning paradigms, and three instances thereof that could help leverage the readily available data and derive valuable insights for modelling healthier, and acceptable human diets.

Keywords: Machine learning · Diet modelling · Consumer preferences

1 Introduction

Current societies are confronted with major challenges. The confluence of population, economic development, and environmental pressures resulting from globalization and industrialization reveals an increasingly resource-constrained world in which predictions point to the need to do more with less and in a more efficient way [1].

Although global food production of calories has kept pace with population growth, more than 820 million people have insufficient food and many more consume low-quality diets that cause micronutrient deficiencies and contribute to a substantial rise in the incidence of diet-related obesity and diet-related non-communicable diseases [2], such as cardiovascular disease, type 2 diabetes, and various types of cancer. As a matter of fact, most NCDs have a root cause in an unhealthy diet [3,4]; a diet that does not fulfill energy and nutrient requirements for healthy growing and aging [5].

The concept of sustainable diets presents an opportunity to successfully advance commitments to sustainable development and the elimination of poverty, food and nutrition insecurity, and poor health outcomes [1]. Sustainable diets can be defined as those with low environmental impacts that contribute to food and nutrition security and to healthy life for present and future generations [6].

Designing and promoting sustainable diets is a complex task. Mathematical and computational models that can capture the complexity of the problem, and

© IFIP International Federation for Information Processing 2020
Published by Springer Nature Switzerland AG 2020
I. N. Athanasiadis et al. (Eds.): ISESS 2020, IFIP AICT 554, pp. 72–80, 2020.
https://doi.org/10.1007/978-3-030-39815-6_7

devise a sustainable nutritional strategy are needed [7]. Moreover, such models can help to set priorities for interventions/policy measure, which might result in a more sustainable consumption pattern that would act as a driver of sustainable production, since current diet and production patterns are among the most important drivers of environmental pressure [8].

Capturing diet modelling complexity is a twofold challenge. Firstly, diet modellers gain their knowledge over the course of many years of education and professional experience, ultimately constructing an immensely convoluted model of what and when a specific diet can or can not be considered healthy. Translating such an intricate biological knowledge system into a set of computer instructions is a nontrivial challenge. Secondly, the goal of diet models is to change – or at least strive towards changing – consumers' dietary patterns, for which they need, at least to some extent, appeal to their preferences. Consumers rarely explicitly state their preferences, let alone explain the reasons behind them. However, in today's data-loaded world, their actions (e.g. recorded supermarket transactions) speak for themselves. The necessity of turning data into actionable insights bodes ill for current diet models, given their inability to do so.

Machine learning, a sub-field of artificial intelligence specialized for automated pattern recognition/feature extraction/(lossy) data compression [9], is a likely candidate for providing algorithmic solutions current diet models could benefit from, namely because of their ability to reshape vast amounts of data into useful information.

In this paper, we consider two machine learning paradigms, and three instances thereof for which we argue to be valuable additions to current diet models. We focus on the two aspects of diet modelling, namely nutrient importance weighting and consumer preferences. For nutrient importance weighting, where the goal is to assign importance weight to every nutrient so as to estimate the overall diet health score, we consider supervised learning approach (binary classification), and suggest two computational methods that could facilitate the translation of expert knowledge into a set of correlated importance weights - the *Principle of maximum entropy* and *gradient boosted decision trees*. For estimating consumer preferences, we consider the concept of recommendation systems, and suggest one possible instance thereof, namely the *Top-N recommendation system based on mutual information and entropy weighting*.

2 Current Diet Modelling Paradigms

The concept of diet modelling dates back to at least 1940s, when the American economist and Nobel laureate Georges Stigler utilized mathematical programming (mathematical optimization) to solve the "diet problem" - a problem of finding the least costly combination of food items that satisfies all nutrient requirements [10].

Mathematical programming remains the principal workhorse behind the majority of today's diet models and can be characterized by the three main components: decision variables, an objective function, and a set of constraints [11].

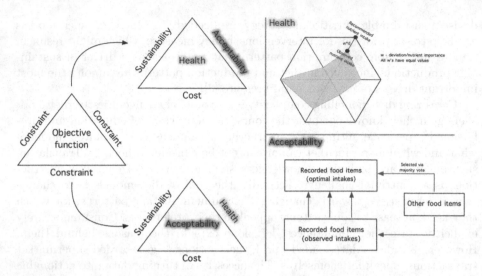

Fig. 1. The majority of diet models are based on some form of mathematical programming, with the two most common objectives: health and acceptability.

It also comes in many forms, depending on the types of decision variables (integers, reals), and the functional form of the objective function. Some of the most prevalent mathematical programming paradigms for diet modelling are linear programming, quadratic programming, mixed-integer programming, and goal-programming [12] (Fig. 1).

During the optimization process, the mathematical programming model aims to search for values for the decision variables that optimize (maximize or minimize) the objective function, while adhering to the preset constraints. In the context of nutrition, diet models based on mathematical programming aim to find the set of food item quantities that optimize a specific objective, (e.g. total diet cost, environmental objective, total deviation from an observed diet), while satisfying constraints such as nutritional recommendations, total energy intake, etc. [12].

2.1   Nutrient Importance and Consumer Preferences

Diet models based on mathematical programming can be classified as hypothesis-driven methods [13], meaning that most of their components are selected based on a priori information. That is, the modeller tries to translate his/her expert knowledge into an appropriate model structure.

For instance, in case of optimizing diet healthiness where the goal is to minimize deviations between observed nutrient intake values and their respective recommended targets, each deviation will be assigned a specific weight, reflecting its relative importance. A total sum of weighted deviations is then equivalent to the overall diet health score, i.e. diet healthiness.

Selecting a set of weights that accurately reflect reality is a challenging task, while almost all diet modellers resort to a uniform set of weights, regardless of the setting [14,15]. We argue that it would be beneficial for diet modellers to have a way of adjusting the weights in case of their disagreement with the uniform set.

Furthermore, in order to generate acceptable optimized diets, diet models have to somehow be able to model the concept of "acceptability", i.e. somehow model preferences of each consumer. This is currently done by taking into account food consumption distribution in the constraints, or by deriving the average observed diet if the aim is to stay as close as possible to current dietary habits [12]. The former approach generally takes a lot of hard-coding, rules of thumb, and has to be re-implemented manually every time the setting changes, whereas the latter might be "too personalized", in the sense that the diet model puts a lot of focus on the observed food items, while disregarding the rest. Moreover, it has been observed that in order to meet nutritional targets, observed individual diets generally have to be expanded with new food items, which tends to be done in an arbitrary fashion [12]. Having a more generic, possibly data-driven approach that can collect and process consumer data from multiple sources, and subsequently deliver personalized food item recommendations, could add a lot of value to the already existing diet models, and possibly bridge the gap between hypothesis-driven and data-driven methods.

3   Data-Driven Approaches to Diet Modelling

3.1   Inferring Function Weights

As described in the previous section, while modelling diets via deviations from the optimal diet, objective function weights represent the "importance" of each deviation. Currently, most diet models resort to a uniform set of weights, regardless of the setting (e.g. different sub-populations and their health weights). Indeed, the weights can be changed manually, however given the multidimensional nature of the problem, it is arguably very hard for the modeller to accurately translate its own beliefs into a set of correlated weights.

We consider two possible methods for dealing with this challenging task, namely the *Principle of maximum entropy (MaxEnt)*, and *Gradient boosted decision trees*. MaxEnt is relatively easy to implement, converges to an exact solution (convex optimization), and is highly usable, because once implemented, it requires almost no prerequisite knowledge or technical skills, apart from nutritional expertise. On the other hand, gradient boosted decision trees tend to be exceptionally successful while dealing with tabular data, giving out state-of-the-art results on many standard classification benchmarks [16]. Both methods are explained in the subsequent sections.

Principle of Maximum Entropy. MaxEnt is a general method for estimating probability distributions from data. The core principle behind MaxEnt is that when nothing is known, the distribution should be as uniform as possible, that is, have maximal information entropy. As bits of information are becoming available, the distribution is updated in a way that adheres to the constraints imposed by the new information, while maximizing the entropy [17].

Essentially, where current models end, MaxEnt begins. That is, starting with a uniform set of weights, diet modellers are able to interact with MaxEnt via pairwise comparisons of diets, i.e. they are presented with diet pairs, and are instructed to select a "better" (e.g. healthier, more sustainable, etc.) diet, according to their expert knowledge. Their classification results get translated into a set of inequalities which will constrain MaxEnt's search space, in order to find a set of weights that are in line with the expert knowledge.

Gradient Boosted Decision Trees. Decision tree learning is a type of predictive modelling approach commonly used within the machine learning/statistics domain, both for regression and classification problems. In order to make predictions, decision trees stratify the predictor space into a number of simple regions, while the splitting rules used for stratification can be represented as a directed acyclic graph whose child nodes can only have a single parent, i.e. a tree, hence their name. In their basic form, they tend not to be as accurate as some other prediction models, however their prediction accuracy can be increased significantly if coupled with some other machine learning methods, such as gradient boosting [16,18]. Furthermore, decision trees tend to be highly interpretable (e.g. each decision can easily be manually inspected), robust (e.g. do not require significant data preprocessing), scalable, and suitable for parallel and distributed computation [18].

Because of their interpretability and high predictive power, we consider a decision tree-based method as a viable option for inferring objective function weights, namely *gradient boosted decision trees*. We cast the problem of inferring function weights as a binary classification problem, where the setting is the same as with the maximum entropy principle - diet modellers are presented with diet pairs and are instructed to select the one they prefer more, with respect to the objective function. By doing so, they generate input-output pairs on which gradient boosted decision trees are then trained/validated. Upon convergence, we select the best performing decision tree, and rank input features according to their importance, which in this case is synonymous with their *total information gain* [18]. We further normalize the results, so as to obtain a proper probability distribution.

Besides inferring objective function weights, the method can provide diet modellers with a variety of other information. For instance, features that appear together in a traversal path are interacting with one another (since the condition of a child node is predicated on the condition of the parent node), which gives modellers the ability to discover interactions among features [16].

3.2   Inferring Consumer Preferences

Diet acceptability modelling has been deemed interesting and important both as a constraint, and an objective, depending on the modelling approach. It is generally modelled as the total deviation between the optimal food item intakes, and the food item intakes of the current diet. The assumption is that if two diets do not deviate significantly in terms of food items and their quantities, they can be considered similar, and almost equally acceptable. This definition of acceptability implicitly takes into account a variety of different factors that might contribute to the diversity of dietary patterns, for instance cultural and lifestyle differences [12].

However, modelling diet acceptability solely through total deviation leaves a lot to be desired. For instance, such approach does not provide the option to search for likely preferable food items that have not been recorded in a consumer's diet, which puts a severe limitation on diet model flexibility. As mentioned before, in order to meet nutritional targets, observed individual diets generally have to be expanded with new food items, which, if done in an arbitrary fashion, could have detrimental effects on diet acceptability. The same thing applies in case a modeller would like to diversify the observed diets by including new food items.

In the following section, we consider a data-driven modelling paradigm based on the concept of *recommendation systems* [19], namely the *Top-N recommendation system based on mutual information and entropy weighting*, that can analyze consumer historical data, and turn it into actionable insights that can complement the already existing diet models. By doing so, we are establishing one of potentially many links between the hypothesis-driven methods, and more data-driven machine learning methods.

Top-N Recommendation System Based on Mutual Information and Entropy Weighting. In order to meet all nutritional constraints, consumers' diets often have to be expanded with new, previously unobserved food items. Most current diet models base their selection of new food items on some form of the majority vote, that is selecting those unobserved foods that are present in e.g. ≥50% of diets in the sample [12]. Although better than random selection, such an approach leaves enough room for improvement.

We consider a recommendation system that can process user data from potentially multiple sources, and leverage algorithmically derived information on consumers' routine behavioral patterns so as to subsequently deliver personalized product recommendations. The recommendation system consists of two computational steps - the preprocessing and pairwise similarity computation.

Preprocessing of the input data can significantly facilitate the extraction of information [20]. It comes in many flavors, ranging from very simple procedures such as normalization and standardization, various kernel functions, weighting functions [21], (non)linear dimensionality reduction methods, to more sophisticated and automatic feature extractors such as deep neural networks [20]. The selection of one or more preprocessing steps will depend on a variety of factors, including, but not limited to, available computing power, and the amount and type of data. Given that the majority of consumer behavior data is not publicly available, diet modellers predominantly leverage relatively scarce data sets obtained via questionnaires [12], hence why we consider a handcrafted weighting function based on the concept of information entropy, which has been shown to perform significantly better than most handcrafted weighting functions in some tasks [22].

As the name suggests, similarity computation step serves for computing either pairwise food item or consumer similarities. Selecting an appropriate similarity measure is of crucial importance. We consider the mutual information, a core information-theoretic quantity that acts as a general measure of dependence between two random variables [23], as opposed to some other commonly employed correlation metrics (e.g. Pearson correlation coefficient), which measure only linear dependence.

Similarity computation ultimately results in a fully connected similarity graph that can be queried in many ways. In case of food item similarities, such a graph can for instance support the prediction of top N likely preferable food items by consumers that have not reported consuming those food items.

For each consumer m_i that has purchased a set U of food items, we compute the set C by taking the union of the k most similar food items for each item $n_i \in U$. After that, we remove all food items from C that are already in U. Then, for each item $c \in C$ we compute its similarity to the set U by summing the similarities between all food items $n_i \in U$ and c, using only the k most similar food items of n_i. Lastly, the food items in C are sorted in non-increasing order with respect to their similarity to the set U, and the first N food items are selected for the recommendation. Clearly, N and k are tunable parameters, and their selection can affect the speed and quality of recommendations [24].

4   Conclusion

Diet models based on mathematical programming have been used extensively during the last couple of decades, and have stood the test of time. With straightforward structure, fast execution, and high usability, mathematical programming poses as an obvious first choice for diet modelling. However, being mainly hypothesis-driven, such diet models often neglect important aspects of today's world - the abundance of user data, and the availability of algorithms that can turn data into actionable insights.

In this paper, we provide just a few examples of available data-driven methods that could greatly facilitate the diet modelling process. With MaxEnt and Gradient boosted decision trees, we provide diet modellers with the means for interacting with their diet models, so as to translate their expert knowledge into a "machine-readable" format. With the Top-N recommendation system, we are enriching the existing diet models with algorithmic and much more information-rich "word-of-mouth" recommendations.

Indeed, data-driven algorithms come with a few caveats. For instance, current state-of-the-art methods are still rather data-inefficient, meaning that they need a significant amount of data to obtain high generalization power. Furthermore, they can also be energy-inefficient, in the sense that large amount of data require significant computational power to be processed in a reasonable amount of time.

References

1. Johnston, J.L., Fanzo, J.C., Cogill, B.: Understanding sustainable diets: a descriptive analysis of the determinants and processes that influence diets and their impact on health, food security, and environmental sustainability. Adv. Nutr. **5**(4), 418–429 (2014)
2. Willet, W., et al.: Food in the anthropocene: the EAT-lancet commission on healthy diets from sustainable food systems. Lancet **393**(10170), 447–492 (2019)
3. Lassale, C., Gunter, M.J., Romaguera, D., Peelen, L.M., Van der Schouw, Y.T., Beulens, J.W.J., et al.: Diet quality scores and prediction of all-cause, cardiovascular and cancer mortality in a pan-European cohort study. PLoS ONE **11**(7) (2016)
4. Minihane, A.M., et al.: Low-grade inflammation, diet composition and health: current research evidence and its translation. Br. J. Nutr. **114**(07), 999–1012 (2015)
5. Fanzo, J.: Ethical issues for human nutrition in the context of global food security and sustainable development. Glob. Food Secur. **7**, 15–23 (2015)
6. Macdiarmid, J.I., et al.: Sustainable diets for the future: can we contribute to reducing greenhouse gas emissions by eating a healthy diet? Am. J. Clin. Nutr. **96**(3), 632–639 (2012)
7. Irz, X., Leroy, P., Requillart, V., Soler, L.: Beyond wishful thinking: integrating consumer preferences in the assessment of dietary recommendations. PLoS ONE **11**(6) (2016)
8. Reisch, L., Eberle, U., Lorek, S.: Sustainable food consumption: an overview of contemporary issues and policies. Sustain. Sci. Pract. Policy **9**(2), 7–25 (2016)
9. Schmidhuber, J.: Deep learning in neural networks: an overview, pp. 7–25. arXiv:1404.7828 (2014)
10. Stigler, G.J.: The cost of subsistence. J. Farm Econ. **27**(2), 303–314 (1945)
11. Danzig, G.B.: Linear Programming and Extensions. Princeton University Press, Princeton (1963)
12. Gazan, R., Brouzes, C.M.C., Vieux, F., Maillot, M., Lluch, A., Darmon, N.: Mathematical optimization to explore tomorrow's sustainable diets: a narrative review. Adv. Nutr. **9**(5), 602–626 (2018)
13. Previdelli, A.N., de Andrade, S.C., Fisberg, R.M., Marchioni, D.M.: Using two different approaches to assess dietary patterns: hypothesis-driven and data-driven analysis. Nutrients **8**(10), 593 (2016)
14. Tyszler, M., Kramer, G., Blonk, H.: Just eating healthier is not enough: studying the environmental impact of different diet scenarios for Dutch women (31–50 years old) by linear programming. Int. J. Life Cycle Assess. **21**(5), 701–709 (2016)
15. van Dooren, C., Tyszler, M., Kramer, G.F.H., Aiking, H.: Combining low price, low climate impact and high nutritional value in one shopping basket through diet optimization by linear programming. Sustainability **7**(9), 12837–12855 (2015)
16. Chen, T., Guestrin, C.: XGBoost: a scalable tree boosting system. In: Proceedings of the 22nd ACM SIGKDD International Conference on Knowledge Discovery and Data Mining, San Francisco, California, USA, pp. 785–794 (2016)

17. Jaynes, E.T.: Information theory and statistical mechanics. Phys. Rev. **106**(4), 620 (1957)
18. Hastie, T., Tibshirani, R., Friedman, J.: The Elements of Statistical Learning. Springer, New York (2001). https://doi.org/10.1007/978-0-387-21606-5
19. Lu, L., Medo, M., Yeung, C.H., Zhang, Y.-C., Zhang, Z.-K., Zhou, T.: Recommender systems. Phys. Rep. **519**(1), 1–49 (2012)
20. Bengio, Y., Courville, A., Vincent, P.: Representation learning: a review and new perspectives. IEEE Trans. Pattern Anal. Mach. Intell. **35**(8), 1798–1828 (2013)
21. Manning, C.D., Raghavan, P.: Introduction to Information Retrieval. Cambridge University Press, New York (2008)
22. Nakov, P., Popova, A., Mateev, P.: Weight functions impact on LSA performance. In: Proceedings of the EuroConference Recent Advances in Natural Language Processing (RANLP 2001), pp. 187–193. (2001)
23. Cover, T.M., Thomas, J.A.: Elements of Information Theory, 2nd edn. Wiley, New York (2006)
24. Karypis, G.: Evaluation of item-based top-N recommendation algorithms. In: 9thProceedings of the Tenth International Conference on Information and Knowledge Management, pp. 247–254. ACM, New York (2001)

AGINFRA PLUS: Running Crop Simulations on the D4Science Distributed e-Infrastructure

M. J. Rob Knapen[1]([✉]), Rob M. Lokers[1], Leonardo Candela[2], and Sander Janssen[1]

[1] Wageningen University and Research, Wageningen, The Netherlands
rob.knapen@wur.nl
[2] ISTI – National Research Council of Italy, Pisa, Italy

Abstract. Virtual Research Environments (VREs) bridge the gap between the compute and storage infrastructure becoming available as the 'cloud', and the needs of researchers for tools supporting open science and analytics on ever larger datasets. In the AGINFRA PLUS project such a VRE, based on the D4Science platform, was examined to improve and test its capabilities for running large numbers of crop simulations at field level, based on the WOFOST-WISS model and Dutch input datasets from the AgroDataCube. Using the gCube DataMiner component of the VRE, and based on the Web Processing Service standard, a system has been implemented that can run such workloads successfully on an available cluster, and with good performance, providing summarized results to agronomists for further analysis. The methods used and the resulting implementation are briefly described in this paper. Overall the approach seems viable and opening the door to many follow-up implementation opportunities and further research. Some of them are indicated in more detail in the conclusions.

Keywords: Distributed computing · e-Infrastructure · Virtual Research Environment · Crop simulation model · WOFOST

1 Introduction

In [10], it is argued that in Agronomy the major Big Data challenges are with variety and veracity, and that tackling the issues with volume and velocity of the data is more generic and to be solved with common industrial Information Technology solutions. Yet, such solutions still have to be created, adapted to, and tried in the field of Agro Informatics. Besides, agronomists and researchers of related domains have to be introduced to them and start making use of these new technologies.

Meanwhile the range of options is getting broader with the rise of container technologies such as Docker (https://www.docker.com), Kubernetes (https://kubernetes.io), and Singularity (https://sylabs.io), and Cloud computing. Platforms familiar to computer scientists and software engineers such as Google Cloud Platform (https://cloud.google.com), Amazon Web Services (https://aws.amazon.com), Microsoft Azure (https://azure.microsoft.com/), are extending their reach by adding tools interesting to other researchers, targeting various domains. While other vendors make more basic compute

I. N. Athanasiadis et al. (Eds.): ISESS 2020, IFIP AICT 554, pp. 81–89, 2020.
https://doi.org/10.1007/978-3-030-39815-6_8

and storage resources still easier accessible at low prices. However, the high-level platforms have the risk of vendor lock-in and unknowingly handing over of data, while the low-level solutions (including direct use of High Performance Computing) require IT proficiency to make proper use of them.

The European Open Science Cloud (EOSC) is an initiative that addresses such issues and promotes a more open, federated, research infrastructure that gives access to compute and storage resources, and support the ideas of Open Science and FAIR data sharing (https://www.force11.org/group/fairgroup/fairprinciples). It is in line with those thoughts that the D4Science platform [3] is being developed.

In the European H2020 AGINFRA PLUS project [2] the D4Science technology is used to create a number of Virtual Research Environments (VRE) specifically targeting research communities in the food and agriculture domain, with the goal to accelerate user-driven innovations of the existing e-Infrastructure. A number of key use cases were selected based on typical work and requirements within each community. This paper will further focus on one of those use cases, being the ability to run crop simulation models at scale on a compute cluster hosted by D4Science, allowing for horizontal scalability to handle large workloads such as running crop simulations for all the crop parcels in the Netherlands.

2   Methods

2.1   D4Science Cloud Computing e-Infrastructure

D4Science [5] promotes open science through the operation of an innovative data and compute infrastructure service, build using the gCube framework [8]. The gCube technology allows easy construction and development of VREs. A VRE in general is a web-based working environment tailored to support the needs of their designated communities, each working on specific research questions. The VRE offers users with domain-specific facilities, e.g. certain computational algorithms, and typically needed datasets, integrated with more common services that support collaboration and cooperation amongst users, e.g. a shared Workspace to store and organize versions of research artifacts, a social networking area, a data analytics platform, and a catalogue-based publishing platform (see [3]).

The data analytics platform (gCube DataMiner, see Fig. 1) is of special interest, since this is the service used to run the crop simulation model. There are two ways to interact with it, one is at a low level where algorithms have to be written using specific Java interfaces that are set up to do map-reduce types of processing [7]. Such algorithms gain access to the 'Worker' cluster, a set of thin nodes ('slow' CPU and limited memory) specifically targeted at this type of data processing. The other option is to write algorithms that can be deployed using the DataMiner importer, which wraps it and deploys it as a Web Processing Service (WPS, a standard from the Open Geospatial Consortium (OGC)) on the 'Master' cluster. These are fat nodes (fast CPU and lots of memory) in the system that handle the queuing, load balancing, and execution of WPS requests.

For both approaches DataMiner automatically provides recording of provenance information using the W3C Prov-O standard [11], so that any run of an algorithm can easily be repeated.

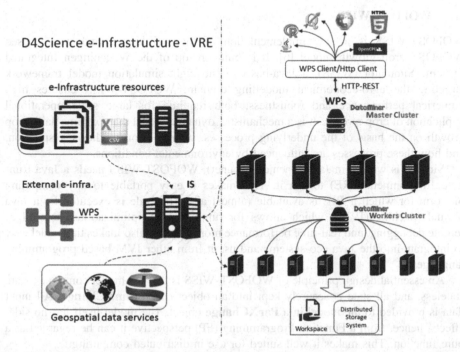

Fig. 1. Architecture of the gCube DataMiner system. With on the right side the two compute clusters and the distributed storage system, and on the left side several e-Infrastructure resources which are indexed on the D4Science Information System (IS).

2.2   The Web Processing Service Standard

The Web Processing Service interface standard is one of the standards of the Open Geospatial Consortium. It is lightweight and XML-based, and easy to use to publish, discover, and execute processes as a service. Processes (e.g. calculations, algorithms, simulation models) can be both simple and complex. Input data for the processes can be included in the HTTP POST request to the WPS service or be made accessible via HTTP URLs. WPS services can also be integrated into workflows by workflow management systems such as Galaxy (galaxyproject.org), Knime (www.knime.com), and Apache Taverna (taverna.apache.org).

WPS has been designed to work with spatially referenced data, but it can be used with any kind of data. It also was not designed to work with distributed computing systems. The main operations defined by the interface are: **GetCapabilities**, **DescribeProcess**, and **Execute**. Allowing to get the list of available services on a system, get a description of the required inputs and the produced outputs, and to execute the process. These do not allow for very dynamic use of a compute cluster. E.g. all outputs of a process have to be specified at process description time, and it is hard to track how busy the system is and how many new requests it would be able to process quickly. In D4Science some of these issues have been addressed.

2.3 WOFOST-WISS

WOFOST-WISS is a new implementation of the well-known and widely used WOFOST crop growth model [6]. It is built on top of the Wageningen Integrated Systems Simulator (WISS), a Java-based, lightweight simulation model framework targeting the agro-economical modelling domain. WOFOST-WISS ensures high numerical performance and robustness, both required for large scale operational application of crop models. It is a mechanistic, dynamic model that explains daily crop growth on the basis of the underlying processes, such as photosynthesis, respiration, and how these processes are influenced by environmental conditions.

Since it is written in Java (openjdk.java.net), WOFOST-WISS needs a Java Runtime Environment (JRE) to run it. This makes it easy portable to any computing platform for which a JRE is available (almost all). The code is executed by a Java Virtual Machine (JVM), which allows for runtime code optimizations, as well as remote debugging, and real-time performance monitoring. It also makes the model easy to integrate into the Java eco-systems and use it from other JVM-based programming languages.

An essential design principle of WOFOST-WISS is that the model components are stateless, and all state is securely kept into an object called **SimXChange**. All input data is provided to the model in a **ParXChange** object. The model itself has no side-effects, hence, from a Function Programming (FP) perspective it can be regarded as a pure function. This makes it well suited for use in distributed computing.

2.4 AgroDataCube

Given that for many applications in the agri-food domain the same basic, large, datasets are always needed, at Wageningen Environmental Research these are being made available as harmonized open data in the AgroDataCube [9], including information about crop fields, crop growth (as indexes derived from remote sensing data), observed weather, terrain height, and soil conditions. Using an access token all data can be retrieved by HTTP GET and POST requests in GeoJSON format (geojson.org) from a REST (https://www.ics.uci.edu/ ~ fielding/pubs/dissertation/rest_arch_style.htm) based Application Programming Interface (API). It is also possible to retrieve sub-field gridded data such as the detailed 10 m × 10 m Normalized Difference Vegetation Index (NDVI).

For the Netherlands the AgroDataCube contains in principle all the data for multiple years needed to run crop simulations at the crop field level. It does however require some further pre-processing of the data, including the mapping of crop codes into the needed crop specific parameters, completing available weather data into a full daily time series of all required weather variables, and calculation of essential soil characteristics from the available soil information.

2.5   Functional Programming and the Actor Framework

The technologies available for building applications continue to evolve at a rapid pace. Systems such as D4Science make it possible to effectively utilize clusters of cores on individual servers and clusters of servers that work together as a single application platform. Costs for memory and disk storage have dropped, and network speeds have grown significantly. This allows for large volumes of data to be collected and processed. However, timely processing typically cannot be done any more on a single traditional computer with limited (vertical) scalability. It requires distributed computing on multiple computers that allow better (horizontal) scalability. And distributed computing is difficult to program without using new programming paradigms such as functional programming.

Functional Programming (FP) is a style of writing computer programs that treats computation as the evaluation of mathematical functions and avoids changing state and mutable data, and side-effects in general. Programming is done by writing expressions or declarations, instead of statements. FP stems from lambda calculus, a formal system developed in the 1930s to investigate computability, amongst others. Lisp (lisp-lang. org), Clojure (clojure.org), Erlang (erlang.org), Haskell (haskell.org), and Scala (scala-lang.org) are some well-known functional programming languages. The latter is a JVM based programming language, hence offers good integration with Java.

Because it avoids side-effects FP fits well for writing programs that are run in distributed computing environments. It is much easier to reason about the execution of (pure) functions, than about multiple computers and threads processing the objects of a program written in an Object-Oriented programming language. Combining FP with a message passing architecture such as the Akka framework [1] allows even further abstraction and isolation, away from the low-level wiring and very technical programming techniques otherwise needed to make efficient use of computational resources.

3   Results

As described, one of the use cases in the AGINFRA PLUS project was to pilot running crop simulations for the crop fields of the Netherlands, using the D4Science distributed infrastructure. Within the project a small cluster was available for testing purposes, with 6 fat nodes, and a slightly larger cluster for operational deployments. A number of VREs have been created, among which one for the Agro-Environmental modelling use cases. This VRE contained the generic components such as the social messaging, the shared Workspace, and DataMiner, as well as more domain specific tools such as access to SoilGrids (soilgrids.org), Jupyter notebooks (jupyter.org), and customized visualizations.

It would certainly have been possible to use the map-reduce approach of DataMiner for running many crop simulations on the system. However, for the long term, this appeared to be a less flexible solution, binding the software directly to the D4Science platform. Being a research organization, future projects might involve running crop simulations in other environments than D4Science, and not in a strictly map-reduce way, making it more appealing to use the WPS based processing of DataMiner.

DataMiner runs the WPS processes on available fat nodes in the cluster. For all incoming WPS requests of the same process it handles the queuing and load balancing. Running the crop simulation models efficiently therefore required implementing two types of algorithms for DataMiner. One that can run as many crop simulations simultaneously per fat node once it gets assigned to one, and another type of algorithm that can divide a total workload of crop simulations to be done for a set of selected crop fields, e.g. all maize fields in the Dutch province Limburg (approx. 15.000 for a single year), into smaller batches, start the crop simulation jobs on DataMiner for each batch, and collect and process all results. In essence the two types of algorithms perform the map-reduce processing via the WPS interfaces.

Both algorithms are implemented using the Akka actor framework, so that they make the best possible use of the machines they get assigned to (within limitations set by the system). The 'worker' algorithm (see Fig. 2) contains WOFOST-WISS and accesses the AgroDataCube in an optimized way, running as many crop simulations in parallel as possible.

Retrieving data from the AgroDataCube is a clear bottleneck that technically should be solved. For now, data retrieved is cached and reused when possible, so after warm-up the algorithm optimizes for running similar crop simulations (e.g. in the same region with little variation in weather and soils). The output of the algorithm is either a CSV

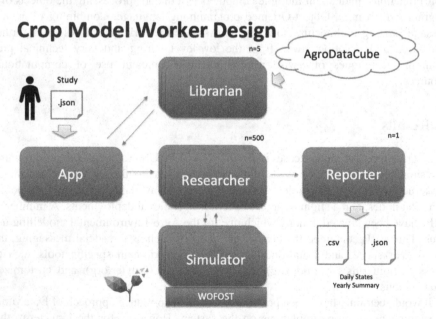

Fig. 2. Actors in the worker algorithm. The user provides a description of a study in JSON format. The Librarians (n = 5) smartly retrieves all required data from AgroDataCube and other data sources. Multiple Researchers (n = 500) run WOFOST crop simulations in parallel via the Simulator. A single Reporter (n = 1) collects and summarizes all results.

file with daily states of all calculated variables in the simulation, in case a single simulation is run, or a JSON file with a summary of the main variables for each simulation run. This keeps the total output manageable and should the detailed data for a specific simulation be needed it can easily be produced.

The 'scheduler' algorithm (Fig. 3) retrieves all IDs of crop fields from the Agro-DataCube that match criteria specified by the user of the system, i.e. crop to process, year to simulate, spatial region the crop fields should be in. And some more technical parameters as well such as the preferred batch size, the maximum number of batches to process, and a timeout value for the total processing. These might be hidden after the system has been tuned and runs in a more operational state. Given the list of IDs the algorithm creates the batches, and for each one sends a WPS request to DataMiner to run the crop simulations algorithm. The scheduler then tracks the status of all algorithm executions in progress. When they all have finished all produced output is analyzed by the algorithm and an overall summary is created and made available in HTML format, giving the research a quick overview of the state of all crop simulations performed.

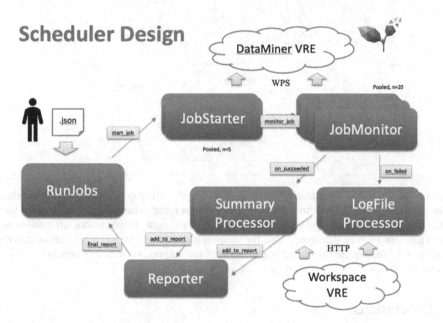

Fig. 3. Actors in the Scheduler algorithm. The user provides a description of a study in JSON format. A number of JobStarters send WPS requests to DataMiner to run the worker algorithm. Once started their execution progress is tracked by JobMonitors. Processing results (all the output files that DataMiner writes to the storage system) are then analyzed by LogFileProcessors and SummaryProcessors, that provide input to a Reporter that creates an overview.

Although improvements still need to be made and many optimizations are possible, it is clear that technically the solution works. Even in this stage and with a limited system of 6 fat nodes in the cluster, round-trip processing of crop simulations runs at about 50 simulations per second. Large workloads can easily be handled by (temporarily) adding more nodes to the cluster. And via WPS both types of algorithms can be called from other applications than the VRE. E.g. a custom web user interface, a mobile application, another WPS client such as QGIS (qgis.org), and so on. To showcase this within the AGINFRA PLUS project a dashboard visualization (see Fig. 4) is also being build, bringing together the input data from AgroDataCube and the output data from crop simulations.

Fig. 4. The Crop Modelling Dashboard. It displays a map with crop fields (top left) from which a parcel can be selected. Data from AgroDataCube is then retrieved and field characteristics such as the crop, previous crops, soil types, etc. are displayed top right. In the bottom left weather and NDVI timeseries can be displayed, while the view on the bottom right side allows running a crop simulation for the selected field and visualization of the outputs, such as leaf area index, above ground biomass, soil moisture, harvest index, etc.

4   Conclusions

The described implementation allows running crop simulations in a standardized environment, with horizontal scalability. For larger workloads required computational time can be decreased by adding more computers to the cluster. Besides, the processes are available via the standardized WPS interfaces and can thus be used in many applications. Or within VREs, tailored to specific user communities and usages. Further fine-tuning of the system is of course needed to turn the current proof-of-concept into an operational solution. With similar data as the contents of the AgroDataCube and proper calibration of the WOFOST-WISS model the same system can also be used for other regions.

Parts of the system will also be used in the Cybele EU H2020 project [4], which looks at the convergence of Cloud Computing services, such as D4Science, and High Performance Computing (HPC). This should make available even more compute power for running crop simulations, opening the door for doing even more advanced studies requiring ever increasing numbers of crop field level simulations to be run, e.g. yield forecasting at the field level based on detailed weather forecasts.

Naturally the real value in the end is to be able to better advice farmers and achieve a more efficient and future-proof agri-food system.

Acknowledgment. This work has received funding from the European Union's Horizon 2020 research and innovation programme under the AGINFRA PLUS project (grant agreement No 731001).

References

1. Akka framework homepage, 30 September 2019. https://akka.io
2. Assante, M., et al.: Realising a science gateway for the agri-food: the aginfra plus experience. In: 11th International Workshop on Science Gateways (2019)
3. Assante, M.: Enacting open science by D4science. Future Gener. Comput. Syst. (2019). https://doi.org/10.1016/j.future.2019.05.063
4. CYBELE EU H2020 project homepage, 30 September 2019. https://www.cybele-project.eu
5. D4science homepage, 30 September 2019. https://www.d4science.org
6. De Wit, A., et al.: 25 years of the wofost cropping systems model. Agric. Syst. **168**, 154–167 (2019)
7. Dean, J., Ghemawat, S.: Mapreduce: simplified data processing on large clusters. Commun. ACM **51**, 107–113 (2008)
8. gCube Framework homepage, 30 September 2019. https://www.gcube-system.org
9. AgroDataCube: A Big Open Data Collection for Agri-Food Applications, 30 September 2019. https://doi.org/10.18174/455759
10. Lokers, R., Knapen, R., Janssen, S., Van Randen, Y., Jansen, J.: Analysis of big data technologies for use in agro-environmental science. Environ. Model Softw. **84**, 494–504 (2016)
11. W3C Prov-O: The PROV Ontology Specification, 30 September 2019. https://www.w3.org/TR/prov-o/

Redefining Agricultural Insurance Services Using Earth Observation Data. The Case of Beacon Project

Emmanuel Lekakis[✉], Stylianos Kotsopoulos, Gregory Mygdakos,
Agathoklis Dimitrakos, Ifigeneia-Maria Tsioutsia,
and Polimachi Simeonidou

Agroapps, P.C. 54-56 Them. Sofouli, 54655 Thessaloniki, Greece
mlekakis@agroapps.gr

Abstract. BEACON is a market-led project that couples cutting edge Earth Observation (EO) technology with weather intelligence and blockchain to deliver a toolbox for the Agricultural Insurance (AgI) sector with timely cost-efficient and actionable insights for the agri-insurance industry. BEACON enables insurance companies to exploit the untapped market potential of AgI, while contributing to the redefinition of existing AgI products and services. The Damage Assessment Calculator of BEACON employs remote sensing techniques in order to improve the quality and cost-effectiveness of agri-insurance by: (i) increasing the objectivity of the experts field inspections; (ii) reducing the cost of field visits and (iii) increasing farmers' confidence in the estimation results, given the significant economic impact of erroneous estimation. This paper provides an analysis of different type of EO data and remote sensing techniques implemented in the operational workflow of BEACON that can be used by AgI companies to provide safe and reliable results on storms, floods, wildfires and droughts damage on crops.

Keywords: Agricultural Insurance · BEACON · Earth observation data

1 Introduction

Agricultural Insurance (AgI) sector is expanding on a global scale and is projected to grow by €50 B, by 2020. This rapid growth is driven by a set of fundamental structural changes directly affecting the agricultural sector like more frequent and severe extreme weather events, growing global population and intensification of production systems [1, 2]. Insurance solutions are set to grow in importance for agricultural management, given that agriculture will continue to be increasingly dependent on risk financing support. However, the development and provision of insurance services/products in the agricultural sector is generally low as compared to other sectors of the economy, and in their majority, suffer from low market penetration [3].

In that frame, the BEACON toolbox was born, that aims to provide insurance companies with a robust and cost-efficient set of services that will allow them (i) to alleviate the effect of weather uncertainty when estimating risk of AgI products; (ii) to

© IFIP International Federation for Information Processing 2020
Published by Springer Nature Switzerland AG 2020
I. N. Athanasiadis et al. (Eds.): ISESS 2020, IFIP AICT 554, pp. 90–101, 2020.
https://doi.org/10.1007/978-3-030-39815-6_9

reduce the number of on-site visits for claim verification; (iii) to reduce operational and administrative costs for monitoring of insured indices and contract handling; and (iv) to design more accurate and personalized contracts. Specifically, BEACON scales-up on EO data and Weather Intelligence services components, couples them with blockchain, to deliver the required functions for Weather Prediction and Assessment and Smart Contracts and offer the required services:

- Crop Monitoring, which provides contract profiling and crop monitoring data together with yield estimations.
- Damage Assessment Calculator, which supports AgI companies in better assess and calculate damage to proceed with indemnity payouts of claims.
- Anti-fraud Inspector, which allows AgI to automatically check the legitimacy of a claim submitted;
- Weather Risk Probability, which provides probabilities maps of extreme weather events that may occur in the upcoming season;
- Damage Prevention/Prognosis – Early Warning System, which provides extreme weather alerts to AgI providers and their customers.

This paper focuses on the Damage Assessment Tool (DAT) service components. It provides an analysis of different type of EO data and remote sensing techniques implemented in the operational workflow of BEACON that can be used by AgI companies to improve the quality and cost-effectiveness of their services.

2 Materials and Methods

BEACON employs a multi-satellite approach to tackle one of the main challenges of AgI, which is damage assessment and handling of claims with a greater accuracy. BEACON estimates damage occurred by hailstorms, windstorms, floods, wildfires, and drought, considered as the most devastating natural hazards of agricultural production worldwide [4]. Damage on a number of arable crops is taken into account, namely wheat, barley, maize, soybean, sunflower and cotton.

The Damage Assessment Calculator (DAC) provides visual damage maps of the affected area accompanied by the appropriate information, aiming in quantifying damage and providing a transparent basis for the indemnity pay-out process with farmers. The general framework under which the DAC is developed, is the implementation of change detection techniques between a pre- and a post-hazard available image. The concept is based on the fact that the spectral behavior of a crop in different zones of the electromagnetic spectrum can be modified by a number of means, including catastrophic phenomena, destruction or decrease in plant chlorophyll content, changes in internal leaf structure and of the morphological characteristics of plant canopy. These changes in spectral behavior can be detected by satellite sensors [5].

Satellite images utilized by BEACON in producing the appropriate vegetation indices (VIs) are: (i) Sentinel-2, Level-2A, Bottom-Of Atmosphere (BOA), surface reflectance products, (ii) Sentinel-1, C-band Interferometric Wide (IW) swath, TOP-SAR data, in GRDH (Ground Range Detected in High resolution) format, with double polarization (VV and VH) and (iii) MODIS Terra 9 × 9 degree Tiles, 8-day NDVI composites. Due to their sensitivity to vegetation condition and abundance, VIs are then employed in image differencing to detect changes related to extreme weather events [6]. Two aspects are critical for the change detection results: selecting suitable image bands or VIs and selecting suitable thresholds to identify the changed areas. For this reason, a number of different techniques were implemented in the DAC, based on the type of the hazardous event.

2.1   Hail and Storms Damage Assessment

In BEACON, to overcome issues in optical data quality and therefore availability, the synergistic use of optical and synthetic aperture radar (SAR) images was included in the workflow of the DAC. Regarding optical data, the NDVI (Normalized Difference Vegetation Index) is used to perform damage assessment between a pre- and a post-hazard acquired image of an insured crop. The index results from the following equation:

$$NDVI = (NIR - RED)/(NIR + RED) \tag{1}$$

where RED and NIR stand for the spectral reflectance measurements acquired in the red and near-infrared regions, respectively. NDVI sensed values are sensitive to a number of perturbing factors including: (i) atmospheric effects (with respect to water vapor and aerosols), (ii) clouds (deep – optically thick and thin clouds – ubiquitous cirrus) and (iii) cloud shadows, that can significantly contaminate the results and lead to misinterpretations in damage assessment. Hailstorm events are usually accompanied by prolonged cloud coverage, impeding the acquisition of cloud free optical images.

SAR sensors are independent of atmospheric and sunlight conditions and therefore can provide the means to overcome the limitations of optical sensors. SAR derived, vegetation indices proposed in the literature are the Radar Vegetation Index (RVI) [7], Radar Forest Degradation Index (RDFI) [8] and Microwave Polarization Difference Index (MPDI) [9]. In BEACON, the MPDI is employed for change detection under this type of damage. The index represents a normalized polarization, calculated from VV and VH images captured by Sentinel-1 satellites. It is expressed as follows:

$$MPDI = \left(\sigma_{VV}^{o} - \sigma_{VH}^{o}\right)/\left(\sigma_{VV}^{o} + \sigma_{VH}^{o}\right) \tag{2}$$

where σ_{VH}^{o} and σ_{VV}^{o} are the backscattering sigma nought values of VH and VV polarization, respectively. The values of MPDI vary between 0 and 1. Low MPDI values (<0.3) refer to high biomass and denser vegetation. Values change gradually to higher values for degraded, damaged or sparse vegetation and during crop maturation.

The MPDI was selected in BEACON for three reasons. Firstly, the numerator (VV-VH) reflects the depolarization ratio. This ratio has an increased sensitivity to surface roughness, as well as vegetation structure. Secondly, the normalization of the depolarization ratio demonstrates sensitivity to vegetation canopy density and water content. Therefore, structural damage caused during hailstorms (e.g. defoliation, stem breakage and uprooting) can easily be detected by MPDI. Furthermore, normalizing the depolarization ratio also serves to reduce potential outliers within the data. Thirdly, VV and

VH present a high level of availability that the Sentinel-1 sensors provide, with a standard revisit time per orbit (ascending, descending) of 6 days (S1-A, S1-B).

2.2   Flood Damage Spatial Distribution

In BEACON, SAR and optical data are utilized for flood damage assessment. SAR data assist in monitoring flood extent, damage and duration and fill the gaps of optical data acquisition [10]. Their synergistic use is intended to enable BEACON to identify the beginning, the duration and the extent of flooding with a significant accuracy.

Optical Data to Detect and Map Flooding Events. In BEACON, mNDWI (modified Normalized Difference Water Index) [11] is used to map and delineate flooded areas. Research has demonstrated that mNDWI can enhance water information and extract water bodies with a significant accuracy [12, 13]. The index is expressed as follows:

$$mNDWI = (GREEN - SWIR)/(GREEN + SWIR) \tag{3}$$

where *GREEN* and *SWIR* stand for the spectral reflectance measurements acquired in the green (visible) and the Shortwave Infrared (SWIR) band, respectively. The value of mNDWI ranges from -1 to $+1$. The higher reflectance of built-up and lower reflectance of water in SWIR band result in negative values of built-up and positive values of water features in the mNDWI derived image. For the separation of water bodies from other land-cover features, several thresholds have been proposed for mNDWI, ranging from 0 to 0.41 [13, 14].

SAR, C-Band Data Processing to Detect and Map Flooding Events. BEACON uses a methodology for flood mapping based on multi-temporal SAR data analysis and the computation of two indices, i.e. the Normalized Difference Flood Index (NDFI) for highlighting flooded areas, and the Normalized Difference Flood in Vegetated areas Index (NDFVI) for highlighting shallow water in short vegetation [15, 16]. According to the method, two SAR multi-temporal layer stacks are created. One contains only reference (pre-flood) SAR images and the other both reference and post-flooding images. Statistical analysis of the backscattering sigma nought, $\sigma°$, of each pixel is then performed in both multi-temporal image stacks (σ^o_{ref} and σ^o_{flood}). For each pixel, the minimum, maximum and mean $\sigma°$ is derived. The calculated temporal statistics are used to compute the NDFI, which aims at highlighting temporary open water bodies:

$$NDFI = \left(mean\langle \sigma^o_{ref} \rangle - min\langle \sigma^o_{ref}, \sigma^o_{flood} \rangle\right) / \left(mean\langle \sigma^o_{ref} \rangle + min\langle \sigma^o_{ref}, \sigma^o_{flood} \rangle\right) \tag{4}$$

To detect shallow water in short vegetation, NDFVI is used, aiming at highlighting the increase of backscatter that happens in those circumstances. NDFVI is used for detecting and delineating flood events in well-developed crops, which is particularly important in BEACON, and is computed:

$$NDFVI = \left(max\left\langle \sigma_{ref}^o, \sigma_{flood}^o \right\rangle - mean\left\langle \sigma_{ref}^o \right\rangle\right) / \left(max\left\langle \sigma_{ref}^o, \sigma_{flood}^o \right\rangle + mean\left\langle \sigma_{ref}^o \right\rangle\right) \quad (5)$$

After the computation of the two indices, a threshold of 0.70 for NDFI and 0.75 for NDFVI is applied to extract flooded areas [15]. In BEACON, the sigma nought for VV polarization is used for both NDFI and NDFVI. Research suggests that VV polarization performs better for water body detection, providing better accuracies than VH [17].

In the workflow for flood detection in BEACON, SAR images, are stored and every time a new image is available, the NDFI and NDFVI are calculated. The two stacks of images contain, on the one hand, the reference image stack and on the other hand, the reference stack and the latest image (presumed as a post-flood image). After the determination of flooded or non-flooded pixels, based on the thresholds imposed, a binary algorithm will be applied. To binarize the image, band math is applied, setting as logical value (true) for values less than the chosen threshold and false for higher values, producing the final "*Water*" image [10].

This methodology adopted in BEACON, exhibits the following advantages: (i) it is fully automated and non-user dependent, especially in terms of defining an appropriate threshold; (ii) it is robust since the same workflow (in particular, the same threshold values) is applied to different floods in different environments by using different SAR sensors, polarizations and resolutions; (iii) the use of time-series improves the robustness of the reference image allowing a more precise mapping; and (iv) it reports shallow water in short vegetation, a product particularly important for flooded crops.

2.3 Wildfires Damage Mapping

Several methods have been proposed for mapping fire-affected areas from multitemporal or single post-fire satellite images [18, 19]. Much of the literature in remote sensing of burn severity has been based on thresholding the arithmetic difference of the Normalized Burn Ratio (dNBR) at two dates. The Normalized Burn Ratio (NBR), is a very sensitive index for burned areas enhancement and severity assessment [20]. The index combines the reflectance in the NIR and $SWIR$ bands. The NBR and the dNBR indices, are expressed as follows:

$$NBR = (NIR - SWIR)/(NIR + SWIR) \quad (6)$$

$$dNBR = NBR_{Pr\,eFire} - NBR_{PostFire} \quad (7)$$

where $NBR_{PreFire}$ and $NBR_{PostFire}$ is the sensed NBR in the satellite image before and after the fire event, respectively. NBR values range from -1 to 1, and dNBR values can range from -2 to 2. Higher NBR values indicate healthy vegetation, and lower values, burned areas.

In BEACON, the Relativized Burn Ratio (RBR) [21] is used for fire damage assessment, mapping and severity classification. RBR is divided by an adjustment to the pre-fire NBR, as follows:

$$RBR = 1000 \cdot dNBR / (NBR_{Pr\,eFire} + 1.001) \qquad (8)$$

RBR index is designed to detect change even where pre-fire vegetation cover is low. The dNBR index receives low values when burned areas are covered with low vegetation, due to low values in the change detection between the pre- and post-fire NBR [22]. This results in the underestimation of the fire severity by the dNBR. The relativized index performs better at detecting high severity effects across the full range of pre-fire vegetation cover [21]. RBR is used in BEACON because it is a robust severity metric applicable across broad geographic regions and fire regimes. Furthermore, RBR thresholds show reduced variability among fires and are more stable compared to other indices like dNBR and RdNBR (Relative dNBR) thresholds, and are thus more transferable among fire types and ecoregions. In terms of the RBR equation usability in an automated workflow, it is expected that the equation will not fail (i.e., reach infinity) for any pre-fire NBR value, will not result in extremely high or low values when pre-fire NBR is near zero, and it will retain the sign of pre-fire NBR, thereby avoiding potential arbitrary bias of taking the absolute value (e.g. RdNBR index) [21, 22].

2.4 Drought Damage Detection

BEACON detects drought damage by monitoring NDVI Anomaly (NDVIA) of an insured crop, throughout the growing season [23]. NDVIA is calculated from the MODIS NDVI, Level-2G product, provided in 8-day composites with a spatial resolution of 250 m (GMOD09Q1). The NDVIA is calculated as follows:

$$NDVIA_{ij} = 100 \cdot \left(NDVI_{i,j} - NDVI_{ave,j}\right) / \left(NDVI_{ave,j}\right) \qquad (9)$$

where i subscript denotes the year, j subscript denotes the 8-day period, and $NDVI_{ave,j}$ is the historical average, based on NDVI values of the corresponding 8-day period from 2001 until present. NDVIA positive values indicate normal conditions while negative values indicate possible drought stress [24]. The use of anomaly isolates the variability in the vegetation signal and establishes meaningful historical context for the current NDVI to determine relative drought severity [25].

3 Results and Discussion

3.1 SAR and Optical Data for Hail and Storms Damage Assessment

In change detection, image acquisition could present a significant irregularity in pre- and post-event dates due to availability issues of a proper cloud free multispectral image. The longer the time period between pre- and post-event images, the most possible it is for change detection techniques to capture different crop phenology stages (physical reduction of chlorophyll content) which will then result in biased damage estimates.

For an effective event coverage, in BEACON, an image acquisition strategy is followed to ensure that the pre- and post-damage imagery are as representative as possible of the insured crop's condition. Afterwards, the Difference Percentage Index (DPI), is calculated with the VI differencing technique, by the pre- and post-hazard satellite image. DPI records the % change of the indices in the pre- and post-hazard crop status, and is used for damage spatial distribution and severity classification in the final image. Differencing is applied on NDVI and MPDI obtained before and after a damage.

$$DPI(\%) = 100 \cdot \left(NDVI_i - NDVI_j\right)/NDVI_i \tag{10}$$

$$DPI(\%) = 100 \cdot \left|(MPDI_i - MPDI_j)/MPDI_i\right| \tag{11}$$

where the subscripts i and j denote the sensed VIs values in the pre- and post-damage satellite images, respectively. The equation is applied in the two available satellite images pixel by pixel, and a third one is produced with the resulting DPI in the pixels.

Since DPI expresses the actual damage, as a percentage of change detection, the incorporation of severity levels generalizes the spatial mapping of damage, providing further information on where the natural hazard event hit the most or where the change was undetectable. From a geoprocessing point of view, the qualitative damage estimation involves the DPI raster value reclassification, into severity levels, classified as light (10–40%), moderate (40–70%) and severe damage (70–100%) [26]. Figure 1 provides an example of hail damage estimated under regular and irregular pre- and post-event time intervals.

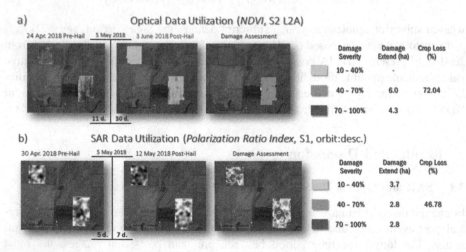

Fig. 1. Wheat crop hail damage spatial distribution and severity levels in Kilkis, Central Macedonia (Greece), on 5 May 2018, estimated with the methodologies implemented in BEACON. (a) Irregular time interval between pre- and post- hazard images due to cloudiness, (b) acceptable time interval between pre- and post- hazard images.

For the validation of the methodology, hail damage in-situ data on wheat, barley, maize, soybean and cotton crops were provided by AgI companies, early adopters of the BEACON solution. Data will be used to derive regression equations between the calculated DPI and levels of damage.

3.2 Flood Duration Identification

Based on the adopted methodology, BEACON applies SAR image change detection for flood mapping and flood extent assessment. Using this methodology synergistically with optical satellite data the flood duration is estimated. Then, crop loss is estimated based on the duration, the crop type and the crop stage. According to the availability of SAR images, the temporal variation of surface backscattering from the pre- to the post-flooding phase is produced, delineating the flood extent by the number of pixels classified as inundated. The same is produced based on the mNDWI sensed values. Every time a new assessment is available, the flood extent is re-estimated and subtracted from the initial extent detected. The days between the pre- and post-flooding images are counted and recorded and a full report is provided to the users through BEACON. This report contains the duration of the flood between the pre- and post-flooding image, as well as, the extent of the flood, until the water fully withdraws. The short revisit cycle of Sentinel-1 satellites (6 days) enables the collection of flood data that allow mapping inundated areas accurately. Figure 2 presents an example of a flooded area estimated with the coupled use of SAR and optical satellite data, with the methodology implemented in BEACON.

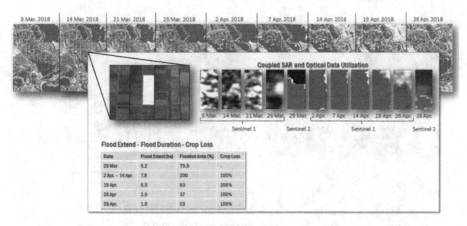

Fig. 2. Wheat crop flood damage assessment (extent and duration) in Tychero, Evros River Basin (Greece), on 29 March 2018, estimated with the methodology implemented in BEACON.

For the assessment of crop loss, BEACON uses the stage-damage exponential functions [27, 28], expressed in the general form:

$$D(\%) = c_1 \exp(c_2 \cdot t) \qquad (12)$$

where D is the flood damage percentage, c_1 and c_2 are coefficients specific for arable crops and t is the duration of flood, in days. These equations take into account the duration of the flood, as well as, the seasonality. Seasonality is introduced by different crop heights. Coefficients c_1 and c_2 are provided for three different crop heights, taking into account, in this way the crop growth stage. The crop heights are 0.2–0.5 m, 0.5–1 m and 1 m and above [27]. In-situ data on flood damage for wheat and barley, provided by AgI companies will be used to validate the stage-damage functions in estimating the damage on these two cereal crops.

3.3   Wildfires Damage Assessment

The fire severity levels are defined based on the RBR values, allowing the spatial mapping of damage intensity. This procedure involves the RBR raster value reclassification, into predefined interval classes. The disaster levels are classified as unburned, moderate-low, moderate-high and high fire severity [21, 22] reflecting the intensity of the damaging agent. RBR values range from lesser than unity to greater than 304. In the crop loss assessment of BEACON, it is assumed that when RBR values are higher than 27, the area is categorized as a burned area and crop is considered totally damaged. Figure 3 provides an example of olive groves fire damage, estimated with the RBR index methodology.

Fig. 3. Olive groves fire damage assessment (spatial mapping and severity levels) in Kotronas, Peloponnese Region, (S. Greece), on 2–5 July 2017, estimated with the methodology implemented in BEACON. $NBR_{Prefire}$, $NBR_{Postfire}$, dNBR, RBR image reclassification, visualization and zonal statistics report on fire damage severity.

3.4 Drought Damage Assessment

In BEACON, NDVI-A product is calculated to characterize the health of vegetation throughout the growing season of an insured crop, and is used as an indicator of declining vegetation health due to drought. BEACON uses this approach to estimate crop damage and loss by the temporal integration of the Absolute NDVI Anomaly (Fig. 4).

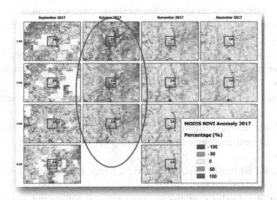

Fig. 4. Niger Case Study, 2017 growing season, multi-crop drought damage assessment estimated with the methodology implemented in BEACON. Crop loss is estimated by the temporal integration of Absolute NDVI-A.

For the validation of the crop loss assessment due to drought, damage data on wheat and barley crops were provided by AgI companies. Drought damage cases were classified in early and late claims, based on the date submitted by the farmers. Depending on the case, an indicator-impact exponential function was then derived by correlating the drought severity with the in-situ assessment of the damage. The drought severity was defined as the sum of the absolute values below zero of the NDVIA during a certain period of time, in the growing season.

4 Summary and Conclusions

BEACON solution employs a multi-satellite approach and a series of change detection techniques in order to provide safe and reliable estimates on crop damage, for any type of Agricultural Insurance. BEACON takes into account damage by hail, floods, wildfires and droughts which are the four most devastating hazards of agricultural production worldwide. This paper presents the methodologies and different types of EO data that synthesize the DAT service of BEACON's toolbox. DAT, supports AgI companies in accurately assessing and calculating damage to proceed with indemnity payouts of claims. The methodologies implemented in the operational workflow of BEACON will be validated by a diverse plethora of ground truth crop damage data.

In-situ data will originate from private AgI companies, most of which are early adopters of the BEACON's solution and will participate in the project's pilot phase.

Acknowledgments. This project has received funding from the European Union's Horizon 2020 Research and Innovation programme under grant agreement N° 821964.

References

1. Rosenzweig, C., Iglesius, A., Yang, X.B., Epstein, P.R., Chivian, E.: Climate change and extreme weather events- implications for food production, plant diseases, and pests. NASA Publications, 24 (2001)
2. Rüegger, M.: Trends in agricultural insurance in the European Union. Milliman (2007)
3. de Leeuw, J., et al.: The potential and uptake of remote sensing in insurance: a review. Remote Sens. **6**, 10888–10912 (2014)
4. FAO: The impact of disasters and crises on agriculture and food security, 2017. Rome (2018)
5. Nuttall, J.G., Perry, E.M., Delahunty, A.J., O'Leary, G.J., Barlow, K.M., Wallace, A.J.: Frost response in wheat and early detection using proximal sensors. J. Agro. Crop Sci. **205**, 220–234 (2019)
6. Lu, D., Mausel, P., Brondízio, E., Moran, E.: Change detection techniques. Int. J. Remote Sens. **25**(12), 2365–2407 (2004)
7. Szigarski, C., et al.: Analysis of the radar vegetation index and potential improvements. Remote Sens. **10**, 1776 (2018)
8. Saatchi, S.: SAR methods for mapping and monitoring forest biomass. In: SAR Handbook: Comprehensive Methodologies for Forest Monitoring and Biomass Estimation. NASA (2019). e-book
9. Chauhan, S., Srivastava, H.S.: Comparative evaluation of the sensitivity of multi-polarised SAR and optical data for various land cover classes. Int. J. Adv. Remote Sens. GIS Geogr. **4** (1), 1–14 (2016)
10. Zoka, M., Psomiadis, E., Dercas, N.: The complementary use of optical and SAR data in monitoring flood events and their effects. In: Proceedings, vol. 2, p. 644 (2018)
11. Xu, H.Q.: Modification of normalised difference water index (NDWI) to enhance open water features in remotely sensed imagery. Int. J. Remote Sens. **27**, 3025–3033 (2006)
12. Du, Y., Zhang, Y., Ling, F., Wang, Q., Li, W., Li, X.: Water bodies' mapping from sentinel-2 imagery with mNDWI at 10-m spatial resolution produced by sharpening the SWIR band. Remote Sens. **8**, 354 (2016)
13. Singh, K.V., Setia, R., Sahoo, S., Prasad, A., Pateriya, B.: Evaluation of NDWI and MNDWI for assessment of waterlogging by integrating digital elevation model and groundwater level. Geocarto Int. **30**, 650–661 (2015)
14. Kwang, C., Osei, E.M. Jr., Amoah, A.S.: Comparing of landsat 8 and sentinel 2A using water extraction indexes over Volta River. J. Geogr. Geol. **10**(1), 1–7 (2018)
15. Cian, F., Marconcini, M., Ceccato, P.: Normalized difference flood index for rapid flood mapping: taking advantage of EO big data. Remote Sens. Environ. **209**, 712–730 (2018)
16. Cian, F., Marconcini, M., Ceccato, P., Giupponi, C.: Flood depth estimation by means of high-resolution SAR images and lidar data. Nat. Hazards Earth Syst. Sci. **18**, 3063–3084 (2018)
17. Twele, A., Cao, W., Plank, S., Martinis, S.: Sentinel-1-based flood mapping: a fully automated processing chain. Int. J. Remote Sens. **37**, 2990–3004 (2016)

18. Roldán-Zamarrón, A., Merino-de-Miguel, S., González-Alonso, F., García-Gigorro S., Cuevas, J.M.: Minas de Riotinto (south Spain) forest fire: burned area assessment and fire severity mapping using Landsat 5-TM, Envisat-MERIS, and Terra-MODIS postfire images. J. Geophys. Res. **111**, 1–9 (2006)
19. Viana-Soto, A., Aguado, I., Martínez, S.: Assessment of post-fire vegetation recovery using fire severity and geographical data in the Mediterranean Region (Spain). Environments **4**, 90 (2017)
20. Key, C.H., Benson, N.C.: Measuring and remote sensing of burn severity: the CBI and NBR. Poster abstract. In Neuenschwander, L.F., Ryan, K.C. (eds.) Joint Fire Science Conference and Workshop, 284 p. University of Idaho and International Association of Wildland Fire (1999)
21. Parks, S.A., Dillon, G.K., Miller, C.: A new metric for quantifying burn severity: the relativized burn ratio. Remote Sens. **6**, 1827–1844 (2014)
22. Suresh Babu, K.V., Arijit Roy, Aggarwal, R.: Mapping of forest fire burned severity using the Sentinel datasets. ISPRS – Int. Arch. Photogramm. Remote Sens. Spat. Inf. Sci. **XLII-5**, 763–769 (2018)
23. Klisch, A., Atzberger, C.: Operational drought monitoring in Kenya using MODIS NDVI time series. Remote Sens. **8**, 267 (2016)
24. Vaani, N., Porchelvan, P.: Assessment of long term agricultural drought in Tamilnadu, India using NDVI anomaly. Dis. Adv. **10**(10), 1–10 (2017)
25. Anyamba, A., Tucker, C.J.: Historical perspective of AVHRR NDVI and vegetation drought monitoring. Remote Sensing of Drought: Innovative Monitoring Approaches, 23 (2012)
26. Zhao, J.L., Zhang, D.Y., Luo, J.H., Huang, S.L., Dong, Y.Y., Huang, W.J.: Detection and mapping of hail damage to corn using domestic remotely sensed data in China. Aust. J. Crop Sci. **6**(1), 101–108 (2012)
27. Herath, S.: Flood damage estimation of an urban catchment using remote sensing and GIS. International Training Program on total disaster management 10–13 June 2003
28. Dutta, D., Herath, S., Musiake, K.: A mathematical model for flood loss estimation. J. Hydrol. **277**, 24–49 (2003)

Producing Mid-Season Nitrogen Application Maps for Arable Crops, by Combining Sentinel-2 Satellite Images and Agrometeorological Data in a Decision Support System for Farmers. The Case of NITREOS

Emmanuel Lekakis[(✉)], Dimitra Perperidou, Stylianos Kotsopoulos, and Polimachi Simeonidou

Agroapps P.C., 54-56 Them. Sofouli, Thessaloniki 54655, Greece
mlekakis@agroapps.gr

Abstract. NITREOS (Nitrogen Fertilization, Irrigation and Crop Growth Monitoring using Earth Observation Systems) is a farm management information system (FMIS) for organic and conventional agriculture which aims in enabling farmers to tackle crop abiotic stresses and control important growing parameters to ensure crop health and optimal yields. NITREOS employs a user friendly, web-based platform that integrates satellite remote sensing data, numerical weather predictions and agronomic models, and offers a suite of farm management advisory services to address the needs of smallholder farmers, agricultural cooperatives and agricultural consultants. This paper provides an analysis of different methodologies employed in the nitrogen fertilization service of NITREOS. The methods are based on the determination of the Nitrogen Fertilization Optimization Algorithm for cotton, maize and wheat crops. Available agro-meteorological data on two distinct agricultural regions were used for the calibration and validation of the recommended Nitrogen rates.

Keywords: Nitrogen fertilization · NITREOS · Earth observation data · FMIS

1 Introduction

Geographic information systems technology has been widely used in fertilization research, through the use of decision support systems. Nitrogen (N) management based on remote sensing technologies is one of the most representative examples as N is found to be one of the most critical nutrients for crop growth. Crop N requirement determination and improvement of Nitrogen Use Efficiency (NUE) has been proved efficient through the use of remote sensing tools [1, 2]. Improving NUE reduces fertilizer costs, improves yield and quality and mitigates environmental pollution caused by loss of N due to deep percolation [3]. Operational applications employ Earth Observation (EO) techniques, Vegetation Indices (VIs) and algorithms, enabling farmers to monitor their fields and acquire advices on the application of N fertilizers [4–6].

© IFIP International Federation for Information Processing 2020
Published by Springer Nature Switzerland AG 2020
I. N. Athanasiadis et al. (Eds.): ISESS 2020, IFIP AICT 554, pp. 102–114, 2020.
https://doi.org/10.1007/978-3-030-39815-6_10

In this paper, a satellite-based fertilization advisory system is presented. NITREOS (https://business.esa.int/projects/nitreos) offers a number of services to farmers and agricultural consultants, namely irrigation scheduling, variable rate fertilization (VRF), crop growth monitoring, yield estimation, as well as short term weather prediction. The VRF service provides in-season optimum N rates for maize, cotton and wheat crops. Zones of equal fertilizer recommendation dose per registered parcel are delivered daily from agro-meteorological data, and updated regularly with the use of high-spatial resolution multispectral satellite images. The VRF service offers:

- a personalized in-season fertilization advice, based on calculation of the Nitrogen Fertilization Optimization Algorithm (NFOA), by taking into account the in-field heterogeneity of the sensed NDVI (Normalized Difference Vegetation Index) and Growing Degree Days (GDD), for variable rate applications;
- the Optimum Time Window (OTW), pointing out the appropriate period for in-season N fertilization, allowing the user to decide upon the level of input, the amount and type of fertilizer (conventional and organic) and the time of in-season application;
- timely delivery of the daily calculated N rates, within the OTW, which consists of maps and suggested fertilizer dose per pixel. The information is published on a dedicated webGIS-platform in order to better plan for fertilizer applications and consequently improve NUE.

This paper focuses on the detailed description of methodological approaches and processing chain employed in NITREOS VRF service. It provides an analysis of the algorithms implemented in the operational workflow of NITREOS. The first calibration – validation results under Greek and Serbian farming conditions, are also presented.

2 Materials and Methods

In the VRF service of NITREOS, the crop heterogeneity captured by the high resolution Sentinel-2 images is considered a valuable add-on information to identify the variability of soil texture and fertility, plant nutrition, or different performance of cropping systems. The concept of the service is based on two main components:

1. the processing of multi-temporal, high-spatial resolution images (Sentinel-2), provided by the EU's Copernicus Program, to timely monitor the crop growth;
2. the estimation of plant N demands, by taking into account weather data (GDD) and the canopy development (through the sensed NDVI) during the appropriate period for mid-season fertilization.

The NFOA was initially proposed for the in-season N fertilization recommendation of winter wheat [8–11], and is based on the Predicted Yield potential with zero-N fertilization (YP_0) and the field-specific NDVI-based Response Index (RI_{NDVI}). The basic steps in the determination of the NFOA include:

1. calculation of YP_0 using the relationship between actual grain yield and INSEY,
2. calculation of the Response Index (RI) at harvest ($RI_{Harvest}$) using RI_{NDVI}, computed as the mean NDVI readings of adequate N rate treatment divided by the mean NDVI readings of the pre-plant N rate. To accomplish this step, NDVI measurements should be collected from particular growth stages,
3. the determination of the Yield Potential (YP) using pre-plant N rates YP_N and equation:

$$YP_N = YP_0 \cdot RI_{NDVI} \tag{1}$$

4. the calculation of the percent N in the grain (PN_G) with a linear relationship between PN_G and YP_N,
5. the calculation of grain N uptake (GN_{UP}) by multiplying YP_N with PN_G,
6. the calculation of canopy N uptake (FN_{UP}) based on an exponential relationship equation between FN_{UP} and NDVI,
7. determination of the in-season N requirement (FNR) using the generalized equation:

$$FNR = (GN_{UP} - FN_{UP})/NUE \tag{2}$$

In the methodology above, INSEY represents the In-Season Estimate of Yield, which is the NDVI divided by GDD and reflects the biomass produced per day for a particular crop [7, 8, 11]. NDVI is calculated with the use of Sentinel-2, Level-2A, Bottom-Of Atmosphere, surface reflectance products. The index is calculated for every parcel registered in NITREOS, through a fully automated procedure, with a spatial resolution of 10 m. NFOA is calculated per pixel and then averaged in four zones of equal treatment. The application offers the choice of downloading geospatial data for variable rate applications. The GDDs or heat summation are computed using the optimum-day method [12], with the equation:

$$GDD = [(T_{max} + T_{min})/2] - T_{base} \tag{3}$$

where T_{max} and T_{min} are the max. and min. daily temperatures (°C). T_{base} refers to a temperature, below which crop growth ceases, equal to 10, 15.5 and 4.4 °C for cotton, maize and wheat, respectively. The RI was introduced to quantitatively characterize the crops' in-season likelihood to respond to additional N [13]. The actual harvested crop grain response to applied N is defined as:

$$RI_{Harvest} = yield\ of\ the\ N\ treatment\ /\ yield\ of\ the\ usual\ N\ practise\ treatment \tag{4}$$

The $RI_{Harvest}$ was well correlated with RI_{NDVI} and was defined as the grain yield from N-adequate plots divided by the yield from the plots receiving the pre-plant N rate [14].

The proposed methodology has been widely applied and confirmed in different agro-climatic conditions and crop types [15–24].

NFOA for Cotton

Previous studies have demonstrated and evaluated the use of NFOA on optimum in-season fertilization on cotton crop [25, 26]. The NFOA for cotton is as follows:

$$NFOA\,(kgha^{-1}) = [(YP_0 \times RI) - YP_0] \cdot percentage\,N\,/\,NUE \qquad (5)$$

where percentage N is the N removed by the crop during the growing season.

For the application of NFOA algorithm, the following steps are followed. Firstly, INSEY, is calculated by dividing the NDVI with the cumulative GDD from planting to sensing (for GDD > 0) [26, 27]. The INSEY value is related to biomass produced per day. Correlation between biomass produced per day and final grain yield has been shown to be highly correlated [7]. Furthermore, NDVI is a good biomass indicator and also implies total N content [28]. In a study for cotton [25], the CumGDD - INSEY was correlated with yield data. Specifically, the CumGDD - INSEY was produced from NDVI readings of cotton, collected between 38 and 90 days after sowing, to produce empirical equations that predict the cotton yield potential. Lint yield data referred to cotton crops receiving a sum of 0, 50, 100, 150 and 200 kgha^{-1} N rates, in pre-planting and in-season N applications. Crops were sown from the 15th to the 18th of May. The nonlinear regression model produced, is as follows [25]:

$$YP_0\,(kgha^{-1}) = 309.72e^{1295.9 \times INSEY} \qquad (6)$$

Apart from the yield potential, the degree to which a crop will respond to additional N is an equally important component in determining in-season N recommendations [11]. The RI is calculated by dividing the yield of a N-rich strip by the yield of the zero-N plot or farmer's practice, where less preplant N is applied. The RI value calculated using the yield is referred to as $RI_{Harvest}$. RI can also be measured mid-season using NDVI values (RI_{NDVI}) collected from the same areas used to determine $RI_{Harvest}$. It has been found that RI_{NDVI} collected midseason is a good predictor of $RI_{Harvest}$ [14]. A linear regression model to describe the relationship between RI_{NDVI} and $RI_{Harvest}$, was proposed as follows:

$$RI_{Harvest} = 0.7324 \cdot RI_{NDVI} + 0.238 \qquad (7)$$

Another study [26] calculated the RI_{NDVI}, by dividing the highest NDVI reading of N-rich strips in the field, by the average NDVI. The average NDVI was received by an area in the field, where the typical farmer's N application practice was followed.

NFOA Implementation for Cotton in NITREOS. NFOA is used in NITREOS to deliver in-season fertilization of cotton. For the calculation of RI_{NDVI} in NITREOS, values were collected from 29 cotton fields registered in the Crop Growth Monitoring

Service of AgroApps P.C. (Greece). In the selected crops, cotton was sown from the 10th to the 25th of April 2018 and the sensing day of NDVI was the 18th of June. The highest NDVI value was considered representative of a N-rich treatment of cotton, while the lower NDVI value was calculated as the average of the remaining measurements. Figure 1 presents the NDVI sensed at the 18th of June per different sowing date.

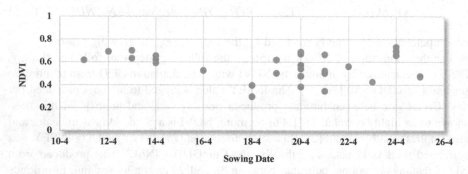

Fig. 1. NDVI at the 18th of June per sowing date of cotton.

Based on the sensed values, the highest NDVI is 0.730 and the average of the readings (excluding 0.730) is 0.553. Dividing the highest NDVI with the average NDVI, results in RI_{NDVI} equal to 1.320, while based on Eq. 7, $RI_{Harvest}$ is 1.205. The RI_{NDVI} is limited at values lower than 2.0 as in-season applications of N would unlikely lead to yield potential being more than two times greater than baseline YP_0 [8].

It is considered that 90 g N per kg of lint and seed, is removed by the cotton crop during harvest, thus the percentage N is set at 0.09 [25–27]. The NUE levels for cotton reported in the literature range from 25 to 60% [25], while 50% is a representative value, since side-dress application of N is expected to be at the higher end of the recorded NUE range [25–27]. Based on the previous calculations and assumptions, the equation providing the optimized, in-season nitrogen fertilization rate ($Kgha^{-1}$), used in NITREOS, is as follows:

$$FNR = \left[\left(1.205 \times 309.72e^{1295.9 \times INSEY} - 309.72e^{1259.9 \times INSEY}\right) \times 0.09\right] / 0.50 \quad (8)$$

It is evident from Eq. (8) that the N recommendation rates change daily with the new calculated CumGGD and newly sensed NDVI values. A daily change is expected due to the nature of the cotton plant having an optimum time for N uptake. In the literature, the maximum N uptake in cotton has been observed between 49 to 71 days from sowing [25, 26, 29, 30]. In NITREOS, the OTW for in-season N application lasts from 38 to 90 days after planting. During that time, recommendations are provided. Figure 2 provides the NITREOS user interface and the fertilizer recommendation dose per zone of equal treatment for a registered cotton field in Greece.

Fig. 2. NITREOS in-season fertilizer recommendation zones of a cotton parcel.

NFOA for Maize

A modification of the NFOA has been proposed for maize [20], as follows:

$$NFOA\,(kgha^{-1}) = [YP_0 \cdot (RI_{NDVI} - 1) \cdot percentage\ N]\,/\,NUE \qquad (9)$$

In this approach, INSEY was calculated by dividing NDVI readings by the number of days from planting to sensing, and was correlated with grain yield data in order to produce empirical equations that predict the maize grain yield potential. Maize yield data referred to plots treated with fixed rates of 0, 67 and 134 kgha^{-1} N, applied in split, pre-plant or side-dress. Crops were sown from the 28th of March to the 12th of April. The nonlinear regression model produced in this case was:

$$YP_0\,\left(kgha^{-1}\right) = 1333e^{122.5 \times INSEY} \qquad (10)$$

The RI was calculated by an adjusted equation of the form:

$$RI_{NDVI} = (1.64 \cdot NDVI_{N-Rich}\,/\,NDVI_{Farmer}) - 0.528 \qquad (11)$$

The equation is derived by dividing the NDVI of a high-N plot by the NDVI of a zero-N plot or farmer's practice. In this study [20] the NDVI readings were collected within the time period of 38 to 60 days after sowing. The highest NDVI value of 0.830 was reported for that period, as well as values of RI equal to 1.43 ± 0.42.

NFOA Implementation for Maize in NITREOS. The NFOA proposed for maize [20] is used in NITREOS to deliver in-season fertilization. For the calculation of RI$_{NDVI}$ in NITREOS, values were collected from 23 maize fields registered in the Crop Growth Monitoring Service of AgroApps P.C. (Serbia). In the selected crops, maize was sown from the 31st of March to the 4th of May 2018. The highest NDVI among the values was considered representative of a N-rich treatment of maize, while the lower value was calculated as the average of the remaining measurements. Figure 3 presents the sowing date and the NDVI sensed at the 2nd of June 2018, for the 23 maize fields.

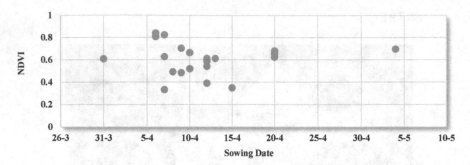

Fig. 3. NDVI at the 2nd of June per sowing date of maize.

Based on NDVI sensed on the 2nd of June, the highest is 0.839 and the average of the readings (excluding 0.839) is 0.594. Therefore, based on the adjusted Eq. (11), RI_{NDVI} is equal to 1.788. The NUE levels reported in the literature for maize range from 33 to 70% [1, 11, 31]. In NITREOS, NUE for maize is set at 0.56 and the N content in grain is 0.0125 kg N per kg grain [20]. Therefore, the general equation providing the optimized, in-season nitrogen fertilization rate in NITREOS, is as follows:

$$NFOA(kgha^{-1}) = \left[0.788\left(1333e^{122.5 \times INSEY} \times 0.0125\right)\right] / 0.56 \qquad (12)$$

Maize N uptake is significant between the 50th and 85th day after sowing. Therefore, the half or one third of the total N fertilizer should be provided in preplant applications, while the rest should be provided in-season. In NITREOS, the OTW for in-season N application lasts from 38 to 90 days after sowing.

NFOA for Wheat
NFOA has been used to estimate the in-season N fertilizer rates for wheat [11]. In this case, INSEY was calculated by dividing NDVI readings with the number of days from sowing to sensing. Including only the days, where GDD > 0, is necessary in order to remove days where growth is not possible in winter wheat. INSEY was correlated with wheat yield data in order to produce empirical equations that predict the potential yield. The model proposed to predict wheat grain yield [10], is:

$$YP_0\left(kgha^{-1}\right) = 992.26e^{142.67 \times INSEY} \qquad (13)$$

In this model, the INSEY was produced from NDVI readings of wheat, collected between 99 to 146 days after sowing. Wheat was sown from the 10th of October to the 20th of November [10]. An improved fit of a linear-linear regression model to describe the relationship between RI_{NDVI} and $RI_{Harvest}$, based on the evolution of RI_{NDVI} values was proposed [20] for wheat. In this case the RI_{NDVI} was calculated by dividing the highest NDVI reading of N-rich strips in the field, by the average NDVI of the farmers practice area. The model is as follows:

$$RI_{Harvest} = \begin{vmatrix} 1.69 \times RI_{NDVI} -0.70 & RI_{NDVI} < 1.72 \\ 0.45 \times RI_{NDVI} +2.20 & RI_{NDVI} > 1.72 \end{vmatrix} \tag{14}$$

NFOA Implementation for Wheat in NITREOS. In NITREOS, INSEY for wheat is calculated by dividing NDVI readings by the number of days from planting to sensing, where GDD > 0. For the calculation of RI_{NDVI}, values were collected from 15 wheat fields registered in the Crop Growth Monitoring Service of AgroApps P.C. (Serbia). Wheat was sown from the 3rd to the 31st of October 2017 and the sensing day of NDVI was the 20th of April 2018. The highest NDVI value was considered representative of a N-rich treatment of wheat, while the lower value was calculated as the average of the remaining measurements. Figure 4 presents the NDVI sensed at the 20th of April per sowing date. Based on the sensed NDVI values, the highest was 0.883 and the average of the readings (excluding 0.883) was 0.614. Dividing the highest NDVI with the average NDVI, results in RI_{NDVI} equal to 1.438, while based on Eq. 14, $RI_{Harvest}$ is 1.730.

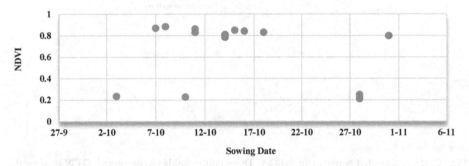

Fig. 4. NDVI at the 20th of April per sowing date of wheat.

In NITREOS, the topdress N requirement for wheat, is calculated as follows [21]:

$$FNR\ (kgha^{-1}) = 0.0239 \frac{1.73 \cdot 992.26e^{142.67 \times INSEY} - 992.26e^{142.67 \times INSEY}}{0.55} \tag{15}$$

where 0.0239 is the percentage of N contained in wheat grain. Published studies report the recovery of applied N at sowing ranging from 30% to 55% while that applied at flowering, ranging from 55% to 80%, thus the NUE is set at 0.55 [9]. Wheat early season N uptake is significant between 123 to 163 days after sowing (leaf sheaths lengthen through first node of stem visible). In NITREOS, the OTW for in-season wheat N application lasts from 100 to 163 days after sowing.

3 Results and Discussion

NFOA Application for Cotton

The calculation of N rates using NFOA was applied in crops registered in the Crop Growth Monitoring Service of AgroApps P.C. For cotton, a Greek region was selected. Data from three cotton crops were used in the calculation of NFOA. The selection criteria were based on the different planting dates for each crop. Cotton was sown on the 8th of April, the 24th of April and the 17th of May, 2018. For the calculation of GDD, max., min. and average temperatures for the region were derived from the Meteorological Service of Agroapps P.C. (1st of April to the 31st of August). The NFOA was calculated from sowing to harvest. The results were produced by averaging the NFOA pixel values of the registered fields in Fig. 5.

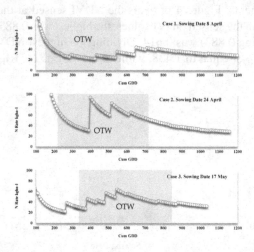

Fig. 5. Recommended N rates with NFOA. Three cotton fields are presented. OTW denotes the Optimum Time Window for the beginning of NFOA calculations (38–90 days after sowing).

It is evident from Fig. 5 that the N recommendation rates change daily due to INSEY and peak values are mainly influenced by the newly sensed NDVI. Based on the calculations of the NFOA, the highest rates were 53.1, 94.2 and 64.4 kg N ha^{-1} with cotton sowing dates 8-April, 24-April and 17-May, respectively. Only the rates in the OTW (38–90 days after sowing) were taken into account. The difference between the predicted doses is attributed mainly to the combination of the sensed NDVI values and the CumGDD. Cotton N requirements have been reported to be highly variable, with a range from 67 to 255 kg N ha^{-1} [29]. In a previous study the use of NFOA on cotton predicted a range of in-season N rate between 26.88 and 51.52 kg N ha^{-1} [25].

NFOA Application for Maize

For maize, a Serbian region was selected. Data from three registered fields were used in the calculation of NFOA. Maize was sown on the 12th, the 20th of April and the 4th of May, 2018. For maize fields, NFOA was calculated from sowing to harvest. The results of the calculations are provided in Fig. 6.

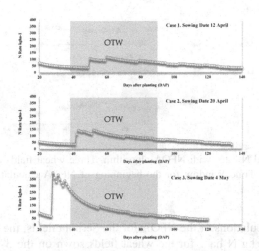

Fig. 6. Recommended N rates with NFOA. Three maize fields are presented. OTW denotes the Optimum Time Window for the beginning of NFOA calculations (38–90 days after sowing).

Based on the calculations of the NFOA for the Serbian fields, the highest rates were 116.5, 144.9 and 273.6 kg N ha^{-1} for the maize crops sown on the 12-April, 20-April and 4-May, respectively. Only the rates in the optimum time window (38-90 days after sowing) were taken into account. For the same period, the average rates were 80.5, 99.8 and 126.6 kg N ha^{-1} for the maize crops sown on the 12-April, 20-April and 4-May, respectively. Optimum N fertilizer rates for maize are highly variable. In a study, optimum N rates for maize, in 198 site-years of published data in the United States (1958–2010), were found to be significantly variable, with an average low of 62 ± 44 kg N ha^{-1} and an average high of 173 ± 55 kg N ha^{-1} [32]. NFOA was appplied in plots of maize and the recommended N rates ranged from 20 to 201 kg N ha^{-1} [20], according to the resolution of the sensed NDVI, the year and the site.

NFOA Application for Wheat

For wheat, a Serbian region was selected. Data from three wheat crops were used in the calculation of NFOA. Wheat was sown on the 3rd, the 28th and the 31st of October 2017. For the calculation of GDD, max., min. and average temperatures for the region were derived from the Meteorological Service of Agroapps P.C. (1st of October to 31st of July). NFOA was calculated from sowing to harvest. The results of the calculations are provided in Fig. 7.

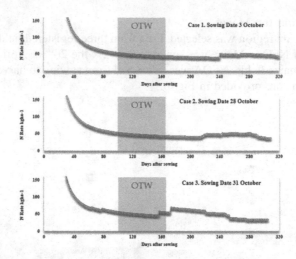

Fig. 7. Recommended N rates with NFOA algorithm. Three wheat fields are presented. OTW denotes the Optimum Time Window for the beginning of NFOA calculations (100–163 days after sowing).

Based on the calculations of the NFOA for the Serbian fields, the highest rates were 52.7, 52.1 and 56.2 kg N ha^{-1} for the wheat fields sown on the 3rd, 28th and 31st of October, respectively. Only the rates in the optimum time window (100–163 days after sowing) were taken into account. For the same period, the average rates were 47, 46.6 and 50.2 kg N ha^{-1}, respectively. NFOA has been applied to winter wheat in previous studies where reported estimated N rates ranged between 5.4 to 72.3 kg N ha^{-1} [33].

4 Summary and Conclusions

NITREOS is a farm management information system for organic and conventional agriculture which aims in enabling farmers to tackle crop abiotic stresses and control important growing parameters to ensure crop health and optimal yields. Among the services of NITREOS, a nitrogen fertilization advisory module is included for the estimation of mid-season N fertilizer rates for cotton, maize and wheat. This paper presents the algorithms for the calculation of plant N demands, by taking into account weather parameters and canopy development, through the use of Sentinel-2 optical imagery. The methodologies are based on the Nitrogen Fertilization Optimization Algorithm (NFOA). The NFOA was calibrated with the use of agro-meteorological data in two distinct agricultural regions (Greece and Serbia) in order to derive crop and site specific parameters, and was validated against actual crops' data, with different sowing dates. The results of the NFOA in terms of N doses, are in agreement with the values reported in the literature, regarding previous studies on NFOA application, under field conditions. Furthermore, the Optimum Time Window (OTW) provided by

NITREOS to point out the appropriate period for mid-season fertilization, falls well within the periods reported in the literature for optimum N uptake, thus leading to maximum crop utilization of in-season applied N.

Acknowledgments. NITREOS - Nitrogen Fertilization, Irrigation and Crop Growth Monitoring using Earth Observation Systems (2018). Project funded by the European Space Agency – ESA. Contract N°: 4000124362/18/NL/NR.

References

1. Fountas, S., Aggelopoulou, K., Gemtos, T.A.: Precision agriculture: crop management for improved productivity and reduced environmental impact or improved sustainability. In: Iakovou, E., Bochtis, D., Vlachos. D., Aidonis, D. (eds.) Supply Chain Management for Sustainable Food Networks, Wiley-Blackwell, Oxford (2016)
2. Bu, H.: Yield and quality prediction using satellite passive imagery and ground-based active optical sensors in sugar beet, spring wheat, corn, and sunflower. Master thesis, Soil Science Department, North Dakota State University (2014)
3. Havlin, J.L., Beaton, J.D., Tisdale, S.L., Nelson, W.L.: Soil Fertility and Fertilizers: An Introduction to Nutrient Management. Pearson Education Inc., Upper Saddle River (2005)
4. Bach, H., Migdall, S., Mauser, W., Angermair, W., Sephton, A.J., Martin-de-Mercado, G.: An integrative approach of using satellite-based information for precision farming: TalkingFields. In: Proceedings 61st International Astronautical Congress, Prague (2010)
5. He, J., Wang, J., He, D., Dong, J., Wang, Y.: The design and implementation of an integrated optimal fertilization decision support system. Math. Comput. Model. **54**, 3–4 (2011)
6. Söderström, M, Stadig, H, Martinsson, J, Piikki, K, Stenberg, M.: CropSAT – a public satellite-based decision support system for variable-rate nitrogen fertilization in Scandinavia. In: Proceedings of the 13th International Conference on Precision Agriculture. Monticello, IL, USA, p. 8. International Society of Precision Agriculture (2016)
7. Raun, W.R., et al.: In-season prediction of potential grain yield in winter wheat using canopy reflectance. Agron. J. **93**, 131–138 (2001)
8. Raun, W.R., et al.: Improving nitrogen use efficiency in cereal grain production with optical sensing and variable rate application. Agron. J. **94**, 815–820 (2002)
9. Lukina, E.V., Freeman, K.W., Wynn, K.J., Thomason, W.E., Mullen, R.W., Klatt, A.R., et al.: Nitrogen fertilization optimization algorithm based on in-season estimates of yield and plant nitrogen uptake. J. Plant Nutr. **24**, 885–898 (2001)
10. http://nue.okstate.edu/Index_NFOA.htm
11. Raun, W.R., et al.: Optical sensor-based algorithm for crop nitrogen fertilization. Commun. Soil Sci. Plant Anal. **36**, 2759–2781 (2005)
12. Barger, G.L.: Total growing degree days. Wkly Weather Crop Bull. **56**, 10 (1969)
13. Johnson, G.V., Raun, W.R.: Nitrogen response index as a guide to fertilizer management. J. Plant Nutr. **26**, 249–262 (2003)
14. Mullen, R.W., Freeman, K.W., Raun, W.R., Johnson, G.V., Stone, M.L., Solie, J.B.: Identifying an in-season response index and the potential to increase wheat yield with nitrogen. Agron. J. **95**, 347–351 (2003)
15. Teal, R.K., et al.: In-season prediction of corn grain yield potential using normalized difference vegetation index. Agron. J. **98**, 1488–1494 (2006)

16. Morris, K.B., et al.: Mid-season recovery from nitrogen stress in winter wheat. J. Plant Nutr. **29**, 727–745 (2006)
17. Inman, D., Khosla, R., Reich, R.M., Westfall, D.G.: Active remote sensing and grain yield in irrigated maize. Precis. Agric. **8**, 241–252 (2007)
18. Ortiz-Monasterio, J.I., Raun, W.R.: Reduced nitrogen and improved farm income for irrigated spring wheat in the Yaqui Valley, Mexico, using sensor based nitrogen management. J. Agric. Sci. **145**, 1–8 (2007)
19. Li, F., Miao, Y., Zhang, F., Cui, Z., Li, R., Chen, X., et al.: In-season optical sensing improves nitrogen-use efficiency for winter wheat. Soil Sci. Soc. Am. J. **73**, 1566–1574 (2009)
20. Tubaña, B.S., et al.: Adjusting midseason nitrogen rate using a sensor-based optimization algorithm to increase use efficiency in corn. J. Plant Nutr. **31**, 1393–1419 (2008)
21. Roberts, D., Brorsen, B., Taylor, R., Solie, J., Raun, W.: Replicability of nitrogen recommendations from ramped calibration strips in winter wheat. Precis. Agric. **12**, 653–665 (2011)
22. Singh, B., Sharma, R., Jaspreet, K., Jat, M.L., Martin, K.L., Yadvinder, S., et al.: Assessment of the nitrogen management strategy using an optical sensor for irrigated wheat. Agron. Sustain. Dev. **31**, 589–603 (2011)
23. Tubaña, B., Viator, S., Teboh, J., Lofton, J., Kanke, Y.: Feasibility of using remote sensing technology in N management in sugarcane production. Int. Sugar J. **113**, 747 (2011)
24. Lofton, J., Tubaña, B.S., Kanke, Y., Teboh, J., Viator, H., Dalen, M.: Estimating sugarcane yield potential using an in-season determination of normalized difference vegetative index. Sensors **12**, 7529–7547 (2012)
25. Arnall, D.B.: Analysis of the coefficient of variation of remote sensor readings in winter wheat, and development of a sensor based mid-season n recommendation for cotton. Ph.D. thesis, Oklahoma State University. Department of Plant and Soil Sciences (2008)
26. Porter, W.: Sensor based nitrogen management for cotton production in coastal plain soils. All Theses. 914. https://tigerprints.clemson.edu/all_theses/914 (2010)
27. Arnall, D.B., Joy, M., Abit, M., Taylor, R.K., Raun, W.R.: Development of an NDVI-based nitrogen rate calculator for cotton. Crop Sci. **56**, 3263–3271 (2016)
28. Raper, T.B., Varco, J.J., Hubbard, K.J.: Canopy-based normalized difference vegetation index sensors for monitoring cotton nitrogen status. Agron. J. **105**, 1345–1354 (2013)
29. Boquet, D.J., Breitenbeck, G.A.: Nitrogen rate effect on partitioning of nitrogen and dry matter by cotton. Crop Sci. **40**, 1685–1693 (2000)
30. Khalilian, A., Henderson, W., Han, Y., Wiatrak, P.J.: Improving nitrogen use efficiency in cotton through optical sensing. In: Proceedings of the Beltwide Cotton Conferences, National Cotton Council of America, Memphis (2008)
31. Miller, E.C., Bushong, J.T., Raun, W.R., Abit, M.J.M., Arnall, D.B.: Predicting early season nitrogen rates of corn using indicator crops. Agron. J. **109**, 2863–2870 (2017)
32. Dhital, S., Raun, W.R.: Variability in optimum nitrogen rates for maize. Agron. J. **108**, 2165–2173 (2016)
33. Butchee, K.S., May, J., Arnall, B.: Sensor based nitrogen management reduced nitrogen and maintained yield. Crop Manag. **10** (2011)

Using Virtual Research Environments in Agro-Environmental Research

Rob M. Lokers[1], M. J. Rob Knapen[1(✉)], Leonardo Candela[2],
Steven Hoek[1], and Wouter Meijninger[1]

[1] Wageningen Environmental Research, Droevendaalsesteeg 3,
6700 AA Wageningen, The Netherlands
rob.knapen@wur.nl
[2] Istituto di Scienza e Tecnologie dell'Informazione,
National Research Council of Italy, Pisa, Italy

Abstract. Tackling some of the grand global challenges, agro-environmental research has turned more and more into an international venture, where distributed research teams work together to solve complex research questions. Moreover, the interdisciplinary character of these challenges requires that a large diversity of different data sources and information is combined in new, innovative ways. There is a pressing need to support researchers with environments that allow them to efficiently work together and co-develop research. As research is often data-intensive, and big data becomes a common part of a lot of research, such environments should also offer the resources, tools and workflows that allow to process data at scale if needed. Virtual research environments (VRE), which combine working in the Cloud, with collaborative functions and state of the art data science tools, can be a potential solution. In the H2020 AGINFRA+ project, the usability of the VREs has been explored for use cases around agro-climatic modelling. The implemented pilot application for crop growth modelling has successfully shown that VREs can support distributed research teams in co-development, helps them to adopt open science and that the VRE's cloud computing facilities allow large scale modelling applications.

Keywords: Virtual research environment · Agro-climatic modelling · Data science · Big data · Crop growth modelling

1 Introduction

Agro-environmental research is highly interdisciplinary, and therefore researchers in the field are generally accustomed to linking with and working together with peers over different scientific domains. However, todays research challenges as captured for instance in the Sustainable Development Goals [1] or in the EU's societal challenges [2] require new approaches, that take advantage of data science and open science practices when combining even more cross-sectoral and cross-discipline knowledge, information and data. Lokers et al. [3] state that recent trends like (1) broadening policy and decision contexts for research; (2) the attention to open data as a public good resource; (3) the tremendous growth of the amount of data available for science and

I. N. Athanasiadis et al. (Eds.): ISESS 2020, IFIP AICT 554, pp. 115–121, 2020.
https://doi.org/10.1007/978-3-030-39815-6_11

(4) the massive increase in computational resources, and better availability and accessibility of them, as well as of data storage in the Cloud, have greatly increased the opportunities for data science to use big data. In Europe, the EC has recognized these trends and has taken action by establishing the European Open Science Cloud (EOSC) [4], which aims to provide researchers better access to high performance distributed compute and storage resources and to better facilities to share their data and tools with the research community in the large.

At present, a lot of research is still carried out in relatively closed communities, with data and knowledge being used and reused in a limited way, among a fairly small network of trusted peers. In operational (data) science, addressing societal challenges and innovating on a global scale usually requires collaboration between multidisciplinary teams. To advance interdisciplinary science and adopt data science and its many opportunities, researchers from different domains and knowledge networks will have to connect, collaborate and co-develop more intensely and on a larger scale than ever before. This can be achieved through the establishment of collaborative, cloud based working environments that enable remote groups to work together efficiently as a team. Such environments use state-of-the-art ICTs to develop, share and reuse resources and to comply with the requirement to publish and process heterogeneous big data resources. Virtual research environments, offering cloud based facilities for collaboration, social interaction and a range of facilities for performing data science, e.g. data discovery and data sharing, data wrangling, distributed computing facilities and visualization, are aiming at providing such environments. In the H2020 AGINFRA+ project, agri-environmental researchers from different domains, infrastructure experts and software developers work together to co-develop a VRE that supports agro-environmental data science and implements typical agri-food and agri-environmental use cases.

2   Virtual Research Environments

In recent years, many infrastructures, science gateways and VREs have been developed, tested and used in scientific practice. Science gateways, virtual laboratories and virtual research environments are all terms used to refer to community-developed digital environments that are designed to meet a set of needs for a research community [5]. Specifically, they refer to integrated access to research community resources including software, data, collaboration tools, workflows, instrumentation and high-performance computing, usually via Web and mobile applications. Such infrastructures support researchers with a tremendous range of different functions. Ahmed et al. [6] examined a large amount of VREs and found them to be most commonly characterized by ICTs that support communities and that allow posting and transferring information, with tools like Databases, Instruments and Computational ICTs being much less common (but also important for more substantive types of VREs). They also found that community ICTs in these VREs were almost entirely dedicated to providing one-way transmission of information and that interactive tools such as chat systems and conferencing systems are almost never incorporated in VREs. Application of VREs can be found over various thematic areas. Zuiderwijk et al. [7, 8] describe multidisciplinary VRE requirements for the use of data coming from governments and publicly-funded research organizations.

They show how meeting these requirements results in a VRE that (1) overlays existing e-Research Infrastructures to provide researchers with integrated open data from different domains, (2) offers Open Government Data in combination with data from publicly-funded research, and (3) stimulates innovation and research collaboration.

In the context of the H2020 AGINFRA+ project it was decided to follow the *system of systems* approach [9] to develop a comprehensive platform enacting to set up and operate several Virtual Research Environments with the as-a-Service delivery model. This platform is implemented by assigning a pivotal role to the D4Science infrastructure and blending together "resources" from "domain agnostic" service providers (e.g. D4Science [10], EGI [11], OpenAIRE [12]) as well as from community-specific ones (e.g. AgroDataCube [13], AGROVOC [14], RAKIP model repository [15]) to build a unifying space where the aggregated resources can be exploited via VREs [16]. The resulting platform is depicted in Fig. 1, described in [17] and made available through a dedicated gateway[1].

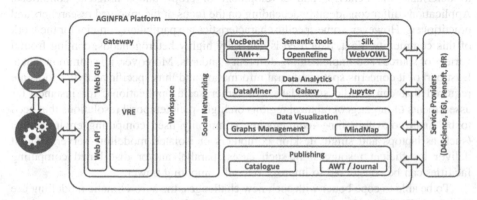

Fig. 1. The AGINFRA+ platform architecture

The D4Science is at the heart of the overall platform, offering core services including (*a*) the AGINFRA+ *gateway*, realising the single access point to the rest of the platform; (*b*) the *authentication and authorisation infrastructure*, enabling users to seamlessly access the aggregated services once managed to log in the gateway; (*c*) the *shared workspace*, for storing, organising and sharing any version of a research artefact, including dataset and model implementation; (*d*) the *social networking area* enabling collaborative and open discussions on any topic and disseminating information of interest for the community, e.g. the availability of a research outcome; (*e*) the *overall catalogue* recording the assets worth being published thus to make it possible for others to be informed and make use of these assets. Most importantly, it offers the facilities for setting up and operating Virtual Research Environments.

These basic facilities for virtual research are complemented by services for the semantic-oriented management of data, data analytics, data visualization, and publishing [17].

---

[1] AGINFRA Gateway https://aginfra.d4science.org/.

3   Virtual Research for Agro-Climatic Modelling in AGINFRA+

3.1   AGINFRA+ and the Agro-Climatic User Community

AGINFRA+ aims at using VREs to bring open science forward in agri-food research. The AGINFRA+ initiative serves a range of scientific user communities in the agri-food domain and implements and evaluates virtual research supported pilots in a variety of use cases that are relevant for these communities. One of the target communities for AGINFRA+ is the agro-climatic modelling community. This group of researchers focusses on developing and calibrating agro-environmental models and algorithms and applying these in research in the agro-environmental and food security domains. They use a variety of agro-environmental data, for instance agronomic data (like crop parameters, crop calendars etc.), weather and climate data, soil data, remote sensing data to determine the behavior and development of crops under different conditions. Applications differ considerably depending on the focus of the involved researchers and practitioners. However, some specific characteristics are particularly crucial for the work of this community. First, data used is generally highly heterogeneous, coming from a variety of sources and implementing different standards. Moreover, it is common that at least part of it concerns spatiotemporal information and thus specific analytics tools are required that can handle such data. For larger scale applications, for instance for assessments of larger geographical regions on high spatiotemporal resolutions that need to be finalized within time requirements, commonly used computing environments (such as laptops and single desktop computers or isolated modelling servers) might deliver insufficient resources. In such cases, parallel and/or distributed computing facilities can be considered to improve overall computing power.

To be able to cope better with such new challenges, the agro-climatic modelling use case in AGINFRA+ focuses on harnessing large scale modelling exercises, requiring substantial computing resources. The network of distributed computing resources is used to run such models in a performant manner, using distributed and parallel computing techniques. Besides, it exploits the typical open science related characteristics of the D4Science environment. Collaborative modelling, where teams of researchers work together to first develop and test models in literate programming environments and then deploy and openly share the developed algorithms can be an important step towards open science. In that way, complying with FAIR principles exceeds the level of only data sharing and reuse and adds the FAIR publication of data science algorithms.

3.2   Use Case – Crop Growth Modelling

One of the AGINFRA+ use cases that was explored and for which typical research applications were implemented and deployed into a VRE, with the aim to demonstrate and evaluate the usability for users of the agro-climatic modelling community, is crop growth modelling. Simulations using crop growth models are one of the important components in yield forecasting, used frequently in food security research and related research areas. Currently, the application of crop growth models is often still limited by the available computing resources. The application piloted in AGINFRA+ , applying

European or global scale crop simulations on the detailed level of agricultural parcels is currently too demanding for many existing research infrastructures in the field. To meet the requirements for such large scale, high-resolution crop growth modelling exercises, the following facilities are indispensable: efficient retrieval of spatiotemporal data streams, spatiotemporal data wrangling and data processing, running models at scale using distributed computing resources and parallel technologies computing, and intuitive spatiotemporal visualization.

In the AGINFRA+ crop growth modelling use case, the preprocessing of spatiotemporal data is an integral part of the AgroDataCube infrastructure. This infrastructure provides Dutch agricultural open data as a service to research and business. The AgroDataCube ingests and merges different spatiotemporal data streams that are relevant for agricultural and environmental applications (among others weather data, agronomic data, parcel geometries, Sentinel-2 satellite data, and soil data). It provides a set of well-documented, ready to use REST services that allow retrieval of the merged data on the parcel level in usable packages and a standardized format (GeoJSON). To cope with the requirement to scale up simulations, the widely used WOFOST crop growth simulation model [18] was embedded into a distributed computing framework that facilitates the distribution of computing jobs over a compute cluster. The resulting modules have been integrated into the VRE as DataMiner algorithms [19], and were published, using the D4Science catalogue service, to make them discoverable and reusable as FAIR algorithms for the whole community. As the requirements for spatiotemporal visualization in this use case were high, a dedicated visualization dashboard, developed on the basis of various VRE components, was developed (see Fig. 2).

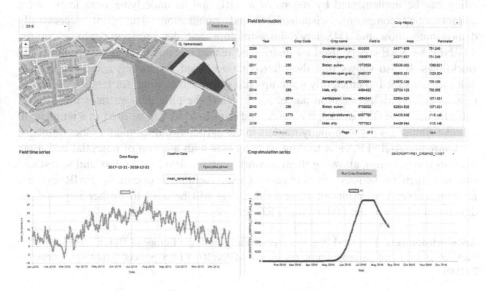

Fig. 2. AGINFRA+ crop growth modelling dashboard

For visual inspections, the dashboard allows geo-spatial and temporal visualization of the various data services provided through the AgroDataCube services that are input to the crop growth simulations. Moreover, it offers its users the opportunity to manually search for, and select a specific agricultural parcel and initiate a WOFOST crop simulation by executing the VRE DataMiner algorithm using input data based on the selected field.

Generated simulation results are stored on the VRE's shared workspace, and the simulated parameters can be visualized as graphs and can be compared and analyzed side by side with the used input data. After being tested and quality checked, the developed models and algorithms and the generated output data can be shared with the broader user community, by publishing them through the VRE's catalogue service. Thus, the VRE is complying with the requirements of FAIR data services and open science in general, adding to that the opportunity to also share algorithms and models in a FAIR manner.

4 Conclusions and Recommendations

AGINFRA+ has explored the usability of the VRE core services and building blocks offered through the D4Science platform for different scientific communities in the agrifood domain, by implementing a range of open science use cases that are typical for the agri-food research community. To demonstrate its value for the agro-climatic modelling community, AGINFRA+ has developed and deployed a pilot application around crop growth modelling, showing how large scale, high resolution crop growth modelling can be implemented by means of a VRE and its underlying core features for collaboration, computing, visualization and publication. The pilot successfully demonstrates how the D4Science infrastructure and the services deployed in the AGINFRA+ VRE can be used by distributed research teams to co-develop modelling workflows. It also shows that the offered cloud based computing and storage technologies are suited to efficiently scale up crop growth modelling, for larger geographic regions and on high-resolution parcel level. While the pilot demonstrates this specifically for the WOFOST model, the developed demonstrator can be used as a template to achieve similar results with many models in the agri-environmental and other domains.

Currently AGINFRA+ is trialing its use cases with a group of potential end users from its communities, allowing them to work with the developed pilots and to test and evaluate them on various criteria: ease of use, usefulness, openness, FAIRness and learning curve. The results of these evaluations will be used to further improve the developed tools and the underlying VRE services.

Acknowledgment. This work has received funding from the European Union's Horizon 2020 research and innovation programme under the AGINFRA PLUS project (grant agreement No 731001).

References

1. United Nations: Sustainable Development Goals. https://sustainabledevelopment.un.org/topics/sustainabledevelopmentgoals. Accessed 29 Sept 2019
2. European Commission: H2020 Societal Challenges. https://ec.europa.eu/programmes/horizon2020/en/h2020-section/societal-challenges. Accessed 29 Sept 2019
3. Lokers, R., Knapen, R., Janssen, S., van Randen, Y., Jansen, J.: Analysis of big data technologies for use in agro-environmental science. Environ. Model. Softw. **84**, 494–504 (2016). https://doi.org/10.1016/j.envsoft.2016.07.017
4. Jones, S., Abramatic, J.F. (eds.): European Open Science Cloud (EOSC) Strategic Implementation Plan (2019)
5. Barker, M., et al.: The global impact of science gateways, virtual research environments and virtual laboratories. Future Gener. Comput. Syst. **95**, 240–248 (2019). https://doi.org/10.1016/j.future.2018.12.026
6. Ahmed, I., Poole, M., Trudeau, A.: A typology of virtual research environments (2018). https://doi.org/10.24251/hicss.2018.087
7. Zuiderwijk, A.: Analysing open data in virtual research environments: new collaboration opportunities to improve policy making. Int. J. Electron. Gov. Res. (IJEGR) **13**(4), 76–92 (2017). https://doi.org/10.4018/ijegr.2017100105
8. Zuiderwijk, A., Jeffery, K., Bailo, D., Yin, Y.: Using open research data for public policy making: opportunities of virtual research environments (2016). https://doi.org/10.1109/CeDEM.2016.20
9. Maier, M.W.: Architecting principles for systems-of-systems. INCOSE Int. Symp. **6**(1), 565–573 (1996). https://doi.org/10.1002/j.2334-5837.1996.tb02054.x
10. D4Science Consortium. D4Science: An e-infrastructure supporting virtual re-search environments. www.d4science.org
11. EGI Foundation: EGI e-infrastructure. www.egi.eu
12. OpenAIRE Consortium OpenAIRE: The European scholarly communication data infrastructure. www.openaire.eu
13. Janssen, H., et al.: AgroDataCube: A Big Open Data collection for Agri-Food Applications. Wageningen Environmental Research (2018). https://doi.org/10.18174/455759
14. Caracciolo, C., et al.: The AGROVOC linked dataset. Semant. Web J. (2013). https://doi.org/10.3233/sw-130106
15. German Federal Institute for Risk Assessment. Foodrisk-labs. https://foodrisklabs.bfr.bund.de/foodrisk-labs/
16. Assante, M., et al.: Enacting open science by D4Science. Future Gener. Comput. Syst. (2019). https://doi.org/10.1016/j.future.2019.05.063
17. Assante M, et al.: Realising a science gateway for the agri-food: the AGINFRA PLUS Experience. In: 11th International Workshop on Science Gateways (IWSG 2019) (2019)
18. de Wit, A., et al.: 25 years of the WOFOST cropping systems model. Agric. Syst. **168**, 154–167 (2019). https://doi.org/10.1016/j.agsy.2018.06.018
19. Coro, G., Panichi, G., Scarponi, P, Pagano, P.: Cloud computing in a distributed e-infrastructure using the web processing service standard. Concurr. Comput.: Pract. Experience **29**(18), e4219 (2017). https://doi.org/10.1002/cpe.4219

Can We Use the Relationship Between Within-Field Elevation and NDVI as an Indicator of Drought-Stress?

Bernardo Maestrini[(⊠)], Matthijs Brouwer, Thomas Been,
and Lambertus A. P. Lotz

Wageningen University and Research, Wageningen, The Netherlands
Bernardo.maestrini@wur.nl

Abstract. Large farmers' datasets can help shed light on agroecological processes if used in the context of hypothesis testing. Here we used an anonymized set of data from the geoplatform *Akkerweb* to better understand the correlation between within-field elevation and normalized differential vegetation index (NDVI, a proxy for biomass). The dataset included 3249 Dutch potato fields, for each of which the cultivar, the field polygon, the year of cultivation and the soil type (clay or sandy) was known. We hypothesize that under dry conditions such correlation is negative, meaning that the lowest portions of the field have more biomass because of water redistribution. From the data, we observed that in dry periods, such as the summer of 2018, the correlation was negative in sandy soils. Furthermore, we observed that early cultivars show a weaker correlation between NDVI and elevation than late cultivars, possibly because early cultivar escape part of the long dry summer spells. We conclude that the correlation between NDVI and elevation may be a useful indicator of drought stress, and deviations from the norm may be useful to evaluate the resistance to drought of individual cultivars.

Keywords: Precision agriculture · Potato · Netherlands · Within-field variability · NDVI · Drought · Elevation · DEM · AHN2 · Actueel hoogtebestand nederland

1 Introduction

The analysis of farmers data is an important opportunity to advance our knowledge of the ecology of agrosystems. One of the most promising approaches to synthesize these data is the use of data-driven approaches where the data drive the construction of models for predictive purposes [1]. Though this approach is powerful for predictive purposes we believe that such large datasets can also be successfully used in the context of traditional hypothesis confirmation studies. Here we seek confirmation in the data for the hypothesis that within-field NDVI variability is driven—also—by the micro-topography (elevation). We do this using a large set of data obtained from "Akkerweb"—a geoplatform popular with Dutch farmers (2,*akkerweb.eu*).

Our main working hypothesis is that the lowest portions of a field are generally more wet and therefore crop growing there is less water-limited. This hypothesis is not novel, for example Kravchenko *et al.* [3, 4] found that yield variability at within-field

© IFIP International Federation for Information Processing 2020
Published by Springer Nature Switzerland AG 2020
I. N. Athanasiadis et al. (Eds.): ISESS 2020, IFIP AICT 554, pp. 122–131, 2020.
https://doi.org/10.1007/978-3-030-39815-6_12

level in corn and soybean fields in the Midwest of the US was associated to topography. Timlin *et al.*, [5] found in the context of a rainfed maize experiment that in dry years the concave parts of the field were more productive than convex parts whereas the effect of terrain curvature disappeared in wet years. Da Silva et al. [6, 7] found that in a Portuguese irrigated maize field, characterized by a high elevation range, topography was driving within-field yield variability and showed that maize yield was higher near the flow lines. These findings on yield-topography correlation were extended by Maestrini and Basso [8] who observed that not only the yield average but also yield temporal variability (stability) was influenced by topography, with the more concave portions of the field being characterized by a higher variability as a result of being either waterlogged in wet years or relatively more wet in dry years.

Here we attempt to prove that elevation is a driver of within-field crop-growth variability even in the Netherlands, a land that is notoriously flat. Further we extend these findings by examining how different soil types and cultivar earliness influence such correlation. We believe that the correlation between NDVI and elevation—once sufficiently corroborated with data—could be used as an indicator of drought stress and deviations from such correlation may help us understand which management strategies (e.g. cultivar choice) alleviate drought stress.

In this study we focus on potatoes,—a major crop in the Netherlands—well represented in our farmers' dataset. Potatoes have been generally regarded as a crop with a shallow root system [9, 10] that makes them vulnerable to drought stress, however there are empirical evidences that their roots can reach one meter [11] and beyond [12].

Therefore, here we hypothesize that also for the Netherlands we can establish a correlation between relative within-field elevation and crop-growth and that such correlation is influenced by both soil type and cultivar earliness. We expect that potato crops on sandy soils as well as late cultivars are more sensitive to dry spells. The sandy soils will be more sensitive because they have a low water holding capacity whereas late cultivars will suffer more when exposed to summer dry spells for longer periods. We apply our hypothesis to a dataset of Dutch farms where the location of the field, the cultivar, the soil type (clay or sandy) is known and the biomass throughout the season is proxied by the normalized difference vegetation index (NDVI) retrieved from satellite images, is known, along with elevation.

2 Materials and Methods

2.1 Data from Akkerweb

Data were collected from farmers' data input to the geo-platform Akkerweb [2] (akkerweb.eu). Through this platform farmers can enter the information about their fields (polygon, crop and cultivar, and sowing dates) and receive information to support their decision making on—among others—in-season fertilization, crop protection, pests like plant-parasitic nematodes and variable rate applications like haulm killing for potatoes.

We received the anonymized data, supplied by the farmers to the Akkerweb geo-platform, through a query that returned the dataset records for which the cultivar, the start and end date of the management plan, and the polygon were available. The query returned the following fields: a key identifier for each field, the field polygon (in well-known text format), the area, the cultivar, the purpose (e.g. for potato consumption, starch, table or seed potatoes), start and end date of the management plan and soil type. The total number of unique records returned was over 100 k. We produced a subset of the dataset where the crop was potato, the purpose was not production of seed potato and the field area was larger than 2 ha and smaller than 100 ha. The fields smaller than 2 ha were excluded because often after the removal of a 10 m buffer there wouldn't be enough pixels left to perform the analysis (particularly if they were characterized by an elongated form). The fields were cultivated in the years 2015 to 2019. Here we will focus on the analysis of the years 2016, 2017 and 2018 because these years are representative of very different weather conditions, particularly 2016 was a wet year, 2017 was a dry spring and a wet summer, and that 2018 was characterized by a very dry summer.

For this analysis we used only a randomly selected subset of records of 3249 fields located on soils classified either as sandy or clay, cultivated with potato (excluding seed potatoes) in the years 2016, 2017 and 2018.

2.2 Publicly Available Data

For each field we retrieved the images from the satellites Landsat 8 and Sentinel 2. For the years before 2017 we only retrieved images from Landsat 8. For each field we also used information from the Dutch digital elevation model (DEM) *Actueel Hoogtebestand*. This digital elevation was produced using airborn lidar data collected between 2007 and 2012 (AHN2). We used the version of the dataset interpolated at a resolution of 0.5 m. This DEM has *"an accuracy of 20 cm for 99.7% of the points. The average point density for AHN2 is between 6 and 10 points per square meter"* [13].

For each cultivar we tried to retrieve data on the cultivar performance, e.g. earliness score or susceptibility to late blight, reported by the cultivar vendor and available on the Akkerweb platform. The performance of individual cultivars are usually scored on a number of indicators on a scale from 1 to 9 (for earliness 1 corresponding to the latest varieties and 9 to the earliest varieties). In this context we used the score on cultivar earliness to make inferences about the influence of the cultivar earliness on the correlation elevation-NDVI.

We used Google Earth Engine [14] to perform calculations on satellite images (Landsat 8 and Sentinel 2) and the Dutch DEM (AHN2 interpolated to 0.5 m). For each polygon we applied the following algorithm (pseudocode):

1. Import the polygon to Google Earth Engine. The information about the polygon were passed in the form of a list of coordinates.
2. Remove a 10 m buffer from the border to make sure that we did not include pixels that were not heterogenous in land cover (e.g. half road and half field).
3. Check the images available in the Landsat 8 and Sentinel 2 surface reflection collection.
4. Remove the clouds and cirrus from Sentinel 2 and clouds and cloud shadows from Landsat 8 using the respective pixel quality bands.
5. Clip the raster regions to the clip polygon setting to "not available" the pixels out of the field.

6. Calculate for each image the following quantities were calculated through a reducer function:
   a. Standard deviation of elevation.
   b. Sperman correlation between NDVI and elevation. To calculate the correlation the elevation dataset was resampled to match the resolution of the vegetation index dataset because this was coarser than the DEM(0.5 m vs 30 m for Landsat 8 and 10 m for Sentinel 2).

If an image was completely covered by clouds, cirrus (for Landsat 8) or cloud shadows (for Sentinel 2) the calculated quantities were set to "not available". The cloud coverage in the images was calculated from the quality band pixels in the two satellites (namely *pixel_qa* for Landsat8, and *QA60* for Sentinel 2).

We retrieved cumulative rain from weather data using the set of weather stations of the Royal Netherlands Meteorological Institute (KNMI, 45 stations). For the purpose of this study we calculated an average Dutch weather for the Netherlands by averaging the values of all the weather stations (Fig. 1 left).

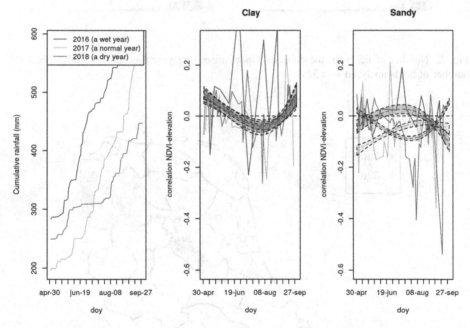

Fig. 1. Here we represent the correlation among over the growing season for the years 2016 to 2018 in contrasting soil types (clay vs sandy). The continuous lines represent the average measured across all the fields in a certain date. The dashed lines and the colored area represent the prediction and the 95% CI interval of the mean calculated using a 3rd degree polynomial equation. (Color figure online)

To approximate the temporal variability of correlation between NDVI and day of the year (DOY) we fitted a 3rd degree polynomial model to the data. This was intended more as a tool to visually interpolate the data rather than a predictive tool or an inferential tool.

2.3   Descriptive Statistics on the Retrieved Dataset

The cultivars present in our subset for which we performed calculations on satellite images are presented—anonymized—in Fig. 2 along with the earliness score.

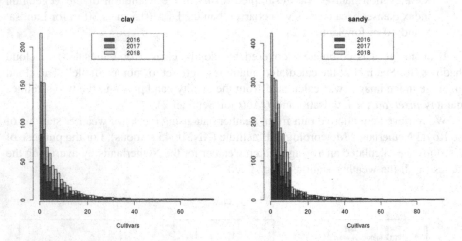

Fig. 2. Number of fields for the cultivars (anonymised) by year used in this study. The total number of fields analyzed was 3249

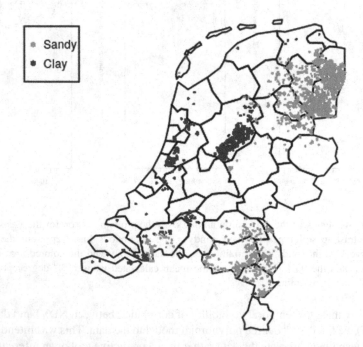

Fig. 3. Geographical distribution of clay and sandy soils in the fields represented in this study.

We analyzed the influence of earliness scores on NDVI-elevation correlation and found that the distribution of cultivar earliness was the following in sandy soils, 3–335 fields, 4–180 fields, 5–548 fields, 6–449, the other earliness classes (1, 2, 7, 8, 9) had less 30 fields. To represent as evenly as possible the late and early classes we defined as late the cultivars with earliness score lower or equal to 5 (6 cultivars with more than 10 fields) and as late the other (3 cultivars with more than 10 fields).

The soil types on the investigated fields are presented in Fig. 3. The main soil types are sandy (in the eastern part of country) and clay (in the western part of the country) for sake of simplicity we excluded the other soil types from the analysis.

Figure 4 shows the distribution of the within-field variability of elevation in the Netherlands. It is well known that fields in the NL are generally very flat. The most uneven fields are located in the western part of the country and in the southern province of Limburg (median standard deviation of elevation being 20 cm) whereas as expected the fields in the region of Flevoland, reclaimed from the sea in the sixties and seventies of last century were the most flat (median standard deviation of elevation typically < 10 cm).

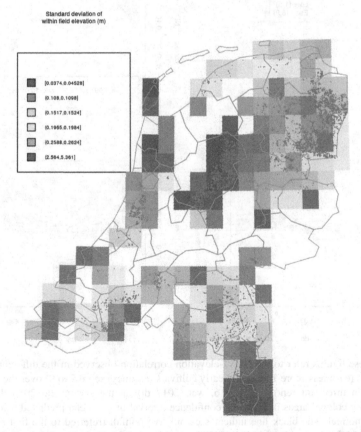

Fig. 4. Median of the standard deviation of the elevation within-fields across the Netherlands. The grey dots represent the field randomly sampled in this study.

3 Results

The correlations that we found were generally weak as the absolute value of the Spearman correlation was on average well below 0.2, but thanks to the high number of observations we were to observe ecologically meaningful trends in them. We found that NDVI was negatively correlated with elevation in sandy soil and dry periods (spring 2017, summer 2018), whereas such negative correlation was not observed for clay soils in all the years and in sandy soil for 2016 (a wet year, Fig. 1).

In clay soils the correlation was positive at the beginning of the season whereas no correlation was observed on average for the rest of the season.

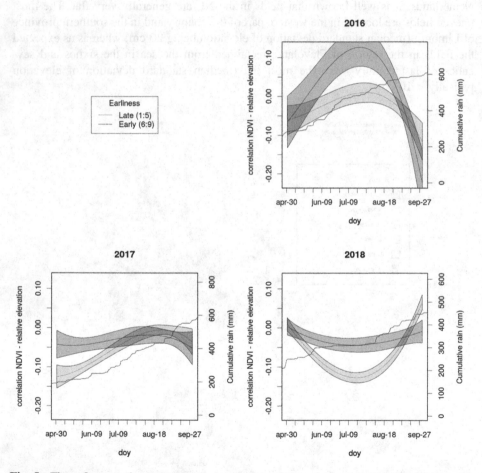

Fig. 5. These figures refer to the NDVI-elevation correlation observed in the different years of late cultivars (earliness score 1 to 5) and early cultivars (earliness score 5 to 9) over the course of the season in three different years (2016, wet, 2017 dry in the spring and 2018 dry in the summer). The colored areas indicate the confidence interval of the mean predicted using a third degree polynomial. The black line indicates cumulative rainfall (referred to the first right axis) and the dashed lines represent the median NDVI over the season (referred to the left axis). (Color figure online)

Also, the earliness score of the cultivar influenced the correlation. In fact the early varieties showed a neutral or positive correlation in wet years (indicating that higher biomasses were observed at relatively higher location), whereas the late developing varieties indicated a predominance of negative correlation in the dry years (Fig. 5).

4   Discussion

The correlations that we observed between the Normalized Difference Vegetation Index (NDVI, a good proxy for biomass) and elevation were generally weak suggesting that their use for prediction purposes at within-field scale is limited, nonetheless on a larger scale the correlation elevation-NDVI may be a useful indicator of cultivars sensitivity to drought stress. We observed that the correlation was negative in dry periods in sandy soils, whereas we hardly observed a negative correlation between within-field elevation and NDVI in clay soils (Fig. 1). The negative correlation for sandy soils may be easily explained by within-field water rerouting and/or distance from the water table and has generally been reported before for different crops (see introduction). The lack of correlation in the clay soils may be explained by geographical position of clay soils. In fact, in our dataset clay soils exhibit the lowest within-field elevation variability because they are mostly located in reclaimed areas (Flevoland province, Fig. 4) and are notoriously very flat. Moreover, clay soil has a higher water holding capacity and is therefore less prone to induce drought stress in the crops, and it has been shown that roots of potatoes in clay soils may grow as deep as one meter possibly because their growth can be facilitated by the presence of cracks in the subsoil [11].

Interestingly we observed a weak positive correlation in the clay at the beginning of the season, irrespective of the year. This could be due to the fact that the higher portions of the fields are less wet and thus warmer at emergence and as a consequence they develop more rapidly.

Our data on the within-field correlation between elevation and NDVI also offer a first insight on how large data from farmers could be used to evaluate differences between cultivars. An evaluation of this correlation for individual cultivars goes beyond the scope of this small study as it would require an evaluation of the performance of the different cultivars under drought for validation. Such scoring is not available to us at the present stage. However, we were able to evaluate how the cultivar earliness score influences the correlation in sandy soils. We found that late cultivars had a stronger negative correlation between NDVI and elevation than early ones. We suggest that early cultivars may escape dry spells because in the summer they have already developed deeper roots, nonetheless we have not yet data to validate this hypothesis.

5 Limitations of This Study

An important factor which we did not consider in this study was irrigation. It is likely that irrigation strongly influenced the correlation between NDVI and elevation, possibly also in unexpected direction. It could be that higher water availability levels-out the differences between the different parts of the field (as the difference in the correlation between wet and dry years would suggest) or it could also be that surface water rerouting exacerbates such differences. We were not able to investigate this aspect with the current dataset, but we believe that information on elevation could be useful to drive precision irrigation.

As we said this methodology has the potential to obtain information about cultivar differences for drought sensitivity. However to be usefully deployed such capability should be made available to breeders, whose plots are too small to be sensed using Landsat or Sentinel. Nonetheless the deployment of new satellites (e.g. *Worldview*) with finer resolution can open important opportunities in this direction.

An important aspect is that the AHN2 dataset has an accuracy (20 cm) that is lower than the field elevation in many cases. This would lower our correlation between vegetation indices and elevation and therefore not impair the validity of our correlation estimates.

6 Conclusion

Using farmers' data we were able to observe a negative correlation—although weak—between NDVI and elevation, and show how this correlation is stronger during dry periods. Because the correlation between the two variables was generally low, elevation has limited predictive power for within-field variability of growth in the Netherlands. Nonetheless we were able to depict how cultivars earliness influences such correlation. The correlation between altitude and vegetation is a parameter that can be virtually measured for every crop and deviations from this parameter, when measured over sufficiently large samples may carry important information about agroecological processes such as cultivars sensitivity to drought-stress.

Acknowledgements. The project was funded by the internal funds of WUR- Agrosystems Research. We are grateful to the Akkerweb Foundation for providing the anonymized dataset and to the two referees for their insightful comments.

References

1. Liakos, K.G., Busato, P., Moshou, D., et al.: Machine learning in agriculture: a review. Sens. (Switzerland) **18**, 1–29 (2018). https://doi.org/10.3390/s18082674
2. Evert, V., Been, T., Booij, A.J., et al.: Akkerweb: a platform for precision farming data, science, and practice. In: 14th International Conference on Precision Agriculture. International Society of Precision Agriculture, Monticello, IL (2018)

3. Kravchenko, A.N., Robertson, G.P., Thelen, K.D., Harwood, R.R.: Management, topographical, and weather effects on spatial variability of crop grain yields. Agron. J. **97**, 514–523 (2005). https://doi.org/10.1016/B978-012348525-0/50026-4
4. Kravchenko, A.N., Bullock, D.G.: Correlation of corn and soybean grain yield with topography and soil properties. Agron. J. **92**, 75–83 (2000). https://doi.org/10.2134/agronj2000.92175x
5. Timlin, D.J., Pachepsky, Y., Snyder, V.A., Bryant, R.B.: Spatial and temporal variability of corn grain yield on a hillslope. Soil Sci. Soc. Am. J. **62**, 764–773 (1998). https://doi.org/10.2136/sssaj1998.03615995006200030032x
6. Marques Da Silva, J.R., Alexandre, C.: Spatial variability of irrigated corn yield in relation to field topography and soil chemical characteristics. Precis. Agric. **6**, 453–466 (2005). https://doi.org/10.1007/s11119-005-3679-3
7. Marques da Silva, J.R., Silva, L.L.: Evaluation of Maize yield spatial variability based on field flow density. Biosyst. Eng. **95**, 339–347 (2006). https://doi.org/10.1016/j.biosystemseng.2006.06.015
8. Maestrini, B., Basso, B.: Drivers of within-field spatial and temporal variability of crop yield across the US Midwest. Sci. Rep. **8**, 14833 (2018). https://doi.org/10.1038/s41598-018-32779-3
9. Haverkort, J.A.: Plant. In: Delleman J, Hanse L (eds.) Potato Handbook. Aardappel BV, pp 121–214 (2018)
10. Lesczynski, D.B., Tanner, C.B.: Seasonal variation of root distribution of irrigated, field-grown Russet Burbank potato. Am. Potato J. **53**, 69–78 (1976). https://doi.org/10.1007/BF02852656
11. Vos, J., Groenwold, J.: Root growth of potato crops on a marine-clay soil. Plant Soil **94**, 17–33 (1986). https://doi.org/10.1007/BF02380587
12. Scott, E.J.A., Scott, R.K.: Principles of agronomy and their application in the potato industry. In: Harris, P.M. (ed.) The Potato Crop, 2nd edn, pp. 816–881. Springer, Dordrecht (1992). https://doi.org/10.1007/978-94-011-2340-2_17
13. Actueel Hoogtebestand Nederland De details van het Actueel Hoogtebestand Nederland. http://ahn.maps.arcgis.com/apps/Cascade/index.html?appid=75245be5e0384d47856d2b912fc1b7ed. Accessed 14 Oct 2019
14. Gorelick, N., Hancher, M., Dixon, M., et al.: Google earth engine: planetary-scale geospatial analysis for everyone. Remote Sens. Environ. (2017). https://doi.org/10.1016/j.rse.2017.06.031

Predicting Nitrogen Excretion of Dairy Cattle with Machine Learning

Herman Mollenhorst[1]([✉]), Yamine Bouzembrak[2], Michel de Haan[1], Hans J. P. Marvin[2], Roel F. Veerkamp[3], and Claudia Kamphuis[3]

[1] Livestock & Environment, Wageningen Livestock Research, Wageningen University and Research, P.O. Box 338, 6700 AH Wageningen, The Netherlands
{erwin.mollenhorst,michel.dehaan}@wur.nl
[2] Toxicology, Novel Foods & Agro Chains, Wageningen Food Safety Research, Wageningen University and Research, P.O. Box 230, 6700 AE Wageningen, The Netherlands
{yamine.bouzembrak,hans.marvin}@wur.nl
[3] Animal Breeding and Genomics, Wageningen University and Research, P.O. Box 338, 6700 AH Wageningen, The Netherlands
{roel.veerkamp,claudia.kamphuis}@wur.nl

Abstract. Several tools were developed during the past decades to support farmers in nutrient management and to meet legal requirements such as the farm specific excretion tool. This tool is used by dairy farmers to estimate the farm specific nitrogen (N) excretion of their animals, which is calculated from farm specific data and some normative values. Some variables, like intake of grazed grass or roughage, are hard to measure. A data driven approach could help finding structures in data, and identifying key factors determining N excretion. The aim of this study was to benchmark machine learning methods such as Bayesian Network (BN) and boosted regression trees (BRT) in predicting N excretion, and to assess how sensitive both approaches are on the absence of hard-to-measure input variables. Data were collected from 25 Dutch dairy farms. In the period 2006–2018, detailed recordings of N intake and output were made during 6–10 weeks distributed over each year. Variables included milk production, feed intake and their composition. Calculated N excretion was categorized as low, medium, and high, with limits of 300 and 450 g/day/animal. Accuracy of prediction of the farm specific N excretion, and distinguishing the low and high cases from the medium ones, was slightly better with BRT than with BN. Leaving out information on intake during grazing did not negatively influence validation performance of both models, which opens opportunities to diminish data collection efforts on this aspect. Further analyses are required to confirm these results, such as cross-validation.

Keywords: Bayesian networks · Boosted regression trees · Nitrogen excretion · Dairy cows

© IFIP International Federation for Information Processing 2020
Published by Springer Nature Switzerland AG 2020
I. N. Athanasiadis et al. (Eds.): ISESS 2020, IFIP AICT 554, pp. 132–138, 2020.
https://doi.org/10.1007/978-3-030-39815-6_13

1 Introduction

Agricultural policy, at least in the Netherlands, is in a transition. Since the second world war, the focus has been on producing as much food as possible in a highly efficient way. Favorable conditions combined with high-level knowledge and expertise, have put Dutch agriculture in a world leading position. However, drawbacks of this policy, become clear in regards to environmental impacts of agriculture and mineral surpluses due to factors such as high imports of animal feed. In 2018, the Dutch minister of agriculture presented a new policy [1], positioning Dutch agriculture as the front runner in circular agriculture, with minimal losses and minimal inputs of artificial inputs (fertilizer, pesticides) and scarce resources (e.g., phosphate, potassium).

Wageningen UR researchers have developed several tools and collected several datasets during the past decades to support farmers in nutrient management to meet the legal requirements. Examples of tools are the Annual Nutrient Cycling Assessment [2], which includes the whole nutrient cycle, or the Excretion Assessment [3], focusing on nutrients excreted in the manure by the animals. The Excretion Assessment is a tool that farmers can use to proof the actual excretion of their animals, in comparison to the excretion standards. The government accepts the results of this tool in order to calculate the manure export of a farm. This tool is based on farm specific data and some normative values modelled in a mechanistic way. However, some variables including intake of grazed grass or roughage, are hard to measure directly, and therefore are measured indirectly or estimated. A data driven approach could help finding structures in data, and identifying key factors determining N excretion. This could lead to possible exclusion of estimates and normative values for hard-to-measure input variables, or to focus on more detailed assessments, on field, group, or individual animal level. This would make the process of monitoring nutrient management more efficient and could be used to elaborate tools with prediction of the effects of possible management interventions. Better monitoring and prediction could support farmers and advisors, in making informed decisions on nutrient management, such as changes in feed ration or manure application.

An earlier study has proven that machine learning can help to predict grass and crop yields at field level, to support decisions on manure application rates [4]. However, it considered only one part of the nutrient circle, but decisions have to be made in more parts of the circle, such as animal nutrition and management. Therefore, in this study we will focus on the excretion of N from the animals, predicted from feed intake and production variables. To make models more explainable, a Bayesian network (BN) approach was applied, which delivers a graphical model that presents probabilistic relationships among a set of variables [5–8]. Next to BN, a less explainable model, boosted regression trees (BRT), was applied, which was also used in the previous study [4].

The aim of this study was to compare BN and BRT in predicting N excretion of dairy cows, and to assess how sensitive both approaches are on the absence of hard-to-measure input variables.

2   Materials and Methods

2.1   Dataset

Data used for this study originated from the project called 'Cows and Opportunities'. In this project, a group of 16 Dutch dairy farmers, together with researchers, searched for opportunities for sustainable and socially accepted agriculture [9]. The farms varied in intensity, scale, soil type, and style of farming. The main aim was to implement expected environmental legislation to monitor environmental, technical, and economic effects at farm level. In this way, each of these farms are a kind of pilot farm.

Data from years 2006 to 2018 were used, and originated from 25 different farms that were part of the project for different periods of time. On each farm detailed recordings were made during 6 to 10 weeks, distributed over the year. Between 14 to 16 farms were present in the dataset per year, which resulted in 108 to 151 weeks with detailed recordings per year. The final dataset contained 1,640 records.

Variables used concerned; milk production, milk composition, feed intake, and feed composition, for milk producing animals, on an average per cow basis. Milk production and milk composition were measured as part of the national milk production registration, according to ICAR regulations. Feed intake was measured through weighing of offered feed and refusals. Feed composition was determined by routine laboratory analyses of feed composition of all feeds. These variables are also used for calculating the N excretion based on formulas described by Oenema et al. [10], which were used as 'observed' values to be predicted with machine learning models. N excretion was categorized as low, medium, or high with limits of 300 and 450 g N per day per animal.

2.2   Machine Learning Models

In this study, two machine learning techniques were applied and benchmarked, namely BN and BRT. Decision tree induction is one of the basic machine learning techniques, is robust against irrelevant input variables, and is able to handle missing values [11, 12]. To alleviate the main disadvantage of decision trees, namely its inaccuracy in prediction, we used the iterative method called boosting. Generalized boosted regression using the Gradient Boosting Machine (h2o.gbm function (h2o version 3.20.0.2)), was applied in this study. BRT, lacked the possibility to clearly show relationships between variables in the model and, subsequently some interpretability. Therefore, BN was applied, which is a class of probabilistic model originating from Bayesian statistics and decision theory combined with graph theory. BN has the ability to integrate different data sources and types such as expert knowledge, measurement data, and feedback experience via Bayes theorem [7, 8]. Hugin software (version 8.7), was used to develop the BN model. Both models were applied on the same training and validation datasets. The validation dataset was a 20% random sample from the original dataset, and the remaining 80% was used for training. Model performance was evaluated by reporting confusion matrices and accuracy indicators. Accuracy was calculated in the conventional method, as well as for the low and high categories only (LHacc). Furthermore, a false alert rate (FAR) was calculated, representing the number of false alerts where an actual low case was predicted to be high or vice versa, over the total number of low and high predictions. All data processing and analyses, except for the BN development, were performed in RStudio (version 1.1.463 running R version 3.6.1).

3   Results and Discussion

Categorization of records concerning N excretion was rather imbalanced with over 88% of cases being medium. Randomization of records over training and validation sets, resulted in a prevalence of 89% medium in the training set and just 85% in the validation set. Especially notable was records categorized high, were over-represented in the validation dataset (Table 1).

Table 1. Number of low, medium, and high cases, and percentage of medium in training and validation datasets

Dataset	# low	# medium	# high	Percentage medium
Training	80	1171	61	89.3
Validation	22	280	26	85.4

Performance of BRT models was better than for BN models, with an overall accuracy for BRT models, just above the prevalence of medium in the validation dataset. The accuracy of predicting for high and low was 8.3% and 10.4%, for BN and BRT respectively (Table 2), both with 0% false alerts for low and high. For both models, this means that they have difficulty distinguishing the low and high cases from the medium ones, and predicting some of these cases corresponds with classifying slightly more (BN) or fewer (BRT) true medium cases incorrectly. When the first hard-to-measure variable, dry matter (DM) intake from grazing, was excluded from the validation set, performance improved slightly for BRT and stayed equal for BN, which means that there was no additional value in this variable for the model (Table 2). Additionally leaving out DM intake from silages and hay, decreased the performance of BRT compared to leaving out only DM intake from grazing, but improved the overall accuracy of the BN model. However, for both BRT and BN, the accuracy of predicting high and low decreased, which means that models tend to predict all records as medium (overall accuracy approaching prevalence of medium in validation dataset of 85.4%, see Table 1), when information on DM intake is left out.

Table 2. Overall accuracy (Accur.), and accuracy for low and high categories (LHacc) of Bayesian Networks (BN) and Boosted Regression Tree (BRT) models, for predicting N excretion with all variables present in the validation dataset or when excluding variables; dry matter intake (DMint) information of grazing, (grass and maize) silages, and hay.

Model description	BN		BRT	
	Accur.	LHacc	Accur.	LHacc
All variables	82.9	8.3	85.7	10.4
All, except DM_{int} grazing	82.9	8.3	86.9	10.4
All, except DM_{int} grazing, silages	84.1	2.1	86.3	6.3
All, except DM_{int} grazing, silages, hay	84.5	2.1	86.0	6.3

Protein content of grazed grass consistently appeared to be the most important variable in all models, often closely followed by variables concerning DM intake of grazed grass, grass or maize silage or their protein content, and milk production. For BRT models, only variable importance could be reported, whereas for BN models also relationships could be made visible (Fig. 1). A remarkable point that should be investigated further is that the DM intake from mineral supplements, which constitutes a minor part of the diet, was rather important in the BN model, with many connections to other variables.

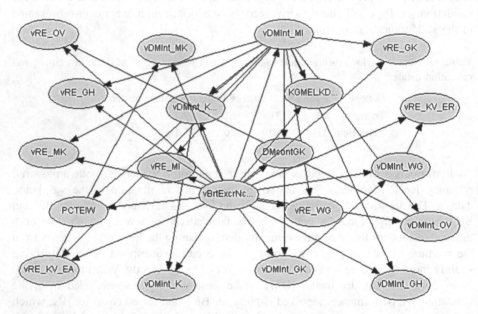

Fig. 1. Graphical representation of Bayesian Network model predicting N excretion (vBrtExcrNc...). (vDMInt = DM intake; vRE = protein content; DMcont = dry matter content; GH = grass hay; GK = grass silage; MI = minerals; MK = maize silage; KV_EA = low-protein concentrates; KV_ER = high-protein concentrates; OV = other feeds; WG = grazing; KGMELKD... = milk production level; PCTEIW = protein content of milk)

Additional analyses were performed to check the consistency of the results. We checked with BRT the effect of leaving out DM intake from both the training and validation dataset. When leaving out DM intake from grazing, this resulted in an increased overall accuracy (87.8%), as well as an increased accuracy for the low and high classes (18.8%), probably indicating that data on DM intake from grazing were noisy data and hampered the development of the prediction model. When also DM intake from grass and maize silage were excluded, accuracy dropped below that of the model containing all variables.

Results in this paper were based on a single split of the dataset and only two machine learning techniques were applied, with their default settings. These results, therefore, need to be confirmed with additional analyses, for example by applying cross-validation or different machine learning techniques.

4 Conclusions

In this study, we developed and benchmarked two machine learning methods (BN and BRT), to predict N excretion of dairy cows. Based on the initial evaluation of models for predicting N excretion from dairy cattle, BRT performed slightly better than BN, both with respect to overall accuracy as well as distinguishing high and low cases from medium ones. We conclude that both BN and BRT have difficulty distinguishing the low and high cases from the medium ones. Further analyses of the relationship between variables in the model, is better facilitated by the graphical representation of the model for BN, whereas for BRT only variable importance is available. Leaving out information on DM intake of grazed grass did not negatively influence the validation performance of both models, which opens opportunities to diminish data collection efforts on this aspect.

Acknowledgements. This research was conducted by Wageningen Livestock Research, commissioned and funded by the Ministry of Agriculture, Nature and Food Quality, within the framework of Policy Support Research theme "Data driven & High Tech" (project number KB-38-001-002 AI in animal and arable systems). Data used were part of the project 'Cows and Opportunities', funded by the Dutch ministries of Agriculture, Nature and Food Quality, and Infrastructure and Water Management, and funded by ZuivelNL (the organization of the Dutch dairy sector), and due to the efforts of the mentioned 25 dairy farmers.

References

1. MinLNV: Landbouw, natuur en voedsel: waardevol en verbonden - Nederland als koploper in kringlooplandbouw (in Dutch). Ministry of Agriculture, Nature and Food Quality, The Hague, The Netherlands (2018)
2. Aarts, H.F.M., et al.: Quantifying the environmental performance of individual dairy farms - the Annual Nutrient Cycling Assessment (ANCA). Grassl. Sci. Eur. **20**, 377–380 (2015)
3. RVO: Handreiking bedrijfsspecifieke excretie melkvee. Rijksdienst voor Ondernemend Nederland, 60 p. (2019)
4. Mollenhorst, H., et al.: Field and crop specific manure application on a dairy farm based on historical data and machine learning (2019, submitted)
5. Marvin, H.J., et al.: Application of Bayesian networks for hazard ranking of nanomaterials to support human health risk assessment. Nanotoxicology **11**(1), 123–133 (2017)
6. Cheng, J., et al.: Learning Bayesian networks from data: an information-theory based approach. Artif. Intell. **137**(1–2), 43–90 (2002)
7. Bouzembrak, Y., et al.: Application of Bayesian Networks in the development of herbs and spices sampling monitoring system. Food Control **83**, 38–44 (2018)

8. Bouzembrak, Y., Marvin, H.J.P.: Impact of drivers of change, including climatic factors, on the occurrence of chemical food safety hazards in fruits and vegetables: a Bayesian Network approach. Food Control **97**, 67–76 (2019)
9. Cows and Opportunities homepage (in Dutch). www.koeienenkansen.nl. Accessed 22 Oct 2019
10. Oenema, J., et al.: Toetsing van de Kringloopwijzer - Gemeten en voorspelde stikstof- en fosfaatproducties van mest en gewas. Wageningen University and Research, Wageningen, The Netherlands. p. 84 (2017)
11. Friedman, J.H.: Greedy function approximation: a gradient boosting machine. Ann. Stat. **29** (5), 1189–1232 (2001)
12. Witten, I.H. Frank, E.: Data Mining: Practical Machine Learning Tools and Techniques. Morgan Kaufmann Series in Data Management Systems, 2nd edn. Elsevier/Morgan Kaufmann, San Fransisco, CA (2005)

Investigation of Common Big Data Analytics and Decision-Making Requirements Across Diverse Precision Agriculture and Livestock Farming Use Cases

Spiros Mouzakitis[1(✉)], Giannis Tsapelas[1], Sotiris Pelekis[1],
Simos Ntanopoulos[1], Dimitris Askounis[1], Sjoukje Osinga[2],
and Ioannis N. Athanasiadis[2] (iD)

[1] Decision Support Systems Laboratory,
National Technical University of Athens, 15780 Athens, Greece
smouzakitis@epu.ntua.gr
[2] Wageningen University, 6700 EW Wageningen, The Netherlands

Abstract. The purpose of this paper is to present the investigation of common requirements and needs of users across a diverse set of precision agriculture and livestock farming use cases that was based on a series of interviews with experts and farmers. The requirements were based on nine interviews that were conducted in order to identify common requirements and challenges in terms of data collection and management, Big Data technologies, High Performance Computing infrastructure and decision making. The common requirements that derived from the interviews and user requirement analysis per use case can serve as basis for identifying functional and non-functional requirements of a technological solution of high re-usability, interoperability, adaptability and overall efficiency in terms of addressing common needs for precision agriculture and livestock farming.

Keywords: Precision agriculture · Livestock farming · Big data analytics · Decision-making · User requirements

1 Introduction

The recent technological advancements in Big Data, Artificial Intelligence (AI), High Performance Computing (HPC), Cloud Services and Internet of Things (IoT) have the potential to enable farmers to overcome long-standing challenges in exploiting the vast amount of data that can be collected, in order to increase efficiency and productivity while reducing the initial farm input costs [1–3]. Big data and AI enable novel precision agriculture opportunities that allow the performing of queries and analytics on a distributed and diverse set of collected data (from IoT devices, images, video, satellite data, etc.) that may lead to better and faster predictions and vital insights for farming decisions. IoT sensors on fields and crops [4–6] can provide a significant amount of information, critical for the decision-making process such as soil conditions, high-fidelity weather conditions [7, 8], fertilising requirements, water availability and pest

I. N. Athanasiadis et al. (Eds.): ISESS 2020, IFIP AICT 554, pp. 139–150, 2020.
https://doi.org/10.1007/978-3-030-39815-6_14

infestations. In addition, aerial images captured by unmanned aerial vehicles [9], or drones, which can patrol fields, can provide early warnings related to potential problems, such as diseases or deviations from expected growth rates; or offer indicators of crop ripeness and quality. Individual plants may also be monitored for nutrients and growth rates. Satellites [10] can facilitate detection of relevant changes in field with captured satellite imagery, identification of crop threats such as nutrients deficiency or insect damage, while GPS units on tractors can help determine optimal usage of heavy equipment and precise management of field operations. At the same time, livestock production management exploits technology to quantitatively measure the behaviour, health and performance of animals, including real-time monitoring of reproduction, health and welfare of livestock and the corresponding environmental impact [11, 12]. The data sources utilised in livestock management include amongst others on-line sound and video observations, feeding intake, drinking behaviour data, data from sensors on the animals and data from milking robots. There is an increasing literature of individual use-cases on precision agriculture and livestock farming applications, nevertheless the identification of common requirements and challenges across different use cases is currently missing.

The purpose of this paper is to present the investigation of common requirements and needs of users across a diverse set of precision agriculture and livestock farming use cases that was based on a series of interviews with experts and farmers.

2 Methods and Approach

2.1 Overall Approach

For the identification of the requirements a close collaboration with twelve agri-food industry stakeholders took place between January and June 2019 and consisted of three phases:

(a) Structured interviews with the stakeholders describing the current situation, the expectations for an ideal, future situation and the challenges to be addressed in between
(b) Using the initial current and future situations from the first phase, nine Usage Scenarios were created in a collaborative manner with data engineers, analysts and HPC experts
(c) A list of common user stories was distilled from all the usage scenarios and were ranked based on their foreseen business impact and technological complexity

The requirement investigation process took into consideration the user-varying dynamics in the precision agriculture and livestock farming scenarios, that is the different sectors, expectations, backgrounds and interests of users involved in different tasks such as data collection, data cleaning, modelling, decision making, and application of the outcome of the tasks for particular purposes.

Each user task is distinguished by several aspects: the data needed for this task, the skills required to perform the task, the timing of this task, and so on. People who assume the role of performing the task can be end users (e.g. farmers, farmer cooperatives), intermediaries (e.g. extension officers, veterinarians, seed providers), companies (e.g. planning institutions), data professionals (e.g. technical assistants, data analysts/scientists), and so on. Nonetheless, the user is not necessarily a person, the term could also describe a device (like a sensor or a satellite), an application program, an HPC cloud function, or any agent performing a task.

In order to avoid confusion around the term 'user', the usage of 'roles' was preferred in the analysis. A role is the particular function a user fulfils when carrying out a particular task, such as the role of data collection or the role of data cleaning. Each role has a body fulfilling that role. Several roles may be combined by the same body of fulfilment. The final user of the use case is not necessarily the same as the end user or stakeholder who benefits from the solution that the use case provides. A use case may end at the point where an intermediary is required to bring the outcome to a farmer in order to help the farmer solve a problem. The farmer himself/herself may not be within the scope of the technological solution, but he is a stakeholder nevertheless. To avoid confusion on that, we use the term 'stakeholder' exclusively for the one who ultimately benefits from use case solutions developed in the context of the ICT solution but who is not necessarily part of the scope of the use case, and hence not necessarily himself/herself a user of the technological solution.

2.2 Interviews

Initially, a set of individual online and physical one-to-one interviews were conducted between March and April 2019. During the interviews, workflow diagrams were identified and drawn together with the interviewees, based on their descriptions. When more than one situation could apply for "current situation" or "future situation", they were all included in the interview. Hence, each interview resulted to a set of workflow diagrams that consisted of at least two, but often more diagrams.

Following, each diagram was discussed with respect to the roles involved in every step of the workflow. These roles were placed in the diagrams, labelled and described as accurately as possible at that time.

Finally, the stakeholders for each use case were identified as well, with elaborated descriptions of how they can be distinguished from one another, and how they inform themselves and communicate within and outside their peer networks. This in-depth description of the stakeholders and the ways they operate guided the process of deriving the requirements that best match their needs and expectations.

2.3 User Scenarios Co-design Process

Following the interviews, nine usage scenarios were co-designed through the collaboration of agrifood-industry stakeholders and technical staff (data engineers, analysts, HPC experts). The usage scenarios are descriptions of hypothetical real-world examples. They are essential in order to highlight the interactions of people and organisations with a system. They contain detailed references to the steps, events, and/or actions which occur during these interactions. More specifically, the scenarios in this document attempt to describe, exhaustively and on a high-level, all the possible ways the users will interact with the proposed technical solutions and accurately depict their critical business actions. Hence, the scenarios show how the various users wish to improve their workflow with available state-of-the-art solutions. Critical properties were specified by the information provided in the scenarios regarding e.g. the type of device the users will access the developed application from, locations where data can be stored, privacy and security constraints, existing solutions. Agrifood stakeholders outlined their business needs and challenges while the technical partners reviewed the scenarios and updated them with proposed state-of-the-art ICT solutions (infrastructure, data workflows, software tools and algorithms). In order for the reader to develop a better understanding of the concept, a summary of an indicative user scenario, as it was designed by the stakeholders of a fish farm, is provided in Sect. 2.4.

2.4   An Example of a User Scenario

Datafish is an SME that develops precision livestock farming ICT solutions for aquaculture by deploying IoT sensors and AI. Datafish wants to develop a platform solution that will aid Cretafish, a fish-farming company in Crete, in monitoring fish behavior in fish tanks and optimizing the decision-making in fish diseases, fish feeding and environmental impacts of the fish farm. Cretafish is currently adjusting the amount of food to be thrown in the cages by observing the fish at the surface level during the feedings.

Datafish will incorporate near real-time processing of aerial drone and satellite images as well as sensor collected data such as water temperature, salinity, maximum chlorophyll index (MCI) etc. Datafish will also include several components that support multiple data operations and visualisations, machine learning modeling capabilities and reporting services, in order to enable the generation of valuable information to be leveraged by Cretafish.

Data Operations and Simple Visualisations Component
- *Data Management.* This module automatically receives relevant data available data to the platform (e.g. weather data). Additionally, it allows for an authorised Datafish employee to gain access to the datasets that are generated by sensors and cameras. She/He can regularly clean and upload them to the solution's platform where they are securely stored in a private cloud.
- *Data Exploration.* This module permits the exploration of each dataset e.g. aerial images for observing fish behaviour, temperature and O2 levels to monitor fish health.
- *Simple Visualisations.* This module provides interactive graphs such as bar-charts that combine generated feeding patterns with weather data in order to assess their correlation.

Experiment/Analytics Environment. An authorised Datafish data analyst, uses this component to gain access to a development environment built to support her/his favorite programming language -e.g. Python- as well as her/his most often-used machine learning algorithms and datasets. She/He writes the code in order to achieve:

- Fish feeding optimisation
- Algae bloom prediction
- Fish disease prediction

Dashboards/Advanced Visualisations Component. The component includes a real-time dynamic heatmap of the fish tank and advanced graphs showing the amount of food, the recommended optimal feeding plan and an overview of adjustable fish parameters. It also provides historical versions of the heatmap for on-the-go comparisons, as well as a camera feed with zoom capabilities that will enable the inspection of individual and group fish behavior and will facilitate disease detection.

Reporting Component. The component enables Datafish to automate the reporting process so that Cretafish receives daily updates that include parts of the Dashboards and a summary report on each cage. Cretafish can also view the dashboards in real-time when feeding is taking place so to optimise future decision-making.

Alerts Component. Cretafish uses this component in order to receive disease warnings based on anomaly detection techniques and alerts relevant to the duration and amount of feeding.

Model Template Component. After approximately six months of application, this system becomes a model template ready to be used by other fish farms through this component.

2.5 Requirements Elicitation and Ranking

A list of user stories was elicited from the case-specific usage scenarios in the form of "As a <Role>", "I want to <user requirement>", "So that <benefit>" and grouped together based on the use cases. Thereafter the stakeholders were asked to rank the derived requirements based on:

(a) Business value: The business value was asked to be provided by the agrifood stakeholders, in a qualitative manner using a scale between 1–5 points, by estimating the importance and foreseen business impact of this requirement for the overall process.
(b) Technical Complexity: The Technical complexity was calculated by the technical partners through voting, on a scale for 1 to 5, with 1 meaning "least complex" and 5 "most complex".

   This methodology poses as an extension to an approach proposed by Lant [13] which calculates a score for every user story, against two different attributes, that of business value and urgency. Through the methodology presented above and by qualitatively examining the requirements and the dependencies among some of them, we concluded on a final set of common requirements for Big Data analysis and decision-making across the nine different use cases of precision agriculture and livestock farming practice.

3   Interview Results Per Use Case

3.1   Organic Soya Yield and Protein-Content Prediction

This use case involves the prediction of yield and protein-content maps based on satellite imagery and additional information concerning electromagnetic soil scans, drone images and sensory data. Time-series of satellite images are very indicative of the relative yield and protein content on the field, i.e. they can pinpoint the areas in which soybean grows better or worse. By knowing the absolute values of yield and protein content on the whole farm, these traits can be reverse-engineered in these specific areas of the field and derive the corresponding maps.

During the interview, the need for data fusion was recognised, as data will be acquired from heterogeneous sources (EC probes, satellites, drones) at different times. Although monitoring in one farm may not be computationally intensive, monitoring the soybean production at field-scale throughout Europe requires huge processing power and smart algorithms, optimised for parallel execution. The size of the dataset and the classification algorithm that has to be trained and executed, require efficient data management and strong processing power through HPC infrastructure and Big Data solutions.

3.2   Climate-Smart Predictive Models for Viticulture

The purpose of this use case is to support complex, highly non-linear, models for vine and grape growth with respect to the extreme number of variables (data types) that have been shown to affect the quality and quantity of the produced yields. Such crop models could estimate vine and grape growth and crop yield at larger scales, with spatial sources of information on soil, water, land use, and other factors. In this way, much larger predictions of yield could be achieved across regional scales.

During the interview it was clarified that this use case involves large matrix operations, which are memory-intensive computations. The limited amount of computer memory available in a non-HPC enabled deployment does not allow for an efficient parallelisation of the data processes entailed in the solution.

3.3   Climate Services for Organic Fruit Production

Integration and comparison of fruit bud development estimation models with temperature and air humidity forecasts and other ancillary data can be used for risk probability mapping in order to establish an early warning system that can help farms to minimise damage effects through protective methods for frost and hail. This use case focuses on climate predictors that are correlated with either frost or hail occurrences and then can be used for planning risk prevention operations.

During the interview the need for examining the integration of a frost and hail early warning system as a climate service into a decision support system for horticultural and fruit-tree farmers was presented. This service is based on exploring and analyzing the best probabilistic predictions of these extreme climate events for site-specific spatial scales. Observational and simulated climate variables need to be integrated with crop modelling approaches to estimate the probable risk. This requires exploration and comparison of different methods together with forecast quality assessment of the predictions, in which synchronous observed and predicted values are compared.

3.4 Autonomous Robotic Systems Within Arable Frameworks

This case considers the provision of autonomous robotic systems within an arable farm. Dictated by the weather, farming tasks have often to be carried out within a short time window. Consequently, equipment has increased in size to complete the work rapidly. One alternative solution is for farmers to manage fleets of smaller, autonomous vehicles and carry out the tasks as required.

During the interview, the to-be situation focused on field robots obtaining sensory data for soil chemical analysis (regularly/monthly) and hyperspectral imaging (HSI) for determining soil and crop conditions. Such data can be used for real time object level plant identification, individual plant harvest readiness assessment (in near harvest periods) and plant-level automated harvesting (which is currently labour intensive). The challenge in this use case lies in the precise processing of sensory data not only for identifying plant, weed and arable land readiness for harvesting, but also for activating nearby actuators distributed across a number of vehicles.

3.5 Optimizing Computations for Crop Yield Forecasting

Crop yield monitoring can be used as a tool for agricultural monitoring (e.g. early warning & anomaly detection), index-based insurance (index estimates) and farmer advisory services to facilitate precision agriculture and timely identify in-field phenomics by helping to provide greater yields and contributing to better food security.

The interview process highlighted that current computation loads over a single server have been reduced to meet hardware limitations. Additionally, more detailed weather forecasts from ECWMF together with parcel-specific data, and data processed for Sentinel Satellite Imagery may allow to predict crop yields at parcel level. Hence, one of the main challenges is distributing the computational load over several computational resources and exploring the potential of machine learning algorithms to forecast yields at parcel level.

3.6 Pig Weighing Optimisation

This use case has three main goals: (1) To estimate the mean and standard deviation of the live weight of grower/finisher pigs in a pen based on video images; (2) To track the weight of individual pigs in a pen based on video images; (3) To incorporate the growth curve estimated by the Convolutional Neural Networks (CNNs) in previously developed models for early warning of diarrhea. Currently there is no video-based weight estimation available and an *eye-balling* estimate is used on common farms due to manual weighing on big farms being a laborious task.

The interview process revealed that the training of the above described CNNs with the already available big data is an inherently immensely computationally demanding task which cannot be handled by limited computational power and memory infrastructures. Moreover, image and video processing and analysis is a task that can highly benefit from HPCs. The sensors that are installed are generating large amounts of video and signal data and this will be an even bigger issue as additional sensors might be installed in the future.

3.7 Sustainable Pig Production

This use case focuses on improving pig health and welfare, works on fulfilling the potential of each pig through its life and on increasing the quality of the end-product for the market and the consumers. This requires the usage and data fusion of various data sources coming from multiple on-farm sensors and software systems, image analysis, management data and slaughterhouse records.

During the interview, the need for exploring techniques for data fusion was identified, particularly for data of different size and sampling frequencies. Additional needs include high-throughput processing of big data with multivariate algorithms and advanced machine learning, as deep learning, to automatically detect data anomalies. The outcomes can include warnings (alerts) of problems with health, welfare or productivity, development of longitudinal trends, and data on individual pigs and prediction of end-product quality.

3.8 Open Sea Fishing

The goal of this use case is to achieve higher sustainability of a fishing fleet, rebuild overfished stocks and prevent overfishing. First, the integration of data from the entire fleet's electronic logbooks is necessary and requires a series of improvements of the on-board database systems of commercial fishing vessels. Additionally, the collection, storage and processing of on-board sensor data is required, together with a visual-based processing of catch imagery deriving from RGB cameras for fish-selection purposes.

During the interview it was revealed that the preprocessing involved is computationally intensive and requiring a scalable infrastructure that offers parallel processing. Moreover, a multivariate analysis model that integrates all available sensor and price data as well as an artificial neural network to find optimal operational parameters for minimal costs is required and is highly computationally intensive.

3.9 Aquaculture Monitoring and Feeding Optimisation

The purpose of this use case is to investigate fish behaviour on a deeper level. To do this, methods like segmentation and region proposal, object tracking, video analysis and machine learning are used to analyse water movements from colour, to detect problems in nets and cages, and to determine fish positions. This information will be combined with other data such as weather information and sensor measurements (mainly related to oxygen and current speed) in order to develop an efficient feed management system that can help companies to make optimal use of the food, reduce costs and also reduce the impact on the environment.

The interview revealed that data processing needs to be performed within short time frame. Being able to process data fast, and extract insights are the big challenges of this use case, demanding high throughput, computational intensity and short turnaround times.

4 Derived Common Requirements from All Use Cases

For each use case presented above, a set of usage scenarios was created along with the corresponding set of user stories. Thereafter all user stories were analysed and classified in eight categories (data management, data storage, data exploration, data analysis, data process, visualisations, support, alerts). Common requirements across all use cases and user stories were identified and are presented in the following Table 1.

Table 1. Common requirements from all use cases investigated

Category	Requirement
Data management	Guarantee data, model & outputs integrity through the entire data value chain in order to develop a trustful relationship between stakeholders (e.g. farmer & buyer)
Data management	Be able to upload new datasets, with different schemas, in a common data repository, from different sources
Data management	Support automated check-in of sensor-collected data
Data management	Daily transfer & access to daily updated data (e.g. parcel specific weather forecasts, satellite imagery data, logbooks, satellite VMS data etc.)
Data management	HPC infrastructure for near real-time image processing in order to allow near real-time notifications
Data management	Ability to share results and visualisations with other users to increase collaboration opportunities and efficiency
Data management	Ability to store as template a whole project, or smaller workflows of it, ready to be trained with new input datasets
Data management	Access to parcel-specific soil data, crop parameters, crop calendars, historical weather archives, regional statistics & historic yield data (parcel-specific N/A but desired) in order to correlate them to conduct analysis and feed them to crop models
Data management	Expose data and results through APIs for increased interoperability with other systems
Data storage	A private cloud storage is required with fine-grained access control
Data storage	Encryption of data on the private cloud storage
Data exploration	Be able to execute user-friendly queries across diverse and distributed datasets of different types and store their results. Desired subsets of whole datasets can be saved & used in latter data analytics
Data exploration	Perform queries on raw, cured or aggregated data, either in batch mode or in real time

(continued)

Table 1. (*continued*)

Category	Requirement
Data analysis	Create and train machine learning models using available datasets to assist in the decision-making process
Data analysis	Reuse models stored in the personal account in different cases in order to save time and use previous experience in new cases
Data analysis	Access to predictions about quantity to be produced (crop yield/fish catch prediction, etc.) on a daily basis in order to improve logistics, increase profits, optimise negotiations & remain reliable to partners
Data analysis	Provide support/integration for a variety of statistical and Big Data tools, like R and MXNet, Tensorflow or Spark frameworks
Data analysis	Upload, train & deploy locally created models to the solution despite the different ML tools used for their development (e.g. by supporting ONNX) for easier comprehension of current situation, predictions and recommended actions
Data analysis	Ability to create models in different programming language (R, python, Scala, Spark MLlib) depending on the expertise/preference of each user. Do not lock-in the use case in a specific programming language
Data analysis	Be able to validate using reference historic data from previous projects to recalibrate or fine tune the system to each user's case in order to leverage existing data and assist the quick training of the models
Data analysis	Ability to enable semi-automatic generation of metadata, in order to save time from manual data input
Data analysis	Support automated detection of anomalies in output from the simulation models that run (executed efficiently on HPC clusters)
Data analysis	Apply classification algorithms on both images and other input variables
Data analysis	Train & optimise Machine Learning and Deep Learning models and evaluate them using different parameters in a parallel way (tool examples: Horvod, Tensorflow)
Data process	Support indications of the parts of the code that are memory or processing intensive and may require parallelisation, i.e. using HPC or Apache Spark functionality
Data process	Process video & image data and extract features within short time windows (near real-time responses)
Data process	Be able to manage the resources being used by the experiments [e.g. Workflow management dashboard (edit, pause, delete, view consumed sources)] in order to be aware and be able to manage resources used respectively to the workload of each task
Data process	Make use of the best distributed frameworks, the best available software libraries for scientific computation (such as MKL or openBLAS)
Data process	Smart distribution of data and parallelisation of tasks based on multi-objective optimisations (e.g. by origin/destination of the data, available resources) and best parameter setting for the productivity model (e.g. according to environmental, regional and weather conditions)

(continued)

Table 1. (*continued*)

Category	Requirement
Data process	Interpolate the available data with many (e.g. at least 20) different weather forecasts and satellite images in order to increase the robustness and practicality of predictions
Visualisations	Be able to create standard and custom visualisations over the data that users with basic ICT knowledge can easily interact with farmers/fishers, etc.
Visualisations	Be able to combine different series of data, create custom visualisations, charts, maps and graphs of selected variables in order to gain intuition over data, models and events and other statistical observations
Visualisations	Support map-based visualisations based on HPC software that require real time data processing
Visualisations	Combine multiple time series in the same graph in order to visually compare and correlate multiple variables in time
Support	Have expert technicians install hardware (cameras and sensors) at the farm (or premises) to enrich the existing databases at minimal cost
Alerts	Ability to receive customisable real-time notifications and warnings in order to make timely decisions

5   Conclusions and Future Work

The present paper presented the interviews conducted in nine (9) diverse precision agriculture and livestock farming cases in order to identify common requirements and challenges in terms of data collection and management, Big Data, HPC infrastructure and decision making.

The interviews outlined and revealed a set of common user requirements and indicated the users' point of view concerning the necessity of a robust and scalable infrastructure that would enable better and faster predictions and data analytics taking advantage of the fusion of different and timely updated datasets. The users put emphasis on the importance of the low cost and the ease of installation and operation of such infrastructure and decision-making tools. A high development and maintenance cost could render the technological solutions inapplicable. The common requirements that derived from the interviews and user requirement analysis per use case can serve as basis for identifying functional and non-functional requirements of a technological solution of high re-usability, interoperability, adaptability and overall efficiency in terms of addressing common needs for precision agriculture and livestock farming.

Future work involves the development of a blueprint architecture and design principles for technological solutions in precision agriculture and livestock farming, as well as the development of a prototype platform that combines HPC, Big Data, Cloud Computing (services) and IoT. Their main purpose will be to provide integrated and unmediated access to a vast number of large-scale datasets of diverse types, coming from a plethora of different sources, as well as to enable the actual generation of value and extraction of insights out of these data.

Acknowledgements. This work has been co-funded by the CYBELE project, a European Commission research program under H2020-825355. We are particularly grateful to the interviewees from the nine CYBELE case study demonstrators.

References

1. Schimmelpfennig, D.: Farm profits and adoption of precision agriculture (No. 1477-2016-121190) (2016)
2. Schimmelpfennig, D., Ebel, R.: Sequential adoption and cost savings from precision agriculture. J. Agric. Resour. Econ. **41**(1835-2016-149552), 97-115 (2016)
3. Janssen, S.J., et al.: Towards a new generation of agricultural system data, models and knowledge products: information and communication technology. Agric. Syst. **155**, 200–212 (2017)
4. Srbinovska, M., Gavrovski, C., Dimcev, V., Krkoleva, A., Borozan, V.: Environmental parameters monitoring in precision agriculture using wireless sensor networks. J. Clean. Prod. **88**, 297–307 (2015)
5. Mahlein, A.K.: Plant disease detection by imaging sensors–parallels and specific demands for precision agriculture and plant phenotyping. Plant Dis. **100**(2), 241–251 (2016)
6. Vuran, M.C., Salam, A., Wong, R., Irmak, S.: Internet of underground things in precision agriculture: architecture and technology aspects. Ad Hoc Netw. **81**, 160–173 (2018)
7. Bendre, M.R., Thool, R.C., Thool, V.R.: Big data in precision agriculture: weather forecasting for future farming. In: 2015 1st International Conference on Next Generation Computing Technologies (NGCT), pp. 744–750. IEEE, September 2015
8. Keswani, B., et al.: Adapting weather conditions based IoT enabled smart irrigation technique in precision agriculture mechanisms. Neural Comput. Appl. **31**(1), 277–292 (2019)
9. Wolf, J., Bhandari, S., Raheja, A.: Unmanned aerial vehicles for precision agriculture in Orchard crops (2017)
10. Gevaert, C.M., Suomalainen, J., Tang, J., Kooistra, L.: Generation of spectral–temporal response surfaces by combining multispectral satellite and hyperspectral UAV imagery for precision agriculture applications. IEEE J. Sel. Top. Appl. Earth Obs. Remote Sens. **8**(6), 3140–3146 (2015)
11. Wolfert, S., Ge, L., Verdouw, C., Bogaardt, M.J.: Big data in smart farming–a review. Agric. Syst. **153**, 69–80 (2017)
12. van der Heide, E.M.M., Veerkamp, R.F., van Pelt, M.L., Kamphuis, C., Athanasiadis, I., Ducro, B.J.: Comparing regression, naive Bayes, and random forest methods in the prediction of individual survival to second lactation in Holstein cattle. J. Dairy Sci. **102**(10), 9409–9421 (2019). https://doi.org/10.3168/jds.2019-1629
13. Lant, M.: How to easily prioritize your agile stories (2010). https://michaellant.com/2010/05/21/how-to-easily-prioritize-your-agile-stories/

Quantifying Uncertainty for Estimates Derived from Error Matrices in Land Cover Mapping Applications: The Case for a Bayesian Approach

Jordan Phillipson[1]([✉]), Gordon Blair[1], and Peter Henrys[2]

[1] School of Computing and Communications, Lancaster University,
Lancaster, UK
j.phillipson@lancaster.ac.uk
[2] Centre for Ecology and Hydrology, Lancaster, UK

Abstract. The use of land cover mappings built using remotely sensed imagery data has become increasingly popular in recent years. However, these mappings are ultimately only models. Consequently, it is vital for one to be able to assess and verify the quality of a mapping and quantify uncertainty for any estimates that are derived from them in a reliable manner.

For this, the use of validation sets and error matrices is a long standard practice in land cover mapping applications. In this paper, we review current state of the art methods for quantifying uncertainty for estimates obtained from error matrices in a land cover mapping context. Specifically, we review methods based on their transparency, generalisability, suitability when stratified sampling and suitability in low count situations. This is done with the use of a third-party case study to act as a motivating and demonstrative example throughout the paper.

The main finding of this paper is there is a major issue of transparency for methods that quantify uncertainty in terms of confidence intervals (frequentist methods). This is primarily because of the difficulty of analysing nominal coverages in common situations. Effectively, this leaves one without the necessary tools to know when a frequentist method is reliable in all but a few niche situations. The paper then discusses how a Bayesian approach may be better suited as a default method for uncertainty quantification when judged by our criteria.

Keywords: Uncertainty quantification · Map assessment · Bayesian · Land cover maps

1 Introduction

National and global scale land cover mappings based on remotely sensed imagery have been shown to be directly useful in many environmental science applications including: carbon emission monitoring [1–4], forest monitoring [5, 6], modelling of soil properties [7], land change detection [8–10], climate dynamics [11–14], natural hazard assessment [15, 16], agriculture, water/wetland monitoring [17, 18] and biodiversity studies [19,

© IFIP International Federation for Information Processing 2020
Published by Springer Nature Switzerland AG 2020
I. N. Athanasiadis et al. (Eds.): ISESS 2020, IFIP AICT 554, pp. 151–164, 2020.
https://doi.org/10.1007/978-3-030-39815-6_15

20]. Because of this, along with the increasing availability of satellite imagery data, national and global scale land cover mappings have attracted significant attention from researchers in the environmental sciences in recent decades.

Satellite imagery alone though is generally not enough to build reliable and meaningful land cover maps. One must also collect reference samples (sometimes referred to as ground truth samples) to both train (when using supervised learning techniques) and validate maps.

When estimating standard performance metrics and area estimates in land cover mapping (e.g. user, producer and overall accuracies and area estimates), a popular method of estimating these quantities is with the use of a post-hoc validation set. This is done by comparing the ground-truth values of these validation samples with their respective predicted values and inferring estimates based on the forms of agreements and disagreements between these values. Since these estimations usually only require the number of different types of agreements and disagreements, it is often convenient to tabulate these results. When this is the case, the subsequent tabulated results are often presented as an error (or confusion) matrix. As a validation set is itself only a sample, such estimations are inevitably going to have uncertainties associated with them. In order for policy makers, stakeholders and other users to have the appropriate level of confidence in such estimations, it is vital that any quantification of these uncertainties are justified.

A major advantage of a using a post-hoc validation sample for estimating these quantities (and subsequently quantifying the associated uncertainties) is that it does not place any requirements on the methods used to create the strata. This means that one is free to build mappings with machine learning techniques (such as Random Forests, Support Vector Machines and Artificial Neural Networks [21]) without needing to be concerned that many of these methods can be black box in nature. Another advantage is that one has much more freedom when collecting training samples. This is because one is not restricted to the specific stochastic structures of sampling, which are necessary when inferring uncertainties directly from a model. This is especially important when dealing with machine learning techniques, as we often have to rely on cheaper, less structured methods, of collecting training data (e.g. polygon sampling, using found data, etc.). Thirdly, it is possible to apply this method with nothing more than the results from an error matrix. This especially useful when analysing historical or third party maps.

The current recommended approach of uncertainty quantification from error matrices is to take a frequentist approach and rely on asymptotic normality estimates to provide confidence intervals [22, 23]. The drawback of this approach is that it is not appropriate when relevant entries of an error matrix are not sufficiently large. Furthermore, because relevant events may be rare (e.g. instances of incorrect labelling between two contrast classes) additional sampling of validation data is not always a practical solution to this problem. Whilst there are methods for dealing with low entry counts in simple situations [24–26], complications arise when one needs to correct estimates for disproportionate sampling across the strata. The main consequences of these complications is that the resultant confidence intervals are of little practical use, either due to their excessively cautious nature, or by the fact the fundamental statement that is implicitly made by confidence intervals (i.e. nominal coverage) cannot be reliably verified.

The goal of this paper is to review existing methods for quantifying uncertainty with the aim of providing an approach that can deal with these aforementioned complications. In what follows, we firstly review the current recommended practice for uncertainty quantification under a frequentist perspective based on the following criteria: transparency, generalisability, suitability when stratified sampling and suitability in low count situations (see Sect. 2 for further details).

We then make a case that a Bayesian approach is more suited as a default for method uncertainty quantification when judged by these criteria.

2 Terminology and Formulating the Problem

We begin by supposing that we have k mutually exclusive strata and that, within in each stratum, instances can be classified as belonging to one of c discrete values. Typically, in land cover mapping applications these instances are single pixels or small clusters of pixels, each approximately of equal size. For the sake of convince we assume that these instances are always at the single pixel level and hence refer to instances as pixels.

Let $p_i \in [0, 1]^c, i = 1, \ldots, k$ denote the proportion vector for population i where $(p_i)_j$ is the proportion of pixels that are within strata i that belong to class j where $j = 1, .., c$. We define a global quantity as any quantity that can be expressed as a function of $p := (p'_1, \ldots, p'_k)'$. i.e. a global quantity is any quantity that can be expressed in the form $g(p)$. Examples of global quantities in land cover mapping applications are performance metrics such as user, producer, and overall accuracies along with large scale measurements such as the total areas. In practice not all entries of p will be needed in the calculation of g. Here we will write "relevant p" as a short hand to "all entries p that are necessary in the calculation of g".

Next suppose that for each of the k strata, we draw a random sample of pixels (with replacement) of size $n_1, \ldots n_k$ respectively and let x_i denote the response vector for strata i with $(x_i)_j$ indicating the number of the n_i pixels drawn from strata i that belong to class j.

Within this notation, the aim of this paper is to review current methods of quantifying uncertainty for estimates of $g(p)$ made with $n := (n_1, \ldots n_k)'$ and $x := (x'_1, \ldots, x'_K)'$.

Note that estimates obtained from an error matrix are a special case of this whereby $k = c$ and x is a vector representation of said error matrix. The evaluation of methods discussed in this paper will be based on the following four criteria.

Transparency – the extent to which one can explicitly state, justify and analyse any assumptions or choices necessary within the method. This is an important criterion as this will influence how likely end users will have confidence in the results of methods.

Generalisability – the suitability and ease of applying a method when considering a wide variety of global quantities or when estimates for global quantities are part of a modelling chain. Essentially, this criterion is included to assess how flexible a given method is to choices of g. This important land cover mapping applications as g is regularly a non-trivial function of the components of p (e.g. ratios, weighted sums etc.). In addition, global quantities are regularly used inputs in other models. Hence, it is common that one may wish to propagate the uncertainty for an estimate of g into another quantity.

Suitability for stratified sampling - how appropriate the method is in situations when a stratified random sampling has taken place. Stratified random sampling has been common practice when collecting test samples as it allows for a more efficient reduction in uncertainty under the currently recommended approach [27]. Hence, it is important that a method of uncertainty quantification can also handle the case of stratified random sampling in order to similar advantage of these practices.

Suitability in low count situations - how appropriate the method is in situations when relevant entries (or combinations of entries) in x are close to, or exactly, zero (around 5 or less). Note, that low sample sizes can cause low count situations but these are not the same thing. For example, a sample of 25 success and 25 failures is not a low count situation but a sample of 499 successes and 1 failure would be a low count situation. It is important that a method of uncertainty quantification can handle low count situations as there serval naturally occurring factors that make them quite frequent. Such factors include a demand for higher resolutions (e.g. thematic, temporal), the relatively high cost of test sampling (reducing the total sample size) and situations when a single class dominates a stratum (making the alternative classes in said strum rare). The latter factor here is interconnected with the efficiency gains that can arise from stratified random sampling. This is because stratified random sampling is most effective when one can create strata in which a single class of pixel heavily dominates each stratum. However, such a stratification is likely to induce a low count situation. This can lead to a peculiar situation in where one can be a victim of one's own success when quantifying uncertainty with a method that cannot handle low count situations.

3   A Motivating Example: Georgian Deforestation

To motivate the work, we consider an example case study of estimating the total deforestation with the use of a land cover change map of Georgia [28].

This case study was chosen as it provides an example in which stratified sampling has taken place and one is in a low count situation for some of the entries of the error matrix. The general problem of monitoring deforestation plays an important role in estimating carbon emissions and is now required as part of recent EU policy [29].

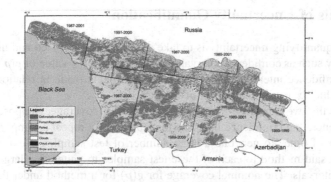

Fig. 1. Change map for Georgia, from circa 1990 to 2000 as presented in [28]

Table 1. Error table for the map presented in Fig. 1. 1 = forest-to-non-forest; 2 = stable forest; 3 = stable non-forest. W_i denotes the total area of the predicted classes in hectares.

		Reference				W_i
		(1)	(2)	(3)	n_i	
Prediction	(1)	51	23	13	87	22,044
	(2)	0	416	15	431	2,694,787
	(3)	1	20	410	431	4,071,576
	Total	52	459	438	949	6,788,387

For the sake of brevity, we shall only consider providing uncertainty quantification for estimates of the total area of deforestation along with the user accuracy and producer accuracy for the deforestation class. In terms of our notation, we define the total area ($\mathcal{A}_1$), user accuracy ($\mathcal{U}_1$) and producer accuracy $\mathcal{P}_1$ for the forest-to-non-forest class as

$$\mathcal{A}_1 = \sum_{i=1}^{k} W_i(\boldsymbol{p}_i)_1, \quad \mathcal{U}_1 := (\boldsymbol{p}_1)_1, \quad \mathcal{P}_1 = \frac{W_1(\boldsymbol{p}_1)_1}{\sum_{i=1}^{k} W_i(\boldsymbol{p}_i)_1} = \frac{W_1\mathcal{U}_1}{\mathcal{A}_1}$$

which we need to estimate from $\boldsymbol{x} := (\boldsymbol{x'}_1, \boldsymbol{x'}_2, \boldsymbol{x'}_3)'$ with

$$\boldsymbol{x}_1 = (51, 23, 13)', \ \boldsymbol{x}_2 = (0, 416, 15)', \ \boldsymbol{x}_3 = (1, 20, 410)'$$

We chose these accuracy quantities as they are standard practice in many land cover mapping applications and will allow us to demonstrate how different methods behave when assessing them against our chosen criteria. The user accuracy for the forest-to-non-forest class is intended to act as simple base case. The total area of deforestation is a quantity in this case in which we are in a low count situation and must account for stratified sampling for a relatively simple function (i.e. a weighted sum). The producer accuracy has the same qualities as total area but considers a slightly more complex case of g that involves a ratio of two unknown values. We also make a note that only $(\boldsymbol{p}_1)_1$ is relevant to $\mathcal{U}_1$ and $(\boldsymbol{p}_i)_1$, $i = 1, 2, 3$ are relevant to $\mathcal{A}_1$ and $\mathcal{P}_1$.

4 Methods of Uncertainty Quantification

One way of quantifying uncertainty is to take a frequentist approach and use measures of uncertainty such as confidence intervals. Here the unknown value of $g(p)$ is assumed fixed and confidence intervals are probabilistic statements made in relation to the test sample, to which x is one realisation of this process.

It is here that we introduce the concept of nominal coverage. Suppose we have a method of generating confidence intervals for $g(p)$ and we repeat a sampling process a large number of times to generate a large number of test samples. Next suppose one was to apply said method to each of these test samples to generate a large number of confidence intervals. The nominal coverage for $g(p)$ for a method under this sampling process is then the proportion of these confidence intervals containing the unobserved true value of $g(p)$. For a method that quantifies uncertainty in terms of confidence intervals the validity of said method in particular situations is determined by how closely the stated level of coverage relates to its nominal coverage. For example, a method that creates a confidence interval at the $100(1 - \alpha)\%$ level is valid in a given scenario if it is reasonable to believe that the nominal coverage is approximately $1 - \alpha$. For the sake of simplicity, this paper will only focus on equal tailed intervals but much of the analysis will extend to the case when tails are not equal.

The use of confidence intervals is currently the recommended practice within the land cover mapping community [22, 23]. We place methods of creating confidence intervals in three categories, exact, heuristic and asymptotic.

Exact methods are methods that rely on using the exact distribution of the sampling processes (in relation to $g(p)$) to generate confidence intervals that have rational gauntness regarding nominal coverage. An example of this is Clopper-Pearson intervals [30].

Heuristic methods are methods that rely on approximations of sampling distributions or make slight amendments to exact methods. Typically, heuristic methods are in response to specific weakness of exact methods or when exact methods are not easily be derivable. An example of a heuristic approaches would be Agresti–Coull intervals [26] or using credible intervals from Bayesian methods with uninformative priors.

Asymptotic methods are methods that rely on asymptotic theory to generate confidence intervals. Whilst they could be considered specific cases of heuristic methods, we have chosen to separate them as they act differently when judge by our four criteria (see Sect. 5). The current recommended practice, that assumes a normal distribution based on asymptotic properties of the central limit theorem and bootstrapping methods [31] are examples of asymptotic methods.

An alternative approach to uncertainty quantification seen in land cover mapping applications is to express uncertainties in the form of probability density functions through **Bayesian inference** [32, 33]. Here allow for the uncertainty of relevant p to be represented as a probability distribution given the observed data and a predetermined prior distribution. From this, we can then quantify uncertainty for $g(p)$, either through direct inference or through simulation based methods.

Because frequentists and Bayesian methods take different perspectives on probability, it does not make sense to judge a Bayesian approach through the assessment of nominal coverage. In a frequentist setting, a confidence interval is a statement related to the behaviour of a large number of (hypothetical) samples. The uncertainty is on the sampling process, not on the parameter itself. Whereas a measure of uncertainty such as a credible interval (often described as a parallel to confidence intervals in a Bayesian setting) is a measure for the spread of the posterior distribution of model unknowns including parameters. This distribution is a rational quantification of uncertainty based on an observed sample and prior knowledge (or belief). Technically speaking, providing that we believe the prior placed on relevant p to be suitable, the resultant posterior distribution for $g(p)$ is valid. A potential difference in results due to set of priors deemed suitable is consistent here. An intuitive interpretation of this is that if two or more actors have different beliefs before observing sample, their beliefs after seeing the sample may also be different if their prior beliefs were sufficiently strong.

Hence when a method takes a Bayesian approach to uncertainty, we shall judge its suitably based on how sensitive the posterior distributions are to **similar** choices of prior distributions.

5 Analysis of Methods

We begin by applying several methods of uncertainty quantification on our Georgian deforestation example. For each method, we calculate an equal tailed confidence (or credible) interval at the 95% level. For the frequentist methods we apply the currently recommended normal approximation method as well as naïve bootstrapping (both asymptotic), a method based on using bounds of multiple Clopper-Pearson intervals for $(p_i)_1$ created at the $100(1 - \sqrt[3]{0.95})\%$ level (exact method) and the 95% credible intervals from the Bayesian methods (heuristic). For the Bayesian methods, we use a set of uninformative priors for each $(p_i)_1$ (Jeffery $(p_i)_1 \sim Beta(0.5, 0.5)$, uniform $(p_i)_1 \sim Beta(1, 1)$, (close to) improper $(p_i)_1 \sim Beta(0.01, 0.01)$).

Table 2. Limits for the confidence and credible intervals under various methods at (equal tailed, 95% level) for the Gregorian deforestation example.

| Method | Forest-to-non-forest | | | | | |
| | User accuracy | | Area (hectares) | | Producer accuracy | |
	Lower	Upper	Lower	Upper	Lower	Upper
Normal approximation	0.4935	0.6975	3734	41002	0.0986	1.0573
Bootstrap (Naive)	0.4944	0.6966	11201	42767	0.2881	1.0000
Clopper–Pearson (+)	0.4862	0.6983	10183	109361	0.0734	6.0035
Bayes (Jeffery)	0.4918	0.6931	14738	61445	0.2075	0.8620
Bayes (Uniform)	0.4913	0.6916	17830	73925	0.1721	0.7174
Bayes (Improper)	0.4923	0.6946	12488	48051	0.2669	0.9804

Form Table 2 we can see that all methods largely agree for the user accuracy of the deforestation class. This is largely expected as all methods will eventually converge to normality and the user accuracy is a relatively simple case. What is particular striking however, is the substantial differences we see for the intervals around the area of deforestation. This is problematic as the choice of method here could potentially have a serious impact on decision making.

In a frequentist setting, one must be able to confirm it is likely that the stated level of confidence is at least close to nominal coverage. However, analysing nominal coverage in general is difficult and will depend on many factors including the sample size n, the level of confidence, g and the value of unknown p. In practice, the dependence on unknown p will generally mean that one will never be able to give the exact nominal coverage. Rather, we may need to consider multiple plausible values of relevant entries of p based on x to build a case of representative coverage.

As an example, let us consider a confidence interval at the 95% level for $(p_1)_3$ generated with the normal approximation method and naive bootstrapping based on a sample size in the presented example (431). In Fig. 2 we can see that both methods suffer from considerable under-coverage if $(p_1)_3$ is close to 0. A low count situation observed in $(x_1)_3$ in the present example is evidence that $(p_1)_3$ may be close to 0.

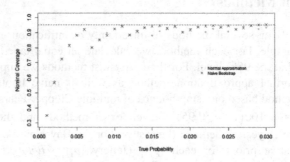

Fig. 2. Coverage plot for the normal approximation method and naïve bootstrapping based on a sample size of 431 (the same as stratum (3) in the Georgian example).

This may call in to question the validity of both these methods when quantifying uncertainty for the total area of deforestation as this quantity replies heavily on $(p_1)_3$ (especially with W_3 being so large). However, a more robust analysis is likely unviable since the relative area relies on three values of p, and so one would need a 3-dimensional equivalent of Fig. 2.

For the other frequentists methods, whilst the Clopper–Pearson (+) intervals are guaranteed to provide sufficient coverage, the unknown over-coverage may be so high that this is also misleading.

For each of the different types of frequentist methods, there is a trade-off between how well they satisfy of each of our criteria. A more systematic analysis of how each type of method meets our criteria is presented in the appendix in Table A1. The major findings are that, most suffer from transparency issues in more complex situations due to the difficulties in coverage assessment. No type of method is likely to be suitable across all four criteria. Of course, not all criteria are relevant in all situations and so some methods may be suitable in individual cases. The problem is that no method is consistent enough across all four criteria to be a good default approach.

In practice, this can mean having to choose between many methods when taking a frequentist approach to uncertainty. This type of approach would rely on expertise in said methods and suitable diagnostic tests (which may not even be available in situations that are more complex).

In comparison, one is more likely to better satisfy our criteria when taking a Bayesian approach to uncertainty quantification (see Table A1 for further details). This is mainly due to three important advantages

The first advantage is that **issues related to coverage are avoided** as Bayesian analysis is an entirely different form of uncertainty quantification.

The second advantage is that **sensitivity to prior choice can be assessed post-hoc**. This means we can effectively "wait and see" if prior sensitivity is going to be an issue at all. In comparison, one must have assurances related to nominal coverage for every new situation with frequentist methods.

Thirdly, **the problem of prior sensitivity is not as detrimental as the problems we face in frequentist settings** due to coverage assessment. This is because the validity of the results is determined how reasonable we believe the priors to be. In practice, a set of standard prior choices is often agreed in advanced by communities (e.g. a set of uninformative priors). We would argue that this is an easier task than say having communities agree which frequentist methods to use in which particular situations.

In the context of the Georgian deforestation example, consider the Bayesian results for the area of deforestation. The results in this case differ by a relatively considerable amount. Whilst this is not ideal, these results are robust and informative for decision makers. This is different to the frequentist setting we have considerably different confidence intervals that are, potentially, misleading due to their level of miss-coverage.

One may be tempted to make a similar statement with the frequentist approaches. The problem with this is that we need to assume that all the individual methods are appropriate to begin with (otherwise, they may act as disinformation). In order to do this, one must assess the coverage for all methods in a given situation, which as we have discussed already, is often very difficult.

6 Discussion and Future Work

So far we have discussed the advantages of a Bayesian approach to quantifying uncertainty from an error matrix produced by single sample and map. However, a Bayesian approach to uncertainty quantification has the potential to offer many more advantages that are not available in frequentist approaches. Whilst an in-depth exploration of these advantages goes beyond the scope of this paper, they do offer some insights in to where future work may lead in terms of uncertainty quantification from a Bayesian perspective. Such work could include:

A Formal Means of Including Prior Information. The inclusion of a prior distribution means that we can formally include information in to our uncertainty quantification before observing our sample. This information may come from historical maps or biased samples (e.g. citizen science data). This could substantially the reduce the sizes of test samples needed to reduce uncertainty to satisfactory levels, especially investigating the prevalence of rare classes (e.g. when monitoring land-use change). Note that prior information cannot be formally incorporated in frequentist approaches, as statements such as confidence intervals are related to the sample itself under fixed parameter values.

Predicting the Impact of Additional Test Samples on Uncertainty Reduction. Suppose we wish to reduce the uncertainty further by collecting a further test sample. When predicting the effects of further test sampling, their impact on the degree of uncertainty is often governed by relevant p, which we can estimate based on an initial test sample. When taking a frequentist approach to uncertainty quantitation, it is difficult to propagate uncertainty in these initial estimates.

However, when the uncertainty for relevant p is represented as a probability distribution, one can propagate this forward. The practical advantage this gives is that one can have a more reliable means of assessing the trade-offs between the cost of additional samples and their likely impact on uncertainty. In addition, it allows us to compare how different distributions across strata may effect uncertainty. This would be a key step in any work assessing the efficiency of different sampling strategies.

7 Conclusion

When making estimates from mappings built with machine learning techniques, one must often rely on error matrices obtained from test sampling to quantify uncertainty for these estimates. The current recommended approach in this setting is a frequentist one that assumes asymptotic normality of estimates. This is often unsuitable when estimating the prevalence of rare classes or when strata are homogenous. Alternative methods may exist for simple cases, but they do not extend to more advanced situations that are relied upon in land cover mapping applications. Furthermore, the assessment of any frequentist method itself is near impossible in more complex situations because of the difficulties in analysing nominal coverage.

In comparison, Bayesian inference can offer an approach to uncertainty quantification that is better suited for land cover mapping applications. It is for these reasons that we recommend that future work related to uncertainty quantification from error matrices should be focused on the development and refinement of Bayesian approaches rather than looking towards more advanced frequentist methods.

Appendix

Table A1. Analysis of the method types based on the four chosen criteria.

Method Type	Transparency	Generalisability	Suitability for stratified sampling	Suitability in low count situations
Frequentists (General)	(+) Coverage can be empirically verified in simple cases. (−) Exact coverage is impossible due to the discrete nature of x. (−) Assurances regarding coverage must be obtained beforehand and is dependent on many parameters (some of which are unknown).	(+) Any method can easily be extended when is when g with only one relevant on a single entry of p. (−) Difficult to verify coverage empirically when g requires multiple entries of p.	(−) Issues arise when analysing nominal coverage empirically when one needs to correct for stratified sampling. (g requires multiple entries of p)	(−) Low count situations, are an indicator of extreme miss-coverage for many popular methods.
Frequentists (Exact)	(+) Sufficient coverage can by ratICnally guaranteed in specific cases. (−) Over-coverage may be extreme in low sample sizes.	(−) Difficult to apply for general g (without relying on overly conservative methods).	(−) Over-coverage becomes more severe as the number of strata increases.	(+) Guaranteed to provide sufficient coverage in low count situations. (−) Over-coverage may be extreme in low count situations.

(continued)

Table A1. (*continued*)

Method Type	Transparency	Generalisability	Suitability for stratified sampling	Suitability in low count situations
Frequentists (Heuristic)	(−) Issues analysing nominal coverage empirically when stratified sampling or g requires multiple entries of p.	(+) Easy to apply, even for more complex forms of g. (±) Theoretically has the potential to be computationally expensive. Mitigatable with aggregation properties and rarely an issue in many applications.	(+) Application can be easily extended when stratified sampling. (+) Theoretical results extend easily when stratified sampling.	(+) Near appropriate coverage is verifiable in simple low count situations.
Frequentists (Asymptotic)	(−) Verifying the assumptions based on asymptotic results is difficult for complex g (−) difficult to know how large sample sizes should be in general.	(+) Theoretical results extend for complex g. (+) Some methods (e.g. bootstrapping) can be calculated with simulation based methods, lowering the mathematical expertise required (useful when as g becomes more complex)	(+) Many asymptotic based methods can be easily applied when accounting for stratified sampling. (e.g. normal approximation, bootstrapping). (+) Theoretical results extend for the case of stratified sampling.	(−) Common methods are verifiably unsuitable in low count situations in simple cases. (e.g. normal approximation, naive bootstrapping).
Bayesian (Simple method)	(+) Credible intervals are a measure of spread of a posterior; hence, one does not need to show sufficient coverage. (+) Differences due to prior choice can be analysed post-hoc.	(+) Easy to apply, even for more complex forms of g. (+) Posterior distributions can be generated through simulation based methods. (±) Can become computationally expensive but this mitigatable with conjugate priors and aggregation properties.	(+) Application can be easily extended when stratified sampling. (−) Increasing the number of strata increases the number of subjective prior choices one has to make.	(±) Results can be sensitive to prior choice in low count situations. Uncertainty quantitation is still viable (if slightly weaker) in prior sensitive situations.

References

1. Birdsey, R., et al.: Approaches to monitoring changes in carbon stocks for REDD+. Carbon Manag. **4**(5), 519–537 (2013)
2. DeFries, R.S., Houghton, R.A., Hansen, M.C., Field, C.B., Skole, D., Townshend, J.: Carbon emissions from tropical deforestation and regrowth based on satellite observations for the 1980 s and 1990 s. Proc. Natl. Acad. Sci. **99**(22), 14256–14261 (2002)
3. Myneni, R.B., et al.: A large carbon sink in the woody biomass of Northern forests. Proc. Natl. Acad. Sci. **98**(26), 14784–14789 (2001)
4. Schwalm, C.R., et al.: Reduction in carbon uptake during turn of the century drought in western North America. Nat. Geosci. **5**(8), 551 (2012)
5. Asner, G.P., Broadbent, E.N., Oliveira, P.J.C., Keller, M., Knapp, D.E., Silva, J.N.M.: Condition and fate of logged forests in the Brazilian Amazon. Proc. Natl. Acad. Sci. **103**(34), 12947–12950 (2006)
6. Potapov, P.V., et al.: Eastern Europe's forest cover dynamics from 1985 to 2012 quantified from the full Landsat archive. Remote Sens. Environ. **159**, 28–43 (2015)
7. Shi, W., Liu, J., Du, Z., Stein, A., Yue, T.: Surface modelling of soil properties based on land use information. Geoderma **162**(3–4), 347–357 (2011)
8. Giustarini, L., Hostache, R., Matgen, P., Schumann, G.J.P., Bates, P.D., Mason, D.C.: A change detection approach to flood mapping in Urban areas using TerraSAR-X. IEEE Trans. Geosci. Remote Sens. **51**(4), 2417–2430 (2013)
9. Hussain, M., Chen, D., Cheng, A., Wei, H., Stanley, D.: Change detection from remotely sensed images: from pixel-based to object-based approaches. ISPRS J. Photogramm. Remote Sens. **80**, 91–106 (2013)
10. Rindfuss, R.R., Walsh, S.J., Turner, B.L., Fox, J., Mishra, V.: Developing a science of land change: challenges and methodological issues. Proc. Natl. Acad. Sci. **101**(39), 13976–13981 (2004)
11. Keegan, K.M., Albert, M.R., McConnell, J.R., Baker, I.: Climate change and forest fires synergistically drive widespread melt events of the Greenland Ice Sheet. Proc. Natl. Acad. Sci. **111**(22), 7964–7967 (2014)
12. Knyazikhin, Y., et al.: Hyperspectral remote sensing of foliar nitrogen content. Proc. Natl. Acad. Sci. **110**(3), E185–E192 (2013)
13. McMenamin, S.K., Hadly, E.A., Wright, C.K.: Climatic change and wetland desiccation cause amphibian decline in Yellowstone National Park. Proc. Natl. Acad. Sci. **105**(44), 16988–16993 (2008)
14. Syed, T.H., Famiglietti, J.S., Chambers, D.P., Willis, J.K., Hilburn, K.: Satellite-based global-ocean mass balance estimates of interannual variability and emerging trends in continental freshwater discharge. Proc. Natl. Acad. Sci. **107**(42), 17916–17921 (2010)
15. Fialko, Y., Sandwell, D., Simons, M., Rosen, P.: Three-dimensional deformation caused by the Bam, Iran, earthquake and the origin of shallow slip deficit. Nature **435**(7040), 295 (2005)
16. Khatami, R., Mountrakis, G.: Implications of classification of methodological decisions in flooding analysis from Hurricane Katrina. Remote Sens. **4**(12), 3877–3891 (2012)
17. Alcantara, C., Kuemmerle, T., Prishchepov, A.V., Radeloff, V.C.: Mapping abandoned agriculture with multi-temporal MODIS satellite data. Remote Sens. Environ. **124**, 334–347 (2012)
18. Anderson, M.C., Allen, R.G., Morse, A., Kustas, W.P.: Use of Landsat thermal imagery in monitoring evapotranspiration and managing water resources. Remote Sens. Environ. **122**, 50–65 (2012)

19. Asner, G.P., et al.: Large-scale impacts of herbivores on the structural diversity of African savannas. Proc. Natl. Acad. Sci. **106**(12), 4947–4952 (2009)
20. Mendenhall, C.D., Sekercioglu, C.H., Brenes, F.O., Ehrlich, P.R., Daily, G.C.: Predictive model for sustaining biodiversity in tropical countryside. Proc. Natl. Acad. Sci. **108**(39), 16313–16316 (2011)
21. Khatami, R., Mountrakis, G., Stehman, S.V.: A meta-analysis of remote sensing research on supervised pixel-based land-cover image classification processes: general guidelines for practitioners and future research. Remote Sens. Environ. **177**, 89–100 (2016)
22. Olofsson, P., Foody, G.M., Stehman, S.V., Woodcock, C.E.: Making better use of accuracy data in land change studies: Estimating accuracy and area and quantifying uncertainty using stratified estimation. Remote Sens. Environ. **129**, 122–131 (2013)
23. Olofsson, P., Foody, G.M., Herold, M., Stehman, S.V., Woodcock, C.E., Wulder, M.A.: Good practices for estimating area and assessing accuracy of land change. Remote Sens. Environ. **148**, 42–57 (2014)
24. DasGupta, A., Cai, T.T., Brown, L.D.: Interval estimation for a binomial proportion. Stat. Sci. **16**(2), 101–133 (2001)
25. Wallis, S.: Binomial confidence intervals and contingency tests: mathematical fundamentals and the evaluation of alternative methods. J. Quant. Linguist. **20**(3), 178–208 (2013)
26. Agresti, A., Coull, B.A.: Approximate Is Better than "Exact" for Interval Estimation of Binomial Proportions. Am. Stat., vol. 52, no. 2, pp. 119–126 (1998). Published by : Taylor & Francis, Ltd. on behalf of the American Statistical Association Stable URL : http://www.jstor.org/stable/2685469 Approximate is Better than " Ex,"
27. Wagner, J.E., Stehman, S.V.: Optimizing sample size allocation to strata for estimating area and map accuracy. Remote Sens. Environ. **168**, 126–133 (2015)
28. Olofsson, P., et al.: Implications of land use change on the national terrestrial carbon budget of Georgia. Carbon Balance Manag. **5**, 4 (2010)
29. O.T.E.U. Council: Regulation (EU) No 2018/841 of 30 May 2018 on the inclusion of greenhouse gas emissions and removals from land use, land use change and forestry in the 2030 climate and energy framework, and amending Regulation (EU) No 525/2013 and Decision No 529/2013/EU, vol. 2018, no. October 2003, pp. 1–25 (2018)
30. Clopper, C.J., Pearson, E.S.: The use of confidence or fiducial limits illustrated in the case of the binomial. Biometrika **26**(4), 404–413 (1934)
31. Davison, A.C., Hinkley, D.V.: Bootstrap Methods and Their Application. Cambridge University Press, Cambridge (1997)
32. Denham, R., Mengersen, K., Witte, C.: Bayesian analysis of thematic map accuracy data. Remote Sens. Environ. **113**(2), 371–379 (2009)
33. Finley, A.O., Banerjee, S., McRoberts, R.E.: A Bayesian approach to multi-source forest area estimation. Environ. Ecol. Stat. **15**(2), 241–258 (2008)

Machine Learning Algorithms for Food Intelligence: Towards a Method for More Accurate Predictions

Ioanna Polychronou(✉), Panagis Katsivelis, Mihalis Papakonstantinou, Giannis Stoitsis, and Nikos Manouselis

Agroknow, 110 Pentelis, 15126 Maroussi, Greece
{ioanna.polyxronou,katsivelis.panagis,mihalis.papakonstadinou,
stoitsis,nikosm}@agroknow.com
https://www.agroknow.com

Abstract. It is evident that machine learning algorithms are being widely impacting industrial applications and platforms. Beyond typical research experimentation scenarios, there is a need for companies that wish to enhance their online data and analytics solutions to incorporate ways in which they can select, experiment, benchmark, parameterise and choose the version of a machine learning algorithm that seems to be most appropriate for their specific application context. In this paper, we describe such a need for a big data platform that supports food data analytics and intelligence. More specifically, we introduce Agroknow's big data platform and identify the need to extend it with a flexible and interactive experimentation environment where different machine learning algorithms can be tested using a variation of synthetic and real data. A typical usage scenario is described, based on our need to experiment with various machine learning algorithms to support price prediction for food products and ingredients. The initial requirements for an experimentation environment are also introduced.

Keywords: Machine learning · Deep learning · Data analytics · Big data · Experimentation method

1 Introduction

Within the field of artificial intelligence, machine learning algorithms have been widely extended and adopted over the last decade [1]. A driving force for this development have been developments made in the area of neural networks with methodologies such as deep learning [2]. Deep learning networks and their implementations within real-life solutions have a large impact that goes beyond the academic world, giving rise to disruptive approaches in industrial applications as well. However, researchers and developers, who use models and algorithms in a variety of projects and contexts, have yet to find interactive, straightforward and

© IFIP International Federation for Information Processing 2020
Published by Springer Nature Switzerland AG 2020
I. N. Athanasiadis et al. (Eds.): ISESS 2020, IFIP AICT 554, pp. 165–172, 2020.
https://doi.org/10.1007/978-3-030-39815-6_16

usable ways in which they may test, execute and parameterise such algorithms, without the need for source code adaptations or additional software installation. Testing methods and tools that may support their systematic implementation and evaluation in the context of near real-life applications are still limited. Experimental testing for these algorithms could be greatly facilitated by interactive experimentation environments that can also offer the computational, memory and storage power that large scale simulations require [3].

In the past, a number of software toolkits and frameworks have been proposed trying to address this need in the area of information filtering systems. Examples include systems like Lenskit [4], MyMediaLite [5], CollaFiS [6]; they are experimentation environments that can be used to set up, parameterize, and evaluate a variety of algorithms over a number of synthetic or real life data sets. In most cases, these have been software libraries and frameworks rather than actual experimentation environments that provide a graphical user interface. They also do not support preparatory tasks such as pre-processing, normalising and splitting the data sets into train and test components. Especially in the context of commercially deployed platforms for data analytics, it is challenging to experiment with a variety of algorithms, to test a variety of parameters to select the ones that seem to perform better over real data, and to customise the version(s) appropriate for each intelligent decision support feature.

In this paper, we propose an extension to the big data platform that supports food data analytics and intelligence. More specifically, we consider the addition of a Prediction Experimentation Panel that has a graphical user interface to help our data scientists, as well as researchers and developers that we collaborate with, test a variety of prediction algorithms in an easy and customisable way and then be able to use a user-friendly dashboard to evaluate experimentation results. First, we describe our existing big data platform for which this extension is considered. Then, we describe a usage scenario that comes from our actual experiments and that is related to food price prediction. Finally, we propose some initial directions towards implementing such a Prediction Experimentation Panel in our big data platform.

2   The Big Data Platform

Agroknow's Big Data Platform is a back-end system responsible for collecting, processing, indexing and publishing heterogeneous food and agriculture data from a large variety of data sources. The platform is organized in a microservice architecture, with different technology components handling different aspects of the data lifecycle. All of the components are interconnected using well-defined connectors and API endpoints, each responsible for storing and processing different types of data. More specifically, the platform includes:

- the **Data APIs** component, which is the machine-readable interface to the different types of data collected in the platform. This part of the architecture is responsible for making data discoverable, but also for submitting new data assets back to the platform,

- the **Data Integration** component, through which data is submitted to the platform through a workflow of four unique steps: data collection, data filtering and transformation, data enrichment and data curation,
- the **Data Indexing** component, which performs data transformation to an appropriate format designed for performance optimization,
- the **Storage** component, which features various storage engine technologies, responsible for the physical archiving of data collections.
- the **Knowledge Classification** component, which provides rules and standards for the organization of data records stored and processed by the platform
- the **Data Processing** component, which is responsible for hosting individual text mining, machine learning and data correlation scripts that can be used in a variety of contexts as standalone pieces of code or as web services through the so-called Intelligence APIs.

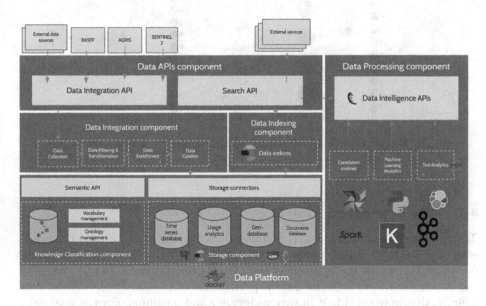

Fig. 1. The Agroknow Data Platform architecture

3   Towards a Method for More Accurate Predictions: The Case of Food Price Prediction

To explore typical design options for parameterization, one can examine the plethora of proposed approaches in machine and deep learning algorithms. These engage various methods and techniques at each step of a prediction workflow, leading to a wide number of parameters that may be useful for scientific experimentation. Those can also be categorized under two generic steps or processes: the **data preparation** process and the **execution and evaluation** process. Figure 2 schematically illustrates a typical experimentation process that our data science team has to follow in order to run only a handful of experiment iterations for just one of the intelligent features that we examine: price prediction for food products and ingredients. In the sections that follow, we describe some of the required steps in more detail so that we illustrate the complexity of the tasks that we would like to support.

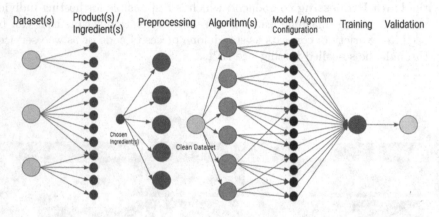

Fig. 2. The workflow followed during our food price prediction experiments

3.1 Data Preparation Process

The data preparation process [7] includes data cleaning, data integration, data selection, and data transformation. *Data Collection* is the process gathering the data that is relevant to the scope of the prediction hypothesis. In the context of the Agroknow Data Platform, data is periodically harvested from different data sources, that may provide it in various formats and mediums. For the food price prediction case, data were collected from the Hellenic Food Market, the European Commission and the Food and Agriculture Organization of the United Nations. *Data collection* corresponds to the *Dataset(s)* in price prediction experiment workflow (Fig. 2). *Data Cleaning* is the process of cleaning, filling the missing values and repurposing data, so that it is well-presented and concise, according to machine-readable standards. Our big data platform performs data cleaning in the way of transforming and filtering values, so that only relevant ones can then end up in machine-readable formats (eg. APIs). An extra process deals with the enrichment of missing or inadequate values of the data. In the case of food price prediction, lots of missing or malformed records and outliers were detected, thus resulting in incomprehensible values, which were automatically corrected. The finalized product was then curated by data experts that validated before making it available for the final step. *Data cleaning* corresponds to the *Preprocessing* in price prediction experiment workflow (Fig. 2).

Data Transformation and Selection: To bring the data in the appropriate format (that is going to be consumed by the prediction model), data needs to follow a specific structure that is understandable by the prediction model. In modern data platforms, this task can be dealt with the use of data indexing mechanisms. Our big data platform made use of its Data Indexing component for bringing slices of data in the desired format. The food price prediction model requires additional data normalization, that is carried out by the indexing software used with the provision of data aggregations or statistics of the indexed data. *Data Transformation and Selection* corresponds to the *Model/Algorithm configuration* in price prediction experiment workflow (Fig. 2).

3.2 Execution and Evaluation Process

Execution and evaluation process includes data mining, pattern evaluation, and knowledge representation. In **Data Mining process**, we have applied methods to extract patterns from the data. Also, this mining includes several tasks, such as classification, prediction, clustering, time series analysis, and so on. In food price prediction case we develop time series prediction algorithms. In this step have been tested six different algorithms that was Moving Average (Standard vs Exponential), K-Nearest Neighbors, LinearRegression, Arima, Long short-term memory and Prophet for more than 800 products. For each algorithm, the data were transformed and consolidated into different forms that are suitable for mining. All these configurations were done directly in the code. The algorithm was executed by running the algorithm in a python environment *Data Mining process* corresponds to the *Algorithms(s)* and *Training* in price prediction experiment workflow (Fig. 2). Last but not list is the **Evaluation** that validates the algorithm's result. The process of evaluating data using analytical and logical reasoning to examine each component of the data provided. If the results are not as expected then the researcher should go back to the previous steps and make changes. *Evaluation* corresponds to the *Validation* in price prediction experiment workflow (Fig. 2).

3.3 Designing a Prediction Experimentation Panel

The Prediction Experimentation Panel helps researchers and developers to develop the processes between transformation and evaluation process via a user-friendly platform. In particular, the user (researcher or developer) can choose from a drop-down menu the dataset that is clean and ready to use, the algorithm that the user wants to experiment with and then, fill in the parameters that each algorithm needs. Finally, the user executes the algorithm. The execution is part of data processing component and in particular part of machine learning analytics (Fig. 1). When the execution finishes the user can evaluate

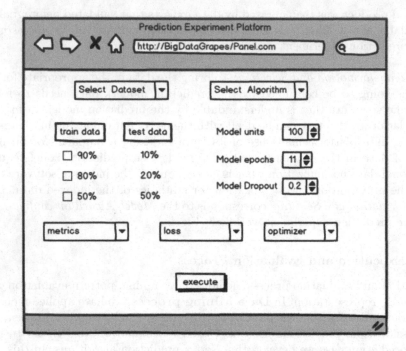

Fig. 3. Initial mockup for prediction experimentation panel

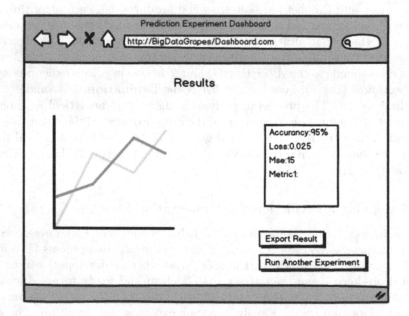

Fig. 4. Initial mockup for prediction experimentation dashboard

the experiment's results using the platform' s dashboards. Results storage in database storage component (Fig. 1). Dashboard includes charts that is line, pie, area, bar, scatter, etc and comments about metrics in order to evaluation the algorithm efficiently.

Data Selection: When a user select a dataset from a drop-down menu, in particular she sends a request to the database through the search API and the response is the selected dataset. The user has the opportunity to parametrize the request by filling in some fields such as date duration and data source. As a result, the response will be a sub-dataset with specific duration and data source. Otherwise, the response is the whole dataset. These parametres are dynamically change in order to fit with the dataset's metadata.

Algorithm Selection: Regarding algorithm selection, user select the algorithm that prefers and fill in the parametres. These parametres dynamically change based on each algorithm needs. This process is part of data processing component (Fig. 1). In a few words the panel adapts dynamically to the requirements of datasets and algorithms Finally, the evaluation involved comparing diagrams of different algorithms.

This process is quite time consuming and developers or researchers need to change the code to make changes to some parameters of an algorithm or a dataset. When it comes to evaluating results, comparing diagrams and metrics is quite difficult when you have so many different algorithms and datasets.

Figures 3 and 4 show initial mockups for prediction experimentation panel. In order to execute Long short-term memory algorithm for price prediction experiment, the panel must have the following parameters which is dataset and algorithm selection from a dropdown menu, the train and the test data, metrics, loss and optimizer in order to evaluate the model (Fig. 3). These parameters have dynamically change for a different algorithms because needs are different. Results are included in a dashboard and the user can export them (Fig. 3).

The figures that are included illustrate the way that we are designing the Experimentation Panel, through a number of graphical mockups that are guiding our implementation work. In order to design a user-friendly Experimentation environment helps researcher and developers to support their experiments, we are in contact with researcher as well as developers that is Agricultural University of Athens (AUA), National Institute of Agricultural Research (INRA), National Research Council (CNR) to get an efficient design for the panel. For this reason, after the implementation of the first demo there will be an evaluation by the users I mentioned above to make the necessary improvements.

4   Conclusions and Next Steps

The implementation of the Experimentation Panel within our big data platform is already undergoing. Our intention is to demonstrate at the workshop a live demonstration of the food price prediction experiment, using the new capabilities of our platform. We believe that such approaches can greatly facilitate the work of data scientists and software developers in companies like ours, as they offer a useful and practical tool that supports extensive experimentation. As part of our R&D work, we are also incorporating novel machine learning algorithms developed by colleagues in academic environments. We want to offer a joint environment in which we can use the rich and heterogeneous data that our big data platform is continuously collecting and processing, to support the experiments of other colleagues in the community. This Experimentation Panel can be an extension to other similar data platforms.

Acknowledgements. This work is funded with the support by European Commission, and more specifically project Big Data Grapes "Big Data to Enable Global Disruption of the Grapevine-powered industries" (Grant No. 780751) (http://www. bigdatagrapes.eu/), which is funded by the schema "Research and innovation actions (RIA)" under the work programme topic "ICT-16-2017 - Big data PPP: research addressing main technology challenges of the data economy". This publication reflects the views only of the authors, and the Commission cannot be held responsible for any use, which may be made of the information contained therein.

References

1. Samek, W., Wiegand, T., Müller, K.R.: Explainable artificial intelligence: understanding, visualizing and interpreting deep learning models. arXiv preprint. arXiv:1708.08296 (2017)
2. Feelders, A., Daniels, H., Holsheimer, M.: Methodological and practical aspects of data mining. Inf. Manag. **37**(5), 271–281 (2000)
3. Manouselis, N., Stoitsis, G.: Towards an e-science environment for collaborative filtering researchers. Int. J. Digit. Libr. Syst. (IJDLS) **4**(1), 41–72 (2014)
4. Ekstrand, M.D., Ludwig, M., Kolb, J., Riedl, J.: LensKit: a modular recommender framework. In: RecSys (2011)
5. Gantner, Z., Rendle, S., Freudenthaler, C., Schmidt-Thieme, L.: MyMediaLite: a free recommender system library. In: RecSys (2011)
6. Manouselis, N., Costopoulou, C.: Designing a web-based testing tool for multi-criteria recommender systems. Eng. Lett. Spec. Issue Web Eng. **13**(3) (2006)
7. Kietz, J.U., Serban, F., Bernstein, A., Fischer, S.: Data mining workflow templates for intelligent discovery assistance and auto-experimentation. In: Third-Generation Data Mining: Towards Service-Oriented Knowledge Discovery (SoKD-10), pp. 1–12 (2010)

Interoperability of Solutions in a Crisis Management Environment Showcased in Trial-Austria

Gerald Schimak[1], Dražen Ignjatović[1(✉)], Erik Vullings[2(✉)], and Maurice Sammels[3(✉)]

[1] AIT Austrian Institute of Technology GmbH,
Giefinggasse 4, 1210 Vienna, Austria
{gerald.schimak,drazen.ignjatovic}@ait.ac.at
[2] TNO, The Hague, The Netherlands
erik.vullings@tno.nl
[3] XVR Simulation, Delft, The Netherlands
sammels@xvrsim.com

Abstract. Crisis Management (CM) is a challenging area when it comes to connecting solutions aiming to support the various tasks involved in handling of CM situations. DRIVER+ [1] an EU-funded project launched in 2014 was setting up a technical infrastructure (so called Test-bed) that allows to interconnect solutions, so they can interact and exchange all crisis relevant information that commanders need, to make their decisions and plan their actions related to a specific crisis.

To verify the DRIVER+ Test-bed as well as the DRIVER+ Trial Guidance Methodology [3] and furthermore, to overcome identified CM gaps [2], a series of Trials was setup. Trial-Austria was the fourth one to be executed.

This Trial was especially challenging as it was held as a field exercise in parallel to a huge European Civil Protection Exercise (called IRONORE2019). The scenario to be dealt with was an earthquake scenario.

The developed methodology, Test-bed as well as various solutions taking part in DRIVER+ are a perfect base and platform to deal with whatever hazard (e.g. chemical, physical, etc.) is endangering our environment or wellbeing.

Keywords: Crisis Management · DRIVER+ · Trial · Earthquake · Interoperability · Innovative solutions · Environmental hazards

1 Introduction/Trial/Scenario

1.1 Introduction

The scale and pace of crises pose enormous challenges to the Crisis Management (CM) sector, with new threats emerging all the time. An already complex field must also strive to integrate new technologies and methods, cope with a rapidly changing infrastructure, understand evolving risks, be effective across cultural, administrative and national boundaries and engage with populations to enhance their resilience.

© IFIP International Federation for Information Processing 2020
Published by Springer Nature Switzerland AG 2020
I. N. Athanasiadis et al. (Eds.): ISESS 2020, IFIP AICT 554, pp. 173–187, 2020.
https://doi.org/10.1007/978-3-030-39815-6_17

Innovation is therefore critical but will only be successful if it is relevant and accessible to practitioners and operators. Many crises involve interfacing diverse CM systems and solutions. Major crises can also frequently involve more than one country or region, which may have differing CM infrastructures and cultures. It is also highly likely that this will necessitate interfacing different systems and combining different solutions. CM innovation must therefore be capable of meeting these multifaceted challenges and delivering solutions that are modular, flexible adaptable and interoperable.

The DRIVER+ Project [1] is dealing exactly with such challenges and within the project's run period (2014–2020) so-called Trials were launched, testing various technical and non-technical solutions.

Furthermore, DRIVER+ seeks to improve the way capability development and innovation management are tackled, by testing and evaluating solutions that address the operational needs of practitioners dealing with Crisis Management (CM).

Understanding the main problems that CM practitioners are currently facing is important to ensure that the project's results correspond to the practitioner's needs.

Thus, DRIVER+ drew up a list of 21 gaps [2] organized in five CM functional domains: decision support; information sharing and coordination; engaging the population; resource planning and logistics, as well as casualty management.

Four Trials (held in Poland, France, Netherlands and Austria) were set up and conducted during the project, which focused on these gaps, by identifying the differences between the current capability and the capability deemed necessary for an adequate performance of one or more crisis management tasks.

2   Trial Guidance Methodology

The Trial Guidance Methodology (TGM) [3, 4] is designed for Crisis Management practitioners as it facilitates a robust assessment of innovative solutions. The TGM provides step-by-step guidelines on how to assess them in non-operational contexts (such as a Trial) through a structured approach.

The methodology consists of three phases: preparation, execution and evaluation. The preparation phase results in a Trial design with multiple elements that are captured within a Trial Action Plan document, whose main outcome is meant to be applied and executed in the second phase. The Trial committee is responsible to ensure that all decisions taken in the first phase can be executed.

Each Trial consists of three elements: the tailoring of the Test-bed in accordance with the Trial design, the finalization and simulation of the identified scenario within the Test-bed, and the ability to carry out an assessment of the three DRIVER+ performance measurement dimensions (i.e. CM-, Trial-, solution dimension).

The execution phase ends with the running of the actual Trial, through the simulation of the pre-defined scenario, the deployment of potential innovative solutions and the collection of relevant data. In addition to the data collected during the Trial, additional feedback from external stakeholders (participating actively as Trial actors or passively as observers) is gathered after the main event.

During the third phase, the gathered data is processed in order to assess and analyse the real impact of the innovative solutions. This information is not only very useful for the CM practitioners but is also valuable for the solution providers concerned with further improvement of their solutions.

DRIVER+ has developed and issued a Trial Guidance Methodology Handbook providing an overview of what crisis managers would need to do in order to depict a specific operation and integrate new socio-technical solutions in their ways of working. The Handbook can be downloaded from [3]. It offers not only a guidance on what to do by whom and when, but also introduce appropriate tools and methods to conduct those tasks. It also provides information about the DRIVER+ Test-bed technical infrastructure.

2.1   Test-Bed

The main purpose of the DRIVER+ technical infrastructure [5, 6] simply called Test-bed is to facilitate preparing, executing and evaluating a Trial. The Test-bed provides a toolkit to connect innovative CM solutions to each other and to integrate legacy systems to enable an exchange of information between them. That means it provides software components to:

- Connect solutions for data and information exchange
- Connect Simulators to create a fictitious, but realistic, crisis
- Create and control the scenario's storylines
- Record and collect observations and logs.

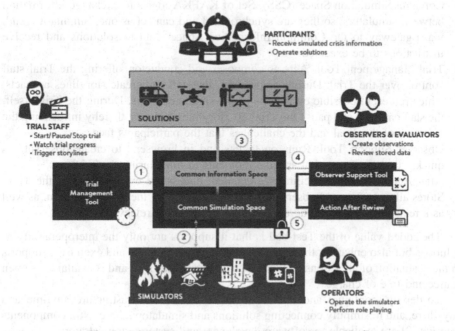

Fig. 1. DRIVER+ Test-bed technical infrastructure [5, 6]

Figure 1 presents the flow of information and interactions between the actors on the one hand and the involved solutions and tools on the other hand.

The flow as indicated in the Fig. 1 is as following:

1. The Trial starts: storylines are activated, and the fictitious crisis evolves.
2. Simulators process storylines and additional operator actions. Simulator data is sent to the solutions.
3. Solutions are fed with simulator data, they share information, and request actions from the Simulators.
4. Observers create observations, which are shared and recorded in the Test-bed.
5. The Trial ends and all logs and observations are collected for evaluation.

The connected components as shown in Fig. 1 are:

- SOLUTIONS: The solutions are assessed during the Trial. They can be connected to the Test-bed via CIS adapters such that they can send and receive data from other solutions and simulators.
- Common Information Space (CIS): Set of KAFKA topics [7] to exchange data between solutions, to receive data from and send commands to simulators.
- SIMULATORS: Provide a fictitious crisis during the Trial for participants and solutions, so solutions can be evaluated effectively in a realistic setting and such that participants feel immersed in the simulated crisis. They offer data and visualizations, such as 3D virtual reality views, flooding plots, fire progressions, panicking crowds and jammed traffic, simulated (social) media messages or a regional/national set of available resources.
- Common Simulation Space (CSS): Set of KAFKA topics to exchange information between simulators, so they are synchronized and can act as one. Simulators send, via a gateway to the Common Information Space, data to solutions and receive instructions to be executed.
- Trial Management Tool: Acts as composer and conductor, offering the Trial staff control over the Trial. During preparation, the staff can create storylines and acts, which represent possible evolutions of the simulated crisis. During the Trial itself, the staff can start and pause the Trial, its storylines and acts, thereby influencing the direction of the Trial and the challenges that the participants face.
- Observer Support Tool: Runs on tablets and in browsers, to create observations quickly that are targeted at specific moments in time during the Trial.
- After Action Review: Facilitates a detailed, data-based evaluation after the Trial. Stores all messages and observations exchanged during the Trial execution, as well as screenshots from running applications, so it can be reviewed together.

The added value of the Test-bed is that it supports not only the interoperability of solutions but also enhances the quality and realism of trainings and exercises, supports in the evaluation of all actions played/executed during the Trial and is available as open source and free of charge.

To deploy, configure and run the Test-bed technical infrastructure anytime and anywhere, and to simplify connecting solutions and simulators, these extra components (see Fig. 2) are available to software developers and system administrators.

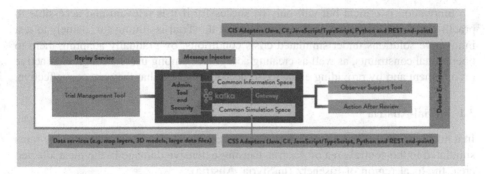

Fig. 2. DRIVER+ Test-bed software for developers and system administrators

- Docker environment: Part of the DRIVER+ website on which you can select the Test-bed components to be installed. It creates one installer containing the Docker images of all the selected components, such that these can be easily installed in one go.
- Replay Service: Developer component to send out a set of pre-recorded messages across one or more KAFKA topics. Can also be used to demonstrate solutions in a realistic context.
- Administrator Tool and security: Developer component to set-up and manage the KAFKA topics and security needed in the CIS and CSS for a specific Trial.
- Message Injector: Developer component to quickly send out a message on one KAFKA topic.
- Gateway: Translates messages from CSS to CIS and vice versa. CIS messages are standardized for use in emergency services communications. CSS messages are optimized for massive throughput and quick handling by simulators.
- Data Services: A set of complementary services to support the Trial, e.g. for storing large data sets, a height model, data from a flooding simulator, a set of fictitious resources, points of interest, map layers, etc.
  A detailed description of the Test-bed can be found at [8].

3   Benefits of Carrying Out Trials

The objective of a Trial is to assess and evaluate solutions in a realistic CM environment by providing a technical infrastructure for them to connect to each other and to provide a possibility for improvements by getting feedback from practitioners using the systems, applications or apps.

The DRIVER+ approach takes as a starting point the fact that there is a strong innovation momentum present in the Crisis Management community. At the same time, there is inertia to change, which can prevent this momentum from resulting in sustainable improvement. This points to the need for a better evidence base for Crisis Management capability investment decisions.

Innovation is critical but will only be successful if it is relevant and accessible to practitioners and operators. This is exactly what the Trial is aiming for, namely to test innovative solutions under simulated crisis conditions, by gradually adapting them to operational constraints, as well as creating acceptance among users through their active involvement and by providing evidence to decision makers that they are cost-effective.

3.1 Trial-Austria

In a nutshell: Trial-Austria focused on a severe earthquake and subsequent heavy rains simulated in the central area of Austria, causing extensive damage in the most affected area, the local region of Eisenerz (in Styria, Austria).

The main objective of Trial-Austria was to find solutions that overcome shortcomings and limitations [2] in the management and monitoring of spontaneous as well as affiliated volunteers on the crisis scene in terms of location, tasking, capabilities and duration of operations. It was also to highlight the ability to merge and synthesize disparate data sources and models in real time (e.g. visualization of resources, critical assets map, damaged objects/infrastructure etc.) to support incident commander decision making, situation assessment and exchanging crisis-related information.

The Trial also focused on (non-technical) solutions for providing psychological first aid and support as well as interaction with population (e.g. foster communication capabilities, registration of affected people, provide safety information, etc.).

Trial-Austria was organized by AIT Austrian Institute of Technology and hosted by the Austrian Red Cross in the centre of Austria at Eisenerz/Münichtal from Thursday 12th to Saturday 14th September 2019. The Trial was conducted as a multi-day field exercise run in parallel to the large-scale European Civil Protection exercise called IRONORE2019 [9].

3.2 Solutions in the Trial

3.2.1 CrowdTasker

CrowdTasker is a solution (from AIT Austrian Institute of Technology) for citizen involvement and community interaction. It supports informing citizens, eliciting contributions to the common operational picture by pre-registered parties and integrating efforts of self-organization. This is achieved by issuing assignments and situational information to a selected group of citizens based on their location and skill set, as well as offering a chatbot interface for emergent groups to participate using their own organizational infrastructure (such as social media groups).

The objective of CrowdTasker is to improve informed decision-making of both crisis managers and citizens. It enables professionals to rapidly query information from users at relevant locations and to provide meaningful assignments to citizens during preparation, mitigation and response. CrowdTasker helps to include several forms of volunteering [10, 11, 17] into the overall relief efforts [18]: spontaneous contributions of individual citizens, requests for contribution that originate from the crisis manager and are then executed by volunteers or even the integration of existing groups for guidance and support (Fig. 3).

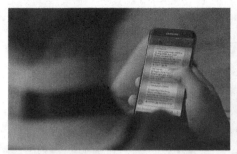

Fig. 3. Emergent groups organizing themselves with CrowdTasker application

During the Trial, CrowdTasker was used to coordinate pre-registered volunteers as well as to evaluate computer-supported interaction with spontaneous, emergent groups that are not registered. Pre-registered volunteers were tasked with confirming observations on site both via the smartphone application and a chatbot interface. Emergent groups were guided in their activity as well as supported in coordinating amongst each other to achieve more complex goals such as setting up tents, providing drinking water, picking up medical equipment from a specific spot, etc.

3.2.2   Airborne Terrestrial Situational Awareness

Real-time aerial imaging significantly enhances situational awareness [19] during major and large- scale disasters. DLR's (German Aerospace Centre's) solution "Airborne and Terrestrial Situational Awareness" comprises of several modules (see also Fig. 4) to provide such a real-time aerial imaging and analysis system.

Module 1 is the ground control station U-Fly, used to plan, engage and monitor aerial missions. The full-size research aircraft D-CODE, which is operated as a drone demonstrator with safety pilots on board, allowing drone-based missions to be executed without regulatory restrictions or safety concerns, executes the missions.

Module 2 is the 3K aerial camera system, specifically developed to acquire and evaluate aerial photographs in near real-time. In addition, it can transfer aerial imagery via data link directly from the aircraft to a mobile ground station to provide the data to decision makers and rescue forces immediately.

Module 3 is the centre for satellite-based crisis information, which analyses aerial imagery and generates crisis information maps.

Module 4, called KeepOperational, has traffic analysis and route planning capabilities.

Within Trial-Austria, the ground control station U-Fly and the 3K system were selected to demonstrate their capabilities. U-Fly was used to create aerial missions based on the request of the operational commander. These can either be missions to assess larger areas of a (simulated) crisis or to monitor and investigate certain points of interest. The 3K system provided live aerial images of these missions to U-Fly to support an assessment of the overall situation on the ground.

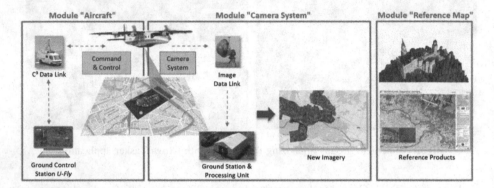

Fig. 4. DLR solution modules used in Trial-Austria

Fig. 5. DLR solution in flight planning in the command centre of the Trial-Austria

During the execution of different scenarios in the Trial, the operational commander requested aerial images of a certain area by informing the U-Fly remote pilot. The remote pilot created a mission based on this request and activated the mission. The drone demonstrator, equipped with the 3K system, collected aerial images of the area and sent them to the ground immediately. The geo-referenced aerial images were displayed in U-Fly in near real-time and was provided to practitioners and other solutions (e.g. vieWTerra Evolution) via the Test-bed (Fig. 5).

3.2.3   vieWTerra Evolution

VWORLD's vieWTerra Evolution [20], vieWTerra Base, vieWTerra Mobile form a combined "GIS & Simulation" suite of products allowing responders to rapidly build a virtual 4D representation (3D synthetic environment + time dimension) of any potential crisis area on Earth. These solutions provide a Common Operational Picture to both the crisis centre and the rescue units out in the field. vieWTerra Evolution is a 4D earth viewer as well as a data & assets integration and development platform. It presents an ellipsoidal model of the earth allowing its users to integrate their own precise datasets anywhere on the globe, without any area coverage limitations, or to access data streams (e.g. imagery, cartography layers).

It can be used to model any type of 3D scene on earth and create scenarios at their real-world location to simulate events in the crisis preparedness phase, and to serve as a global repository for building a custom earth-wide GIS, either used perfectly off-line or ported on to an on-line architecture in order to allow sharing of multiple information, data and assets from disparate sources between all stakeholders in the crisis response phase (3D entities, icons, shapefiles, geotagged reports, photos, videos, sound, multiple overlays such as disaster maps, heat maps, tactical situation, etc.).

Within Trial-Austria, it was used to instantly visualize newly-acquired imagery from drone acquisition and photos taken from the field, shared in real-time with the crisis centre and displayed into/mixed with the 3D view. vieWTerra Mobile complementary software allows display of the same data & assets database in a plug-in free web-browser-based HTML5 app.

vieWTerra Evolution was used as the Trial's data sink, which means that all information output from each solution was provided via the Test-bed technical infrastructure to vieWTerra Evolution where it was visualized to support the decision-making process of the crisis managers (Figs. 6 and 7).

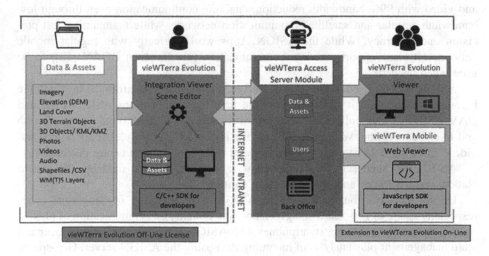

Fig. 6. VWORLDs vieWTerra suite

Fig. 7. vieWTerra Evolution visualizes in 3D the simulated environment all incoming crises relevant data and information

3.2.4 ASIGN

ASIGN is a solution by AnsuR Technologies [22] that helps reducing critical emergency and disaster response time. It is a complete all-in-one disaster assessment software tool for easy collection, optimal communication and effective management of operationally relevant critical information. ASIGN supports collection and communication of photos, videos, geo-texts, tracking, geo-zones, geo-alerts and assessment forms in a very bandwidth-efficient manner. Specifically, it can communicate photos and video with 99% bandwidth reduction, enabling communication even through low bandwidth cellular and satellite communication networks while maintaining full precision and accuracy. While the ASIGN Apps work perfectly with regular mobile networks, it also supports satellite communication (via Inmarsat BGAN [12]) to be used when needed.

ASIGN is comprised of the ASIGN Server, a cloud-based platform from which the incoming information is managed, plus the field user applications ASIGN PRO and UAV-ASIGN, which collect and send information from the field to the server, all with end-to-end encryption. With up to 99% saving in cost and capacity, ASIGN photos and videos from the field can arrive 100x faster at their coordination centre destination.

ASIGN has been actively developed with, and used in the field by, the United Nations, police forces and civil protection entities.

During the Trial the main tasks of ASIGN were: marking of dangerous zones (especially usage of geo-zones and geo-alerts functionality); Communication of photos, videos, text and tracks using smartphones with ASIGN software applications; User and team management plus analysis of incoming data using the ASIGN server; Geo-spatial photo and video clip communication, with mapping integration, for providing improved visual situational understanding; Use of 360° videos in addition to regular photos; Use of satellite communication via BGAN [12] where little bandwidth was available or no internet connection was possible by mobile devices (e.g. smartphones) (Fig. 8).

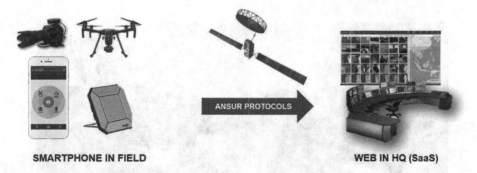

SMARTPHONE IN FIELD   WEB IN HQ (SaaS)

Fig. 8. ASIGN modules

3.2.5   PFA – Psychological First Aid

The psychological first aid (PFA) training (provided by the Danish Red Cross – as a non-technical solution) for spontaneous volunteers is a one-day training course, in which participants learn and get to practice the main skills needed to give good PFA in a crisis situation. They learn the internationally recognized principles of Look Listen Link, developed by the World Health Organization (WHO) [20]. The training includes sessions on these three principles as well as role plays, discussion sessions, sharing of knowledge and experience between the participants. Organizations responding to a crisis can implement the training to leverage the resources that spontaneous volunteers bring to a crisis in a positive and safe way.

The leadership seminar for engaging with spontaneous volunteers in crisis response combines the WHO's Look Listen Link principles for PFA, knowledge of caring for volunteers and theory on power relations to build the skills of field level leaders working for crisis response organizations to engage with spontaneous volunteers during crisis response. Through a series of exercises, analytical sessions, roleplays and discussion and reflection sessions, the participants activate their own experience and knowledge and learn from each other to be better placed to engage positively and constructively with spontaneous volunteers.

The ultimate goal of the solution is to alleviate human suffering and foster resilient societies.

The training contributes to this goal by supporting crisis management organizations' staff, so they can engage positively with spontaneous volunteers, and by building the capacity of PFA providers to deliver quality support.

Psychological first aid is a method of helping people in distress, so that they feel calm and supported in coping with their challenges. It is a way of assisting someone to manage their situation and make informed decisions. The basis of psychological first aid is caring about the person in distress. It involves paying attention to the person's reactions, active listening and, if needed, providing practical assistance, such as problem solving or help to access basic needs.

Both the leadership seminar as well as the PFA training for spontaneous volunteers where given during the Trial-Austria and practiced in different exercises throughout the course of the Trial (Fig. 9).

Fig. 9. Psychological first aid and leadership training held by the Danish Red Cross as a non-technical solution in Trial-Austria

3.3   Solutions Connected, Monitored and Evaluated via the Test-Bed Technical Infrastructure

Figure 10 provides the final data exchange diagram for Trial-Austria. It shows all solutions used during the Trial and which output they give to participants and how these participants interact with them. It also illustrates data flows of these solutions to/from the Test-bed technical infrastructure and which components of the Test-bed technical infrastructure are used.

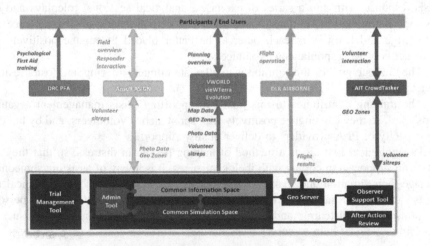

Fig. 10. Solutions' interactions via Test-bed

4 Conclusion

Trial-Austria was the last one in the series of four Trials. All Trials were organized to operationalize and test Crisis Management solutions. A final demonstration will take place in November 2019 and will incorporate the outcomes of all previous Trials.

The first results and recommendations have already been provided for Trial Poland (May 2018) and Trial France (October 2018) on the dedicated Trial section of the DRIVER+ website [13]. Subsequent paragraphs, however, are intended.

A first analysis of the feedbacks given for Trial-Austria was that commanders rated the exchanged and provided information as very valuable, impressive and innovative regarding decision making in the view of Crisis Management. All practitioners were impressed by the engagement and spirit of the solution providers working together in the Trial-Austria. One of the statements was "I got in contact with great experts of different countries' professionals and researchers from all over EU!".

Solution providers found it very valuable to see practitioners interacting with the operators of the solutions, on the one hand commanding them (learning the commander's speech) and on the other hand getting immediate recommendations and insight what functionality could be improved or was missing in their solution. This helped each solution provider to identify room for improvements and implement additional functionalities.

All outcomes (e.g. feedbacks to the Trial from Trial observers, Trial practitioners, Trial committee, etc.) as well as lessons learnt will be reported in an Evaluation Report Deliverable by the end of the project (in April 2020).

For now, we can only provide some first initial lesson learnt statements:

- TGM has proven to be valuable support tool for setting up Trials.
- Setting up a Trial as a field exercise (e.g. including the testing of field components) can quickly become an enormous organisational and logistical challenge. Reducing the number of solutions to be tested would help to reduce the overall complexity. The same is true for testing solutions in parallel.
- The Test-bed technical infrastructure has proven stable in the way that all solutions could connect and exchange the requested information and data (e.g. images from the DLR solutions, videos from AnsuR solutions, messages from AIT's solutions) in the needed timeframe.
  Still, the adaptation work for the solutions to connect to the Test-bed as well as to implement use-cases for the Trial scenario and to test them all is very time consuming.
- Installation of international observers and practitioners needs a lot of preparation, coordination and training efforts.
- Support tools (e.g. Observer Support Tool, Trial Management Tool, etc.) are very valuable when it comes to evaluation of questionnaires and performance of solutions, but the time needed to prepare all the questionnaires related to injects played within the scenarios and sub-scenarios should not be underestimated.
- … more lessons learnt, and recommendation will be provided in the Evaluation Report Deliverable. So please keep track on the DRIVER+ website [13] on all upcoming reports and deliverables.

Finally, to mention is that all solutions tested in the Trials can be found in DRIVER+ Portfolio of Solutions (PoS) [14, 15]. It is an online catalogue to access information about innovative solutions for Crisis Management. For each solution, practitioners can share their user experiences and solution providers can give background information and offer support. The PoS is currently being scaled up and has the ambition to become the leading platform and one-stop-shop for Crisis Management solutions in Europe.

Acknowledgement. This project has received funding from the European Union's Seventh Framework Programme for research, technological development and demonstration under grant agreement no. 607798. The information and views set out in this publication are those of the author(s) and do not necessarily reflect the official opinion of the European Union.

This Trial owes a lot to the professionals of the Austrian Red Cross acting as commanders during the Trial as well as the link to the IRONORE2019 [9] exercise, which brought their professionalism, suggestions and recommendations for further improvements to the Trial, and demonstrated a very impressive and gratifying commitment in the management and execution of the various Trial scenarios but also in the feedback discussion that followed.

The observers, with their professional experience as commanders, teachers and evaluators to this Trial brought a precious methodological perspective for the evaluation, as well as an encouraging feedback.

The students and teachers from the Young Business School in Eisenerz (BHAK) [16] acting as volunteers for the emergent group scenarios testing the CrowdTasker application and taking part in the PFA training and providing their valuable feedbacks on solutions as well as on the trainings.

We would like to express our gratitude to all of them.

References

1. Project DRIVER+. https://www.driver-project.eu
2. D922.11: List of CM gaps. DRIVER+ Deliverable (March 2018)
3. Trial Guidance Methodology. https://www.driver-project.eu/trial-guidancemethodology/
4. D922.21 - Trial guidance methodology and guidance tool specifications, DRIVER+ Deliverable (March 2018)
5. DRIVER+ Test-Bed Specification. https://driver-eu.gitbook.io/test-bed-specification
6. Vullings, E., van Campen, S., Hameete, P., Hendriks, M.: An interoperability framework for trials and exercises. In: ITEC 2019 Conference Stockholm (April 2019)
7. Apache Kafka. https://kafka.apache.org
8. DRIVER+ Test-Bed Design. https://driver-eu.github.io/test-bed-design
9. IRONORE2019 Project. https://www.ironore.eu
10. Middelhoff, M., et al.: Crowdsourcing and crowdtasking in crisis management: lessons learned from a field experiment simulating a flooding in city of the Hague. In: Proceedings of the International Conference on Information and Communication Technologies for Disaster Management (December 2016)
11. Drews, P., Eiser-Mauthner, J., Kloyber, C.: Spontaneous volunteer management programs for emergency management – a European perspective. In: Proceedings of the 4th International Conference on Healthcare System Preparedness & Response to Emergencies & Disasters (IPRED IV), Tel Aviv, pp. 154–156 (January 2016)

12. AnsuR and Inmarsat Solutions: Presentation of the BGAN satellite communication device. Inmarsat company (March 2014). https://www.inmarsat.com/wp-content/uploads/2014/04/AnsuR_and_Inmarsat_Solutions_Indon_Case_Study_e.pdf
13. DRIVER+ Trials. https://www.driver-project.eu/events/trials/
14. DRIVER+ Portfolio of Solutions. http://pos.driverproject.eu/
15. Ignjatović, D., Havlik, D., Neubauer, G., Turptil, S., Gonzales, F., Regeczi, D.: The portfolio of solutions. In: Proceedings of the 27th Interdisciplinary Information Management Talks, Kutná Hora, Czech Republic, 4–6 September 2019, pp. 199–206 (2019)
16. Bundeshandelsakademie Eisenerz: Young Business School. https://www.bhak-eisenerz.at/home/
17. Auferbauer, D., Tellioğlu, H.: Centralized crowdsourcing in disaster management. In: Proceedings of the 8th International Conference on Communities and Technologies - C&T 2017, pp. 173–182. ACM Press, New York (2017)
18. Neubauer, G., et al.: Crowdtasking – a new concept for volunteer management in disaster relief. In: Hřebíček, J., Schimak, G., Kubásek, M., Rizzoli, A.E. (eds.) ISESS 2013. IAICT, vol. 413, pp. 345–356. Springer, Heidelberg (2013). https://doi.org/10.1007/978-3-642-41151-9_33
19. Römer, H., et al.: Using airborne remote sensing to increase situational awareness in civil protection and humanitarian relief – the importance of user involvement. In: The International Archives of the Photogrammetry, Remote Sensing and Spatial Information Sciences, XXIII ISPRS Congress, Prague, Czech Republic, 12–19 July 2016, vol. XLI-B8, pp. 1363–1370 (2016). https://doi.org/10.5194/isprs-archives-XLI-B8-1363-2016
20. WHO: War Trauma Foundation and World Vision International (2011). https://www.who.int/mental_health/publications/guide_field_workers/en/. Accessed 28 Nov 2019
21. vieWTerra Evolution. https://www.viewterra.com
22. AnsuR Technologies. https://www.ansur.no

ELFIE - The OGC Environmental Linked Features Interoperability Experiment

Kathi Schleidt[1]([✉]), Michael O'Grady[2], Sylvain Grellet[3], Abdelfettah Feliachi[3], and Hylke van der Schaaf[4]

[1] DataCove e.U., Robert Hamerling Gasse 1/14, 1150 Vienna, Austria
kathi@datacove.eu
[2] UCD Dublin, Belfield Dublin 4, Ireland
michael.j.ogrady@ucd.ie
[3] BRGM, 3 avenue Claude-Guillemin, BP 36009,
45060 Orleans Cedex 2, France
{s.grellet,a.feliachi}@brgm.fr
[4] Fraunhofer IOSB, Fraunhoferstr. 1, 76131 Karlsruhe, Germany
hylke.vanderschaaf@iosb.fraunhofer.de

Abstract. The OGC Environmental Linked Feature Interoperability Experiment (ELFIE) sought to assess a suite of pre-existing OGC and W3C standards with a view to identifying best practice for exposing cross-domain links between environmental features and observations. Environmental domain models concerning landscape interactions with the hydrologic cycle served as the basis for this study, whilst offering a meaningful constraint on its scope. JSON-LD was selected for serialization; this combines the power of linked data with intuitive encoding. Vocabularies were utilized for the provision of the JSON-LD contexts; these ranged from common vocabularies such as schema.org to semantic representations of OGC/ISO observational standards to domain-specific feature models synonymous with the hydrological and geological domains. Exemplary data for the selected use cases was provided by participants and shared in static form via a GitHub repository. User applications were created to assess the validity of the proposed approach as it pertained to real-world situations. This process resulted in the identification of issues whose resolution is a prerequisite for wide-scale deployment and best practice definition. Addressing these issues will be the focus of future OGC Interoperability Experiments.

Keywords: Open geospatial standards · Linked data · Environmental features

1 Introduction

Environmental data is becoming ever more ubiquitous; this poses many difficulties going forward as data pertaining to an arbitrary real world situation will differ according to the perception of the provider as to what is contextually important. Advances in geospatial technologies continue to resolve many of the problems entailed in spatial data provision; nonetheless, certain domains, for example, the hydrological and geological domain, often require more comprehensive information on how spatial objects interrelate than is innately apparent from their topological relationships alone.

© IFIP International Federation for Information Processing 2020
Published by Springer Nature Switzerland AG 2020
I. N. Athanasiadis et al. (Eds.): ISESS 2020, IFIP AICT 554, pp. 188–193, 2020.
https://doi.org/10.1007/978-3-030-39815-6_18

Open Geospatial Consortium (OGC) data models and services are lacking when it comes to exposing cross-domain links between environmental domains and sampling features. The existing suite of OGC Web Services (OWS) follows classic web service design patterns. Data encoding is done in XML, only fragile linkages between spatial objects are possible via xlink; however, the semantic context behind these links is difficult to include. There is no clear guidance on xlink targets and resolution mechanisms. Ultimately, current OWS are still driven by simple feature concepts that assume discrete standalone datasets; there is little support for interlinkage beyond the boundaries of virtual dataset concepts.

Linked open data has the potential to radically transform the normal OGC service pattern (GetCapabilities request followed by lengthy introspection and further DescribeFeatureType requests to understand contents) [1] by encoding associations between features as linked data predicates. The potential of Linked Data in the geospatial domain has been acknowledged by the academic community. To elucidate briefly: A framework for utilizing geospatial Linked Data with the Web Feature Service (WFS) has been proposed and evaluated within the biodiversity domain [2]. Additionally, The Open European Location Services project, a collaboration between the national mapping agencies of Finland, the Netherlands, Norway and Spain, demonstrated the capabilities of linked data for international geospatial data provision [3]. Closely related to this project was an initiative in the Netherlands that focused on the visualization of linked geospatial data [4].

The OGC foresees the concept of Interoperability Experiments (IE) for the structured exploration of potential future topics; thus, as specific implementation conventions and best practices are not available, an OGC IE was initiated to explore how linked data might be best harnessed in OGC services and identify a roadmap for future activities.

The Environmental Linked Features Interoperability Experiment (ELFIE) [5] "focused on encoding relationships between cross-domain features and linking available observations data to sampled domain features" within the hydrogeological domain, adopting and integrating relevant concepts from the semantic community. In order to keep the experiment within scope, the ELFIE specifically focused on linked data requirements and encoding options; in this process, diverse areas of future work were identified and documented for potential future IEs.

2 Problem Statement

The ELFIE seeks to define a method of interlinking domain features and observations of them, whilst maintaining a focus on the semantics of these linkages. An additional objective concerned the provision of a simple solution that would be easily adoptable by developers and users across software platforms whilst leveraging existing standards and best practices (notably SDW BP 2&3 [6]) and, as far as possible, integrating standard taxonomies and ontologies.

At the onset of the ELFIE, work on the specification of an OGC API [7] was still very much a work-in-progress (as WFS3). Thus, the ELFIE also aims at illustrating how RESTful and Linked Data principles can be leveraged to create a reusable approach for encoding information models specified in cross-disciplinary applications, independent of any specific web-API pattern. In addition, the possibility of defining multiple "views" of the same data resource, with each view providing a specific subset of the linked-data graph, was explored during the IE.

Keeping within the parameters of the IE, environmental domain models were thus limited to landscape interactions with the hydrologic cycle. Data was constrained to surface water, groundwater, well/borehole structure and soil moisture. The following data models, where utilized, serving as proto-ontologies: WaterML2, GroundwaterML 2, GeosciML 4 and SoilML. Topics pertaining to network architecture, default behavior when dereferencing an identifier, and discoverability were all deemed as being of utmost importance, but out-of-scope for this IE.

Initially, a wide range of potential use cases was considered with topics ranging from floods to droughts, water quality and quantity, as well as causes and impacts. Additional data sources ranging from meteorological data (both measurement and forecast), elevation data, and critical infrastructure (transport networks, bridges and so forth) and known critical discharge locations (for example, mines) were also identified and integrated.

These use cases were then iteratively reduced to a smaller but representative set for testing and prototyping of the developed concepts; relevant aspects identified in those use cases not utilized were retained in order to assure a comprehensive solution.

In addition to spanning environmental domains, a key feature of the selected use cases was that their constituent data was often administered within different institutions or even countries.

The following use cases were then examined in greater detail - the final two may be regarded as flagships demonstrating the intrinsic usefulness of linked data in environmental/cross-domain contexts:

1. Water budget summary: integrating water budget data with data on the hydrographic network, watershed boundary and outlet, this use case strives to give the user a summary overview of the water budget for a watershed.
2. Flood risks and impacts: by linking available hydrographic information on a watershed with meteorological and water level information as well as the relevant transport networks, real time information of benefit to decision-makers can be provided.
3. Groundwater level monitoring: integrating boreholes and other monitoring facilities with aquifers, thereby gaining a better understanding of groundwater levels.
4. Surface-groundwater networks interaction: provides a comprehensive overview of a water system by applying a linked data approach to all relevant domain features as well as measurements being taken on these features.
5. Watershed data index: by applying linked data principles to monitoring sites and watersheds, data stemming from water quality and quantity sensors is brought into context with the hydrographic network, allowing for a wide array of linked watershed information use cases.

3 Proposed Solution

OGC data models were used extensively in the ELFIE. The Observations and Measurements (O&M) conceptual model provided a high level organizing framework for most ELFIE documents. The OGC-W3C Spatial Data On the Web Working Group implementation of O&M (Sensor, Observation, Sample, and Actuator (SOSA) and Semantic Sensor Networks (SSN)) [8] was used directly because of its applicability to the linked data technology pursued in the ELFIE. The GeoSPARQL [9] ontology was also used directly for representing geometries and spatial relations between features, and to overcome the technology gap between GeoJSON and JSON-LD.

Domain specific data models such as HY_Features [10], GWML2 [11] and GeoSciML [12] were also used for feature types and relations in the ELFIE linked data documents.

As the ELFIE seeks to provide a pragmatic and implementable solution while leveraging the power of linked data, it was decided to explore the potential of JSON-LD; this decision was further influenced by ongoing work in the OGC towards the adoption of JSON. JSON-LD Context files were created for attributes that were deemed important for the use cases considered; in line with the approach of providing multiple views of the same data object, context files were created to support two exemplary conceptual views - "preview" and "network". Well established vocabularies were referenced within the contexts, ranging from schema.org, skos and geosparql for general concepts, the W3C Semantic Sensor Network (SSN) and Sensor, Observation, Sample, and Actuator (SOSA) ontologies for observational models to various domain models such as GWML2, HY_Features and GeoSciML (Fig. 1).

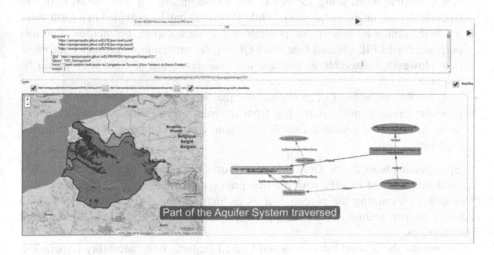

Fig. 1. BLiv viewer for exploration of linked JSON-LD resources

Exemplary data files were created for each use case, whereby in most instances it was decided to provide a small representative set of files, and to only provide these statically on GitHub. In addition, for the Surface-groundwater Networks Interaction Use Case (Number 4), a wrapper built on top of an OGC SensorThings API deployment was created for the provision of dynamic data. Various GUIs were developed for exploration of the provided data. Exceptional among these is the BLiv viewer developed by BRGM, providing the user with parallel views on the raw data, the underlying semantic graph, as well as a conventional map.

4   Issues and Future Work

While the ELFIE was successful in reaching its primary objectives, this exercise also served to highlight various issues that must be further investigated within future IEs. These issues are summarized as follows:

- Resolvable Identifiers: when utilizing existing OGC services for data provision, a specific feature could only be referenced via a complex and unstable request URI. Rewriting approaches were successfully tested, but there was a consensus that this could only ever be a work-around; APIs allowing resolution of URI based identifiers would be essential.
- Domain Feature Model: while the standard vocabularies utilized in the JSON-LD contexts are well suited for referencing, issues were encountered pertaining to the domain vocabularies only available in conceptual (UML) form, as well as those relying on XML Schema. Ongoing work on the OGC Register should provide valuable insights going forward.
- Spatial Representation: utilization of GeoJSON structures for spatial representation is not possible when using JSON-LD due to the underlying RDF based structure (specifically the unordered arrays). While Point data can be provided in a form valid for both standards, this is not possible for more complex geometries. For this purpose, the ELFIE utilized GeoSPARQL for the provision of geometry information. However, being able to leverage the widespread use of GeoJSON would be valuable
- Multiple Representations of an Object: one real-world-object can have multiple data representations, at times stemming from different organizations, or exposing different facets of the available data. Mechanisms for maintaining alignment must be explored.

Specification work on the OGC API (previously WFS3) has been progressing since the finalization of the ELFIE, with the first prototypes becoming available. Currently, there is work exploring the potential of extending the OGC API with JSON-LD, to allow for implementation of the concepts developed within the ELFIE via standardized OGC services.

At present, the Second Environmental Linked Features Interoperability Experiment (SELFIE) is carrying this work further, focusing on feature identification, referencing real world objects, and URL resolution. Special focus is on the relation between the real-world-objects being described and their digital representations.

Acknowledgements. Interoperability Experiments are by their nature group efforts. Thus many thanks to all participants within the ELFIE:

David Blodgett, Byron Cochrane, Ingo Simonis, Rob Atkinson, Sylvain Grellet, Abdelfettah Feliachi, Alistair Ritchie, Eric Boisvert, Marcus Sen, Mickaël Beaufils, James Passmore, Boyan Brodaric, Katharina Schleidt, Chuck Heazel, Steve Richard.

References

1. Open Geospatial Consortium: Web Services Context Document (OWS Context). https://www.opengeospatial.org/standards/owc
2. Vilches-Blázquez, L.M., Saavedra, J.: A framework for connecting two interoperability universes: OGC web feature services and linked data. Trans. GIS **23**(1), 22–47 (2019)
3. Ronzhin, S., et al.: Next generation of spatial data infrastructure: lessons from linked data implementations across Europe. Int. J. Spat. Data Infrastruct. Res. **14**, 84–106 (2019)
4. Folmer, E., Beek, W., Rietveld, L.: Linked data viewing as part of the spatial data platform of the future. Int. Arch. Photogrammetry Rem. Sens. Spat. Inf. Sci. **42**(4), 49–52 (2018)
5. Open Geospatial Consortium: Environmental Linked Features Interoperability Experiment. https://opengeospatial.github.io/ELFIE/
6. OGC W3C Spatial Data on the Web Best Practices. https://www.w3.org/TR/sdw-bp/
7. Open Geospatial Consortium: OGC API (OAPI) Common Specification. https://github.com/opengeospatial/oapi_common
8. OGC W3C Semantic Sensor Network Ontology. https://www.w3.org/TR/vocab-ssn/
9. Open Geospatial Consortium: GeoSPARQL - A Geographic Query Language for RDF Data. https://www.opengeospatial.org/standards/geosparql
10. Open Geospatial Consortium: WaterML 2: Part 3 - Surface Hydrology Features (HY_Features) - Conceptual Model. http://docs.opengeospatial.org/is/14-111r6/14-111r6.html
11. Open Geospatial Consortium: OGC WaterML 2: Part 4 – GroundWaterML 2 (GWML2). http://docs.opengeospatial.org/is/16-032r2/16-032r2.html
12. Open Geospatial Consortium: Geoscience Markup Language 4.1 (GeoSciML). https://docs.opengeospatial.org/is/16-008/16-008.html

Real-Time Visualization of Methane Emission at Commercial Dairy Farms

Dirkjan Schokker[1]($\boxtimes$), Herman Mollenhorst[2], Gerrit Seigers[3],
Yvette de Haas[1], Roel F. Veerkamp[1], and Claudia Kamphuis[1]

[1] Wageningen Livestock Research (Animal Breeding and Genomics),
Wageningen University and Research,
PO Box 338, 6700 AH Wageningen, The Netherlands
dirkjan.schokker@wur.nl
[2] Wageningen Livestock Research (Livestock and Environment), Wageningen
University and Research, PO Box 338, 6700 AH Wageningen, The Netherlands
[3] Facility and Services (Information Technology), Wageningen University
and Research, PO Box 59, 6700 AB Wageningen, The Netherlands

Abstract. The Dutch government has set an objective to reduce greenhouse gasses (GHG) emissions to 116 Mton CO_2-equivalent in 2030. The agriculture sector aims for 11–23 Mton of GHG emission by 2050 and thus contributes to this objective. For this sector, the major contributor to the GHG emission in the Netherlands is the dairy sector. Before any mitigation strategies can be enrolled, some key facts need to be measured regarding the GHG emission on a farm. One of these key facts is the establishment of the baseline of GHG emission on a farm (and per cow). For this, we previously have built an infrastructure to measure and collect methane and carbon dioxide (near) real-time on a farm. The next challenges, addressed in the current study, were to (1) combine the private methane data, collected real-time through the infrastructure, with open source weather information, and (2) visualize both data streams for farmers, by developing an application that can be viewed on a web or mobile phone platform.

Keywords: Farm · Cow · Methane emission · Real-time · Visualization

1 Introduction

1.1 Background

The objective for the Netherlands is to achieve a greenhouse gasses (GHG) emissions reduction of 49% in 2030 (compared to 1990). In 1990, the total GHG emissions were approximately 228 megaton CO_2-equivalent. This means that in 2030, the GHG emissions has to be reduced to 116 Mton CO_2-equivalent. Five sectors have been indicated, including electricity, industry, mobility, houses, and agriculture. For agriculture the objective for 2050 is to have a 90% reduction, in other words a maximum of 11–23 Mton of GHG emission. To establish a baseline for the methane emission of a farm and of an individual cow, and more importantly to identify the most successful strategies to reduce these emissions, it is necessary to have (real-time) methane data.

© IFIP International Federation for Information Processing 2020
Published by Springer Nature Switzerland AG 2020
I. N. Athanasiadis et al. (Eds.): ISESS 2020, IFIP AICT 554, pp. 194–200, 2020.
https://doi.org/10.1007/978-3-030-39815-6_19

This continuous monitoring of methane emission from livestock production systems, including dairy farming, is needed to understand which aspects contribute to the methane emissions and to what extent. Moreover, this knowledge is needed to develop mitigation strategies. The available data can be used to visualize the impact of these strategies.

A large intensive research program has been started in 2018 by the Dutch Ministry of Agriculture, Nature and Food [1], to identify strategies to reduce methane emission in the agricultural-sector. Part of this program involves continuous monitoring of methane, by means of sensor measurements, both at the barn and individual animal level. The research program involves several animal production domains, including dairy farms. Therefore, monitoring of methane takes place at 17 commercial Dutch dairy farms. At these farms, methane is measured by methane analyzing sensors. These so-called sniffers use a nondispersive infrared sensor (NDIR) for methane and carbon [2]. These sniffers generate a constant analogue signal that is linearly related to gas concentrations. By placing these sniffers in the milking robot, we ensured that all milking cows at a farm were monitored for their methane emission while being milked. To collate these data from several sniffers in the field and to link this information to individual barns and animals we developed a flexible infrastructure [3]. This infrastructure continuously monitors sniffer functioning and data quality to bring loss of data to a minimum, and allows for a cheap but trustworthy data transfer from the sensors to a cloud storage platform (in our case: Microsoft Azure). The infrastructure is also flexible in accepting other types of information. One can think of other sensor data, but also animal and farm data that are often stored in separate farm management programs. Another part of the flexibility of the infrastructure links to the scalability, i.e. handling data from new farms in case the number of farms, where methane is monitored, increases.

In this study we worked on two challenges. The first challenge was to combining the real-time sniffer data, which is private data, with open source weather information from IBM through Akkerweb (www.akkerweb.eu). This combination is important because it is expected that wind and relative humidity affect methane emissions [4, 5]. The second challenge was to developed a tool that visualizes the incoming sniffer and weather data, two data streams that differ in veracity, for web and mobile applications using Power BI, an interactive tool to visualize data developed by Microsoft (https://powerbi.microsoft.com/).

1.2 Objectives

Our objectives were (1) to integrate private methane data with open source weather data and (2) to visualize methane emission data on dairy farms in (near) real-time to in an application for web and/or mobile.

2   Materials and Methods

2.1   Infrastructure

Up till now, 18 sniffers were installed at 17 commercial Dutch dairy farms, using the same set-up as described by Huthanen et al. [2]. These sniffers have a nondispersive infrared (NDIR) sensor, a simple spectroscopic sensor, here used to detect methane and carbon dioxide. The sniffer sends the corresponding values every 30 s to the connected Arduino (microchip Atmel SAMD21, 32 bit Arm Cortex Arduino compatible and a uBlox Sara R410M, all NB-IoT bands, LTE-M). Subsequently, the Arduinos were programmed to push the data every 3 min to the Azure cloud. This was done via the Internet of Things (IoT) network, to avoid potential problems with low coverage of e.g. a WIFI signal.

In Azure, a Microsoft cloud platform (https://azure.microsoft.com), an IoT hub was built which was subscribed to the data stream, meaning getting and loading the data. Here, different alerts were coded, for example when the data stream pushed by the Arduino had down-time (out of action) or when measured values were outside a predetermined expected range, the data owner received an email [3]. To visualize the data stream from the IoT hub, we used Power BI (Version: 2.72.5556.801 64-bit, August 2019), which provides interactive visualizations to create dashboards and reports. Additionally, we integrated an additional open data source, i.e. current weather data. Here, we have used the IBM weather data, by querying the current weather via an API at Akkerweb. The following weather fields were retrieved: temperature, wind speed, precipitation (last 24 h, 6 h, or 1 h), UV strength, and the relative humidity. These values were visualized within Power BI for the city in which a farm is located. The associated city names were transformed to "latitude-longitude" by using https://www.latlong.net/, to ensure proper working of the API. A schematic overview of the data flows is presented in Fig. 1.

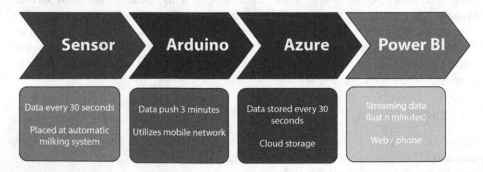

Fig. 1. Data-flow diagram. The sensor is placed in the area of the milking robot. The data is captured by an Arduino sends it to Azure in the cloud. In Azure the data is loaded into an IoT hub. Lastly the data is visualized in Power BI.

3 Results and Discussion

3.1 Methane Visualization

We were able to visualize sniffer data in (near) real-time for individual commercial Dutch dairy farms. A lesson we learned when performing the data push from the cloud Azure to Power BI is that the data needed to be in a so-called "star" schema. The center of the star has one fact table (in our case the farm) and a number of associated dimension tables (in our case methane and weather data). This star schema is needed to have a more efficient performance on the visualization side in Power BI, compared to a so called "snowflake" schema. Figure 2 shows data from one sniffer, equaling methane emission data from one milking robot unit on a farm, for a 90 min period. This figure shows fluctuations around zero, indicating the absence of a cow in the milking robot. On the other hand, a peak indicates the presence of a cow in the milking robot. From these data, it is not evident yet when one cow enters or leaves the milking robot. It would be worthwhile to combine these sniffer data to other farm management software and/or measurements, to assess more precisely when a cow enters or leaves the milking robot. When further developing this visualization application further development is needed regarding the integration of the individual cow data. The main advantages of such additional data are to have improved emissions estimates at farm level, and the possibility to generate a cow specific methane profile. This will open-up new possibilities to reduce methane emission, by feeding and/or breeding strategies, as well as management [6].

3.2 Integration with Additional Data Streams

The sniffer data may fluctuate due to characteristics of the barn. For example, its construction and air flow through the barn and the location of the milking robot may influence the measurement. Furthermore, outside weather may also exert an influence, like temperature, wind flow, and humidity. The current weather data was pulled into Power BI and subsequently visualized for the village the farm is located (for example Cornwerd, a city in the northern province Friesland, see Fig. 3).

While developing this part, we experienced Power BI was not yet optimally designed in handling the data streams. Mainly because Power BI is designed to visualize data from data warehouses and the new data was appended to the database. Power BI will load the whole database each time after a refresh. In our case we have combined data streams from private and open data, simultaneously. The methane data stream was loaded into an SQL database in the cloud and subsequently a subset of the data was pushed to Power BI. Power BI was subsequently used to developed a prototype application for both web and mobile (Fig. 4). This application now demonstrates the cumulative methane emission per day, which resets every day (122.63 K in Fig. 4). Additionally, the methane emissions from the last 60 min are visualized, as well as the current outdoor temperature (°C), relative humidity (%), and wind-speed (km/h).

The current study faced the challenge to combine private data, collected near real-time with open source data. This combining of different data sources, with a variety of formats, scale, and veracity will become increasingly important in the future. For

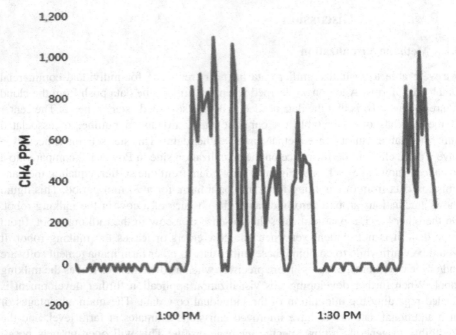

Fig. 2. Results of the last 90 min for a single sensor. The x-axis depicts the time, here from approximately 12.30 PM to 2.00 PM. Whereas the y-axis depicts the concentration methane in the air, in parts per million (CH4_PPM).

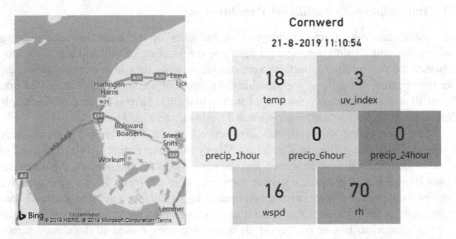

Fig. 3. Overview of the current weather of a participating farm, here in Cornwerd. The left panel shows the location on the map of the Netherlands, whereby the view is zoomed in on the province of Friesland. The right panel shows the city name, data, time and below the temperature in degrees Celsius and the UV-index. Furthermore, the precipitation of the last hour, previous six hours, or past 24 h, and the current wind speed, and the relative humidity.

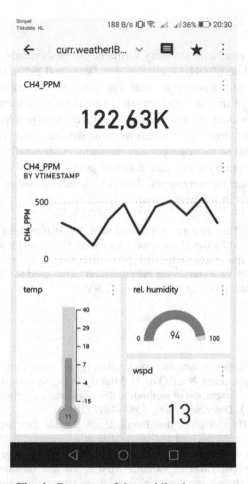

Fig. 4. Prototype of the mobile phone app.

example, when developing digital twins (of e.g., a farm) it can be expected that a plethora of sensors will monitor different aspects of the farm; including individual feed intake, animal health status, animal behavior, and GHG emission. Our study contributed to that future by exploring the possibilities to retrieve data real-time, combine it with open source data, and to visualize it for farmers. Moreover, combining the sniffer methane data with other information like age of the cow, which is a factor known to influence emission [7, 8]. Such information would be an addition to our application, to better interpret the sniffer data or to enrich the visualizations by coloring per age group. In addition, further development is needed regarding the application (web and mobile), particularly to integrate the individual cow data. The main advantages of such additional data is to generate a cow specific methane profile. This will open-up new possibilities to reduce methane emission, by feeding and/or breeding strategies, as well as management [6].

4   Conclusion

To reduce the GHG emissions on dairy farms in the Netherlands, it was necessary to first establish a baseline of GHG emissions per farm (and per individual cow). To do so, we built a data infrastructure for real-time collection of methane measurements. Subsequently, we have shown (near) real-time visualization of methane measurements, enriched with open source (weather) data. Visualization is performed on an interface via a web and mobile phone. The current methane data stream is visualized, as well as the cumulative amount of methane per day per farm. Additionally, the current weather data is integrated to enrich the methane data and possibly identify influences, e.g. wind speed, on the methane measurements. The data handling for visualization could be enrolled on 100 farms in the near future.

Acknowledgement(s). This research was conducted by Wageningen Livestock Research, commissioned and funded by the Ministry of Agriculture, Nature and Food Quality, within the framework of Policy Support Research theme "Data driven & High Tech" (project number KB-38-001-004 Smart and Privacy conserving infrastructures). Data used for this study was collected within the Climate Envelop project of Ministry of LNV.

References

1. Schouten, C.: Agriculture, nature and food: valuable and connected. The Netherlands as a leader in circular agriculture. N.a.F.Q.o.t.N. Ministry of Agriculture, Editor (2018)
2. Huhtanen, P., et al.: Comparison of methods to determine methane emissions from dairy cows in farm conditions. J. Dairy Sci. **98**(5), 3394–3409 (2015)
3. Kamphuis, C., de Haas, Y., van den Bergh, E.: A flexible data architecture to automate collection of (near) real-time methane sensor data at commercial dairy farms. In: Scientific Symposium FAIR Data Sciences for Green Life Sciences, Wageningen (2018)
4. Saha, C.K., et al.: The effect of external wind speed and direction on sampling point concentrations, air change rate and emissions from a naturally ventilated dairy building. Biosyst. Eng. **114**(3), 267–278 (2013)
5. Schmithausen, A.J., et al.: Quantification of methane and ammonia emissions in a naturally ventilated barn by using defined criteria to calculate emission rates. Animals **8**(5), 75 (2018)
6. de Souza, W., et al.: Mitigation of enteric methane emissions through pasture management in integrated crop-livestock systems: trade-offs between animal performance and environmental impacts. J. Clean. Prod. **213**, 968–975 (2019)
7. Ramirez-Restrepo, C.A., Clark, H., Muetzel, S.: Methane emissions from young and mature dairy cattle. Anim. Prod. Sci. **56**(11), 1897–1905 (2016)
8. van Gastelen, S., Dijkstra, J., Bannink, A.: Are dietary strategies to mitigate enteric methane emission equally effective across dairy cattle, beef cattle, and sheep? J. Dairy Sci. **102**(7), 6109–6130 (2019)

Design of a Web-Service for Formal Descriptions of Domain-Specific Data

Jannik Sidler[✉], Eric Braun, Thorsten Schlachter, Clemens Düpmeier, and Veit Hagenmeyer

Institute for Automation and Applied Computer Science,
Karlsruhe Institute of Technology, Karlsruhe, Germany
{jannik.sidler,eric.braun2,thorsten.schlachter,clemens.duepmeier,
veit.hagenmeyer}@kit.edu

Abstract. The growing relevance of Big Data and the Internet of Things (IoT) leads to a need for an efficient handling of this data. One key concept to achieve efficient data handling is their semantic description. In the environmental and energy domain, these issues become more relevant since there are measurement stations that produce large amounts of data that software systems have to deal with. In the context of cloud-based infrastructure and virtualisation via containers, microservice architectures and scalability become important aspects in software engineering. This article presents the design of a web service providing software systems with semantic descriptions of data fostering a microservice architecture. It implements key concepts such as domain modelling, schema versioning and schema modularisation. It is evaluated and demonstrated in the context of a current environmental use case.

Keywords: JSON Schema · Semantic description · Schema service · Semantic web services · Big Data · Internet of Things

1 Introduction

In the past few years, Big Data and the Internet of Things (IoT) have become topics of big significance. Consequently, many resources are invested in research of concepts and technology to improve the overall ability to make use of them in an efficient manner. One important aspect is the management and storage of Big Data that comes along with modern data platforms. Problems of Big Data storage are often symbolised by four words beginning with the letter "v": *volume, velocity, variety* and *veracity*. Especially, the variety of data semantics is a key problem since Big Data storage solutions have to cope with many different types of data, where each type has its own semantic structure. Therefore, most Big Data storage solutions, for example NoSQL database systems such as time series [12,13] or document-oriented databases [14,15], are schema-less, i.e. do not enforce static schemas for data storage. Still, Big Data applications often require a certain degree of structural and semantic understanding of the data, which

© IFIP International Federation for Information Processing 2020
Published by Springer Nature Switzerland AG 2020
I. N. Athanasiadis et al. (Eds.): ISESS 2020, IFIP AICT 554, pp. 201–215, 2020.
https://doi.org/10.1007/978-3-030-39815-6_20

cannot be acquired by internal database schemas anymore. However, a formal description of the structure of data can also be achieved by externalizing the semantic description and creating additional metadata schemas of the respective data. This data is stored in an external schema service. This service can deliver a description of how data of a certain type has to be interpreted and therefore simplify data management and processing.

Furthermore, an external semantic schema description covers another important aspect: connections and relationships between data items. If relations are not formally defined, it is difficult for humans and even more difficult for machines to identify them. In software systems (for example search engines), identifiable relations between data lead to a better search interface e.g. connecting search results in a knowledge graph. By using schemas, such relations can be formalised and consequently used by software that has the need for such information. Linked metadata schemas can be used to create Linked Data [18,19], e.g. the data providing services annotate the data with semantic description elements from the schema descriptions. Externalised schemas are frequently used in semantic web applications, in the context of IoT as described in [5–7], in the context of big datasets [8], or for referring to comparability of data [9].

Another very popular approach in software development is the microservice architecture [23]. The main idea of this architecture is to divide functionality into blocks of a reasonable small size and make these blocks part of a greater, overall functionality, but keeping them independent of each other. This principle contrasts to monolithic architectures, where functional blocks are not implemented independently and the implementations of different functionalities are closely linked to each other. While separating functionality of an application into separate services, single microservices can be far more generic. They can be used even in different application contexts. This advantage of the microservice architecture becomes relevant in many projects and applications today. In environmental projects, it is often necessary to measure various properties of the environment, for example, air pollution properties, such a carbon dioxide emissions, water quality or radioactivity. If the application-specific part of the semantics of such measurements is separated from the meta information such as a metric identifier (identifying the property), a timestamp and a value, a generic time series service can be used to store many different kinds of measurements. Similarly, the important aspects of the measured physical property (name, unit identifier, relation to a measurement device) can be stored in a separate generic service called master data service (more details can be taken from [22]). Therefore, a schema service can provide a formal semantic description of how "time series data" is structured within the time series service [22], how corresponding master data is structured in the master data service and how certain master data is related to a time series metric. By doing this, it is possible to describe the semantic interpretation context of the time series data, i.e. the physical property and related information which is associated with time series data corresponding to a certain metric.

Motivated by the previously mentioned problem setting, the goal of this article is to describe the design and basic concepts of a microservice that is able to manage and administer schemas describing the application semantics of specific application domains. Such meta knowledge about data is relevant for many modern application areas like Big Data and IoT, as mentioned before [5–9] and furthermore, the importance of generic microservices which can be used, deployed and executed in a cloud-based environment in a generic application independent way rises continuously. For the design of such microservices and their interoperability with a schema service adding application-specific meta knowledge, there are several requirements that have to be considered.

The first requirement is related to the basic functionality of the service. It is intended to be used in a productive environment, which implies that it is necessary to offer basic data operations for users who work with it. These operations are derived from the CRUD principle (Create, Read, Update and Delete). In the context of this article, schemas have to be accessible via an appropriate REST API [11,16] that offers such operations.

Additionally, it is necessary to control the formal correctness of metrics and data in general. For this purpose, an automatic schema/metadata validation mechanism is necessary. This mechanism has to supervise the formal correctness of available data by validating it against an appropriate schema before a create/update operation is executed. Consequently, an update of data is only allowed to be executed if the validation of the data is successful.

Another requirement is the need for a versioning concept. Client applications may have to work with a specific version of data, structured accordingly to a certain version of the application schemas, while higher versions of the schema are already created for working with next generation clients. In this case, in order to provide backward compatibility, it is necessary that older data versions are supported although a newer version is already available (and possibly even recommended for usage). Versioning also guarantees the availability of a history feature, which is crucial for supporting old data that still can be of interest. If the data format changes in a certain period of time, old versions of data may not be possible to be processed correctly anymore. In this case, the availability of older schema versions is necessary to process old data.

To model relations between different schemas, it is necessary to include references that point to related schemas. This is supported by the usage of a specific vocabulary, for example JSON Schema [1,2] It allows the usage of a special keyword which offers the inclusion of external data in order to mark relations between schemas and to enable a modular schema structure with low redundancy. Linked resources are identified by a Uniform Resource Identifier (URI). For an efficient usage of references, it is mandatory to have a suitable domain concept that relates every resource to its corresponding domain.

The remainder of this article is organised as follows: Sect. 2 deals with related work that examines similar content referring to this article. Section 3 describes solutions for the main concepts mentioned above. Section 4 evaluates the presented concepts. In Sect. 5, a conclusion is given as well as an outlook for further work.

2   Related Work

This section deals with publications that are related to the general idea of the present article and to parts of the requirements.

The article by Chervenak and Foster et al. [8] deals with the management of datasets of large volume in scientific contexts. They describe the design of a data grid and suggest a concept for a schema service describing the data in which they decide to distinguish schema information between payload and metadata. The payload in this case is the actual content of the schema that describes the underlying data, whereas the metadata is a piece of information that defines meta attributes of the schema. As reasons for this distinction, they mention increased flexibility regarding the storage system implementation and less effort when changing behaviours that affect one metadata or payload description. Additionally, metadata is divided into different kinds of metadata which are application metadata, replica metadata and system configuration metadata, where each of these respectively covers different tasks. The article emphasizes that the separation of metadata and payload is an important matter for many years and that the design of a metadata service in combination with Big Data was already reasonable in the year 2000. A similar approach can also be found in [6]. The approach described later divides information in schema documents into "payload" and "metadata".

Another related article is given by Krylovskiy, Jahn and Patti [5]. t deals with the design of a smart city IoT platform by using the microservice architecture. The presented platform architecture consists of applications, a service platform, containing middleware services and smart city services, and information models. Additionally, it contains components for the management of platform metadata. Data can be accessed by a client application via a REST API and is stored in a document-oriented database. Data with more semantic structure is stored in a triplestore database and can be accessed by a semantic web client. The article describes the advantages of the microservice architecture in the context of its service platform, the most important ones are the componentisation of functionality, decentralised governance and data management, which lead to technology heterogeneity, resilience, good scaling and composability. The separation of metadata and payload consequently can be covered by using a microservice architecture, which may lead to a separate service only dealing with metadata. However, the work presented in [5] describes metadata in an abstract way, and does not mention aspects like an appropriate metadata model or a distinction of metadata depending on their respective domain.

Additionally, related to the present article is the work given by Agocs and Le Goff [10]. It deals with the architecture of a web service using a REST API and JSON Schema to construct knowledge graphs for data visualisation. They describe the need for descriptors that are used to validate data. Moreover, they suggest an ontology-like hierarchy as data structure. The latter requirement is applied by using JSON Schema's referencing functionality. Agocs's and Le Goff's design of the web service is similar to the one that is described in the present article as they use a microservice architecture as well as a REST API, which provides basic CRUD operations for applications using the knowledge graph.

However, concepts that are not discussed in Agocs's and Le Goff's work are a versioning concept, which will be included in the present work. Additionally, the creation and management of domain concepts for different applications in the same schema service and a metadata model are not addressed by Agocs's and Le Goff's work but will be discussed in the following chapters as part of the solution presented in this paper.

3   Concept and Architecture

In this chapter, a solution for the problems described in the introduction is presented.

3.1   Domain Model

First, the term **Domain-specific Data** is discussed. It refers to different categories of data for different application domains, for example environmental data or energy data. These two application domains serve as examples in the context of the present article as they already have good and well known semantic models for their data. Domain-specific data is hierarchically categorised according to its domain-specific meaning. A category defines a more specific type of data which can be divided into more specific subgroups on its own. This process is repeated until the scope of the grouped data items is specific enough that the structure of the data can be defined by a formal description. The category names can be associated with a more formal definition of a vocabulary of domain terms with precise semantics within the application domain, which can also be described by a thesaurus. Adding structural information to certain categories, results in a domain model. Figure 1 shows an example of such a hierarchical categorisation and is a visualisation of the air/climate domain model given by the Umweltbundesamt [17]. The air/climate domain model contains more terms in the hierarchy, which are not depicted in Fig. 1 to keep it clear.

At the level of "gaseous pollutant", i.e. emissions of gas into the air, an associated data schema can be basically defined by the name or type of the pollutant (ozone, nitrogen dioxide) and its concentration, which can be seen as a measurement value MV (see Fig. 1) if there are means for measuring or calculating it from measurements. This contrasts to air pollutants which are not gaseous but particles (e.g. particulate matter). The size of the particle and the particle type mix is important besides the concentration. Therefore, both concepts lead to different schemas.

A set of such schemas which define the data semantics of all data belonging to certain domain terms (e.g. "gaseous pollutant") is called **schema domain**. The schema service discussed in the present article allows to create as many schema storage containers as required to provide schema domains as sets of schemas to different applications. These applications can have different application domains

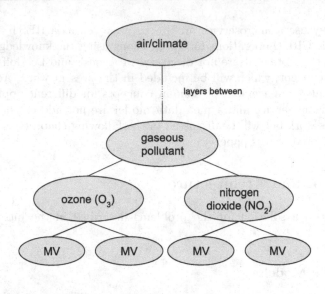

MV = Measured Value

Fig. 1. Excerpt from the air/climate domain model, extended by measured values.

as well. Each schema domain can contain many schemas which define the structure of certain types of data within the domain.

As schemas can reference other schemas to implement relations between them, schemas defining the data structure of a certain application domain are closely related to each other. If the structure of schemas is enhanced over time, new versions of schemas are created, and not all versions of different schemas are compatible with each other regarding their relationships. Therefore, it is necessary to have a versioning concept for schema domains and for single schemas.

3.2   Versioning Concept

In this section, the versioning concept is discussed. Principally, there are different methods and use cases how versioning can be applied to schemas. In the present article, three approaches are discussed. The first one is Domain-specific Versioning, which attaches a version number to a whole schema domain. In this approach, all schemas that belong to the same domain have the same version number as the schema domain. Consequently, updating a single schema in a (sub)domain leads to an update of the version number of all schemas in this domain. The mechanism is depicted in Fig. 2. It shows an update request which is handled by an interface managing the update of the domain. This leads to a consistent version number in the entire domain, which is a crucial feature for using software applications. However, this uniform version comes along with a disadvantage. To keep the version consistent, every update leads to a large number of update requests. Even if a schema contains no changes for a new

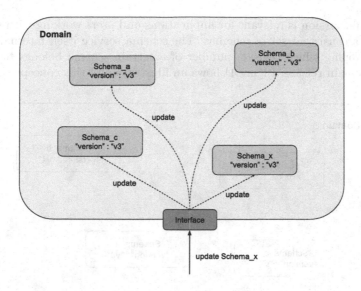

Fig. 2. Schema updating with Domain-specific Versioning.

version, the version number must be incremented. Depending on the frequency of updates, the effort for incrementing the version number may be too high to be negligible.

This problem is the motivation for a second versioning approach, the Schema-specific Versioning. In this approach, every schema has its own version number, which implies that every schema can be updated independently of each other. Figure 3 shows the updating of a schema using the Schema-specific Versioning method. As depicted, the updating of a single schema does not affect other schemas in the domain. The advantage of this strategy lies in the efficiency as only the affected schema is updated. This concept is well-known from versioning source code files in software development processes [20,21] and suitable for authoring schemas since changes of schemas are tracked by the revision number and different revisions can be compared to each other. However, as a consequence, there is no consistent and uniform version number which may lead to difficulties as schemas are linked to each other, and applications have no precise view on which version of a schema is linked to which version of another schema.

For this reason, the third approach combines both formerly presented concepts. The combination is similar to the versioning concepts applied to software code where each source code file has a revision number. Each schema (e.g. analogous to a source code file) has an internal version that is called revision number. It is only relevant for authoring and managing schemas and schema domains but not propagated to applications that are working with the data. Additionally, there is a domain version applied to a schema domain as a whole which can be considered as the version number of a schema domain release, which can be a set of consistent schema definitions that are used by applications.

The domain version is relevant for applications and users working with schemas to access a consistent set of schemas. The schema service itself internally manages a mapping which revision number of a certain schema belongs to a given schema domain release. Figure 4 shows an illustration of this concept.

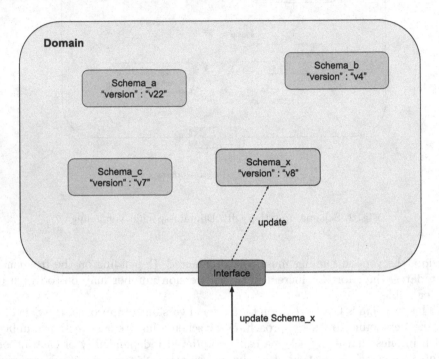

Fig. 3. Schema updating with Schema-specific Versioning.

Related to this approach is the question of an updating strategy. Typically on demand of application developers, schema authors have to evolve schemas to add new functionalities. This is performed by preparing new schema domain releases. The combined version approach supports this: schema authors work on new releases by committing new versions of single schemas or single schema sets analogous to the versioning of software source code which results in new instances of the schema objects internally having an incremented revision number. When a new set of consistent schema instances is finalised, a new schema domain release is prepared by assigning the corresponding revision numbers of the schemas to the new schema domain release. Afterwards, the consistent set of schemas is released to be usable for applications. The applications refer to the new release by the new schema domain version number. To provide backward compatibility, the schema service has to provide more than one release of the same schema domain to clients according to the version number the client application uses. For maintaining consistency across all schemas of a domain release, it is important that schema revisions are fixed and not changeable anymore when they are assigned to a released schema domain version.

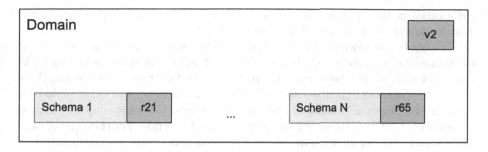

Fig. 4. Updating using combined strategy of Domain-specific Version and Schema-specific Version.

3.3 Modularisation

Another important topic in the context of this article is the modularisation of schemas. Modularisation is a consequence of using references in schemas to divide large schemas into smaller pieces. This approach has various advantages. Redundancy is significantly reduced by using references. This leads to a concept where schema information is stored exactly once, which means that schemas are reusable. Consequently, updating is less expensive since an update request affects only smaller parts of a schema. Strongly related to this is reusability which is a desired feature as it reduces the efforts for updating and further editorial work. Such reusable, "common" schemas are helpful for authors who need them as they can include them instead of creating them again. Additionally, schemas become more readable for humans.

Related to the usage of references is their resolving. A reference is a URI that points to a specific schema at a specific location described by the reference itself. The resolving indicates the process of replacing the reference's URI by the referenced schema itself. As there may be applications that are not able to resolve references by themselves, the service contains a functionality that performs the resolving on demand. As internal references (where the referenced schema is part of the schema itself, in which it may be used multiple times) can be resolved implicitly by the usage of JSON Schema [1,2], external references (where the referenced schema is located in a separate document) have to be treated differently. JSON Schema's "$ref" keyword uses URIs to define the location of a specific linked schema. To resolve external references, an algorithm is needed that locates all the corresponding references, queries the linked schemas using the URI and writes them to the correct location in the schema. The algorithm exactly fulfills the described requirements by recursively iterating through the schema, detecting all references, querying the respective reference schema and editing the base schema correctly. Whenever it detects the "$ref" keyword in a schema, it uses the value of this key to query the corresponding schema from the database and writes it to the proper location, adding all necessary syntactical characters. Whenever another keyword is detected, it is checked if there is a nested schema. The complexity of the algorithm depends on the number of nested schemas that are located in the main schema. The more nested the schema structure is, the more recursive steps the algorithm has to perform.

Related to the modular schema structure that uses references is the usage of a classification concept which divides the set of schema documents belonging to a schema domain into more modular parts (in the following called *package*). In many (sub)domains, schemas can be divided into several groups of reusable base schemas, for example basic data attribute definitions, basic data objects, such as measurements or more complex application object schemas. For this type of classification as well as for assigning internal revision numbers to schemas, metadata attributes are required to be assigned to schema documents. As discussed before, it is desirable to separate payload and metadata in a schema document. By using JSON Schema, a possible representation of the schema document structure is shown in Listing 1.1. This example contains the different sections for metadata and payload (schema).

```
"metadata" : {
        "class": "measurement",
        "package": "DO",
        "revisionNumber": "r44",
        ...
}
"schema": {
        ...
}
```

Listing 1.1. Structure of schema documents within a storage container of a document-oriented database of the schema service (related to one schema domain).

The metadata section contains three properties:

- the "class" property, which describes the type of the schema and the derived objects which are instances of that schema
- the "package" property, which defines the package to which a schema definition belongs to (e.g. DO for Data Objects)
- the "revisionNumber" property, which represents the internal revision version

Moreover, Fig. 5 models the validation process that is used in JSON Schema and in the schema service. It consists of three different layers. The lowest one is the object layer, where objects are given in the JSON data format [3,4]. They are validated against a certain JSON Schema that serves as formal prototype for the object. This schema, on the other hand, defines the structure of the objects. JSON Schemas are the middle layer in the model given by Fig. 5. They are validated themselves against the upper layer, the JSON Meta Schema or JSON Schema Draft. This draft defines the keywords and their functionality and thereby, it defines the JSON Schemas in the middle layer. Figure 6 depicts the architecture of the schema service. It consists of different components containing different tasks needed in the context.

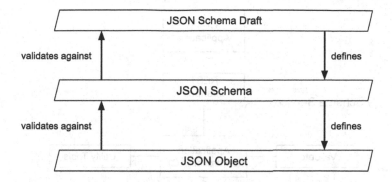

Fig. 5. Hierarchy in the validation process with JSON Schema.

The service is used by client applications. Examples for client applications are dashboards or other visualisation components. For the applications, the service provides a REST Interface (REST API) containing the necessary functionality to process client requests. Requests are received and processed by the Application Controller (AC). The AC uses a configuration file to manage necessary system parameters, for example ports or authentication/authorisation information. If the request contains a request body (in case of create/update requests), it is validated by the validator first. If the validation is successful, the AC uses a database interface to translate the request to the corresponding database query. The query is sent to the database where the desired data is stored. If the validation fails or the requested data is not available, the client receives an error request with the corresponding HTTP status code.

3.4 Prototype Architecture

Figure 6 depicts the architecture of the schema service. It consists of different components performing different tasks needed in the context. The service is used by client applications. Examples for client applications are dashboards or other visualisation components. For the applications, the service provides a REST Interface (REST API) containing the necessary functionality to process client requests. The REST API is designed accordingly to [11]. Requests are received and processed by the Application Controller (AC). The AC uses a configuration file to manage necessary system parameters, for example ports or authentication/authorisation information. If the request contains a request body (in case of create/update requests), it is validated by the validator first. If the validation is successful, the AC uses a database interface to translate the request to the corresponding database query. The query is sent to the database where the desired data is stored. If the validation fails or the requested data is not available, the client receives an error request with the corresponding HTTP status code.

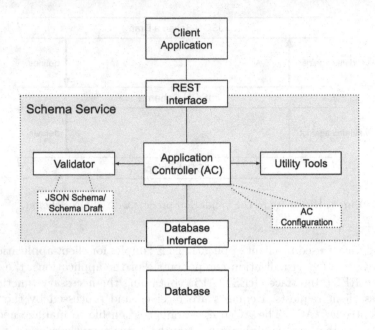

Fig. 6. Architecture of the service and connected systems.

4   Evaluation

To evaluate the concept provided within this article, the service was tested within an application of the Landesanstalt für Umwelt Baden-Württemberg (LUBW), Germany. The application beside other usages instruments a google maps chart with an additional layer that shows the nitrogen dioxide content in the air (see Fig. 7) at different measurement points in Baden-Württemberg. On the right side of the figure, the meaning of the different measurement point colors is shown, which changes with a rising or falling value of nitrogen dioxide in the air depending on which predefined range of values contains the value.

In this example context, the schema service provides advantages for the application. On the one hand, data that is stored in the system can be validated. This helps to reduce the existence of error values which contain an illegal format or illegal values. On the other hand, time series data used in the measurements can be schematically linked with master data objects which provide the domain specific interpretation context to the measurement values. They share information about the chemical property measured (as nitrogen dioxide), the unit of the measurement value, the time resolution, the measurement environment (measurement station equipment) and the location of the station. The service that delivers the data to the map client component is able to resolve the references for concrete instance data and to provide an aggregated data object, which contains all the information beside the measurement values that is required to have the coloring information and the legend information available to render the data

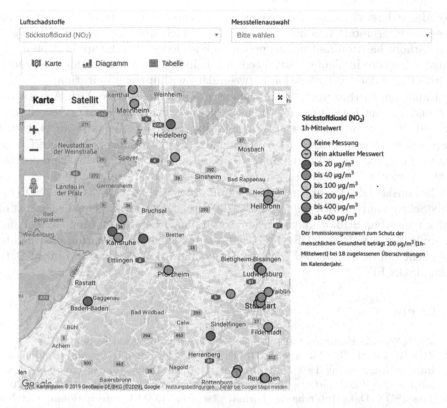

Fig. 7. Map with measurement data that shows the nitrogen dioxide (NO_2) content in the air.

on the map. Additionally, schemas are useful for preconfiguring components as selectors (e.g. for filtering data) based on classification information according to the schema of the corresponding dataset.

5   Conclusion

In the present article, the need for semantic descriptions of data objects in an application domain and the usefulness of an external schema service for it were motivated. Afterwards, related works and needed functionalities of such a service were discussed. First, the versioning of semantic descriptions were discussed and an appropriate concept was presented which is analogous to the versioning of source code and releases in software development. Second, the data format of a schema document within the schema service and its metadata for management of schemas were described. Furthermore, a short overview of the overall archi-tecture of the schema service was presented. Finally, the evaluation described in the evaluation chapter showed that a larger environmental software project can benefit from the presented concepts of the schema service in different ways. It provides stricter checking of data consistency, can link data to meta information given an interpretation context for the data which can be used by an application without hardcoding the interpretation knowledge into the application itself. Thus, it helps to implement advanced, but helpful functionalities for users, such as filtering of data or navigation between data within the application.

Important further work lies in the extension of the service API. A basic set of functions that is required for the usage of the service has already been implemented. Still, additional features such as extended filtering and an extended search would improve the API. Additionally, a more powerful user interface is needed for updating and managing schemas. It simplifies the verification process of the service API and makes it more reliable. Moreover, different data formats can be considered. One of the service's limitations is that it works with JSON/JSON Schema only, which are the most widespread data formats in the context of web engineering. Still, it may be useful to support other data formats as well, for example XML/XSD or RDF/OWL. Especially, schema information returned to the client can be augmented with semantic annotations leading to Linked Data using JSON-LD.

References

1. JSON Schema Homepage. http://json-schema.org. Accessed 13 Sept 2019
2. Zyp, K., Court, G., Galiegue, F.: JSON Schema: core definitions and terminology, Internet Engineering Task Force, Internet-Draft draft-zyp-json-schema-04, August 2013. https://tools.ietf.org/html/draft-zyp-json-schema-04. Accessed 20 Aug 2019
3. The JSON Data Interchange Format, 1st edn. ECMA International, October 2013. http://www.ecma-international.org/publications/files/ECMA-ST/ECMA-404.pdf. Accessed 23 Aug 2019
4. Bray, T.: The JavaScript Object Notation (JSON) Data Interchange Format, IETF RFC 7158, October 2015. https://rfc-editor.org/rfc/rfc7158.txt. Accessed 23 Aug 2019
5. Krylovskiy, A., Jahn, M., Patti, E.: Designing a smart city Internet of Things platform with microservice architecture. In: 2015 3rd International Conference on Future Internet of Things and Cloud, Rome, 24–26 August 2015. https://doi.org/10.1109/FiCloud.2015.55
6. Mattmann, C., Crichton, D., Medvidovic, N., Hughes, S.: A software architecture-based framework for highly distributed and data intensive scientific applications. In: Proceedings of the 28th International Conference on Software Engineering, ICSE 2006, Shanghai, pp. 721–730, 20–28 May 2006
7. Kolchin, M., Klimov, N., Shilin, I., Garayzuev, D., Andreev, A., Mouromtsev, D.: SEMIOT: an architecture of semantic Internet of Things middleware. In: 2016 IEEE International Conference on Internet of Things (iThings) and IEEE Green Computing and Communications (GreenCom) and IEEE Cyber, Physical and Social Computing (CPSCom) and IEEE Smart Data (Smart Data). https://doi.org/10.1109/iThings-Green-CPSCom-SmartData.2016.98
8. Chervenak, A., Foster, I., Kesselman, C., Salisbury, C., Tuecke, S.: The data grid: towards an architecture for the distributed management and analysis of large scientific datasets. J. Netw. Comput. Appl. **23**, 187–200 (2000). https://doi.org/10.1006/jnca.2000.0110

9. Kettouch, M., Luca, C., Hobbs, M.: Using semantic similarity for schema matching of semi-structured and linked data. In: 2017 Internet Technologies and Applications (ITA). https://doi.org/10.1109/ITECHA.2017.8101923

10. Agocs, A., Le Goff, J.-M.: A web service based on RESTful API and JSON Schema/JSON Meta Schema to construct knowledge graphs. In: 2018 International Conference on Computer, Information and Telecommunication Systems (CITS). https://doi.org/10.1109/CITS.2018.8440193

11. Giessler, P., Gebhart, M., Steinegger, R., Abeck, S.: Checklist for the API design of web services based on REST. Int. J. Adv. Internet Technol. 9(3&4), 41–51 (2016)

12. Jensen, S.-K., Pedersen, T.-B., Thomsen, C.: Time series management systems: a survey. IEEE Trans. Knowl. Data Eng. 29(11) (2017). https://doi.org/10.1109/TKDE.2017.2740932

13. Influx DB. https://www.influxdata.com/. Accessed 09 Sept 2019

14. MongoDB. https://www.mongodb.com/. Accessed 09 Sept 2019

15. Elasticsearch. https://www.elastic.co/. Accessed 09 Sept 2019

16. Fielding, R.: Architectural Styles and the Design of Network-Based Software Architectures. University of California, Irvine (2000)

17. Environment Thesaurus of the Umweltbundesministerium. https://sns.uba.de/umthes/de/hierarchical_concepts.html. Accessed 27 Nov 2019

18. Leadbetter, B., Smyth, D., Fuller, R., O'Grady, E., Shepherd, A.: Where big data meets linked data: applying standard data models to environmental data streams. In: 2016 IEEE International Conference on Big Data (Big Data). https://doi.org/10.1109/BigData.2016.7840943

19. Al Rasyid, M., Syarif, I., Putra, I.: Linked data for air pollution monitoring. In: 2017 International Electronics Symposium on Knowledge Creation and Intelligent Computing (IES-KCIC). https://doi.org/10.1109/KCIC.2017.8228565

20. Hildenbrand, T., Rothlauf, F., Geisser, M., Heinzel, A., Kude, T.: Approaches to collaborative software development. In: 2008 International Conference on Complex, Intelligent and Software Intensive Systems. https://doi.org/10.1109/CISIS.2008.106

21. Hata, H., Mizuno, O., Kikuno, T.: Historage: fine-grained version control system for Java. In: Proceedings of the 12th International Workshop on Principles of Software Evolution and the 7th annual ERCIM Workshop on Software Evolution, IWPSE-EVOL 2011, September 2011. https://doi.org/10.1145/2024445.2024463

22. Prasad, S., Bhole, A.: Application of polyglot persistence to enhance performance of the energy data management systems. In: 2014 International Conference on Advances in Electronics, Computers and Communications (ICAECC). https://doi.org/10.1109/ICAECC.2014.7002444

23. Newman, S.: Building Microservices. O'Reilly Media Inc., Newton (2015)

Models in the Cloud: Exploring Next Generation Environmental Software Systems

Will Simm[1](✉), Gordon Blair[1], Richard Bassett[2], Faiza Samreen[1],
and Paul Young[2]

[1] School of Computing and Communications, Lancaster University, Lancaster, UK
w.simm@lancaster.ac.uk
[2] Lancaster Environment Centre, Lancaster University, Lancaster, UK
http://www.ensembleprojects.org

Abstract. There is growing interest in the application of the latest trends in computing and data science methods to improve environmental science. However we found the penetration of best practice from computing domains such as software engineering and cloud computing into supporting every day environmental science to be poor. We take from this work a real need to re-evaluate the complexity of software tools and bring these to the right level of abstraction for environmental scientists to be able to leverage the latest developments in computing. In the Models in the Cloud project, we look at the role of model driven engineering, software frameworks and cloud computing in achieving this abstraction. As a case study we deployed a complex weather model to the cloud and developed a collaborative notebook interface for orchestrating the deployment and analysis of results. We navigate relatively poor support for complex high performance computing in the cloud to develop abstractions from complexity in cloud deployment and model configuration. We found great potential in cloud computing to transform science by enabling models to leverage elastic, flexible computing infrastructure and support new ways to deliver collaborative and open science.

Keywords: Cloud computing · Environmental modelling · Data science

1 Introduction

Models in the Cloud is a three year project which sets out to explore the opportunity for a paradigm shift in the support offered by cloud computing for the execution of complex environmental models. Cloud computing is having a major and transformative impact on many areas of society, including in smart cities, eCommerce and eGovernment. Significant advances are being made in these areas and cloud computing is proving to be of significant benefit in minimising up-front investment, achieving economies of scale, supporting elasticity in the

© The Author(s) 2020
I. N. Athanasiadis et al. (Eds.): ISESS 2020, IFIP AICT 554, pp. 216–227, 2020.
https://doi.org/10.1007/978-3-030-39815-6_21

underlying computational/storage capacity and out-sourcing of the infrastructure management [6].

These advances present a new opportunity for configuring computing on demand, and provide a fabric of services that can be configured and combined to support new modes of working. In visioning the future, consider that the code for a software model of the environment is constrained by the computer system it is to be deployed upon, traditionally a desktop computer or a high performance parallel computing environment. Here, the experiment is designed to fit the available computer. Now consider that cloud computing effectively allows you to design a computer around your experiment, removing constraints in a flexible, on demand, dynamic environment, then the potential opportunities for science are vast.

In his call to action for software engineers, Easterbrook [3] specifically identifies 'Computer-Supported Collaborative Science' as a fundamental way in which software engineering can contribute to addressing the grand challenge of climate change. He identified that through supporting earth system models with software engineering tools and techniques we can accelerate the process of getting scientific ideas into working code.

Blair et al. [2] laid out a roadmap of 10 challenges for research in data science of the natural environment. These research challenges cross-cut the themes of data acquisition, infrastructure, methods and policy making and are summarised here: (1) supporting a cultural shift towards more open and more collaborative science; (2) build on cloud computing, extending the levels of abstraction for the domain of science; (3) address complexity more fundamentally and explicitly, e.g. data science techniques to address extremes and emergent behaviours; (4) provide the tools to reify uncertainty and reason about cascading uncertainty; (5) seek adaptive techniques such as adaptive sampling or adaptive modelling driven by uncertainty considerations; (6) seek approaches that deal with epistemic uncertainty in environmental modeling and links with dealing with emergent behavior in complex and irreducible phenomena; (7) seek novel data science techniques, especially those that can make sense of the increasing complexity, variety and veracity of underlying environmental data; (8) seek innovations in modeling by combining process models with data-driven or stochastic modeling techniques; (9) incorporate sophisticated spatial and temporal reasoning, including reasoning across scales; and (10) discover new modes of working, methods and means of organization that enable new levels of cross-disciplinary collaboration.

In this work we primarily address challenge (2) and see running models in a collaborative, elastic cloud environment is fundamental to underpin many of the other challenges. In supporting new modes of science, it is critical to provide tools at the right level of abstraction for uptake by scientists in their work, and it is through the lens of abstraction that this project focuses to ascertain what is in place and what is required to leverage cloud computing.

Abstracting from underlying compute infrastructure and defining interfaces and datastores for environmental models will allow models to be connected and run more efficiently, and to allow scientists to concentrate on the science, resulting in a better understanding of phenomena and uncertainties which would hopefully be reflected in better policy informed by results. This work forms a core pillar of technology enabling the concept of 'models of everywhere' - a vision to have models of everywhere, models of everything and models at all times, being constantly re-evaluated against the most current evidence [1].

In prior work we published a qualitative study with environmental modellers, and an implementation and associated feedback from modellers on a cloud deployment of a complex weather model [9]. This paper summarises that work, adds further analysis and describes the next steps taken.

The aim of this research is to determine if the principles and approaches exist to leverage cloud computing at a usable level of abstraction, and to inform the development of new tools and practices. This paper contributes the approach we took, the lessons learned from qualitative and experimental work, and adds reflections on lessons learnt to inform taking this work forward.

2   Methodology

As part of an interdisciplinary team of researchers [1], we undertake agile research. This involves relatively short cycles of "Plan - Act - Reflect", with each cycle informing the next. Supporting this work is an evolution of the Speedplay research methodology [4], rooted in participatory design that sees the computer scientists and environmental scientists in equal partnership, developing together. In this research we will go full circle, not just unravelling and understanding the opportunity, but designing and building technologies with end users embedded in the process.

We had end users as collaborators embedded throughout the project, the research team was comprised of experienced computer scientists and environmental modellers. We first did a qualitative study phase with environmental modellers from across the spectrum of the modelling community, this allowed us to up skill in understanding, shared language and get a handle on the challenges faced by modellers. It also helped focus the resources of the study.

We went onto an experimental phase where we began 'learning through doing' - exploring the application of abstraction technologies to this domain, putting models into cloud architectures and learning about the challenges in doing this both from computing and environmental science perspectives. This is the 'Act' part of the cycles in which feedback and reflection is embedded in directing the research.

3   Qualitative Phase

We undertook a study consisting of semi-structured interviews and demonstrations with a diverse group of five environmental scientists engaged in writing

---

[1]   https://www.ensembleprojects.org/.

software to model a variety of environmental systems and processes. The purpose of the study was to gain an understanding of how environmental models are developed and deployed, and the computing tools and architectures which are used. These sessions also up skilled both computer and environmental scientists in their domain languages (e.g. cloud in the sky vs cloud computing, environmental model vs software model) and understanding of each other's domain. Further detail is in Simm et al. [9] but the findings are summarised and analysis extended here.

We selected our 5x participants from those working with a range of model complexities, from small scale statistical models of insect population to community developed global climate models. This was to enable us to gain an understanding of the challenges and opportunities at each scale. We grouped findings under Technical, Scientific and Human headings, for brevity just the main technical findings are summarised here [9]:

Computational Demands and Resources required by models varied from desktop machines to institutional high performance computing (HPC) facilities. When running models on HPC, in depth systems administration skills are required such as file system preparation, shell script writing and good command line familiarity. Data is input and output in flat files not data stores, and sorted and downloaded by FTP and shared by email. Projects are not costed to include projected compute costs or support form experienced software engineers.

In terms of **Computational Skills and Expertise** each of the participants had self-taught programming and systems admin without a formal education in computing. Code is frequently written as a monolith with little thought to code reuse or defining interfaces or structure.

Code Understanding - models are written in scientific languages such as Fortran, Matlab and R, often models are configured and run with Bash scripts and results are analysed using Python and R. Code is often not well commented and is difficult for others to understand, and Integrated Development Environments (IDEs) are not used often except for Matlab and R.

Version Control systems are not widely used, code (and data) being shared by email amongst collaborators rather than using version controlled repositories which leads to confusion about the 'latest version' and why changes are made and by whom.

Fault Tolerance and Resilience is good in large community models, allowing them to restart after a crash. However many models are difficult to debug and understand why crashes have occurred.

(In)efficiency arises from needing to download large data files (sometimes 10's of GiB) to extract the small amount of data for focus as data is stored in flat file format rather than query-able data stores. Code reuse is poor, languages like R do not enforce object orientated styles, and the choice of language is sometimes sub optimal, e.g. R is good at statistical modelling but often used for many other things.

Compatibility - the interfaces for running models are not abstracted from the models - in depth knowledge of the model is required to configure, parameterise and run models. Data input and output is usually flat file CSV, netCDF and Excel spreadsheet format.

This phase of embedding computer scientists in the environmental modelling domain allowed us to grasp the challenges faced by environmental modellers and understand what appropriate abstractions over computing complexity might be. The main finding of this phase of work from the perspective of this project is that the code of environmental models is deeply entwined with the architecture of the conventional computing systems and the working practices of environmental scientists. There is a great desire to move the science on from this complexity, which we believe could be achieved through abstraction. Indeed, to foster greater understanding of uncertainty in models of environmental systems, models runs may need to be more efficient and run many more times in many more places with approaches such as models of everywhere [1]. Software engineering achieves the separation of concerns through abstraction using modularity, frameworks and defined interfaces; these practices are not often seen in day to day environmental modelling, possibly due to a lack of SE training, but mainly due to the absence of tools at a usable level of abstraction for this domain.

The offline mode of working makes sharing and collaborating difficult, we found our participants indicated closer collaboration would be desirable for science. Code is not released to the community because it is not considered robust or efficient; usually this is because of concerns about input data, misunderstood bugs or the specifics of a system such as configuration of dependencies. A software engineer can see much of this could be resolved through abstraction (e.g. by using pre-built data cleaning libraries rather than unique data cleaning code), changes to code writing style to make debugging easier, and using dependency management tools.

3.1   Opportunities for Abstraction

Computational abstraction alone will not address the problems identified in the qualitative work, social factors are important as well, but beyond the scope of this paper. However we believe abstracting from computational complexity can play a significant role at multiple levels:

1. At the **model code** level: Software frameworks and robust software engineering practices such as defined interfaces and modular code architectures would allow code reuse, reduce dev time and reduce the need for debugging.
2. At the **infrastructure** level: By removing the reliance on the desktop and HPC there is the opportunity to deploy models to new and flexible architectures provided by cloud computing. There are multiple additional benefits here of opening access to experiments for collaborative science, and access to data stores and data science tools already present in cloud offerings.
3. At the **model configuration** level: Complex models have interdependence across a huge volume of configurations, the interaction of which needs to be understood, and sometimes the same value needs to be specified in multiple places.

4. At the **model parameterisation** level: There is a range of methods to parameterise models, often involving multiple model runs before settling on a suitable parameter set.

The first opportunity is perhaps symptomatic of a lack of core software engineering skills within the community writing software models. It cannot be addressed without significant re-engineering of models; our participants pledged to learn about best practice but software frameworks for developing and running models would support this.

The second is one area in which we chose to focus our efforts by deploying models to the cloud to explore the opportunity, and look for tools at the right level of abstraction to enable an environmental modeller to configure and deploy a suitable infrastructure for their experiment.

The third is another area we looked at, and felt their was an opportunity for techniques such as Model Driven Engineering (MDE) to build a software model of the complexities in configuration of environmental models.

The fourth we have considered and propose that techniques from AI and machine learning can reduce the parameter space and help the scientist to select the most suitable parameters for their experiment, but only if models exist in an on demand, flexible cloud infrastructure supported by fit for purpose data stores and powerful data science machines.

4 Experimental Phase

This phase describes approaches to abstracting over (i) the complexity in the configuration and deployment of an environmental model (abstraction 3 above) and (ii) the complexity in cloud deployment of the model (abstraction 2 above). We created a tool for the configuration experiments, and a cloud deployment of the Weather Research and Forecasting (WRF) model. Here, we raise the level of abstraction through reducing the complexity of configuration and deployment, leveraging the on demand scale-ability of cloud architecture.

4.1 WRF

The Weather Research and Forecasting (WRF) model [10] is a large community-based endeavour (around 40,000 users), supported by the National Center for Atmospheric Research (NCAR). The model is primarily used for atmospheric research and forecasting across a wide range of scales (thousands of kilometres to meters). The diverse range of extensively validated science WRF can simulate includes regional climate, air quality, urban heat islands, hurricanes, forest fires, and flooding through coupling with hydrological models.

WRF is chosen as a case study here for the following reasons: (i) WRF installation is viewed as a barrier to use; (ii) cloud resources will enable WRF users to conduct simulations beyond current capability [7]; (iii) WRFs open-source nature and portability; and (iv) benefits will impact WRFs large community user base.

4.2   Configuration and Collaboration

Model Driven Engineering (MDE) is an approach to managing complexity in software systems and to capture domain knowledge effectively [8]. Domain knowledge is captured in a software model of the system, this model is configured using Domain Specific Languages (DSLs) that relate to the application domain and potentially the underlying platform features. Code is then generated by the model using transformation approaches to configure and deploy the system being modelled. This approach has been applied successfully in a variety of areas [8] including in industry settings [5].

In this work we investigated using this approach to develop DSLs to allow scientists to describe an experiment, with the underlying software model managing the generation of code to configure the environmental model appropriately, deploying the model to appropriate flexible cloud infrastructure and returning results. In exploring the tools available, we found they are not able to support such a vision at the current state of readiness. There are so many complexities and flexibility required in configuring models like WRF for the many different uses, that to hard code a set of rules into a DSL was not an approach that was likely to be successful.

Instead we decided to use a general purpose language to manage the configuration and deployment, and proposed embedding a future 'learning' approach that would match experimental configurations to infrastructures, and would be able to recommend an appropriate architecture for an experimental configuration. In our qualitative phase we found our participants were familiar with languages such as R and Python, often used to process data and produce visualisations.

In taking this MDE-lite approach, we produced a Python object based model of a WRF experiment configuration, that allows configuration using standard Python constructs. The Python package f90nml[2] allows the object to generate Fortran 90 namelist files that are used to configure WRF, these are auto-uploaded to the WRF instance for deployment. This provides a layer of abstraction over the skills required to login to an instance, navigate the file system, and edit the Fortran namelist file without introducing errors. No configuration dependencies are managed in this first iteration, but this can be added to the Python model in future.

Code notebooks such as Jupyter[3] are now widely used in the data science community to collaborate and annotate data analysis. They are online environments, often hosted in the cloud (but not necessarily publicly available) that allow code to be edited and run with multiple collaborators. They allow mixed mode documentation, with in line code and output visualisation from many modern programming languages, including Python and R. They are able to pull in data from outside sources and write out data to attached cloud native stores or via API.

---

[2] https://pypi.org/project/f90nml/.
[3] https://jupyter.org/.

For our purposes a Jupyter code notebook provides an ideal space for environmental scientists to control modelling experiments. Whilst it would not be possible to run a complex model such as WRF in the notebook, it is possible to configure a run experiments via system APIs. The model can be configured using our Python object based configuration tool, and the experiment run outside of the notebook (either on the same machine or an external 'cloud burst') with output data returned to the notebook for collaborative analysis. The notebook allows the experiment to be documented (supporting scientific reproducibility) and shared, extending the reach of the experiment.

4.3   Cloud Deployment of WRF

We built a scripted cloud deployment of WRF, and evaluated usability, performance and cost metrics. This installation script dealt with dependencies and the configuration and compilation required to run WRF on the Microsoft Azure cloud platform. The script is automated as far as possible, however in a number of places unavoidable user input is requested from the WRF installer.

The architecture of the WRF model itself is complex, described by [10]. Our standard cloud configuration consisted of a Message Passing Interface (MPI) supported cluster of 9 standard compute nodes from the Microsoft Azure Dsv3-series each having a 3.2 GHz Intel Xeon E5-2673 v4 (Broadwell) processor. One node is a master node taking care of all the compilation and providing a means of sharing the storage and computation with all the nodes.

We used a predefined image of Ubuntu Server 16.06 LTS for each of the cluster machines and each node has 8 processors with 32 GiB RAM and temporary storage of 64 GiB that is considered a secondary storage for each compute node. We used the GNU Fortran and GCC compilers. The cluster provides primary storage of 100 GiB shared amongst nodes via the Network File System (NFS). The shared location contains all the simulation related input/output data and files required for WRF configuration as well as compilation. All the cluster nodes and storage are deployed in Western Europe under one secure virtual network and have friction-less access to enable data sharing and execution of MPI jobs.

An expert user group of 6 regular WRF users agreed that our automated WRF deployment successfully abstracted over the major hurdle of initially installing the model. They helped to develop the use cases that we used in developing the work: (A) removing barriers to entry for new users, allowing them to immediately run experiments; (B) users wanting to run the model in a standard way to feed results into other models; and (C) power users wishing to deploy massively in parallel and without waiting for institutional HPC queue times [9].

4.4   Mechanisms for Cloud Computing Configuration

To build on this scripted installation, we investigated key mechanisms to abstract over the complexities of configuring compute architecture, by exploring different modes of cloud deployment. We wanted to retain as much flexibility in the deployment whilst retaining usability for our use cases.

Portal Configuration. The scripted installation described above requires the manual configuration of the cluster from the Azure web portal, or defined in code using their Infrastructure As Code (IAC) offering, which are general purpose interfaces and require a deep understanding of the desired infrastructure. Because of this knowledge required, it is perhaps not a suitable interface for our use cases except perhaps (C) the power user who may have an understanding of the relative merits of different cluster configurations and be able to fine tune to their experiment manually. Since the WRF installation is not fully automated, it still requires user interaction.

Containerisation is a mechanism whereby the software environment including dependencies for a particular application is defined in code. These containers are infrastructure agnostic, so can be deployed to any suitable provider. However the MPI architecture of the WRF model makes it unsuitable for containerisation - MPI is the mechanism by which messages are transferred between nodes, and we found little support for this in existing technologies. This situation is changing, with a number of providers beginning to offer support for MPI [4].

LibCloud is a Python library for interacting with many cloud providers, abstracting from their specific IAC offering. This allows a provider agnostic configuration of a cloud infrastructure from a notebook, however it is again general purpose and does not encompass every offering from every provider. It is designed for the computer scientist, and does not really abstract from the complexity of deploying a cloud computing system, just from the differences that individual cloud providers might have for their standard machines. It also does not get around the user interaction required for installing WRF so perhaps only suitable for use case (C).

Infrastructure As A Service (IAAS) allows the replication of predefined and configured machine images, allowing standard node with WRF installed to be instantiated on demand. In Azure this can be in their machine image library for anyone to use, and other providers have similar facilities.

In summary, the IAAS approach was selected as being most suitable for our WRF cloud deployment as it means deployment is instantaneous with no user interaction required in getting a system running WRF running, so good for use cases (A) and (B). However this reduces flexibility for (C) in terms of virtual machine specification as it is tied to a specific standard machine type offered by our cloud provider. Without re-engineering the WRF installer, or WRF itself it was not possible at this time to create a cloud-native, provider agnostic system without user input in the installation.

4.5 Experimental System

The IAAS approach whilst reducing ultimate flexibility in infrastructure, allowed us to explore how WRF might be configured and deployed from a notebook environment. We built a demonstrator using the Azure SDK for Python to configure and deploy a WRF cluster from within a Jupyter notebook running on an

---

[4] https://www.stackhpc.com/the-state-of-hpc-containers.html.

instance of Azure data science machine and so far a number of test experiments have been run.

Ongoing Work: The next stage in developing this system is to integrate the WRF namelist configuration tool to the same notebook, and return results as an attached data store to the machine. The same Jupyter notebook can then be used to sort output data and prepare data visualizations. In this way the whole experiment can be orchestrated through a single collaborative notebook interface, which is version controlled and can be archived easily. Figure 1 shows this visually.

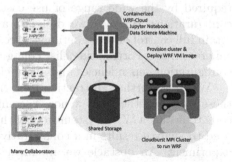

Fig. 1. WRF-cloud system architecture

5 Reflections

The key successes of this project were in using the WRF case study to navigate available technologies to create useful abstractions not only to enable the scientist to focus on science, but in support of Easterbrook's vision of the next generation of computer supported collaborative science [3]. A vision where models form part of a service fabric of technologies that can be recombined and run an unlimited number of times to explore the specifics of place and rationalise about uncertainty. The work underpins Blair's ten challenges to environmental data science community [1] and leverages the elasticity and flexibility of cloud computing to provide on demand, scale-able computing.

Adapting WRF to a cloud computing infrastructure and attempting to leverage the latest advances was bound to face some challenges. WRF has been developed over decades and consists of about half a million lines of Fortran code. Fortran is especially good at large scale numerical simulation, however it is not a typically supported language in the modern software industry and hence cloud computing platforms. The MPI libraries for parallelising code were written for Fortran and C++, and support for these is low in cloud native technologies such as containerisation, although this is changing as more cloud providers consider supporting scientific applications. Containerisation allows complete abstraction from underlying compute architecture, and would make deployment on new generations of machines possible. As such it was not possible during the project to leverage these cutting-edge technologies to run WRF, and we had to step back to an IAAS approach of using machine images to explore our ideas.

Installing and compiling WRF on new machines is a chore, and requires an advanced computing skill set. Our demonstrator of an auto-install of WRF to the cloud was an eye-opener for many of our participant scientists. The ability to simply spin up a virtual machine pre-installed with WRF is beginning to be used in teaching labs, instead of requiring students to go through the long error-prone process. This was a successful exercise in abstraction from complexity.

We found the tools developed by the MDE research community to be unable to capture the complexity of WRF deployment without reducing the flexibility required by the wide range of use cases - they required hard coding a set of configurations. However we designed a Python tool to allow the scientist to retain full control of the experimental configuration, without risking errors in the generation of a Fortran namelist configuration file, that in future could manage configuration dependencies and abstract from configuration complexities.

We added further abstraction from the cloud provider's interface by bringing these tools together into a now becoming familiar Jupyter notebook, writing code to deploy a WRF system from within the notebook, which can then also be used to analyse results in a collaborative environment that describes the whole experiment. An obstacle we are facing in completing this vision is the poor support of WRF's netCDF output files, which are designed for flat file stores. Other groups are working on this, for example Unidata at UCAR[5].

6   Conclusion

In this project we aimed to find out if the principles and approaches exist to leverage cloud computing at a usable level of abstraction in environmental modelling, and we found we were able to make usable abstractions from complexity in deployment of the WRF model to cloud, and the configuration of WRF. We found a notebook based approach supports new practices in collaborative and open science through the ability to describe and run an experiment in a single notebook document that can be shared and examined by others. Our findings can be generalised to other complex models, specifically MPI based models but learning is applicable to many others.

The abstractions proposed and explored through this project mean that WRF could form part of a cloud service fabric consisting of many models, data stores and data science services that could run as many times and in as many combinations as desired. Add in cloud based machine learning facilities and a system could propose its own infrastructures based on the experiment to be run, as well as help to reduce the workload of scientists in terms of reducing parameter spaces when parameterising models. These abstractions also have potential to be significant when operationalising code which needs to run continuously and effectively, allowing code to be run on diverse and shared architectures.

Future work will involve 'closing the loop' by returning outputs from WRF to the notebook by connecting output data to a cloud native data store, thus enabling the analysis of output within the same notebook, but also powerfully interfacing output to other models as part of the aforementioned service fabric. This work primarily focused on technical factors, but equally there are many social factors at play in defining the software and hardware architectures in use in environmental science. Future work could include exploring the barriers these present to the take up of new computing technologies.

---

[5] https://www.unidata.ucar.edu/blogs/news/entry/netcdf-and-native-cloud-storage.

Acknowledgements. Thanks to the wider Ensemble team (https://www.ensemble projects.org/) for their support. This work is supported by "Models in the Cloud: Generative Software Frameworks to Support the Execution of Environmental Models in the Cloud" EPSRC: EP/N027736/1 and a Microsoft Azure AI for Earth grant.

References

1. Blair, G.S., et al.: Models of everywhere revisited: a technological perspective. Environ. Model. Softw. **122**, 104521 (2019). https://doi.org/10.1016/j.envsoft.2019.104521
2. Blair, G.S., et al.: Data science of the natural environment: a research roadmap. Front. Environ. Sci. **7**, 121 (2019). https://doi.org/10.3389/fenvs.2019.00121
3. Easterbrook, S.M.: Climate change: a grand software challenge. In: Proceedings of the FSE/SDP Workshop on Future of Software Engineering Research, FoSER 2010, pp. 99–104. ACM, New York (2010). https://doi.org/10.1145/1882362.1882383
4. Ferrario, M.A., Simm, W., Newman, P., Forshaw, S., Whittle, J.: Software engineering for 'social good': integrating action research, participatory design, and agile development. In: Companion Proceedings of the 36th International Conference on Software Engineering, ICSE Companion 2014, pp. 520–523. ACM, New York (2014). https://doi.org/10.1145/2591062.2591121
5. Hutchinson, J., Whittle, J., Rouncefield, M., Kristoffersen, S.: Empirical assessment of MDE in industry. In: Proceedings of the 33rd International Conference on Software Engineering, ICSE 2011, pp. 471–480. ACM, New York (2011). https://doi.org/10.1145/1985793.1985858
6. Johnson, R.E.: Frameworks = (components + patterns). Commun. ACM **40**(10), 39–42 (1997). https://doi.org/10.1145/262793.262799
7. Powers, J.G., et al.: The weather research and forecasting model: overview, system efforts, and future directions. Bull. Am. Meteorol. Soc. **98**(8), 1717–1737 (2017). https://doi.org/10.1175/BAMS-D-15-00308.1
8. Schmidt, D.C.: Guest editor's introduction: model-driven engineering. Computer **39**(2), 25–31 (2006). https://doi.org/10.1109/MC.2006.58
9. Simm, W.A., et al.: SE in ES: opportunities for software engineering and cloud computing in environmental science. In: Proceedings of the 40th International Conference on Software Engineering: Software Engineering in Society, ICSE-SEIS 2018, pp. 61–70. ACM, New York (2018). https://doi.org/10.1145/3183428.3183430
10. Skamarock, W., et al.: A description of the advanced research WRF version 3 (2008). https://doi.org/10.5065/D68S4MVH

An Environmental Sensor Data Suite Using the OGC SensorThings API

Hylke van der Schaaf[1(✉)], Jürgen Moßgraber[1], Sylvain Grellet[2],
Mickaël Beaufils[2], Kathi Schleidt[3], and Thomas Usländer[1]

[1] Fraunhofer IOSB, Fraunhoferstr. 1, 76131 Karlsruhe, Germany
{hylke.vanderschaaf,juergen.mossgraber,
thomas.uslaender}@iosb.fraunhofer.de
[2] BRGM, 3 avenue Claude-Guillemin, BP 36009, 45060 Orléans Cedex 2, France
{s.grellet,m.beaufils}@brgm.fr
[3] DataCove e.U., Robert Hamerling Gasse 1/14, 1150 Vienna, Austria
kathi@datacove.eu

Abstract. In many application domains sensor data contributes an important part to the situation awareness required for decision making. Examples range from environmental and climate change situations to industrial production processes. All these fields need to aggregate and fuse many data sources, the semantics of the data needs to be understood and the results must be presented to the decision makers in an accessible way. This process is already defined as the "sensor to decision chain" [11] but which solutions and technologies can be proposed for implementing it?

Since the Internet of Things (IoT) is rapidly growing with an estimated number of 30 billion sensors in 2020, it offers excellent potential to collect time-series data for improving situational awareness. The IoT brings several challenges: caused by a splintered sensor manufacturer landscape, data comes in various structures, incompatible protocols and unclear semantics. To tackle these challenges a well-defined interface, from where uniform data can be queried, is necessary. The Open Geospatial Consortium (OGC) has recognized this demand and developed the SensorThings API (STA) standard, an open, unified way to interconnect devices throughout the IoT. Since its introduction in 2016, it has shown to be a versatile and easy to use standard for exchanging and managing sensor data.

This paper proposes the STA as the central part for implementing the sensor to decision chain. Furthermore, it describes several projects that successfully implemented the architecture and identifies open issues with the SensorThings API that, if solved, would further improve the usability of the API.

Keywords: Open geospatial standards · Sensor data management · Architecture

© IFIP International Federation for Information Processing 2020
Published by Springer Nature Switzerland AG 2020
I. N. Athanasiadis et al. (Eds.): ISESS 2020, IFIP AICT 554, pp. 228–241, 2020.
https://doi.org/10.1007/978-3-030-39815-6_22

1   What Is the OGC SensorThings API

The OGC SensorThings API [9,15] is a standard for exchanging sensor data and metadata. It is, in many ways, a redesign of the older OGC Sensor Web Enablement (SWE) standards, targeted at the Internet of Things (IoT). The OGC SensorThings API (STA) currently consists of two parts: "part 1: Sensing" and "part 2: Tasking". The Sensing part can be seen as a successor to the OGC Sensor Observation Service, while the Tasking part overlaps specifically with the Sensor Planning Service. One of the goals of the development of the STA was to make a service that is lighter weight and easier to use than the SWE standards based on SOAP/XML that already existed, by moving to a REST approach as architectural style (see below). The API adapts the OASIS OData standard for this REST interface, offering simple data navigation, powerful filtering and the ability to customise the results to minimise the amount of data transferred and the number of necessary requests. Furthermore, the API supports push-messages to notify clients of changes in the data.

The API specifies not only the methods used to interact (Create, Read, Update, Delete) with the data in the service but also the data model that describes the data that is stored in the service.

1.1   REST as Architectural Style

Service-orientation has been a best-practices approach in industrial software engineering for many years. However, several architectural styles addressing how to realize the service paradigm on the concrete technological level are competing [20]. Some years ago, service orientation focused upon Web services that follow the classical architectural style of remote invocation of operations with arbitrary semantics in its behaviour, however, sometimes only specified to a certain degree leading to difficulties in semantic interoperability. On the other hand, there are the so-called RESTful Web services [16] that rely upon uniquely identifiable resources with a limited set of well-defined operations (e.g. get, set, create, delete), following the Representational State Transfer (REST) architectural style of Fielding [4].

Within the OGC SWE domain several architectural styles are co-existing. Originally starting with Web services, see the Sensor Observation Service and the Sensor Planning Service as stated above, the current development of the STA is focussing on the REST-based architectural style.

1.2   Data Model

The data model of the STA is depicted in Fig. 1. It is based on the ISO Observations and Measurements (O&M) conceptual model [7,14] and consists of 8 entity types, their properties, and the relations between the entity types.

The following entity types are defined in the API:

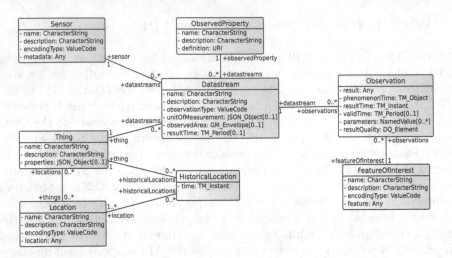

Fig. 1. The data model of the OGC SensorThings API part 1 – Sensing.

Thing. What a thing is, depends completely on the individual use case. In the case of environmental monitoring, the environmental monitoring station may be a Thing, but a river, river section or ship can also be defined as a Thing.

Location. The location defines where the Thing is. It can hold a machine-readable GeoJSON object describing this location, or a human-readable description, like an address.

HistoricalLocation. In some cases, Things move. Every time the Location of a Thing changes, a new HistoricalLocation is created, that stores when the Thing was at the given Location.

Sensor. The sensor holds the description of the device or procedure that created an Observation. This can be a relatively simple electronic device, or a complicated procedure, executed by a technician in a laboratory.

ObservedProperty. The Observed Property describes the property that is being observed, like "temperature", "humidity" or "traffic density"

Datastream. A Datastream connects a set of Observations, of the same ObservedProperty, made by same Sensor, to a Thing. The Datastream also holds the unit of measurement of the Observations.

Observation. The Observation object holds the actual result value of the measurement made by the Sensor. This result can be a numeric value, but can also be any other valid JSON type, including a complete JSON Object or Array.

FeatureOfInterest. The FeatureOfInterest gives the Observation a location. In many cases, this will be the same as the Location of the Thing that is linked to the Observation through the Datastream, but in the case of a moving Thing, or in the case of remote sensing, the FeatureOfInterest can be different from the Location of the Thing.

Each of these entity types have several entity properties that describe exactly what data can be stored in each entity. Most of these properties are self explanatory, like name or description. Some noteworthy properties are:

Observation/phenomenonTime. The phenomenonTime is the time at which the phenomenon that was observed existed. In many cases, with in-situ sensors, this is the time at which the measurement was made. In the case of ex-situ measurements, where a sample is taken that is sent to a laboratory to be analysed, it is the time when the sample was taken. In the case of predictions, the phenomenonTime can be in the future. Furthermore, the phenomenon-Time can be either a time instant, or a time interval. In the case that the observation is an average over a certain time interval, the phenomenonTime can exactly reflect this time interval over which the average was taken.

Observation/result. The result can be a numeric value, but can also be any other valid JSON type, including a complete JSON Object or Array.

Thing/properties. The "properties" property of Thing and the parameters property of "Observation" are of the type JSON Object. The user is free to store any data in these fields. Depending on the server implementation, these fields are also searchable.

Besides entity properties, entity types also have relations, called navigation properties. Most relations are one-to-many, like the Thing-Datastream relation, and the Datastream-Observation relation. This means a Datastream has exactly one Thing, but a Thing can have zero to many Datastreams. On the "one" side of the relation, the relation is mandatory, meaning that a Datastream must have a Thing, a Sensor and an ObservedProperty and the service must ensure this requirement is met. There is one many-to-many relation in the base specification: Thing-Location. A thing can be linked to zero-to-many Locations, and each Location can be linked to zero-to-many things.

1.3 HTTP (REST) Interface

The main interface for the SensorThings API is the HTTP interface. It is based on the OASIS OData interface, but does not follow the OData specification completely. The base URL of a SensorThings API service always ends in the version number of the specification that the service implements. This makes it clear for both client and server which version of the specification is used. The 8 entity types described above each have an entity collection through which these entities can be accessed. Fetching the base URL of the API with a HTTP Get returns an index document listing the URL of each of the available entity collections.

A HTTP-Get request on a collection returns a list of the entities in the collection. Each entity can also be fetched individually by appending the entity ID, in parentheses, to the entity collection. Besides its specific properties, each entity has an ID, listed in JSON as "@iot.id", a self link, under "@iot.selfLink" and links to other entities as described in the data model. For example, a

Thing can have relations to multiple Datastreams. Therefore, each Thing has a navigation link to a collection of Datastreams, listed in its JSON under "Datastreams@iot.navigationLink", to .../v1.0/Things(id)/Datastreams. Likewise, each Datastream is linked to exactly one Thing. Therefore each Datastream has a navigation link to this Thing, listed under "Thing@iot.navigationLink", to .../v1.0/Datastreams(id)/Thing.

A request to a collection is subject to pagination, based on the request parameters and server settings. A client can request the number of entities returned to be limited using the "$top" query parameter. The server will not return more than this number of entities, but it can return fewer if it is configured with a lower maximum. If there are more entities to be returned than allowed in a single request, the server adds a link to the result, named "@iot.nextLink", that returns the next batch of entities. The client itself can also request a number of entities to be skipped, using the query parameter "$skip". For example, a client can request entities 11 to 15 using $top $=5$&$skip $=10$.

Entities in a collection can be ordered using the "$orderby" query parameter. The entities can be ordered by one or more of their properties, in ascending or descending order.

If a client is not interested in all properties of the requested entities, it can limit which properties are returned, using the query parameter "$select". For example, the query to .../v1.0/Things?$select $=$ id, name returns only the id and the name of all Things.

When requesting entities from a collection, a filter can be applied to the entities with the "$filter" query parameter. This filter can act on any of the properties of the entities in the collection, or any of the properties of related entities. It is, for example, possible to request all Observations that have a phenomenonTime in a certain time range, or all Observations that have a Datastream that has an ObservedProperty with a certain name. The filtering options are quite extensive and include geospatial, mathematical and string functions. Multiple filters can be combined with "and", "or", and "not" keywords and parenthesis.

When requesting entities, it is possible to have related entities be directly included in the response, by using the "$expand" query parameter. The expanded items can be subjected to all query parameters, including the "$expand" query parameter itself. This makes it possible to request, in a single request, a Thing, including its ObservedProperty and Datastreams, and the latest Observation for each of these Datastreams.

Besides requesting data with HTTP-Get, new entities can be created with a HTTP-Post to the collection of the entity, entities can be updated with a HTTP-Patch or HTTP-Put to the self-link of the entity, or entities can be deleted with a HTTP-Delete to the self-link of the entity.

1.4   MQTT Interface

Besides the main HTTP interface, the SensorThings API specifies a MQTT interface as an optional extension. This MQTT interface can be used to receive push messages when a new entity is created or when an entity is updated. The

MQTT topics used to distribute these messages are the same as the URL patterns for fetching data using the HTTP interface. A subscription on the topic "v1.0/Things" receives a message whenever a Thing is created or updated. The topic "v1.0/Things(id)" receives a message when this specific Thing is updated and "v1.0/Datastreams(id)/Observations" receives a message when an Observation is added to, or updated in the given Datastream. The $select option can also be used to only receive the specified properties of the created or updated entities.

The MQTT interface can also be used to create new Observations, by sending a message to the topic "v1.0/Observations", "v1.0/Datastreams(id)/Observations" or "v1.0/FeaturesOfInterest(id)/Observations".

1.5 Extensions

The SensorThings API defines several other extensions next to the MQTT extension. The MultiDatastream extension defines a new entity type: Multi-Datastream. A MultiDatastream is very similar to a normal Datastream, but instead of only one ObservedProperty and UnitOfMeasurement, a MultiDatastream can have more than one ObservedProperty, and the same number of UnitsOfMeasurement. An Observation linked to a MultiDatastream has an array as result value, that holds the same number of elements as the MultiDatastream has observed properties. MultiDatastreams are very useful for Observations of related observed properties that are always measured and used together, like wind speed and direction, or aggregate values like an average, minimum, maximum and standard deviation.

The DataArray extension defines a more efficient encoding when fetching or posting a large number of Observations. Instead of each Observation consisting of a JSON Object with name-value pairs for each property, the returned document contains a header that lists which properties are present for each Observation in the document, and the values of these properties are encoded in a single nested array.

An issue with version 1.0 of the SensorThings API is that it is not possible for a client to get a list of the extensions that a server implements. For some extensions, like the MultiDatastream extension, this is not a problem, since the presence of the extension can be deduced from the responses of the server, but for other extensions this is a problem. It is for example impossible for a client to find out if a service implements the MQTT extension, and if it does, how to connect to the MQTT service. The upcoming version 1.1 of the specification intends to solve this problem by adding the list of extensions that a service implements to the landing page, and allowing each extension to add additional information as well.

2   Architecture: From Sensor to Display

The basis for any decision is awareness of the current situation, how the current situation came to be, and how the situation is likely to change in the future. In many application domains, data from sensors and forecasting algorithms contribute an important part to this situational awareness and thus an architecture is needed to deal with the broad variety of sensors and algorithms that supply data that needs to reach the decision makers' displays [11]. This architecture needs to deal with the ingestion of sensor data, the processing and analysis of this data, and searching and display of the data. By basing the communication in the architecture on open standards, it becomes easier to mix and match data sources and potentially more information becomes available to the decision maker.

The OGC SensorThings API defines an interface for creating, updating, deleting, reading and searching data, with a versatile data model with custom data fields, and push messaging. This makes the SensorThings API suitable as a central component in a sensor data management architecture (see Fig. 2).

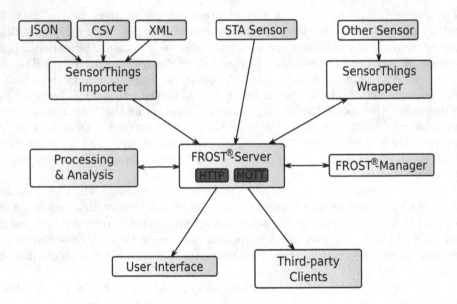

Fig. 2. An architecture for a sensor data management suite.

2.1   Components

The central component is a server that implements the SensorThings API. Any compliant server implementation that supports the features and extensions required for the use case can fill this role. An implementation, which is available as open-source is FROST® [17]. It provides a fully standard compliant and certified implementation of the entire specification, including all extensions. It uses PostgreSQL with the PostGIS extension as data store.

In an ideal world, all sensors would be able to directly communicate using the SensorThings API. However, in the real world sensors mostly do not directly speak STA. Often sensor data needs to be imported from separate data files in non-standardised formats like CSV. To convert between the different formats, additional tools are required. Fortunately, since all that is needed to insert an Observation into a SensorThings API conformant service is an HTTP Post with a simple JSON payload, any scripting language can be used to write such importers. In more complex situations, when connecting to a data source that supplies data for multiple different sensors, like a LoRa network server, the unique identifier of the sensor in the external system can be stored in the metadata of the Sensor or the Datastream in the SensorThings server. That way the wrapper can find the matching entities in the SensorThings server with a simple search.

Processing and Analysis is an important part of sensor data management. For instance, when dealing with long time-series, statistics like hourly, daily or yearly average, minimum, maximum and standard-deviation are required to efficiently handle the data. These statistical values can be seen as (virtual) sensor data and stored in the SensorThings service together with the source data. A client that wants to visualise sensor data over a longer time frame can check which aggregation levels are available, and choose the appropriate source. This use-case of visualising aggregate values is also a good example of where the MultiDatastream extension is very useful. By using a MultiDatastream, the average, minimum, maximum and standard-deviation for an aggregation period can all be stored together, and a client does not have to fetch these values separately and match them together. The feature that the phenomenonTime of an Observation can be a time interval means there is no ambiguity as to the time interval over which the aggregate is calculated, since the start and end times of this interval can be explicitly stated. The processing algorithm can monitor the relevant Datastreams using the MQTT interface of the SensorThings API, so it is notified as soon as a new Observation is entered into the service. Since processing results are entered back into the service, they can be used as input for other algorithms. As a result, one new Observation can trigger a chain of processing runs.

While scripting is the preferred way to deal with automatic data flow, often manual access to the data is required to make small changes or correct small errors. FROST®-Manager is a GUI for interacting with SensorThings API servers. It can browse though the server and is very useful for making small updates to the metadata of entities.

Users will access the data through either the "official" user interface, usually a website of the data provider, or by using their own software. A big advantage that the SensorThings API brings for clients is the powerful query and search functionality. There is no need for a client to "download all data" just to be able to find the bits that the client really needs. Finding out what kind of data is served by an STA instance is also trivial. In most cases a simple web-browser is sufficient, since all entities can be reached by simply following the navigation links that the API offers.

2.2   Added Properties

The Thing entity type has a property called "properties" of type JSON Object, that allows users to store any meta data in a structured way. Because this is a structured data type, unlike for example the description text field, a server implementation can support direct querying on this data. If a service holds Things that are rivers or stations, the type of each Thing can be stored in "properties/type". When a client is interested in the Things of type "station", it can do the following request to only get the Things of this type:

   .../v1.0/Things?$filter = properties/type eq 'station'

One issue with version 1.0 of the SensorThings API is that only Things and Observations have such a property for storing structured custom data. In many cases, the ability to store structured custom data on other entity types is also needed. For instance, when calculating hourly and daily aggregate values for a Datastream, it is important to be able to store the source Datastream of the aggregate data, and the aggregation level. Having this data in a structured way allows clients to better search for all aggregate MultiDatastreams for a given Datastream. To solve this deficiency, FROST® has implemented a custom extension that adds such "properties" fields to the other entity types.

Given the proven usefulness of these "properties" fields, they are also scheduled to be added to the upcoming version 1.1 of the SensorThings API.

3   Projects

In the following, first a project is presented from the environmental domain, which already successfully applied the proposed technologies. After that, two European Horizon 2020 projects are presented, which used FROST® in the domains of climate change, crisis management and cultural heritage. To widen the perspective the applicability to the INSPIRE Directive is discussed as well as an example from the industrial domain.

3.1   BRGM and French Water Information System Hub'Eau

The French water information system monitors the quantity and quality of all surface and ground water bodies in France. This includes data like surface and ground water levels, water flow through rivers and concentrations of over 1500 different chemical substances. These data can be a great asset for policy and decision makers, if it can be accessed in an easy and efficient way.

The French water information system architecture is traditionally based on XML webservices that serve data according to a nationally defined semantic. This architecture has been running for 20 years and the conclusion is that data interoperability practices evolve and that the "entry ticket" to access data should be easier to maximize data reuse. Thus, an innovation project started in 2015 and an API-fication process of major national wide water related database is going on under the project 'Hub'Eau'. Swagger (OpenAPI) APIs are now progressively deployed for those. But, this solves the problem stated above only half-way as each of those API comes with its own ad-hoc API operations and semantics.

Through the French IT Research Center 'INSIDE' [5], BRGM successfully tested SensorThings API as an alternative to those home-specified APIs on the following topics (each time on national scale data): surface water levels, raw ground water levels and surface water quality. Each of those exercise proved that

- the semantic needs required by domain expert can be covered using Sensor-Things API;
- the required operations to search, find, reuse data are covered in SensorThings API. Actually SensorThings API goes beyond the needs expressed when it comes down to filtering and traversing the data graph;
- performance expectations for production environment are covered by FROST® (the SensorThings API implementation identified during the tests). The surface water quality database contains more than 130 Millions observations and filtering through all of them is performant and allows the deployment of GUIs on top.

As a result, those experimentations are progressively moved to production with a target to replace the home-specified APIs.

BRGM is also deploying the SensorThings API as the reference API to serve its raw groundwater levels in near real time using the API both in Write (REST, MQTT to push observations from field sensors) and Read modes. Another side effect of all those tests is that the French national database on polluted soils observations is also being exposed using SensorThings API.

3.2 beAWARE

The main goal of the Horizon 2020 project beAWARE [1] (Enhancing decision support and management services in extreme weather climate events) is to provide decision support in all phases of an emergency incident. It proposes an integrated solution that includes early warning, forecasting and analysis of multi-modal data, including sensor data. The sensor data management part of the project uses an architecture [11] as described here, centered around the OGC SensorThings API. Data is imported from a variety of external systems, using a variety of interfaces and data formats. Processing algorithms are triggered either over the MQTT interface, by subscribing to the relevant entity changes, or periodically, with result either flowing back into the SensorThings service, or pushed to other components in the system.

One of the issues identified is that support for filtering of time intervals is limited. For example, take a set of observations, where the phenomenonTime of each observation is a time interval. When drawing a diagram of a time-based subset of these observations, one would expect to see all observations that have a phenomenonTime that overlaps with the displayed time interval. However, when requesting all observations greater than the start of the interval, and smaller than the end of the interval, this leaves out those observations that start before the displayed interval, but end in it, and those observations that start in the displayed interval, but end after it. An "overlaps" filter function does not exist for time, but would be very useful in this situation. Adding more filter functions covering Allen's interval algebra [3] would be a good addition to the standard.

3.3 HERACLES

Environmental factors, worsened by the increasing climate change impact, represent significant threats to European Cultural Heritage (CH) assets. In Europe, the huge number and diversity of CH assets, together with the different climatological sub-regions as well as the different adaptation policies to Climate Change adopted by the different Nations, generates a very complex scenario. The Horizon 2020 project HERACLES [2] has the objective to design responsive solutions for effective resilience of CH against climate change effects. Part of the developed solution is an ICT platform [6,12] able to collect and integrate multi-source information, to provide situational awareness and decision support. Examples of relevant sensor data flowing into the platform are measurements of the environmental factors monitoring data of existing damage to CH sites and climate forecasts. Together, these data can be used analyse how climate change may impact CH sites and which measure are needed to minimise damage.

One such set of monitoring data comes from a set of accelerometers, measuring vibrations in the "Palazzo dei Consoli" in the town of Gubbio, at a data rate of 100 Hz. This large data volume is dealt with by storing time-series of half an hour per Observation, with the exact begin and end time of the series stored as time interval in the phenomenonTime, instead of creating a new Observation for each data point. This is possible in this use-case, since the sensor has a fixed measuring frequency, so the exact measuring time of each data point can be calculated from the time series. By calculating aggregate values for each minute, hour and day, the data can still be efficiently handled by clients.

3.4 INSPIRE

While less of a project in its own right, the work towards integrating SensorThings API within INSPIRE could be seen as the mother of many future projects. The European Union INSPIRE Directive laid down the foundation of a pan-European Spatial Data Infrastructure (SDI) where thousands of public sector data providers make their data, including sensor observations, available for cross-border and cross-domain reuse. This massive data pool has the potential of becoming a key source of information for decision makers in many domains, but this will only come to fruition if the data is easily findable and accessible. Current guidance documents recommend the provision of this data via OGC services, foreseeing utilization of WMS, WFS, SOS and WCS for data provision. As technology and standards have progressed, the various additional technical requirements have been raised by SDI stakeholders, foremost:

- the need for adoption of RESTful architectures
- alternative (to GML) data encodings, such as JavaScript Object Notation (JSON) and binary exchange formats
- adoption of asynchronous publish–subscribe-based messaging protocols.

This inspired us to explore the suitability of SensorThings API for fulfilling the requirements laid down by the INSPIRE Directive pertaining to:

- Data Scope: Within INSPIRE, data models have been defined encompassing all attributes of a spatial feature deemed relevant within that spatial data theme. The challenge lay in mapping existing SensorThings API attributes to those foreseen within the INSPIRE themes. For attributes required by INSPIRE where a suitable mapping could not be made, additional attributes within the extended properties section foreseen within the 1.1 version of SensorThings API where defined [8].
- Download Service Requirements: INSPIRE lists various functionalities required by network services within COMMISSION REGULATION (EC) No 976/2009 of 19 October 2009 implementing Directive 2007/2/EC of the European Parliament and of the Council as regards the Network Services (OJ L 274, 20.10.2009, p. 9) [19]. At present, work is progressing on showing how all these requirements can be fulfilled either by SensorThings API as it currently stands, or via extensions planned for the upcoming 1.1 version of the standard [18].

At present, an INSPIRE Good Practice is being set up to finalize this work, and illustrate how SensorThings API can be utilized to fulfill INSPIRE requirements while providing the available data in a simple and easy to use manner.

3.5 AutoInspect

Although the main application domain of the STA is environmental information and risk management systems, the STA may also be applied in other domains of the Internet of Things (IoT). The industrial branch of the IoT, the Industrial IoT (IIoT), comprises application domains such as energy management, logistics or industrial production. For example, manufacturing plants encompass quality inspection activities, sometimes offline in dedicated inspection stations, but more and more inline, e.g. camera-based systems that try to detect defects in body parts of automobiles. Such inspection activities may be modelled by means of the STA-based sensor data model. Their results (e.g. images or roughness maps) are observations of these inspection tasks. The benefit of applying the STA is to have a common interface and data model for all kind of inspection activities which reduces the engineering effort to feed the individual inspection results into overarching quality management systems of a production plant. The STA perfectly complements other standards that are widespread in automation technology such as IEC 62541 OPC UA (Open Platform Communications Unified Architecture) of the OPC Foundation [13]. Fraunhofer IOSB currently experiments with both standards, the STA and OPC UA together with the open source

OPC UA implementation hosted at https://open62541.org/, in its automotive quality inspection pilot site entitled AutoInspect. Here, OPC UA is used for controlling and managing the individual inspection tasks, whereby the SensorThings API is used to store and retrieve the inspection results in raw and aggregated or interpreted form.

4   Conclusions

The OGC SensorThings API already proved its value as the central part of implementing the sensor to decision chain in several scientific as well as real world projects. It can be facilitated to implement the storage of heterogeneous data, attach semantic annotations, as well as trigger processing algorithms with the new Tasking extension of the standard.

It supports advanced filtering, not just on the properties of the entities being queried, but also across the relations of those entities, including the structured, custom meta-data. The MQTT extension allows clients to receive push notifications when entities are added or changed. All this makes the OGC SensorThings API a good core in a sensor data management architecture as demonstrated here. One improvement that would greatly increase the functionality of the API is adding a properties field to all other entity types besides the Thing entity type. Fortunately, this change is coming in the upcoming version 1.1 of the API.

A second issue that was identified is that it is not possible to see if a server implements the MQTT extension, and if it does, how to connect to this MQTT service. The upcoming version 1.1 of the standard is scheduled to solve this issue by adding a list of implemented extensions to the landing page of the service, and allowing each extension to add additional information. The MQTT extension can use this to list the connection details that a client can use to connect to the MQTT service.

The standard lacks functions for effective filtering when dealing with time intervals, which is noticeable when dealing with observations that have a "validTime", or a "phenomenonTime" that is an interval. This lack of filter functions that support time interval logic can be addressed with an extension to the standard, that adds a set of functions covering Allen's interval algebra.

Future work will include using the Tasking part of the SensorThings API [10] to control on-demand processing. This will allow the processing algorithms to be started that do not have a clear trigger based on incoming data, but are run on-demand based on user interaction.

Acknowledgments. The HERACLES project has received funding from the European Union's Horizon 2020 research and innovation programme under grant agreement No 700395.

The beAWARE project has received funding from the European Union's Horizon 2020 research and innovation programme under grant agreement No 700475.

Funding for BRGM work is provided by its joint IT Research Center 'INSIDE' dedicated to innovation in Environmental Information Systems with the French National

Agency for Biodiversity (AFB), French Museum of Natural History (MNHN) and French Marine Agency (IFREMER).

References

1. beAWARE Project. https://beaware-project.eu/
2. HERACLES Project. http://www.heracles-project.eu/
3. Allen, J.F.: Maintaining knowledge about temporal intervals. Commun. ACM **26**(11), 832–843 (1983). https://doi.org/10.1145/182.358434
4. Fielding, R.T.: Architectural styles and the design of network-based software architectures. Ph.D. thesis, University of California, Irvine (2000)
5. Grellet, S.: Implementation of OGC sensorthing API for environmental data (2018). https://github.com/INSIDE-information-systems/SensorThingsAPI
6. Hellmund, T., et al.: Introducing the heracles ontology-semantics for cultural heritage management. Heritage **1**(2), 377–391 (2018). https://doi.org/10.3390/heritage1020026
7. ISO/DIS: 19156:2011 geographic information - observations and measurements (2011). https://www.iso.org/standard/32574.html
8. Kotsev, A., et al.: Extending inspire to the Internet of Things through sensorthings API. Geosciences **8**(6), 221 (2018). https://doi.org/10.3390/geosciences8060221
9. Liang, S., Huang, C.Y., Khalafbeigi, T.: OGC SensorThings API part 1: sensing, version 1.0, 15–078r6 (2016). http://docs.opengeospatial.org/is/15-078r6/15-078r6.html
10. Liang, S., Khalafbeigi, T.: OGC SensorThings API part 2: Tasking core, version 1.0, 17–079r1 (2016). http://docs.opengeospatial.org/is/15-078r6/15-078r6.html
11. Moßgraber, J., et al.: The sensor to decision chain in crisis management. In: Boersman, K., Tomaszewski, B. (eds.) Conference Proceedings of the 15th International Conference on Information Systems for Crisis Response and Management, pp. 754–763, May 2018
12. Moßgraber, J., Lortal, G., Calabro, F., Corsi, M.: An ICT platform to support decision makers with cultural heritage protection against climate events. In: Geophysical Research Abstracts, vol. 20, April 2018. https://meetingorganizer.copernicus.org/EGU2018/EGU2018-13962.pdf
13. OPC Foundation: Unified architecture (2008). https://opcfoundation.org/about/opc-technologies/opc-ua/
14. Open Geospatial Consortium: Observations and measurements (2011). https://www.opengeospatial.org/standards/om
15. Open Geospatial Consortium: OGC SensorThings API (2016). https://www.opengeospatial.org/standards/sensorthings
16. Richardson, L., Ruby, S.: RESTful Web Services. O'Reilly Media, Newton (2008)
17. van der Schaaf, H., Jacoby, M.: FROST-Server (2016). https://github.com/FraunhoferIOSB/FROST-Server
18. Schleidt, K.: SensorThings work at DataCove (2018). https://github.com/DataCoveEU/SensorThings
19. The Commission of the European Communities: Commission regulation (EC) no 976/2009 of 19 October 2009 implementing directive 2007/2/ec of the European parliament and of the council as regards the network services (2009). https://eur-lex.europa.eu/eli/reg/2009/976/2010-12-28
20. Usländer, T.: Service-oriented design of environmental information systems. Ph.D. thesis, Universität Karlsruhe (2010). https://doi.org/10.5445/KSP/1000016721

WISS a Java Continuous Simulation Framework for Agro-Ecological Modelling

D. W. G. van Kraalingen$^{(\boxtimes)}$, M. J. Rob Knapen , A. de Wit ,
and H. L. Boogaard

Wageningen University and Research, Droevendaalsesteeg 3, 6708 PB,
Wageningen, The Netherlands
{daniel.vankraalingen, rob.knapen, allard.dewit,
hendrik.boogaard}@wur.nl

Abstract. A simulation framework is presented (WISS, Wageningen Integrated Systems Simulator) which targets the agro-ecological modelling domain. Especially simulation for a large number of locations, such as in detailed regional and global simulation studies. The framework strengths are in modularization, control, speed, robustness and computational protection (multiple system checks during simulation). The WOFOST model is currently implemented in WISS, through which it is used in a number of Wageningen University and Research projects. WISS is written in Java and the framework code is freely available.

Keywords: Simulation · Agro ecology · Modelling · WOFOST · Crop modelling · Framework

1 Introduction

In crop modelling there has been a tendency over the years for more modularization and looser coupling of software code describing the principal physiological and physical processes. The software architectures that were used had to evolve as model descriptions became more complex requiring increased modularization, understanding of reality improved and demands on speed, robustness and versatility increased (Holtzworth et al. 2015; Donatelli et al. 2010). But these trends also required solutions for communication of data among modules. In some implementations large arguments lists of variables were moved around, where in some cases people could hit the maximum of 255 arguments in some Fortran implementations. In other cases, large blocks of global storage were used (such as 'common blocks' in Fortran). Other solutions tended to introduce a software component responsible for the exchange of state and other variables by lookup in long lists. In all such solutions, ownership of state variables is with the software code where the states are calculated, but basically copies of these variables are communicated and are supplied on request by the communication component to other parts of the model, providing some greater flexibility and protection.

© IFIP International Federation for Information Processing 2020
Published by Springer Nature Switzerland AG 2020
I. N. Athanasiadis et al. (Eds.): ISESS 2020, IFIP AICT 554, pp. 242–248, 2020.
https://doi.org/10.1007/978-3-030-39815-6_23

The BioMa framework ([1]Donatelli et al. 2010) facilitates modularization and heterogenous model compositions but source code of the framework itself is not provided and its dependency on the .NET platform limits its use on non-Microsoft operating systems.

Another force behind the WISS development was the need for the WOFOST crop model (Wit et al. 2019) to be able to run for very large numbers of situations, where speed, robustness and versatility of the code are of utmost importance. An example where WOFOST as implemented using WISS is applied is the Agro Data Cube (https:// agrodatacube.wur.nl/).

WISS is implemented in Java, which was chosen for its speed, language features, market penetration and machine independence (Microsoft Windows, Linux, mac OS), requiring no recompilation of the code. An installation of a JavaVirtual Machine (JVM) is required though (VMs are available for all relevant platforms).

2 WISS Approach to Agro-Ecological Modelling

In this short paper we present a different approach which has clear advantages over more traditional techniques of inter-module communication of data. In the WISS framework (Wageningen Integrated Systems Simulator), we have developed a technique whereby states are not dispersed and kept permanently in software code describing model processes (the classic approach) but are kept in a special object which manages all states. This approach we call the "shared state approach".

Having all states together in one object during the whole simulation implicates the huge advantage that this object can be queried not only during simulation, but also after simulation. Not only can final values be obtained through simple functions, but also more advanced functionality like the highest and lowest value of a state variable during simulation, the change in value between the first and the last date, the average value and more can be programmed in a very generic way even without knowledge of the names of the state variables!

A consequence of the centralized state principle is that a module has to obtain the value(s) of its own state variables from the central object before starting calculations for the new time step, next to obtaining the value for other state variables it may need, but does not own. The calculations provide rates of change to the central state object. At the start of the new time step, the central state object integrates all states for which it has received rates. Having this kind of architecture enables us to override state variables to specific values without any code change in the module that calculates its rates. In fact, there is no way of knowing for this module whether a state value it received was overridden or not.

The central state object has several advanced features that help to maintain simulation integrity and support modularity. First of all, it accepts states in a particular unit and deliver it in another unit to a module requesting it, of course only if the unit conversion is valid. This improves flexibility in coupling modules together into one

---

[1] Biophysical Model Applications, https://en.wikipedia.org/wiki/BioMA.

model, whereby each module can have its own set of units (which may differ from the units used by another module in the system), e.g. weight per area conversions from kg. ha-1 to g.m-2, or temperature conversions from degrees Celsius to Kelvin.

Second, the central state object can also safeguard calculations during simulation as the state variables can be registered with a valid range (e.g. zero to infinity, between zero and one etc.). Violation of these bounds will be detected by the central state object on acceptance of the rate of change of the state variable and simulation will be interrupted. Running the model with well-established bounds results in a higher quality model implementation and more confidence in the final results. Calculations can also be protected against accidental changes of state variables by other model components, through a strict ownership mechanism.

Finally, the central state object also enables us to suspend and resume the calculations of a model on a particular date during simulation, since the state of the system is completely defined by the states in the central object. This is an important feature particularly for more complicated models, for instance in the case of simulations that track near real time weather, as the simulation can start where it left off in the previous run.

Several other ambitions led to the development of the WISS framework. We wanted a framework in which the model can be called as a fast numerical function without any file based input and file based output. This is an essential requirement for models intended to run for a large number of geographically different units, e.g. in a distributed computing environment. We also wanted a framework in which model components can be run together with as little code changes to the model components as possible, and we wanted to have great flexibility in making those compositions (run a water balance for a bare soil, or one with a crop on top of it, rotations etc.). Flexibility was also required in starting and stopping subsystems during one simulation period, e.g. a crop on top of a soil water balance. Obviously, the crop module needs to be terminated at harvest (the crop is gone), but the water balance must continue to run.

3   Time Steps and Integration

WISS is targeted at the agro-ecological modelling domain. In this domain, daily time steps in numerical integration are most common (basically driven by the nature of daily weather data, hourly being much harder to obtain). Systems with flexible (=variable) time steps tend to introduce a level of complexity that would make programming a WISS model much less straightforward, and would slow down development of the initial framework. Simulation with flexible time steps may be introduced in future versions, should the need arise. Concurrent with daily time steps, rectangular integration (Euler) is the provided integration method. Remember it is the central state object doing the actual integration.

4   WISS Model Components

Besides the WISS framework components, a model implemented in WISS must have at least one so called SimObject, and one so called SimController. A SimObject is the place where the calculations for a model component are programmed, providing separation of calculations. It normally consists of a section where the states it will produce are registered and a place where the states it needs are registered. There must also be a rate calculation section where the rate of change for each state variable must be calculated. Prior to the calculations, the latest values for the required states must be obtained from the central state object, which is called SimXChange. A SimObject, however, does nothing while the model is running unless it is started (=instantiated) by a so called SimController which's sole responsibility is to start and stop one or more SimObjects, providing separation of control. Not only can there be one or more SimObjects, there can also be one or more SimControllers (e.g. one for 'seeding' a crop, one for harvesting a crop).

A SimObject which is not started will do nothing, but if started it will need model parameters and initial states to properly initialize. This is where another important WISS model component kicks in, ParXChange. This component works like a key value list which is meant to hold parameters by name and is able to accept and provide the numerical value for that name. Similarly, for initial values for states, these are given to the ParXChange component, which provides it to SimObjects requesting it. Typically a ParXChange object is filled with data prior to starting the simulation.

The central state object is called SimXChange in WISS terminology. It is empty at the start of the simulation but gets filled with data as simulation proceeds. During simulation it constantly accepts rates of change and provides values to the running SimObjects. After termination of the model, it is loaded with all simulated data of every time step and ready for final processing or exporting the results of part of whole of the simulation period.

The simulation loop, in simplified form is given in Fig. 1.

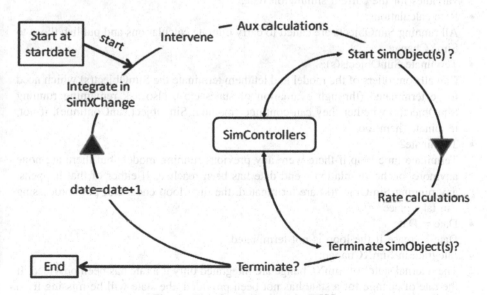

Fig. 1. The simulation loop in WISS

The schema in Fig. 1 shows the sequence of events that take place in WISS while the model is running. The implementation in code is in the TimeDriver class. Execution is in clockwise order, starting from "Start at start date". The following steps are made:

- Start one or more SimControllers (depending on the model, not shown here for clarity). These will oversee the simulation and start and stop the SimObject(s) if necessary (but starting is actually done later in the loop).
- Intervene:
  The Intervene step is an opportunity for every running SimObject in the system to override (=force) any state variable in the provided SimXChange object. Here adding or taking away part or whole of a state variable is allowed (if within the registered bounds). The provided SimXChange object will report these forcings in a special report with the date of overriding, the old and the new value. Examples are an external mowing event in case of grass simulation, a crop growth model in which the leaf area index needs to be forced by the values from a field experiment.
- Aux calculations:
  All running SimObjects are called to provide, if it is the SimObject's responsibility, time dependent driving data to provided SimXChange for SimObjects to use during the rate calculation step. Examples are air temperature, air carbon dioxide concentration etc. After this point, all existing states and time dependent driving data are up to date for the current simulation date!
- Start SimObject(s)?:
  All running SimControllers are asked whether additional SimObject(s) must be started. All started SimObject(s) also have their AuxCalculations method called (not shown here). At this point the system is up to date for the new states and auxiliary variables for the current simulation date.
- Rate calculations:
  All running SimObjects are called to carry out rate calculations and publish those to SimXChange.
- Terminate SimObjects(s):
  Call all controllers of the model and let them terminate the SimObject(s) which need to be terminated (through evaluation of states etc.), also ask remaining running SimObject(s) whether they can continue (method: SimObject.canContinue), if not, terminate them too.
- Terminate?:
  Terminate time loop if there were any previous running models but there are none anymore, or the simulation's end date has been reached. If either of that happens, any running SimObject(s) are terminated, the time loop ends, and post processing can take place.
- Date = Date + 1:
  Date increase if the loop is not terminated.
- Integrate in SimXChange:
  The internal states of SimXChange are integrated only if a rate has been provided. If the rate of change for a state has not been provided, the state will be missing from the new date until the end date. An error will occur if a SimObject tries to 'revive' a state variable by providing a rate. The state can only exist for one contiguous period.

5 Implementation Aspects

The above mentioned features are nice but we also strived for excellent execution performance. This is achieved by introducing a registration mechanism for state variables whereby the native unit and value bounds have to be provided. This registration returns a token which essentially contains the internal SimXChange's fixed array location of the state variable so that when communication takes place with SimXChange using this token the central state object immediately knows the name and other attributes of the state variable.

WISS is designed to safeguard valid simulation as much as possible. In general simulation will be terminated by a run-time exception whenever something goes wrong. Beit a non-existing unit conversion, a bounds check error, a required external variable not there etcetera. The principle being that if an error occurs, simulation results are unreliable anyway, so there is no need to continue. Best is to present the error with as much information as possible to the user, so the error can be located easily and repaired.

Extensive logging features are available in the WISS framework for the error, warning, info, debug and trace level.

6 Availability

The current version of the WISS framework is version 1 and it is available as open source software but the exact license still needs to be discussed (request the author of this paper for more information). WISS is available on https://github.com/DanielVanKraalingen/.

Currently 2 models have been implemented in WISS of which WOFOST is the most complicated one, the other one being a Lotka/Volterra prey predator model for demonstration purposes.

The current version of WOFOST (for which you'll need the WISS framework) is 7.2 but we will not automatically provide the Java source code. However, you can work with the jar file enabling you to run the WOFOST model with all valid inputs and program all possible outputs because the user has full control of the SimXChange object after simulation.

7 Real World Application

The WISS version of WOFOST is applied within the EU funded project AGINFRA+. AGINFRA+ is a D4Science Virtual Research Environment (VRE) and a use case was developed to perform parcel specific crop simulation taking data from the AgroData-Cube. The AgroDataCube provides a large collection of open data at parcel level for use in agri-food applications in the Netherlands (https://agrodatacube.wur.nl/). Through the VRE, the user has access to a computer cluster, of scalable size. The DataMiner core component of the D4Science platform provides handles adding and running algorithms on the cluster, while also making them available through OGC WPS (Web

Processing Service) interfaces. On top of that, a dashboard has been created to select crop parcels, activate WISS-WOFOST and visualize and inspect results.

8 Future

We are currently finalizing the freely available manual of the WISS framework version 1.0. With that manual, and the software for WISS 1.0 (including the prey/predator example) you should be able to start your own WISS model. Contact the author for more details.

We intend to expand WISS as a modelling framework as well as expand the process descriptions of WISS-WOFOST with a true multi-layer water balance model.

References

Donatelli, M., et al.: A component-based framework for simulating agricultural production and externalities. In: Brouwer, F., Ittersum, M. (eds.) Environmental and Agricultural Modelling. Springer, Dordrecht (2010). https://doi.org/10.1007/978-90-481-3619-3_4

Holzworth, D., et al.: Agricultural production systems modelling and software: current status and future prospects. Environ. Model Softw. **72**, 276–286 (2015). https://doi.org/10.1016/j.envsoft.2014.12.013

de Wit, A., et al.: 25 years of the WOFOST cropping systems model. Agric. Syst. **168**, 154–167 (2019)

Mathematical Estimation of Particulate Air Pollution Levels by Multi-angle Imaging

Or Vernik[1]([✉]) and Barak Fishbain[2]([✉])

[1] Department of Applied Mathematics, Faculty of Mathematics,
Technion - Israel Institute of Technology, Haifa, Israel
orvernik@gmail.com
[2] Department of Environmental, Water and Agriculture Engineering,
Faculty of Civil and Environmental Engineering,
Technion - Israel Institute of Technology, Haifa, Israel
fishbain@technion.ac.il

Abstract. Air pollution control and mitigation are important factors in wellbeing and sustainability. To this end, air pollution monitoring has a significant role. Today, air pollution monitoring is mainly done by standardized stations. The spread of those stations is sparse and their cost hinders the option of adding more. Thus, arises the need for cheaper and available means to assess air pollution. In this article, a method for assessing air pollution levels by means of multi angle imaging is presented. Specifically, the focus is on estimating images' blur as an indication for PM (Particulate Matter) ambient levels. The suggested method applies back-projection Radon transform. By back projection methodology, particles' concentration at each voxel in a 3D space is reconstructed from photos taken from a few different angles.

Keywords: Air pollution monitoring · Multi-angle imaging · Filtered Back Projection

1 Introduction

Exposure to PM is known to be one of the predominant factors in morbidity and mortality, causing the premature death of millions of people a year. This is especially true in developing countries with growing industry [1]. Thus, measuring and monitoring PM pollution is a very important task the world needs to deal with in order to ensure public health.

Currently, PM monitoring is standardly done by Air Quality Monitoring (AQM) stations that are considered accurate [2]. Due to their size and cost, the stations are sparsely dispersed and so we get a low-resolution concentration map. This limitation is typically addressed by interpolation schemes. However, the interpolation is a complicated task as PM concentrations are characterized by high spatial variability and may present different behaviors for different fractions

© IFIP International Federation for Information Processing 2020
Published by Springer Nature Switzerland AG 2020
I. N. Athanasiadis et al. (Eds.): ISESS 2020, IFIP AICT 554, pp. 249–257, 2020.
https://doi.org/10.1007/978-3-030-39815-6_24

and geographical areas [3]. These drawbacks have lead researchers to seek other approaches such as Micro Sensing Units (MSUs) for air pollution monitoring [2,4–6], either high-resolution methods or less costly and portable monitors. Those methods can be used for taking measurements, validating new technologies or giving hints in interpolating existing in-situ measurements.

Here we focus on *visual* means for assessing PM levels in the atmosphere. To this end, an image processing technique for evaluating the extinction coefficient using visibility cameras was suggested by Graves and Newsam [7]. The extinction coefficient is a measure that quantifies local radiance attenuation and is used as a standard for measuring atmospheric visibility. Using this measure, an image-processing method to extract a quantitative measurement of atmosphere transmission (the ability of radiation to pass through the atmosphere) from standard photos was presented. The transmittance has a closed form relationship with the extinction coefficient (inversely related), that then can be computed. The research here aims at improving this notion by looking at a 3D volume with changing concentrations at each voxel, as opposed to the method above, which assumes a homogeneous area.

Methods for retrieving PM by multi-angle imaging are in use by satellites. Instruments such as Multi-angle Imaging SpectroRadiometer (MISR) and Airborne Multi-angle SpectroPolarimetric Imager (AirMSPI) are currently applied for remote aerosols sensing [8,9]. However, these methods have low temporal resolution, as it takes a satellite few hours (or few days) to complete their orbit (latitude dependent), but more importantly, these devices measure the full vertical atmospheric column, which makes it less relevant to the amount of pollution at ground level that can indicate health hazards [10]. On top of these, this method is expensive and cannot be easily deployed.

The underlying assumption here is that due to the particles' optical properties of scattering, different concentrations of particles will cause the light field to scatter differently [10]. The higher the concentration of scatterers is, the more refractions the light will go through. Refracted light impairs human visibility and expression for this phenomenon is evident in standard photos [7]. A photo acquires a snapshot of the light field coming from all angles, refracting by the objects and particles in the scenery and eventually hits the camera lens. Particles suspended in the air cause a level of blurriness in the acquired photo. Having this relationship between blurriness and amount of scatterers in the air leads us to the approach of estimating the particles' concentration by measuring image blurriness.

The blur of an image is positively correlated with the integral of the attenuation (extinction) coefficient over the Line Of Sight (LOS) to the object. Thus, by measuring the blurriness of one image we cannot infer the concentration at each voxel. The intensity of the light's direct transmission is attenuated by the scattering (absorption by particulate matter is negligible) and is computed by:

$$I = I_0 e^{-\int_{LOS} \beta(l) dl} . \tag{1}$$

Where, I_0 is the initial intensity of the radiation source. Our objective then is to find β, which is strongly related with the PM concentration denoted n, by:

$$\beta(\bar{x}) = \sigma \cdot n(\bar{x}) . \tag{2}$$

Where, $n(\bar{x})$ is the PM concentration at position $\bar{x}$ in space and σ is the extinction cross section. σ is depended upon the light's wavelength and the particle's shape and size, thus for our purposes it will be assumed constant. Assuming we know the values of the extinction coefficient integral from a large number of angles (having a correlation with the blurriness measure), the inverse problem is mathematically solvable by the Radon transform [11].

Radon transform is widely used in Computational Tomography (CT) applications, allowing us to reconstruct the object being scanned from its measured projections. The classically used form of the Radon transform and that we are going to describe, is the 2D Radon. A projection is the integral on the extinction coefficient which equals to:

$$p(y) = \int \underbrace{\beta(x,y)}_{\substack{\text{our} \\ \text{objective}}} dy = \underbrace{-\ln\left(\frac{I(y)}{I_0}\right)}_{\text{assumed known}} . \tag{3}$$

The most effective way for reconstructing β from the projections is by using Filtered Back Projections (FBP) that is equivalent to the Inverse Radon Transform (IRT) but less computationally costly.

The Radon Transform:

$$p_\theta(r) = \int \beta(r \cdot \cos\theta - s \cdot \sin\theta, r \cdot \sin\theta + s \cdot \cos\theta)ds . \tag{4}$$

FBP:

$$I(x,y) = \int_0^\pi p(r,\theta) * q(r)d\theta . \tag{5}$$

$q(r)$ is the LPF, for example Ram-Lak filter [12].

Relying on these principals, this research will define a method for three-dimensional PM concentrations reconstruction by multi-angle imaging. The proposed method will be visibility cameras based, aimed to be a simple, cheap and portable technique for air pollution assessment.

2   Monte-Carlo Simulation

To illustrate the potential of the suggested method, a simulation of the image acquisition process of the light field in a 3D volume, taken from few different angles is presented. The simulation allows for the reconstruction of PM suspended at each voxel in the volume.

We relate to the physical behavior of light propagating through a volume containing PM in different concentrations as a random process [13]. The light, taken in its particulate sense of photons, passes a medium, which has spatially variable optical depth (a measure of the light ability to propagate through the medium) denoted by τ. At each stage, τ is sampled from the optical depth Cumulative Density Function (CDF):

$$F(\tau) = \int_0^\tau e^{-\tau'} d\tau' = 1 - e^{-\tau} \ . \tag{6}$$

Using Monte-Carlo method, we get a random optical depth sampled from its CDF. For this, we use the uniform distribution U[0,1] CDF for sampling a random number u, and get τ by:

$$\tau = F^{-1}(u) \ , \ u = rand() \ . \tag{7}$$

By using the random τ we sampled, we can determine l, the distance the ray propagates until the next diffraction, by the relationship:

$$\tau = \int_0^l \beta(x, y, z) dl = \int_0^l \sigma \cdot n(x, y, z) dl \ . \tag{8}$$

Where β is the extinction coefficient, σ is the extinction cross section and n is the PM concentration at each voxel with its coordinates denoted by $\{X, Y, Z\}$. l is found by numeric integration.

Once l is found, the scattering angle after the collision has to be determined. The angle is computed in a similar fashion, assuming randomness in the process and relying on Mie scattering theory under the assumption of spherical particles [14]. The Mie Theorem provides a physical solution for the scattering of an electromagnetic wave by spherical uniform particles about the size of the light wavelength. Using Monte-Carlo, we will sample a random number from the CDF of the Mie scattering angle on the intersection plane [13] and a fully random $[0, 2\pi)$ zenith angle. The found angles, will give us the new direction of the ray's propagation.

We repeat this process of finding new distance to the next collusion, new direction and the intensity at each stage, until the ray exits our volume at some point. This will be done for each ray in the packet of rays entering from each radiated voxel. For now, the image acquisition process is done by summing the values of the exiting rays' intensities for each pixel at the volume's boundaries (visualization of the simulation shown at Fig. 1).

The received photos (each received from different angle) are used to estimate the level of pollution by applying the Blur Metric (BM) suggested by Frederique Crete [15]. The BM estimation of the image blurriness is based upon the notion that once an image is blurred, blurring it again will result in smaller differences than blurring a sharp image. We thus receive a value between zero and one indicating the effective blurriness of the image from which we can deduce the general level of pollution (amount of scaterrers).

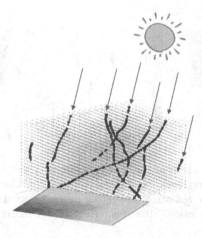

Fig. 1. Sun rays hit the medium and scattered until exiting the grid boundaries. Image is received on the bottom plane as a result of rays intersecting the plane.

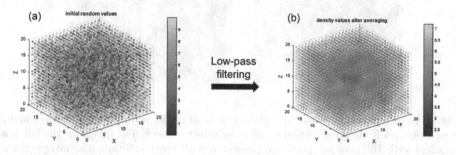

Fig. 2. Initial uniform random values in the range $[0, 10]$ (a) and the smoother version with smaller spatial gradients in concentration (b).

3   Preliminary Results

As for now, we have created a volumetric grid containing random, uniform distributed PM concentration at each voxel (Fig. 2a). In order to create a more realistic distribution we smoothed the outcome with a 3D box filter (Fig. 2b).

We then simulated with Monte-Carlo method the rays enter the volume at specific points and angle and diffracting by the particles. The ray's entrance angle determines which faces of the cube are going to be affected by the radiation. The code is designed to plot random number of rays track as demonstrated in Fig. 3. For each voxel in the face that the radiation intersects with, we simulate a beam that hits the voxel and propagating through the volume until exiting from the grid boundaries.

All rays start with some initial intensity, which will be reduced by the collisions with the aerosols in the volume by the following connection:

$$I_{after} = I_{before} \cdot \bar{\omega} \,. \tag{9}$$

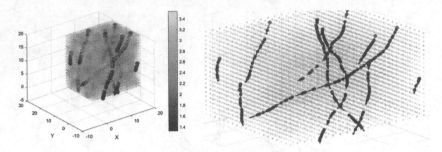

Fig. 3. On the left, simulation of random rays entering the experiment volume with same angle, and scattering until exiting the volume. On the right, same simulation zoomed in; we can see the red arrow indicating entrance point and angle and the blue arrows indicating new directions after scattering. (Color figure online)

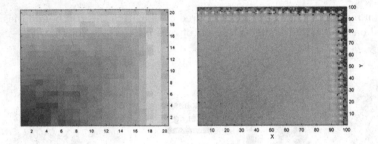

Fig. 4. Received images at the X-Y plane (the floor of the volume). Sun light is coming from the top left corner direction to all three affected faces. The image on the left was acquired with 100 rays per pixel and presented with low resolution. The image on the right has higher spatial resolution (x5 than the left image) and 500 rays per pixel.

where, $\bar{\omega}$ is the single scattering albedo (the attenuation in intensity) (SSA) of PM and I is the intensity.

For better understanding of the results we repeated our experiment, this time instead of all rays having the same initial intensity, we used a black and white image of 'Lena' [16] that will filter our rays when entering the upper face of the volume. The rays are now coming in a straight angle from above. The results are a highly noisy image of the original Lena at the bottom plane (Fig. 5). Repeating the same initial conditions only with growing levels of PM concentrations and measuring the blurriness of the image using our blur metric, gives us a strong correlation between the effective image blur and the level of pollution as we can see in Fig. 1. Those results will be better examined, evaluated and validated as we continue our work.

  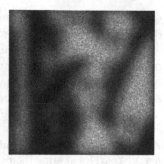

Fig. 5. From left to right. 1. Lena's original B&W image. 2. Bottom plane received image. 3. Using LPF on the received image.

Table 1. The measure of blurriness increases with the rise in PM pollution level as we can see in different ranges we examined and different scattering simulations.

Range of random concentrations	random scattering	Mie scattering
[0,5]	0.4961	
[4,9]	0.5185	
[8,13]	0.6396	
[12,17]	0.7141	
[0,0.5]		0.4763
[0,0.25]		0.4689
[0,0.1]		0.4533

4 Conclusions

The preliminary results indicate a certain connection between image blur and pollution level. As for now, this study's concept is theory based. We have reason to believe that the results will be highly correlated with real-life measurements. The system discussed here is integral based. Hence, it tends to be stable and presents small perturbation at the system's output as a result of small perturbation at its inputs. Therefore, we expect this theoretical exercise to show similar results in real-life applications. Albeit, this is still a work in progress, the study needs to continue and establish the found correlation. The model is not yet fully built and there are no concrete reconstruction results to test at this stage.

At next stage, a full back projection (FBP) based reconstruction scheme will be used for finding the original concentrations in space, having only the images as input. Currently, the most simplified model is used. We aim to gradually add more layers of accuracy, better modelling of the physical phenomena, using enhanced air pollution dispersion modelling tools (e.g. GRAL) [17], adding effects of light polarisation and effects of ground and background reflections.

Once the model is complete, sensitivity analysis will be done as well as validating concentrations against ground truth values and cross validation. Future work will also aim at testing the scenario simulation in real life. Our proposed method has the potential to be cheaper, more feasible and with higher spatial and temporal resolution than existing standard methods (remote sensing, AQM stations, etc.). Those advantages add up to the simplicity of the method which may be deployed by anyone with the possession of commodity cameras.

Acknowledgments. The authors would like to thank Holodovsky Vadim and Schechner Y. Yoav, for sharing their code for Mie scattering, that has helped to push the paper forward in terms of accuracy.

References

1. Apte, J.S., Marshall, J.D., Cohen, A.J., Brauer, M.: Addressing global mortality from ambient PM2.5. Environ. Sci. Technol. **49**, 8057–8066 (2015)
2. Moltchanov, S., Levy, I., Etzion, Y., Lerner, U., Broday, D.M., Fishbain, B.: On the feasibility of measuring urban air pollution by wireless distributed sensor networks. Sci. Total Environ. **502**, 537–547 (2015)
3. Pinto, J.P., Lefohn, A.S., Shadwick, D.S.: Spatial variability of PM2.5 in urban areas in the united states. J. Air Waste Manag. Assoc. **54**, 440–449 (2012)
4. Castell, N., et al.: Can commercial low-cost sensor platforms contribute to air quality monitoring and exposure estimates? Environ. Int. **99**, 293–302 (2017)
5. Fishbain, B., et al.: An evaluation tool kit of air quality micro-sensing units. Sci. Total Environ. **575**, 639–648 (2017)
6. Lerner, U., Hirshfeld, O., Fishbasinl, B.: Optimal deployment of a heterogeneous environmental sensor network. J. Environ. Inform. **34**(2), 99–107 (2018)
7. Graves, N., Newsam, S.: Using visibility cameras to estimate atmospheric light extinction. In: 2011 IEEE Workshop on Applications of Computer Vision (WACV), pp. 577–584 (January 2011)
8. Diner, D., Beckert, J., Reilly, T., Bruegge, C., Conel, J., Kahn, R.: Multi-angle imaging spectroradiometer (MISR) instrument description and experiment overview. IEEE Trans. Geosci. Remote Sens. **36**, 1072–1087 (1998)
9. Diner, D., Xu, F., Garay, M.J., Martonchik, J.V., Rheingans, B.E., Geier, S.: The Airborne Multiangle SpectroPolarimetric Imager (AirMSPI): a new tool for aerosol and cloud remote sensing. Atmos. Meas. Tech. **36**, 2007–2025 (2013)
10. Etzion, Y., Broday, D., Fishbain, B.: Analysis of image color and effective bandwidth as a tool for assessing air pollution at urban spatiotemporal scale. In: Proceedings of SPIE - The International Society for Optical Engineering, vol. 8657 (February 2013)
11. Yaroslavsky, L.: Digital Holography and Digital Image Processing: Principles, Methods, Algorithms. Springer, Berlin (2013). https://doi.org/10.1007/978-1-4757-4988-5
12. Bernal, J., Sanchez, J.: Use of filtered back-projection methods to improve CT image reconstruction (September 2009)
13. Levis, A., Schechner, Y., Aides, A., Davis, A.: Airborne three-dimensional cloud tomography, pp. 3379–3387 (December 2015)
14. Hansen, J.E., Travis, L.D.: Light scattering in planetary atmospheres. Space Sci. Rev. **16**, 527–610 (1974)

15. Crété-Roffet, F., Dolmière, T., Ladret, P., Nicolas, M.: The blur effect: perception and estimation with a new no-reference perceptual blur metric. Hum. Vis. Electron. Imaging **12**, 03 (2007)

16. Munson, D.C.: A note on Lena. IEEE Tran. Image Process. **5**, 3–3 (1996)

17. Ottl, D., Sturm, P.-J., Almbauer, R.: Application of the Lagrangian dispersion model GRAL to assess the air quality in the city of Graz. In: 12th Symposium on Transport and Air Pollution, pp. 75–79 (2003)

Interpolation of Data Measured by Field Harvesters: Deployment, Comparison and Verification

Tomáš Řezník, Lukáš Herman[✉], Kateřina Trojanová,
Tomáš Pavelka, and Šimon Leitgeb

Department of Geography, Faculty of Science, Masaryk University, Kotlářská 2,
611 37 Brno, Czech Republic
`tomas.reznik@sci.muni.cz`, {`herman.lu`, `ktrojanova`,
`pavelka.tomas`, `leitgeb`}`@mail.muni.cz`

Abstract. Yield is one of the key indicators in agriculture. The most common practices provide only one yield value for a whole field according to the weight of the harvested crop. On the contrary, precision agriculture techniques discover spatial patterns within a field to minimise the environmental burden caused by agricultural activities. Field harvesters equipped with sensors provide more detailed and spatially localised values. The measurements from such sensors need to be filtered and interpolated for the purposes of follow-up analyses and interpretations. This study verified the differences between three methods of interpolation (Inverse Distance Weighted, Inverse Distance Squared and Ordinary Kriging) derived from field sensor measurements that were (1) obtained directly from the field harvester, (2) processed by global filters, and (3) processed by global and local filters. Statistical analyses evaluated the results of interpolations from three fully operational Czech fields. The revealed spatial patterns, as well as recommendations regarding the suitability of the interpolation methods used, are presented at the end of this paper.

Keywords: Data filtering · Field harvester · Interpolation · Inverse Distance Squared · Inverse Distance Weighted · Ordinary Kriging · Yield mapping

1 Introduction

The main goals of precision agriculture (or precision farming) generally include the minimisation of negative environmental impacts on the one hand, and the maximisation of economic profit on the other hand [3, 17]. Geospatial information is highly valuable for these purposes [24, 25], in particular when based on Semantic web principles [16]. A differentially corrected Global Navigation Satellite Systems (GNSS) equipped yield monitoring system on field harvesters enables collection of georeferenced yield data [10, 18]. These data can be processed within Geographic Information system (GIS) using several interpolation techniques in order to generate detailed yield maps [5, 19]. On their basis, farmers can more precisely determine where exactly to put which inputs and in what quantities, because data from field harvesters represent the most detailed source of yield information. Unfortunately, these measurements usually contain errors

© IFIP International Federation for Information Processing 2020
Published by Springer Nature Switzerland AG 2020
I. N. Athanasiadis et al. (Eds.): ISESS 2020, IFIP AICT 554, pp. 258–270, 2020.
https://doi.org/10.1007/978-3-030-39815-6_25

which influence results of complex spatial analyses [7]. As suggested for example by [2], as well as [4], such errors might arise for the following reasons: the occurrence of unexpected events during the harvesting process leading to unusual behaviour on the part of the machine; the trajectory of the field harvester; and errors caused by the wrong calibration of the yield monitor. Therefore, the measurements need to be processed and filtered (different types of filters can be used; see Sect. 2.2 for more details).

Other aspects requiring further investigation include the influence of the individual interpolation methods on the quality of the resulting yield maps. The objective of this paper is to investigate the influence of three interpolation methods (Inverse Distance Weighted, Inverse Distance Squared and Ordinary Kriging) commonly used to generate of yield maps. To compare them, we used descriptive statistics, Mean Prediction Error, Root Mean Square Prediction Error and Map Algebra. Interpolation methods were applied on three fields from Rostěnice Farm (Czech Republic). See details in Sect. 2.1.

2 Materials and Methods

2.1 Study Site

Data measured by a cereal field harvester were used to analyse and evaluate the approaches of spatial filtering and interpolation. Data acquisition was conducted at the Rostěnice cooperative farm in the south-eastern part of the Czech Republic (Fig. 1). The farm, Rostěnice a.s. (N49.105 E16.882), manages over 8,300 ha of arable land in the South Moravian region of the Czech Republic (see Fig. 2).

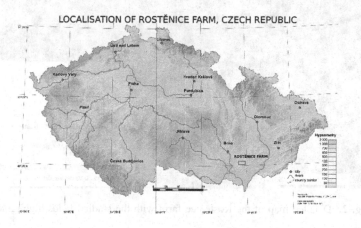

Fig. 1. Overview map of the Rostěnice farm.

The average annual temperature is 8.8 °C and the average annual rainfall is 544 mm. Within the managed land, the most prevalent soil types consist of Chernozem, Cambisol, haplic Luvisol, Fluvisol near bodies of water, and, occasionally, also Calcic

Leptosols. The fields are located mainly in sloping terrain. The main programme consists in plant production, where the main focus is on the cultivation of malting barley,
maize for grain and biogas production, winter wheat, oilseed rape, and other crops and
products such as soybean and lamb. The high spatial variability of soil conditions in the
southern part of farm has led to the adoption of precision farming practices, such as the
variable application of fertilisers (since 2006) and crop yield mapping by field harvesters
(since 2010).

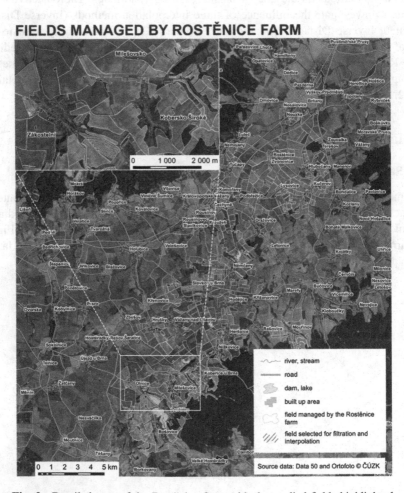

Fig. 2. Detailed map of the Rostěnice farm with the studied fields highlighted.

2.2 Sensor Measurement and Processing

Data were measured for three fields by a CASE IH AXIAL FLOW 9120 field harvester
equipped with an AFS Pro 700 monitoring unit in 2017. The measurements were of
GNSS-RTK (Real Time Kinematics) quality. Measurements were taken continuously

each second at an average speed of 1.55 m.s^{-1}, recommended as optimal at the Rostěnice farm for cereal harvesting by the CASE IH AXIAL FLOW 9120 harvester. The harvesting width was 9.15 m. The monitoring of yield was conducted as on-the-go mapping by recording grain flow and moisture continuously over the whole plot area. The crop type did not influence the spatial density of the performed measurements. The measurements were stored directly in the field harvester and manually copied to a USB flash drive after the end of operations on the pilot fields.

As mentioned above, data from field harvesters contain different types of errors. These data errors corrupt the results, which means the datasets need to be processed and filtered. Filtering of data from field harvesters was described, e.g., by [6, 12, 22]. We used the approach introduced [20]. This approach comprises two subsequent steps – global filtering and local filtering. Global filtering removes non-reliable measurements (data point values) within the whole dataset by means of a statistical analysis of measurement values and related attributes. Local filtering then focuses on some parts of the dataset in a higher detail (Table 1), and it is mostly based on the analysis of the neighbourhood of data point values.

In the approach used [20], global filters detect incorrect outliers based on:

– the range of possible yield values,
– the speed of a field harvester,
– the direction of harvesting.

Local filtering brings the most accurate results regarding domain knowledge, e.g. measurements, data processing and yield history, as well as knowledge of the data, of the situation, and of the whole range of issues in general. Local filtering comprises a set of subjective methods (points are excluded manually). In the approach used [20] local filters identify potentially incorrect values when the following situations occur in datasets:

– the crossings in harvester trajectory,
– the neighbouring rows in harvesting trajectory are too close to each other,
– the gaps in measurements within one row of trajectory.

Table 1. Absolute number of sensor measurements, relative percentage of data points after global and local filtering.

Name	Measured data		Global filtering		Global and local filtering	
	Points	%	Points	%	Points	%
Zákostelní	28 658	100.00	24 509	85.52	23 877	83.32
Milešovsko	8 406	100.00	6 652	79.13	6 331	75.32
Kobersko Široké	18 462	100.00	13 498	73.11	12 817	69.42

2.3 Interpolation Methods

There are many spatial interpolation methods applied in various environmental-related disciplines and many diverse factors affect the performance of these methods [13]. From the wide range of interpolation methods mentioned by [13], only a few are used in precision agriculture to process field harvester data. [11] used punctual and block kriging. [21] applied IDW in addition to the aforementioned two methods. [23] compares Ordinary Kriging (OK), Inverse Distance Weighted (IDW) and Inverse Distance Squared (IDS). We decided to test these three interpolation methods, firstly because they are used in precision agriculture and, secondly, because they are the most commonly used interpolation methods in environmental sciences (see [13]).

IDW is a popular deterministic method for spatial analysis. IDW is multivariate interpolation, which means it is a function for more than one variable. The method is used to predict the unknown points in specific locations. The unknown values are calculated as a weighted average from the known available values [15]. Inverse Distance Squared (IDS) is very similar to IDW, but power of IDW is equal to 1 and power of IDS is equal to 2. IDW is referred to as linear interpolation, while equation of IDS is squared. IDW and IDS are deterministic methods [1, 23].

Table 2. Basic settings of the OK interpolation for the selected fields.

	Zákostelní			Milešovsko			Kobersko Široké		
	Measured data	Global filtering	Global and local filtering	Measured data	Global filtering	Global and local filtering	Measured data	Global filtering	Global and local filtering
Lag size	0.000354	0.000619	0.000875	0.001199	0.000033	0.001369	0.000067	0.001523	0.01493
Number of lags	12	12	12	12	12	12	12	12	12

Kriging – also known under the acronym BLUE (Best Linear Unbiased Estimator) – is a stochastic (geostatistical) interpolation method which uses geostationary estimation methods. The interpolated values are calculated by a Gaussian process and controlled by covariances. Local estimate is used for kriging, which means that the expected values of the variable are calculated from available data in a relatively small neighbouring area. There are several types of kriging, where ordinary kriging is the most frequently used one. Ordinary Kriging (OK) is spatial interpolation, where the error variance is minimised [8]. OK provides estimate values in points or in blocks for which a variogram is known. Data in the neighbourhood of the predicted value are used for the estimate [26]. An alternative to OK that is another variant of kriging and that can be used to process yield data is, for example, Simple Kriging (see [20]).

The three algorithms mentioned above represent both deterministic (IDW, IDS) and stochastic methods (OK). IDS and IDW methods can be considered simpler in terms of setting their input parameters. All three interpolations were computed in ArcGIS 10.6 software. The parameters were computed by means of Exploratory Spatial Data Analysis.

2.4   Verification Methods

The differences between observed and calculated values can be evaluated using simple descriptive statistics, Mean Prediction Error, Root Mean Square Prediction Error and Map Algebra. Within the methods of descriptive statistics, we investigated the mean, and especially the minimum and maximum, to determine whether the studied interpolation methods overestimate or underestimate the results compared to the original data.

Mean Prediction Error (MPE) is the average difference between the measured and the predicted values (Formula 1). The error values of the estimates should be impartial and their average should be zero [9].

$$MPE = \frac{\sum_{i=1}^{n}(\hat{Z}(s_i) - z(s_i))}{n} \tag{1}$$

Where:

$\hat{Z}(s_i)$: predicted value,
$z(s_i)$: measured value,
n: number of observations.

Root Mean Square Prediction Error (RMSE) is the standard deviation of the prediction errors. It is the square root of the average of squared differences between predicted and measured values (see Formula 2). Smaller value of the RMSE means the model is more suitable, because the calculated values are closer to the measured values [9].

$$RMSE = \sqrt{\frac{\sum_{i=1}^{n}(\hat{Z}(s_i) - z(s_i))^2}{n}} \tag{2}$$

Where:

$\hat{Z}(s_i)$: predicted value,
$z(s_i)$: measured value,
n: number of observations.

To visualise and describe spatial patterns of the differences between interpolation algorithms, Map Algebra was used. Map Algebra and especially the relative difference method provide insights into variances between values in overlapping raster data [14]. The relative differences (d_v) were used as defined in Formula 3. Relative differences are often used as a quantitative indicator of quality assurance and quality control for repeated measurements/calculations where the results are expected to be similar or the same.

$$d_v = \frac{i_a - i_b}{i_a} \times 100 \tag{3}$$

Where:

i_a: reference interpolated value,

i_b: compared interpolated value.

All these verification methods were computed in ArcGIS 10.6 software. Verification methods were calculated for all three studied fields (Zákostelní, Milešovsko and Kobersko Široké – see Fig. 2) and interpolated surfaces from all three steps of data filtration (Measured data; Global filtering; Global and Local filtering).

3   Results

Interpolations were made for all datasets, with nine different interpolated surfaces for each field (see the example of Kobersko Široké field provided in Fig. 3). Relative yield values were used for more suitable comparison. The size of the pixels of the interpolated surfaces was 3.5 × 3.5 m. OK parameters are presented in Table 2. For filtered data, spatial extents were smaller due to the filtration process, which removes measurement points at the edges of fields. In order to achieve homogeneous (consistent) and comparable results, we decided not to use extrapolation methods because their precision in the respective areas would be debatable.

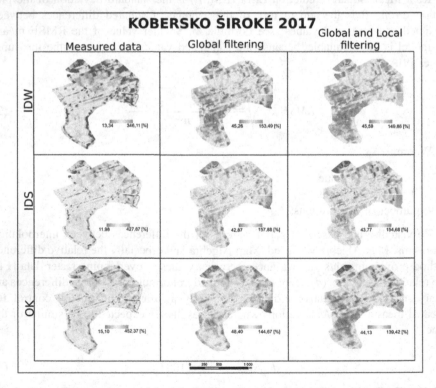

Fig. 3. Interpolations of measured, globally filtered, and both globally and locally filtered data for the Kobersko Široké field [relative yield values in %].

As the first step in comparison of the interpolation algorithms used, descriptive statistics were calculated. Figure 4 shows the mean values and the total range of values, both for the input data and the interpolated surfaces. At the same time, it is clear that especially global filtering removes extreme outliers and considerably reduces the overall range of values (Fig. 4 – compare the columns Measured data and Global filtering). A similar but much smaller effect in reducing the range to the measured data is also detectable in all three interpolation algorithms used (Fig. 4 – compare the columns Input data and the others).

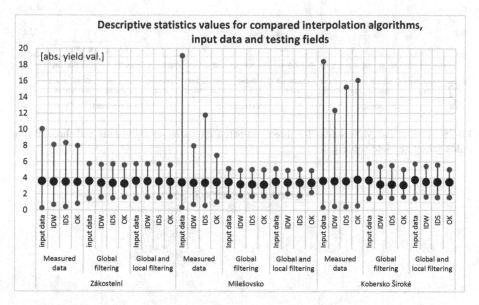

Fig. 4. Minimal, mean and maximum values for three compared interpolation algorithms, input data and three testing fields [absolute yield values].

The second step in comparison of the interpolation algorithms used was based on MPE and RMSE calculation. Results are presented in Fig. 5. Both MPE and RMSE express average model prediction error, but RMSE also expresses extreme errors.

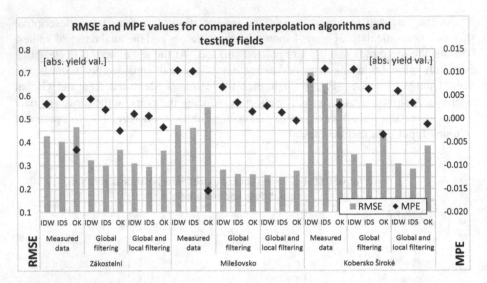

Fig. 5. RMSE and MPE values for three compared interpolation algorithms and three testing fields [absolute yield values].

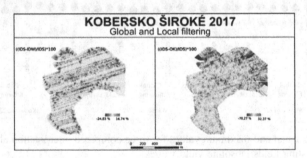

Fig. 6. Relative differences between IDS and IDW (left) and IDS and OK (right) for both globally and locally filtered data from Kobersko Široké field [in %].

Figure 6 depicts the relative differences between the compared interpolation methods. We chose the Kobersko Široké field for this visualization, because there are evident differences between interpolation algorithms (see Fig. 5). Figure 6 shows also the spatial pattern of the calculated relative differences. Relative differences occur in both pairs of compared algorithms at the field edges. However, the biggest relative differences exist between OK and IDS in some field passes; this is since IDS is an exact interpolator, which gives the most weight to near input points, while OK is rather a spatial estimator.

4   Discussion

When comparing individual interpolation algorithms (IDW, IDS and OK), we focus primarily on their applicability within the three above-mentioned steps of processing data from field harvesters (measured data, global filtering and local filtering). The analysis of differences between fields in which algorithms have been compared lies beyond the scope of this paper as these differences are influenced by multiple natural and artificial factors (i.e., field shape, topography, soil, water regime, fertilisation, harvesting strategy). A set of various methods have been used in the comparison: descriptive statistic, MPE, RMSE and Map Algebra. RMSE is the most commonly used method for comparing the individual interpolation methods. However, a combination of multiple methods provides a more comprehensive comparison, although it cannot be interpreted as unambiguously as the result of a single indicator. [21] also reach similar conclusions.

It seems that IDW and IDS are more suitable for interpolation of directly measured (unfiltered) data. For the data used in this paper, IDS is characterised by the fact that the average, minimum and maximum values in the interpolated surface are closer to the input data. IDS is also characterized by lower RMSE values. These differences can be partially explained by the number of neighbouring measurement points used in the interpolations. For example, IDS increases weight of the nearest measurement points and, therefore, it essentially reduces the number of measurement points used in the interpolation, thus better capturing the local variability in the data. Similar conclusions are also provided by [23].

When comparing interpolation algorithms for filtered data (for globally filtered and especially globally and locally filtered data), the differences between IDW, IDS and OK have been considerably smaller. Also, with regard the filtered data interpolations, the lowest RMSE values were achieved for IDS. Regarding MPE it was also closest to zero on all three fields. An interesting fact is that MPE values for OK were less than zero in all three fields, which shows that OK tends to underestimate the interpolated results. In general, ordinary kriging acted as a spatial estimator, rather than an exact interpolator [21].

Essential settings for IDW/IDS calculation are simpler than the settings necessary for OK interpolation. Basically, it is necessary to set the cell size of the resulting raster and the power value (1 for IDW; 2 for IDS). Thus, we can conclude that IDW and IDS are more suitable for less experienced users of the GIS technology such as farmers. OK is more difficult to set up, but these additional parameters have a positive effect on the accuracy of the interpolation, especially if there are large gaps without measurement points in the input datasets appearing, e.g., when yield data are filtered.

The obvious limit of this research certainly lies in the fact that we have tested only a limited number of interpolation algorithms (and their settings). However, these interpolation algorithms are also used by other authors for yield data processing [11, 21, 23] and, according to [13], IDW, IDS and OK are generally the most commonly used interpolation algorithms in the environmental sciences.

5   Conclusions and Future Work

This paper compared three interpolation techniques in terms of their usability in yield mapping: Inverse Distance Weighted, Inverse Distance Squared and Ordinary Kriging. The measurements from a field harvester equipped with a GNSS unit need to be filtered and interpolated for follow-up analyses. This study verified the differences between the three aforementioned methods of interpolation used on data that were derived from field sensor measurements. These measurements were (1) obtained directly from the field harvester, (2) processed by global filters, and (3) processed by both global and local filters. Statistical analyses evaluated the results of interpolations from three fields (Zákostelní, Milešovsko and Kobersko Široké) cultivated by a fully operational farm (Rostěnice, the Czech Republic).

So far, existing approaches evaluated positional accuracy only with respect to the Root Mean Square Prediction Error. The outcomes of this study have confirmed that a different interpolation method has to be chosen when taking into account: (1) solely the Root Mean Square Prediction Error, or (2) a combination of Mean Prediction Error, Root Mean Square Prediction Error, in combination with descriptive statistics and Map Algebra. In general, Inverse Distance Squared seems to be the most suitable interpolation method, especially when it comes to interpolating unfiltered data. Both Inverse Distance Squared and Inverse Distance Weighted methods are exact interpolators and it is relatively easier to define their input parameters. Ordinary Kriging appears to be relatively the least suitable, but its importance grows especially when a dataset contains missing/removed measurements. However, as in previous studies, no universally valuable advice could be given as to which interpolation method is the best. More general recommendations, but only for yield mapping domain, can be formulated after additional testing on multiple datasets from different fields with different crops etc.

The conducted study will also serve as a resource for further research that will attempt to compare the measured yield with that predicted based on yield productivity zones. Interpolated surfaces serve as the yield productivity zones for both measurement and prediction. The resulting interpolated surfaces are considerably influenced by the applied interpolation method. Interpolation algorithms and their settings therefore influence the evaluation of yield productivity predictions when confronted with the measured values.

Acknowledgments. This paper is part of a project that has received funding from the European Union's Horizon 2020 research and innovation programme under grant agreement No. 818346 titled "Sino-EU Soil Observatory for Intelligent Land Use Management" (SIEUSOIL). Kateřina Trojanová, Tomáš Pavelka and Šimon Leitgeb were also supported by funding from Masaryk University under grant agreement No. MUNI/A/1576/2018. The authors would like to thank all persons from the Rostěnice Farm who participated in the study.

References

1. Almasi, A., Jalalian, A., Toomanian, N.: Using OK and IDW methods for prediction the spatial variability of a horizon depth and OM in Soils of Shahrekord, Iran. J. Environ. Earth Sci. **4**(15), 17–27 (2014)

2. Arslan, S., Colvin, T.S.: Grain yield mapping: yield sensing, yield reconstruction, and errors. Precision Agric. **3**(2), 135–154 (2002)
3. Auernhammer, H.: Precision farming – the environmental challenge. Comput. Electron. Agric. **30**(1–3), 31–43 (2001)
4. Blackmore, S., Moore, M.: Remedial correction of yield map data. Precision Agric. **1**(1), 53–66 (1999)
5. Charvat, K., et al.: Advanced visualisation of big data for agriculture as part of databio development. In: IEEE International Geoscience and Remote Sensing Symposium, pp. 415–418 (2018)
6. Gozdowski, D., Samborski, S., Dobers, E.S.: Evaluation of methods for the detection of spatial outliers in the yield data of winter wheat. Colloquium Biometricum **2010**(40), 41–51 (2010)
7. Hoskova-Mayerova, S, Talhofer, V., Hofmann, A., Kubicek, P.: Spatial database quality and the potential uncertainty sources. In: Studies in Computational Intelligence, pp. 127–142 (2013). https://doi.org/10.1007/978-3-642-32903-6_10
8. Huisman, O., By, R.A.: Principles of Geographic Information Systems: An Introductory Textbook, 4th edn. International Institute for Geo-Information Science and Earth Observation, Enschede (2009)
9. Krivoruchko, K.: Spatial Statistical Data Analysis for GIS Users, 1st edn. ESRI Press, Redlands (2011)
10. Kubicek, P., Kozel, J., Stampach, R., Lukas, V.: Prototyping the visualization of geographic and sensor data for agriculture. Comput. Electron. Agric. **97**(9), 83–91 (2013)
11. Lee, K.H., Chung, S.O., Choi, M.-C., Kim, Y.-J., Lee, J.-S., Kim, S.-K.: Post processing software for grain yield monitoring systems suitable to Korean full-feed combines. In: Proceedings of the 13th International Conference on Precision Agriculture, pp. 1–15 (2016)
12. Leroux, C., Jones, H., Clenet, A., Dreux, B., Becu, M., Tisseyre, B.: A general method to filter out defective spatial observations from yield mapping datasets. Precision Agric. **19**(5), 789–808 (2018)
13. Li, J., Heap, A.D.: A review of comparative studies of spatial interpolation methods in environmental sciences: performance and impact factors. Ecol. Inform. **6**(3–4), 228–241 (2010)
14. Longley, P.A., Goodchild, M.F., Maguire, D.J., Rhind, D.W.: Geographic Information Science and Systems, 4th edn. Wiley, Hoboken (2015)
15. Lu, G.Y., Wong, D.W.: An adaptive inverse-distance weighting spatial interpolation technique. Comput. Geosci. **34**(9), 1044–1055 (2008)
16. Palma, R., Reznik, T., Esbrí, M., Charvat, K., Mazurek, C.: An INSPIRE-based vocabulary for the publication of agricultural linked data. In: Tamma, V., Dragoni, M., Gonçalves, R., Ławrynowicz, A. (eds.) OWLED 2015. LNCS, vol. 9557, pp. 124–133. Springer, Cham (2016). https://doi.org/10.1007/978-3-319-33245-1_13
17. Řezník, T., et al.: Open farm management information system supporting ecological and economical tasks. In: Hřebíček, J., Denzer, R., Schimak, G., Pitner, T. (eds.) ISESS 2017. IAICT, vol. 507, pp. 221–233. Springer, Cham (2017). https://doi.org/10.1007/978-3-319-89935-0_19
18. Reznik, T., et al.: Monitoring of in-field variability for site specific crop management through open geospatial information. ISPRS Arch. Photogramm. Remote Sens. Spat. Inf. Sci. **XLI-B8**, 1023–1028 (2016)
19. Reznik, T., et al.: Disaster risk reduction in agriculture through geospatial (big) data processing. ISPRS Int. J. Geo-Inf. **6**(8), 1–11 (2017)

20. Reznik, T., Pavelka, T., Herman, L., Leitgeb, S., Lukas, V., Sirucek, P.: Deployment and verifications of the spatial filtering of data measured by field harvesters and methods of their interpolation: Czech cereal fields between 2014 and 2018. Sensors **19**(22), 1–25 (2019)

21. Robinson, T.P., Metternicht, G.: Comparing the performance of techniques to improve the quality of yield maps. Agric. Syst. **85**(1), 19–41 (2005)

22. Spekken, M., Anselmi, A.A., Molin, J.P.: A simple method for filtering spatial data. In: 9th European Conference on Precision Agriculture, pp. 259–266 (2013)

23. Souza, E.G., Bazzi, C.L., Khosla, R., Uribe-Opazo, M.A., Reich, R.M.: Interpolation type and data computation of crop yield maps is important for precision crop production. J. Plant Nutr. **39**(4), 531–538 (2016)

24. Stampach, R., Kubicek, P., Herman, L.: Dynamic visualization of sensor measurements: context based approach. Quaestiones Geographicae **34**(3), 117–128 (2015)

25. van Wart, J., Kersebaum, K.C., Peng, S., Milner, M., Cassman, K.G.: Estimating crop yield productivity zones at regional to national scales. Field Crops Res. **143**(1), 34–43 (2013)

26. Wackernagel, H.: Ordinary kriging. In: Multivariate Geostatistics, pp. 74–81 (1995)

Author Index

Printed in the United States
By Bookmasters